BOTTLES

Identification and Price Guide

THIRD EDITION

BOTTLES

Identification and Price Guide

THIRD EDITION

Michael Polak

Quill
A HarperResource Book
An Imprint of HarperCollinsPublishers

BOTTLES: IDENTIFICATION AND PRICE GUIDE, THIRD EDITION. Copyright © 2000 by Michael Polak. All rights reserved. Printed in the United States of America. No part of this book may be used or reproduced in any manner whatsoever without written permission except in the case of brief quotations embodied in critical articles and reviews. For information address HarperCollins Publishers Inc., 10 East 53rd Street, New York, NY 10022-5299.

HarperCollins books may be purchased for educational, business, or sales promotional use. For information please write: Special Markets Department, HarperCollins Publishers Inc., 10 East 53rd Street, New York, NY 10022-5299.

First Quill printing, Third Edition: September 2000
First Avon Books printing, Second Edition: August 1997
First Avon Books printing, First Edition: March 1994

ISBN 0-380-72815-X

00 01 02 03 04 /RRD 10 9 8 7 6 5 4 3 2 1

This Third Edition is dedicated to three special gentlemen: LeRoy Fowler, Alex Kerr, and William Wright.

During 1998 the bottle collecting world lost LeRoy Fowler of the Los Angeles Historical Bottle Club and William Wright of the Las Vegas Bottle Club. Then, in March 1999, another friend said good-bye: Alex Kerr, also a member of the Los Angeles Historical Bottle Club. Each of these three gentlemen had been involved with antique bottle collecting most of their lives and were well known in the west as major collectors possessing a wealth of knowledge. But most of all, they will be remembered for their genuine friendship, constant encouragement, endless helpfulness, inspiration, and their overall contribution and legacy they left to the hobby of bottle collecting.

Good-bye guys, we'll miss you.

Acknowledgments

When I began gathering information to write the Third Edition of this book, it became obvious that I would need additional help from fellow collectors, dealers, and many friends. Once again, I had plenty of help from those individuals with real expertise, and I'd like to say *thank you* to the following special people:

David Finnern—Thanks for your contribution to the Third Edition with the special chapter on "Diving for Bottles," the great underwater photographs, and an education on the world of diving.

Jim Hagenbuch (*Antique Bottle & Glass Collector Magazine*, Glass Works Auctions)—Thank you for the great assortment of photographs, pricing inputs, and overall support of the project.

Norm Heckler (Heckler Auctions)—Thank you for your contribution of photographs and your support of the project.

Fred Holabird—Thanks for your continued help with understanding the Bottles of Nevada and your great friendship.

Bob Kay—Thanks for your contribution of pricing inputs on Miniature Beer Bottles and your support of the project.

Jacque Pace Polak—A special thank you to my wife for your continued patience and invaluable moral support.

Mark Lutsko (Antique Bottle Connection)—Thanks for all of the photographs and your pricing inputs on Montana Bottles.

John Pastor—Thanks for the great photographs of Nursing Bottles and the inputs and information on pricing and history.

Steve Ritter (Steve Ritter Auctioneering)—Thanks for your help in obtaining the ACL Soda Bottle photographs and your help with the pricing inputs.

Gary and Vickie Lewis—Thank you for your contribution of the great assortment of ACL Soda Bottle photographs and your overall support of the project.

Photo Credits

David Finnern
Jim Hagenbuch (*Antique Bottle & Glass Collector Magazine*, Glass Works
    Auctions)
Norman C. Heckler (Norman C. Heckler and Company, Auctions)
The H. J. Heinz Company
Bob Glover
Terry Guidroz
Fred Holabird
Gary and Vickie Lewis
Mark Lutsko (Antique Bottle Connection)
Dale Mooney
John Pastor
Steve Ritter (Steve Ritter Auctions)
Jan Rutland (National Bottle Museum)
Rick Sweeney
David Spaid
Jennifer M. Tai
Jeff Wichmann (Pacific Glass Auctions)
Willy Young

Contents

Introduction

Welcome again to the world of antique bottle collecting. Once again, **thank you** to all of my readers for your support in making the Second Edition of *Bottles: Identification and Price Guide* a huge success. I continue to receive positive and valuable input and helpful comments from bottle collectors, clubs, and dealers across the United States, Europe, and Asia-Pacific. In fact, a large number of collectors and dealers have given the book the nickname of "***The Bottle Bible,***" for which I thank everyone. I have enjoyed writing the Third Edition just as much as the Second, and I am grateful to have been able to incorporate all of the positive feedback.

In order to make it the best, most informative reference and pricing guide available, I have updated and revised the Third Edition to provide the beginner and veteran collector with an even broader range of detailed information. Based on your responses, the Third Edition continues to include, with updates, essentials of the hobby, such as the history and origin of bottles, information on how the beginning collector gets started, and detailed sections on basic bottle facts, bottle sources, and bottle handling techniques. In response to the numerous requests from collectors, there are two new chapters on the fastest growing segments of bottle collecting, "Soda Bottles—Applied Color Label (ACL)" and "Nursing Bottles." To complement the chapter on "Digging for Bottles," there is also a new chapter on "Diving for Bottles" written by guest author David Finnern, a noted expert on underwater exploration and treasure hunting. The Third Edition also provides a complete pricing update for both Old Bottles (Pre–1900) and New Bottles (Post–1900). To help you better understand the details of how to price a bottle, I've added a chapter titled "Determining Bottle Values." For reference and research purposes, I have updated and expanded the sections on Trademarks, Bottle Clubs and Bottle Dealers, as well as the Bibliography and Glossary of common terminology. Two hundred new photographs have also been added throughout the book.

Interest in bottle collecting continues to grow and new bottle clubs are forming throughout the United States and Europe as more and more people are spending their free time digging through old dumps, foraging through old ghost towns, digging out old "out" houses (that's right), exploring abandoned mine shafts, and searching out their favorite bottle or antique show, swap meet, flea market, or garage sale. In addition, the Internet now offers collectors numerous opportunities to buy and sell bottles without even leaving the house. I'm not sure that it is as much fun, but it has provided the collector with many new sources for many more bottles. Bottle collecting also continues to grow as a business, as evidenced by the increasing prices in this book and the many auction websites now available to the collector.

Most collectors, however, still look beyond the type and value of a bottle into its origin and history. In fact, I find that researching the history of bottles has at times proved to be more interesting than finding the bottle itself. I enjoy both pursuits for their close ties to the rich history of the settling of the United States and the early methods of merchandising. My goal has always been to enhance the hobby of bottle collecting for both beginner and expert collectors and experience the excitement of antique bottle collecting, especially the thrill of making that special find. I hope that the Third Edition of *Bottles: Identification and Price Guide* continues to bring you an increased understanding and enjoyment of the hobby of bottle collecting. If you would like to provide additional information or input regarding the Third Edition, or just talk bottles, I can be contacted at either my e-mail—bottleking@earthlink.net— or my Web site—www.bottlebible.com. Good bottle hunting.

How to Use This Book

This book is designed to assist collectors—from the complete novice to the seasoned veteran. The Contents clearly indicates those chapters, such as "The Beginning Collector," that veterans may want to skip over. However, other introductory sections, including those on history, facts, sources, and handling, and the new chapters, "Diving for Bottles," "Soda Bottles—Applied Color Label (ACL)," "Nursing Bottles," and "Determining Bottle Values," will contribute information and resource material to even the expert's store of knowledge about bottles and collecting.

The pricing information is divided into two main sections. The first begins on page 57 and covers older collectibles, those manufactured almost exclusively before 1900 (some categories—such as Beer Bottles, Fruit Jars, and Barber Bottles—reflect dates starting with 1900 but are considered to be in the older section by collectors and dealers), broken down into categories based on physical type and the bottle's original contents. Where applicable, trade names are listed alphabetically within these sections. In some categories, such as Flasks, trade names were not embossed on the bottles, so pieces are listed by embossing or other identification that appears on the bottles themselves. Descriptive terms used to identify these pieces are explained in the introductory sections and are also listed in the Glossary at the end of the book. The second pricing section, which begins on page 299, is a guide to pieces produced after the turn of the century, broken down by manufacturer alone.

Since it is difficult to list prices for every available bottle, I've produced a cross section of collectibles in various price ranges. The dollar amount attached to any listing indicates the value of that particular piece. Similar but not identical bottles could be more or less valuable that those specifically mentioned. This listing will provide a good starting point for pricing pieces in your collection or you are considering as additions.

What's Happening in the World of Bottle Collecting?

Between the Second and Third editions of this book, great bottle discoveries have been made and an awareness of the hobby has been growing, as evidenced by an increase in the number of bottle clubs, collectors, dealers, and bottles show and events. One of most exciting and biggest events in the world of bottle collecting was the "Great Dig of the Century," which took place in San Francisco, California, on the corner of 4th and Bryant streets in the oldest part of Downtown during a three week period during February and March 1998.

The Dig of the Century, which started out as just a dig by a small group of collectors with some inside information, ultimately produced approximately 7,000–9,000 bottles, including many rare finds. The first week was fairly unexceptional by digging standards. But by the middle of the second week, the second gold rush of Northern California was in full gear and the excavation action a crazy frenzy. We're talking about Jackhammers, floodlights, sledge hammers, picks, and shovels. By Thursday of the second week, the wild digging gave up some of the most rare and best finds: 2 Bryant's Megaphones, 6 Lacquer's Bitters, and 1 Cassin's bitter. Bryant's Bitter bottles are among the rarest of all bitter bottles. Some of the other bottles found were as follows: 8 to 12 Lacour's Sarsaparilla Bitters, more than 100 Pacific Congress Water, more than 100 San Francisco Jamaica Gingers, and a number of Barrel Bitters such as Greeley's, Sachem's, and Roback's. And these are only the bottles we know about. Many diggers kept their finds a secret. The majority of the bottles dated from the 1850s to the 1860s, with a few dating back to the 1840s and some into the 1880s. A large quantity of European gold-rush era items along with a number of rare pot lids were also found. Truly a bottle digger's dream.

These weren't the only discoveries in the last few years. In 1998, marine archeologists using an undersea robot to prowl the floor of the Mediterranean Sea discovered what may be the largest concentration of ancient shipwrecks ever found. The find included five Roman ships dating from 100 B.C. and A.D. 400 and one Islamic ship from the late eighteenth century. As part of this discovery, there were hundreds of Roman pots, jugs, bottles, and other vessels intended to store wine, olive oil, sauces, and medicines.

Also in 1998, an American Revolution gunboat which had been under the command of Benedict Arnold and sunk in a major battle with the British in 1776, was located on the bottom of Lake Champlain near Vergennes, Vermont. The excavation is now in progress and is expected to reveal many artifacts such as Ale and Flask bottles from that period.

The Federation of Historical Bottle Collectors teamed up with The Museum of American Glass at Wheaton Village to present a featured exhibit for 1997–1998 in the main bottle gallery of more than 150 American historical flasks in many rare molds and colors. The museum has also accepted the Federation's offer to place annual exhibits in various categories of glass containers in the bottle gallery with the category for 1998–1999 being Fruit Jars, corresponding with the 140th anniversary of Mason's patent in 1858.

In addition, the commercial world has finally realized that antique bottles can sell a product. A number of companies are using photographs of pre–1900 bottles to convey a message. One of the best I saw is an ad from a telecommunications company that featured an 1880s medicine bottle with a message in the bottle and the following slogan: Communicating statically to your audience via the Web is like sending your message in a bottle.

As you can see, interest in bottle collecting and the resources available to collectors continue to grow at a rapid pace.

Bottles: History and Origin

Glass bottles are not as new as some people might think. In fact, the glass bottle has been around for about 3,000 years. In the late first century B.C., the Romans began to make glass bottles that the local doctors and pharmacists used to dispense pills, healing powders, and potions. These were small cylindrical bottles, 3 to 4 inches in length and very narrow. As we will read later, the majority of early bottles produced after Roman times were sealed with a cork or glass stopper, whereas the Romans used a small stone rolled in tar to seal vials. Also, the finished bottles contained many impurities such as sand particles and bubbles caused by the crude glass-producing process. Because of the thickness of the glass and the crude finish, Roman glass was very resilient compared to the glass of later times, which accounts for the survival and good preservation of some Roman bottles that have been dated as 2,500 years old. The Romans also get credit for originating what we think of today as the basic store bottle and early merchandising techniques.

The first effort to manufacture glass in America is thought to have taken place at the Jamestown settlement in Virginia around 1608. It is interesting to note that the majority of glass produced at the Jamestown settlement was in fact earmarked for shipment back to England (owing to England's lack of resources) and not for the new settlements. As it turned out, the Jamestown glasshouse enterprise ended up being a failure almost before it got started. The poor quality of glass produced simply couldn't support England's needs.

The first successful American glasshouse was started in 1739 in New Jersey by Caspar Wistar, a button manufacturer who immigrated to the

Roman bottles, jars, and glass objects, 1st–3rd Centuries A.D. Found in the baths and necropolises of Cimiez Nice, France.

United States from Germany. The next major glasshouse operation was started by Henry Stiegel in the Manheim, Pennsylvania, area between 1763 and 1774. He later established several more. The Pitkin glassworks was started in East Hartford, Connecticut, around 1783 and was the first American glasshouse to provide figural flasks. It also became the most successful glasshouse of its time, until it closed around 1830 because of the high cost of wood for fuel. In order to understand early glasshouse history, both the successes and far more numerous failures, we need to understand the problems of availability of raw materials and the concerns of constructing the glasshouse itself.

The glass factory of the nineteenth century was usually built near abundant sources of sand and wood or coal, and in close proximity to numerous roads and waterways for transportation of the raw materials to the glasshouse and the finished products to major eastern markets such as Boston, New York, and Philadelphia. Finding a suitable location was usually not a problem, but once production was under way resources would quickly diminish.

The glasshouse building itself was usually a large wooden structure, which housed a primitive furnace that was shaped like a beehive about

9 feet in diameter. A major financial drain on the glass companies, and the major reason so many of the businesses went broke, was the large pot that fit inside the furnace to hold the molten glass. The melting pot, which cost about $100 and took eight months to build, was made by hand from a long coil of clay and was the only substance known that would not melt when the glass was heated to 2,700°. Although the material could withstand the temperatures, the life span of each pot was only about eight weeks; the high temperatures over a long period of time caused the clay itself to turn into glass. The cost of regularly replacing these melting pots proved the downfall of many an early glass factory.

Throughout the nineteenth century, glasshouses continued to come and go because of changes in demand and technological improvements. Between 1840 and 1890, there was an enormous demand for glass containers to satisfy the whiskey and beer businesses and the medicine and food-packing industries. Owing largely to this steady demand, glass manufacturing in the United States finally expanded enough to become a stable industry. This demand was caused in large part by the settling of the western United States and the great gold and silver strikes between 1850 and 1900. Unlike other industries of the time that saw major changes in manufacturing processes, the technique for producing glass bottles remained the same. This process gave each bottle special character, producing unique shapes, imperfections, irregularities, and various colors until 1900.

At the turn of the century, Michael J. Owens invented the first fully automated bottle-making machine. Although many fine bottles were manufactured between 1900 and 1930, Owens's invention ended an era of unique bottle design that no machine process could ever duplicate. In order for a bottle collector, especially a new bottle collector, to better understand the history and origin of antique bottles, it is important to take a look at the chronological history of bottle manufacturing.

Free-Blown Bottles: First Century B.C. to 1860 (Figure 1)

During the first century B.C., the blowpipe, which was nothing more than a long hollow metal rod, was invented. The tip was dipped into molten glass, and by blowing into the other end, a glassblower formed the desired bottle, bowl, or other container.

Free-Blown Bottle-Making Process
Figure 1

1. The blowpipe was inserted into the pot of red-hot metal and twisted to gather the requisite amount onto the end of the pipe.

2. The blowpipe was then rolled slowly on a metal table to allow the red-hot metal to cool slightly on the outside and to sag.

3. The blower than blew into the pipe to form an internal central bubble.

4. The gathered amount of metal was further expanded and sometimes turned in a wooden block that had been dipped in cold water to prevent charring by the hot metal, or possibly rolled again on the metal table.

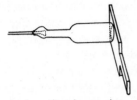

5. The body and neck were then formed by the bottom of the bottle being flattened with a wooden paddle called a Battledore (named after a glassblower who designed the paddle concept).

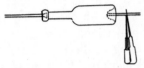

6. One of the irons (pontil) was attached to the center bottom of the bottle for easy handling during the finishing of the bottle neck and lip. At this time, a kick-up could be formed in the bottom of the bottle by pushing inward when attaching the iron.

7. The bottle was whetted, or cracked off the blowpipe, by touching the hot glass at the end of the pipe with a tool dipped in cold water.

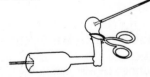

8. With the bottle held on a pontil, the blower reheated the neck to polish the lip and further smoothed it by tooling.

Pontil Marks: 1618 to 1866

Once the bottle was blown, it was removed from the rod through the use of a three-foot metal pontil rod, which was dipped into the tank of molten glass and applied to the bottom of the bottle. The neck of the bottle was then touched with a wet rod or stick, which separated it from the blowpipe.

The finishing process could include a variety of applied and tooled rings and collars. In the final step, an iron was inserted into the neck of the bottle, or held by tongs, while the pontil was separated from the bottle. If the bottle was to be molded for body form, the gather was inserted in a mold and further expanded to take on the shape of the interior of the mold, usually cylindrical, square, or polygonal.

Snap, Cases, Snap-Cases: 1860 to 1903 (Figure 2)

Between 1850 and 1860, the first major invention for bottle making since the invention of the blowpipe appeared, an instrument known as the snap, which replaced the pontil. The basic snap-case was a 5-foot metal rod that had claws to grasp the bottle. A snap locked the claw into place in order to hold the bottle more securely while the neck was being finished. It should be noted that each snap-case was tailor-made to fit bottles of a certain size and shape. These bottles have no pontil scars or marks, which left the bases of the bottles free from lettering or design. There may, however, be some minor grip marks on the side as a result of the claw device.

The snap-case instrument was used for small-mouth bottle production until the automatic bottle machine came into existence in 1903.

Molds: First Century B.C. to 1900

The use of molds in bottle making, which really took hold in the early 1800s, actually dates back to the first century with the Romans. As detailed earlier, in the free-blown process the glassblower shaped the bottle, or vessel, by blowing and turning it in the air. When using a mold, the glassblower would begin in the same way, then take a deep breath while lowering the red-hot shaped mass into the hollow mold. The blower would continue blowing air into the tube until the glass compressed itself against the sides of the mold to acquire the finished shape.

Molds were usually made in two or more sections in order to enable the mold to come apart. The hardened bottle could then be easily re-

Snap, Cases, Snap-Cases: 1860–1903
Figure 2

Snap Case Open

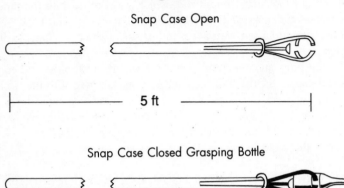

Snap Case Closed Grasping Bottle

moved. Since it was impossible to have the molds fit precisely, the seams show on the surface of the finished article, giving a clue about the manufacturing methods used in the production of the bottle. The molds were categorized as "open," where only the body of the bottle was forced, with the neck and lip being added afterward, and "closed," in which the neck and lip were part of the original mold (Figure 3). Later two specific types of molds came into use: the three-piece mold, in use from 1809 to 1880, which consisted of two main types; and the turn mold or paste mold, in use from 1880 to 1900. The three-piece mold helped the bottle industry become stronger in the nineteenth century.

Molds: First Century B.C.-1900
Figure 3

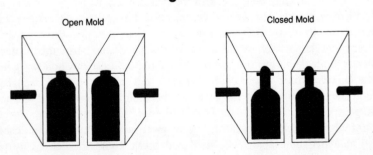

Open Mold   Closed Mold

Three-Piece Mold
Figure 4

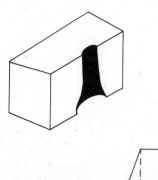

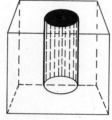

Three-Piece Molds (Figure 4)

Three-piece dip mold—the bottom section of the bottle mold was one piece, and the top, from the shoulder up, was two separate pieces. The mold seams appeared circling the bottle at the shoulder and on each side of the neck.

Full-height molds—the entire bottle was formed in the mold and the two seams run vertically to below the lip on both sides of the bottle.

Turn Mold or Paste Mold

Wooden molds used in the manufacture of bottles were kept wet to prevent them from igniting, but as the hot glass came into contact with the mold, the walls of the mold became charred. By turning the mold, however, manufacturers discovered that they could erase seams and mold marks, give a high finish to the completed bottle, and prevent charring. After metal molds replaced wooden ones, manufacturers used a paste inside the mold that allowed the bottle to slide easily during the turning process, which explains the origins of the terms "turn mold" and "paste mold."

Full height metal mold, front view.

Full height metal mold, side view.

Mason Food Jars: 1858

In 1858, John Mason invented the wide-mouth jar that became famous as a preserved food container. His new screw-top neck was formed in the same mold as the body. The jar was then broken away from the blowpipe and sent to the annealing oven to temper the glass, making it more resistant to breakage. After this, the jagged edges of the rims were ground down. In fact, earlier jars can be distinguished from later ones by looking for rough and sharp edges produced by this grinding process.

Press-and-Blow Process: 1892

In 1892, a semiautomatic process called "press and blow" was invented. This process could only be used in the production of wide-mouth containers formed by pressing molten glass into the mold to form the mouth and lip first. Then a metal plunger was inserted through the mouth and applied air pressure formed the body of the bottle. This process was utilized for the production of early fruit jars and milk bottles.

The Automatic Bottle-Making Machine: 1903

Michael J. Owens is recognized as the inventor of the first automatic bottle-making machine. Owens first introduced his invention in 1899, but the machine was not perfected until 1903. In the beginning, the Owens machine made only heavy bottles since the demand for them was the greatest. In 1909, improvements to the machine made it possible to produce small prescription bottles. Between 1909 and 1917, numerous other automatic bottle-making machines were invented and soon all bottles were formed automatically throughout the world.

In 1917, another invention of mechanized bottle manufacturing provided a way of forming a measured amount of molten glass from which a bottle could be blown. It was called a "gob feeder." In this process, a gob of glass is drawn from the tank and cut off by shears.

One last note about bottle making concerns the process of producing screw-top bottles. Early glassblowers produced bottles with inside and outside screw caps long before the bottle-making machines mechanized the process. Because early methods of production were so complex, screw-top bottles produced before the 1800s were considered specialty bottles and expensive to replace. Today they are considered to be rare and quite collectible. In fact, the conventional screw-top bottle did not become common until after 1924, when the glass industry standardized the threads.

Now that you have learned something about the history and origin of bottle making, it's time to provide information about how to approach the hobby of bottle collecting, as well as suggestions on books and reference guides, start-up costs, old versus new bottles, and some information on bottle clubs.

So, what approach should you take toward getting started, and what might influence that approach? The first thing to understand about antique bottle collecting is that there aren't any rules. Everyone's finances, spare time, available storage space, and preferences are different and will influence his or her approach. As a collector, you will need to think about whether to specialize and focus on a specific type of bottle or group of bottles, or whether you're more of a general or "maverick" collector who acquires everything that becomes available. The majority of bottle collectors I have talked with over the years, me included, took the "maverick" approach as new collectors. We grabbed everything in sight, ending up with bottles of every type, shape, and color. Now, after twenty years of collecting, my recommendation to newcomers is to specialize. Of course, taking the more general approach in the early years has given me a wider spectrum of knowledge about bottles and glass in general. But specializing has distinct advantages over the "maverick" approach:

- It reduces the field of collection, which helps organize study and research.
- The specialist becomes an authority on bottles in a particular field.

- Trading becomes easier with other specialists who may have duplicate and unwanted bottles.
- By becoming more of an authority within a specialty, the collector can negotiate a better deal by spotting those bottles that are underpriced.

I need to mention, however, that specialized collectors will always be tempted by bottles that don't quite fit into their collections. So they cheat a little and give in to that maverick urge. This occasional cheating sometimes results in a smaller side collection, or, in extreme cases, turns the collector away from a specialty and back to being a maverick. But that's all right. Remember, there are no set rules, with the exception of having a lot of fun.

Now, what does it cost to start a collection and how do you know the value of a bottle? Aside from digging excursions, which have travel and daily expenses, starting a collection can be accomplished by spending just a few dollars or maybe just a few cents per bottle. Digging, which we will discuss in detail later, is in this writer's opinion the ultimate way of adding to your collection.

Knowing what and where the best deals are obviously takes some time and experience. But the beginner can do well with just a few pointers.

Over the years, I've developed a quick-look method of buying bottles by grouping candidates into one of three categories:

1. **Low end or common bottles:** Bottles reflect noticeable wear and the label is usually missing or not very visible. In most cases the label is completely gone and there is never embossing. The bottle is dirty (which can usually be fixed), with some scrapes, and free of chips. These bottles are usually clear and colorless.
2. **Average grade/common bottles:** Bottles reflect some wear and a label may be visible but is usually faded. They are generally clear in color and free of scrapes or chips. Some of these may have minimal embossing.
3. **High end and unique bottles:** These bottles can be empty or sometimes partially or completely full, with the original stopper and label or embossing. The color is clear and the bottle has no chips or scrapes and very little or no wear. If it has been stored in a box it is very likely in good condition. Also the box must be in good condition.

*   *   *

I discuss price ranges just briefly here since values will be covered in detail in the two price sections. Usually, low-end bottles can be found for $1 to $5, average-grade bottles will range from $5 to $15, and basic high-end bottles will range from $15 to $50. Anything over $50 should be looked at closely by someone who has been collecting for a while.

As a rule, I try not to spend more than $2 per bottle for the low end and $5 for the average grade. It's easier to stick to this guideline when you've done your homework, but sometimes you just get lucky. During the 1992 Reno, Nevada, Bottle and Antique Show (one of the best, by the way), I stopped at a table where the seller had "Grab Bags," shopping bags full of bottles for $2 a bag. Well, I couldn't pass up this bargain. Later, when I had time to examine my treasures, I discovered a total of nine bottles, some purple, all earlier than 1900, in great shape, with embossing, for a total cost of 22¢ per bottle. Now what could be better than that! In the high-end category, deals are usually made after some good old horse trading and bartering. But, hey, that's part of the fun. Always let the seller know that you are a new collector with a limited budget. It really helps. I have never run across a bottle seller who wouldn't work with a new collector to try to give the best deal for a limited budget.

A collector should also be aware of old bottles versus new bottles and what distinguishes an antique bottle from an old bottle, and either from a new bottle. Quite often, new collectors assume that any old bottle is an antique and that if a bottle isn't old it is not a collectible. By collectible, I mean a relatively rare and/or valuable bottle, or one that holds special interest for the collector (for its historical value, perhaps). This is not necessarily the case. In the antique world, an antique is defined as any article more than 100 years old. But you will see quite a number of bottles listed in this book that are less than 100 years old and are in fact just as valuable, perhaps more so, than those that are antiques. I'm referring to bottles made between 1900 and 1950. As we discussed earlier, the history, origin, background, use, and rarity of the bottle can possibly gain more points with the bottle collector than how close the bottle comes to the 100-year mark.

The number and variety of old and antique bottles is greater than the new collectible items in today's market. On the other hand, the Jim Beams, Ezra Brooks, Avons, and recent Coke bottles, figurals, and miniature soda and liquor bottles manufactured more recently, are very desirable and collectible and are in fact made for that purpose. If you decide you want to collect new bottles, the best time to buy is when the first issue comes on the market. When the first issues are gone, the collectors' market is the only available source, and limited availability will drive prices up considerably. In mid-1992, the Coca-Cola Company reissued the 8-ounce junior-size Coke bottle in the Los Angeles area in an attempt to garner attention in a marketplace full of cans. This 8-ounce bottle has the same contour as the 6½-ounce bottle that was a Coke standard from the 1920s into the 1950s. (The 6½-ounce bottle is still available in a few parts of the United States, most noticeably in Atlanta, where Coca-Cola has its headquarters.) When the 8-ounce bottles were issued in Los Angeles, the "heavy-duty collectors" literally paid in advance and picked up entire case lots from the bottling operations before they hit the retail market.

For the beginning collector, and even the old-timer, books, reference guides, magazines, and other similar literature are readily available at libraries and bookstores. I still make it a point to read as much as possible since someone is always discovering something new. As a help, there is a bibliography in this book of various types of literature since clubs pool numerous sources of information as well as offer occasional digging expeditions. Various bottle clubs and dealers are also listed at the end of this book, beginning on page 464.

Now, get out to the antique shops, flea markets, swap meets, and antiques and bottle shows. Pick up those bottles and handle that glass. Ask questions, and soon you will be surprised by how much you have learned, not to mention how much fun it is.

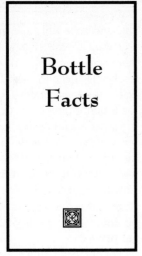

Bottle Facts

In order for a new bottle collector to understand the hobby better, there are certain specifics such as age identification, bottle grading, labeling, and glass imperfections and peculiarities that are very important to familiarize yourself with.

As mentioned in the introduction, usually the first question from a novice is "How do you know how old a bottle is?" or "How can you tell that it is really an antique bottle?" Two of the most common methods for determining the age are by the mold seams and the color variations. Also, details on the lip, or top of the bottle, will provide some further clues.

Mold Seams (Figure 5)

Prior to 1900, bottles were manufactured with a blowpipe using the free-blown method or with a mold (in use after 1860). In either process, the mouth or lip of the bottle was formed last and applied to the bottle after completion (applied lip). An applied lip can be discerned by examining the mold seam, which will run from the base up to the neck and near the bottom of the lip. In the machine-made bottle, the lip is formed first and the mold seam runs over the lip. Therefore, the closer to the top of the bottle the seam extends, the more recent the bottle.

For the earliest bottles, manufactured before 1860, the mold seams will end low on the neck or at the shoulder. On bottles made between 1860 and 1880, the mold seam stops right below the mouth, which makes it easy to detect that the lip was formed separately. Around 1880, the closed mold was utilized, wherein the neck and lip were mechanically shaped and the glass had to be severed from the blowpipe. The ridge that resulted was evened off by hand sanding or filing. This mold seam usually

14

Age Identification Mold Seams of Bottles
Figure 5

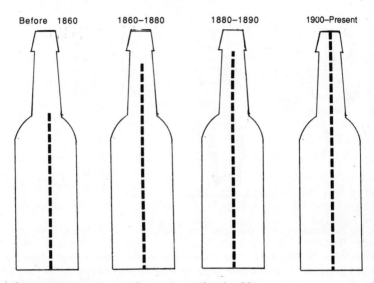

Before 1860: Seams extend to just over the shoulders.
1860–1880: Seams go most of the way up the neck of the bottle.
1880–1890: Seams continue through the top but not through or over the lip.
1900–present: Seams extend the full length of the bottle and over the lip.

ends within ¼ inch from the top of the bottle. After 1900, the seam extends clear to the top. Since the lips, or tops, were an integral part of the bottle-making process, it is important to understand some of that process.

Lips and Tops (Figures 6 and 7)

One of the best ways to identify bottles manufactured prior to 1840 is the presence of a "sheared lip." This type of lip was formed by cutting, or snipping, the glass free of the blowpipe with a pair of shears, a process that leaves it with a stovepipe look. Since hot glass can be stretched, some of these stovepipes have a very distinctive appearance. Around 1840, bottle manufacturers began to apply a glass ring around the sheared lip, forming a "laid-on-ring" lip. Between 1840 and 1880, numerous variations of lips or tops were produced by utilizing a variety of different tools. After 1880, manufacturers started to pool their processing

Neck-Finishing Tools
Figure 6

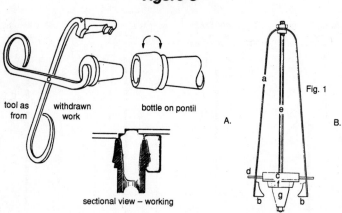

tool as   withdrawn   bottle on pontil
from   work   A.   B.

Fig. 1

sectional view – working

A. The line drawings were developed from a description that appeared in the seventh edition (1842) of the *Encyclopaedia Britannica*, vol. X, p. 579: "The finisher then warms the bottle at the furnace, and taking out a small quantity of metal on what is termed a ring iron, he turns it once round the mouth forming the ring seen at the mouth of bottles. He then employs the shears to give shape to the neck. One of the blades of the shears has a piece of brass in the center, tapered like a common cork, which forms the inside of the mouth, to the other blade is attached a piece of brass, used to form the ring." This did not appear in the sixth edition (1823), though it is probable the method of forming collars was practiced in some glasshouses at that time.

B. The exact period in which neck-finishing tools evolved having metal springs with two jaws instead of one, to form collars, is undetermined. It doubtless was some time before Amosa Stone of Philadelphia patented his "improved tool," which was of simpler construction, as were many later ones. Like Stone's, "the interior of the jaws [was] made in such shape as to give the outside of the nozzle of the bottle or neck of the vessel formed the desired shape as it [was] rotated between the jaws in a plastic state . . ." U.S. Patent Office. From specifications for (A. Stone) patent No. 15,738, September 23, 1856.

information, resulting in a more evenly finished and uniform top. As a rule, the more uneven and crude the lip or top, the older the bottle.

Closures/Stoppers (Figure 8)

As discussed earlier, the Romans used small stones rolled in tar as stoppers. Later centuries saw little advancement in the methods of clo-

Bottle Lips/Tops Identification
Figure 7

1. Tooled, rounded, rolled-over collar
2. Tooled, flanged, with flat top and squared edges
3. Tooled, rounded above ¾-inch flat band
4. Tooled, flat ring below thickened plain lip
5. Tooled, narrow beveled fillet below thickened plain lip
6. Tooled, broad sloping collar above beveled ring
7. Tooled, plain broad sloping collar
8. Tooled, broad sloping collar with beveled edges at top and bottom
9. Tooled, broad flat collar sloping to heavy rounded ring
10. Tooled, broad flat vertical collar with uneven lower edge
11. Tooled, double rounded collar, upper deeper than lower, neck slightly pinched at base of collar
12. Tooled, board round collar with lower level

sure. For most of the fifteenth and sixteenth centuries, the closure consisted of a sized cloth tied down with heavy thread or string. Beneath the cover was a stopper made of wax or bombase (cotton wading). Cotton wool was also dipped in wax to be used as a stopper, along with coverings made of parchment, paper, or leather. Corks and glass stoppers were still used in great numbers. The cork was sometimes tied or wired down for use with effervescent liquids. When the "close mold" came into existence, however, the shape of the lip was more accurately controlled, which made it possible to invent and manufacture many different capping devices.

One of the most unique was developed in 1873 when a British inventor, Hiram Codd, invented a bottle with a glass marble confined inside its neck so that when it was used with an effervescing liquid, the pressure of the gas forced the marble to the top of the neck, sealing the bottle. From 1879 to the early 1900s, the Hutchinson stopper became a com-

S.A. Whitney, Bottle Stopper
No. 31,046 Patented January 1, 1861
Figure 8

Drawing 1   Drawing 2

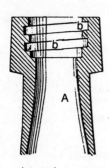
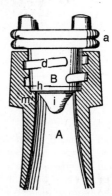

From Samuel A. Whitney's specifications for his "Bottle Stopper," patent No. 31,046, January 1, 1861. Drawing 1 shows the grooves in neck of the bottle. Drawing 2, on which "h" is a cork washer, shows the stopper in place. "The stopper is formed by pressing or casting the molten . . . glass in molds of the desired shape. . . . Although . . . applicable to a variety of bottles and jars, it is especially well adapted to and has been more especially designed for use in connection with mineral-water bottles, and such as contain effervescing wines, malt liquors, &c., the corks used in this class of bottles, if not lost, being generally so mutilated as to be unfit for second use when the bottles are refilled." (U.S. Patent Office.)

mon bottle closure. It used a heavy wire loop to control a rubber gasket that stayed inside the neck of the bottle. The Lighting stopper, used from 1880 to the early 1900s, was a porcelain or rubber plug anchored to the outside of the bottle by means of a permanently attached wire. The wire formed a bar that controlled the opening and closing of the bottle.

In 1897, William Painter invented the crown cap, which revolutionized the soft drink and beer bottling industry. A crown cap was formed from a circular tin plate crimped on the outer edge to fit tightly over the rolled lip of the bottle. The inside of the cap was filled with a cork disk that created an airtight seal. A modified version of this cap is still used on beer and soft drink bottles today.

Finally, in 1902, threads were manufactured on the outside of the lip to

Glass
stoppers,
1850–1900.

Glass stoppers, 1850–1900.

enable a threaded cap to be screwed onto the mouth of the bottle. This was not a new idea. Early glassblowers had produced bottles with inside and outside screw caps long before bottle-making machines came along. Early methods of production were so complex, however, that screw-top bottles produced before the 1800s were considered specialty bottles. They were expensive to replace and today are considered rare and quite collectible. In fact, the conventional screw-top bottle did not become common until after 1924, when the glass industry standardized the threads.

Glass Color

The next most common method for determining the age of a bottle is by examining the color of the glass. The basic ingredients for glass production (sand, soda, and lime) have remained the same for 3,000 years. These ingredients, when mixed together, are collectively called the "batch." When the batch is heated to a molten state, it is referred to as the "metal." In its soft or plastic stage, the metal can be molded into objects that when cooled become the solid material we know as glass.

Producing colored and perfectly clear glass were major challenges for glass manufacturers for centuries. In the thirteenth and fourteenth centu-

Dumfries Ale (English) depicting inside threads.

Dumfries Ale (English), full-bottle view depicting inside threads.

ries the Venetians produced clear glass by using crushed quartz in place of sand. In 1668, the English tried to improve on this process by using ground flint to produce clear glass, and by 1675, an Englishman named George perfected lead glass. Today, this lead glass is referred to as "Flint glass." Prior to 1840, intentionally colored or colorless glass was reserved for fancy figured flasks and vessels. The coloration of bottles was considered unimportant until 1880, when food packers began to demand clear glass for preserved food products. Since most glass produced prior to this time was green, glass manufacturers began using manganese or delenium to bleach out the green tinge produced by the iron content of the sand. Only then did the clear bottle become common.

Iron slag was used up to 1860 and produced a dark olive-green or olive-amber glass that has become known as "black glass" and was used for wine and beverages that needed protection from light. Colors natural to bottle glass production are brown, amber, olive-green, and aqua.

The true blue, green, and purple colors were produced by metallic oxides added to the glass batch. Cobalt was added for blue glass, sulfur for yellow and green, manganese and nickel for purple, nickel for brown, copper or gold for red, and tin or zinc for milky colored glass (for apothecary vials, druggist bottles, and pocket bottles). Since these bright colors were expensive to produce, they are very rare and are sought after by most collectors.

"Purple glass" is the product of a number of imposed and natural forces and many collectors prize it above other colored glasses. As discussed earlier, the iron contained in sand caused glass to take on a color between green and blue. Glass manufacturers used manganese, which counteracted iron's blue effect and produced clear glass. Glass with this manganese content, which was most common in bottle production between 1880 and 1914, takes on a rich purple color when exposed to ultraviolet rays. This "purple glass" has come to be known as "desert glass" or "sun-colored glass" since the color is actually a result of exposure to the sun. One last note, glass that was produced between 1914 and 1930 is most likely to change to an amber or straw color.

Imperfections

Imperfections and blemishes are also clues to how old a bottle is and often add to the charm and value of an individual piece. Blemishes usually show up as bubbles or "seeds" in the glass. In the process of making glass, air bubbles form and rise to the surface, where they pop. As the "fining out" or elimination process became more advanced (around 1920), these bubbles or seeds were eliminated.

Another peculiarity of the antique bottle is uneven thickness of the glass. Often one side of the base has a 1-inch-thick side that slants off to paper thinness on the opposite edge. This imperfection was eliminated with the introduction of the Owens bottle-making machine in 1903. In addition, the various marks of stress and strain, sunken sides, twisted necks, and whittle marks (usually at the neck, where the wood mold made impressions in the glass) also give clues to indicate that a bottle was produced before 1900.

Labeling and Embossing

While embossing and labeling were a common practice in the rest of the world before 1850, American bottle manufacturers did not adopt the inscription process until 1869. These inscriptions included information about the contents, manufacturer, distributor, and slogans, or other messages advertising the product. Raised lettering on various bottles was produced with a plate mold, sometimes called a "slug plate," which was fitted inside the casting mold. This plate created a sunken area, and these bottles are of special value to collectors. Irregularities such as a misspelled name add to the value of the bottle, as will any name embossed with hand etching or another method of crude grinding. These bottles are very old, very collectible, and very valuable.

Inscription and embossing customs came to an end with the production of machine-made bottles (1903) and the introduction of paper labels. In 1933, with the repeal of Prohibition, the only letter embossing on bottles, usually those containing alcohol, is "Federal Law Forbids Sale or Re-Use of this Bottle."

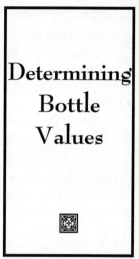

Determining Bottle Values

Determining an old bottle's value is dependent upon a number of variables. The following factors are most often used by collectors and dealers to determine a bottle's value and are consistent with the methods that I have used over the years.

1. Rarity, supply, and demand for the specific bottle
2. Age, condition, and historic appeal and significance
3. Embossing, labeling, and design
4. Color—purple (amethyst), cobalt blue, black and milk colored glass
5. Unique features such as Pontil marks, Whittle marks, glass imperfections, and slug plates.

In order to better understand bottle valuation, it's important to also know how to judge a bottle's condition and rarity.

Conditions

Mint—An empty or full bottle (preferably full) with a label or embossing. This bottle must be clean and have good color, with no chips, scrapes, or wear. If the bottle comes in a box, the box must be in perfect condition too.

Extra Fine—An empty or full bottle with slight wear on the label or embossing. Bottle must be clean with clear color, and no chips or scrapes. There is usually no box, or, a box not in very good condition.

Very Good—Bottle reflects some wear and label is usually missing or not very visible. Most likely there is no embossing and no box.

Good—Bottle reflects additional wear and label is completely absent. Color is usually faded and bottle is dirty. Usually some scrapes and minor chips. Most likely there is no box.

Fair or **Average**—Bottle reflects a large amount of wear and the label is missing.

Rarity

Unique—A bottle is considered to be unique if only one is known to exist. These bottles are also the most valuable and expensive.

Extremely Rare—A bottle is considered extremely rare if there are only 5 to 10 known specimens.

Very Rare—A bottle is considered very rare if there are only 10 to 20 known specimens.

Rare—A bottle is considered rare if there are only 20 to 40 known specimens.

Very Scarce—A bottle is considered very scarce when there are no more than 50 bottles in existence.

Scarce—A bottle is considered scarce when there are no more than 100 bottles in existence.

Common—A bottle that is considered common, such as clear 1880–1900 medicine bottles, exist in abundance and are easy to acquire and usually very inexpensive. A great bottle for the beginning collector.

Even with the above guidelines, it is important to always have additional resources, especially for those rare and unique bottles. The bibliography, bottle club, and dealer chapters in this book will provide some of those additional references. And remember, never miss a chance to ask other collectors and dealers for help and assistance.

Bottle Sources

Antique or collectible bottles can be found in a variety of different locations and sometimes where you least expect them. Excluding digging for bottles, which we'll discuss later, the following sources are good potential hiding places of that much sought after bottle.

The Internet

In the twenty-five years that I've been collecting, I've never seen anything impact the hobby of Bottle Collecting as much as the Internet. Simply go to the Internet and type in Antique Bottle Collecting. You'll be amazed at all of the data at your fingertips. There are numerous Web sites throughout the United States, Canada, and Europe that provide information about clubs, dealers, antique publications, and auction companies. These sites have literally opened up the entire world to the collector and are very inexpensive and valuable resources for the collector and dealer.

Flea Markets, Swap Meets, Thrift and Secondhand Stores, Garage Sales, Salvage Stores

For the beginner collector, these sources will likely be the most fun (next to digging) and yield the most bottles at the best prices. As we discussed earlier, a little bit of homework can result in opportunities to purchase bottles of endless variety for an extremely low cost. As a rule, the majority of bottles found at these sources will fall into the common or common but above average category.

When looking around at flea markets, swap meets, and thrift stores, be sure to target those spots where household goods are being sold. It's a good bet they will have some type of bottles. When targeting garage sales, try to concentrate your search in the older areas of town since the items being presented for sale will be noticeably older, more collectible, and more likely to fall into a rare category. Salvage stores or salvage yards are great places to search for bottles since these businesses deal with companies that have contracts to demolish old houses, apartments, and businesses, and on occasion will come across treasures. One New York salvage company that was contracted to clean out some old storage buildings came across an untouched illegal prohibition set-up complete with bottles and unused labels and equipment. What a find!

Local Bottle Clubs and Collectors

By joining a local bottle club or working with other collectors, you will find yet another source for your growing collection. Members will usually have quantities of unwanted or duplicate bottles which they will sell very reasonably, trade, or sometimes simply give away especially to a enthusiastic new collector. In addition, bottle clubs are always a good source for information about digging expeditions.

Bottle Shows

Bottle shows not only expose you to bottles of every type, shape, color, and variety but provide you with the opportunity to talk with many experts in specialized fields. In addition, there are usually publications for sale relating to all aspects of the bottle collecting hobby. Bottle shows can be a rewarding learning experience for the beginner collector in particular but also for the veteran collector. These bottle shows take place almost every weekend all across the country. There is always something new to learn and share and, of course, bottles to buy or trade. One last note: make sure you look under the tables at these shows. Many bargains in the form of duplicates and unwanted items may be lurking there.

Auction and Estate Sales

Auction houses have become a good source of bottles and glassware over the last ten years. When looking for an auction, try to find an auction house that specializes in antiques and estate buy-outs. To promote itself and provide buyers with a better idea of what will be presented for sale, an auction house usually publishes a catalog that provides bottle descriptions, conditions, and photographs. Auctions are fun and can be a very good source of bottles at economical prices. I do recommend, however, that you visit an auction first as a spectator to learn a little about how the whole process works before you decide to participate and buy at one. When buying, be sure of the color and condition of the bottle, and terms of the sale. These guidelines also apply to all Internet auctions. Note: The Bibliography includes some auction houses that specialize in bottles and related items.

Estate sales are great sources for bottles if the home is in a very old neighborhood or section of the city that has historical significance. These sales are a lot of fun, especially when the people running the sale let you look over and handle the items for sale to be able to make careful selections. Prices are usually good and are always negotiable.

Knife and Gun Shows

What, bottles at a knife and gun show? Quite a number of gun and knife enthusiasts are also great fans of the West and keep an eye open for related artifacts. Every knife and gun show I've attended, or sold at, has had at least 10 dealers with bottles on their tables (or under the tables) for sale. And the prices were about right since they were more interested in selling their knives and guns than the bottles. Plus, these dealers will often provide information on where they made their finds, which you can put to good use later.

Retail Antique Dealers

This grouping includes those dealers who sell bottles at or near full market prices. Buying from a dealer has its upside as well as its downside. They usually have a large selection and will provide helpful information and details about the bottles. It is a safe bet that the bottles for sale are authentic and have been priced in accordance with the true condition of the bottle.

On the other hand, trying to build up a collection from these dealers can be very expensive. But their shops are a good place to browse, learn, and try to fill out a collection.

General Antique and Specialty Shops

The difference between a general shop and a retail dealer is usually the selection (more limited with a general shop) and the pricing of a bottle, which is happily much lower. This is partly because these dealers are not as knowledgeable about bottles and therefore may incorrectly identify a bottle, overlooking critical areas that determine the value. If a collector can become knowledgeable, these general dealers may create the opportunity to acquire quality underpriced merchandise.

Digging
for
Bottles

There are many ways to begin your search for collectible bottles, but as I have mentioned before, there are few searches as satisfying and fun as digging up bottles yourself. While the goal is to find a bottle, the adventure of the hunt is as exciting as the actual find. From a beginner's viewpoint, digging is a relatively cheap and excellent way to start a collection. The efforts of individual and bottle club digging expeditions have turned up numerous important historical findings. These digs surfaced valuable information about the early decades of our country and the history of bottle and glass manufacturing in the United States. The following discussion of how to plan a digging expedition covers the essentials: locating the digging sites, equipment and tools, general rules, and helpful hints, as well as a section on privy/outhouse digging for the real adventurer.

Locating the Digging Site

Prior to any dig, you will need to learn as much as possible about the area you plan to explore. Do not overlook valuable resources in your own community. Chances are, you can collect important information from your local library, local and state historical societies, various types of maps, and city directories (useful for information about people who once lived on a particular piece of property). The National Office of Cartography in Washington, D.C., and the National Archives are also excellent resources.

In my experience, old maps are the best guides for locating digging areas with good potential. These maps depict what the town looked like in an earlier era and provide clues about where stores, saloons, hotels, red light districts, and the town dump were located. All are ripe for exploring. The two types of maps that will prove most useful are Plat maps and Sanborn Fire Insurance maps. A Plat map, which will show every home and business in the city or area where you wish to dig, can be compared to current maps to identify the older structures or determine where they once stood. The Sanborn Insurance maps are the most detailed, accurate, and helpful of all for choosing a digging site. These maps, which have also been published under other names, provide detailed information on each lot illustrating the location of houses, factories, cisterns, wells, privies, streets, and property lines. These maps were produced for nearly every city and town in the country between 1870 and 1920 and are dated so that it's possible to determine the age of the sites you're considering. Figure 9 depicts an 1890 Sanborn Perris map section of East Los Angeles. This map section was used to locate an outhouse in East Los Angeles that dated between 1885 and 1905. A dig on that site turned up more than fifty bottles. Knowing the appropriate age of the digging site also helps to determine the age and types of bottles or artifacts you find there.

The local chamber of commerce, law enforcement agencies, and residents who have lived in the community for a number of years can be very helpful in your information search. Another great resource for publications about the area's history are local antiques and gift shops, which often carry old books, maps, and other literature on the town, county, and surrounding communities.

Since most early settlers handled garbage themselves, buried bottles can be unearthed almost anywhere, but a little thinking can narrow the search to a location that's likely to hold some treasures. Usually, the garbage was hauled and dumped within 1 mile of the town limits. Often, settlers or store owners would dig a hole about 25 yards out from the back of their home or business for garbage and refuse. Many hotels and saloons had a basement or underground storage area where empty bottles were kept.

Ravines, ditches, and washes are also prime digging spots because heavy rains or snow melt often washed debris down from other areas. Bottles can quite often be found beside houses and under porches. Residents would store or throw their bottles under their porches when porches were common building features in the late nineteenth and twentieth centuries. Walk down abandoned roads where houses or cabins once stood, investigate old wagon trails, railroad tracks, and sewers. If it is

Figure 9

legal, and you should check first, old battlegrounds and military encampments are excellent places to dig. Cisterns and wells are other good sources of bottles and period artifacts.

The first love of this bottle hound, and high on the list of most collectors, is an expedition to a ghost town. It's fun—and a lesson in history. The best places to conduct a search in ghost towns are near saloons, trade stores, the red light district, train stations, and the town dump (prior to 1900). The Tonopah, Nevada, town dump was the start of my digging experiences and is still a favorite spot.

Privy/Outhouse Digging

"You've dug bottles out of an old outhouse? You've got to be kidding!" Telling your family and friends about this unique experience will usually kick the conversation into high gear. I'm quite serious when I say that one of the best places to find old bottles—old bottles that can be very rare and in great condition—is in an old outhouse. Prior to 1870, most bottles were not hauled out to the dump. Why would people bother when they could simply toss old bottles down the outhouse hole in the back of a house or business? In fact, very few pontil-age (pre–Civil War) bottles are ever found in dumps. At that time people either dug a pit in their backyard for trash or used the outhouse. These outhouses, or privies, have been known to yield all kinds of other artifacts such as guns, coins, knives, crockery, dishes, marbles, pipes, and other household items.

To develop a better sense of where privies can be found, it is important to have an understanding of their construction and uses. The privies of the nineteenth century (you'll find the best bottles in privies that date from the nineteenth century) were deep holes lined with wood slats or brick, called "liners." You'll find privy holes were dug in a variety of shapes: square,

Terry Guidroz, Schriever, LA, standing by a "wet privy" in New Orleans, LA (holding a Cathedral Pickle Bottle), and John Gautreaux, Schriever, LA, digging in the "wet privy" in New Orleans, LA.

Terry Guidroz, Schriever, LA, digging in the "wet privy" in New Orleans, LA.

round, rectangular, and oval. (The table opposite summarizes the different types of privy holes, their locations, and their depth.)

In general, privies in cities are fairly deep and usually provide more bottles and artifacts. Privies in rural areas are shallower and do not contain as many bottles. Farm privies are very difficult to locate and digs often produce few results.

How long was an outhouse used? Well, the life span of a privy is anywhere from ten to twenty years. It was possible to extend its useful life by cleaning it out or relining it with new wood, brick, or stone. In fact, nearly all older privies show some evidence of cleaning.

At some point, old privies were filled and abandoned. The fill materials included ashes, bricks, plaster, sand, rocks, building materials, or soil that had been dug out when a new or additional privy was added to the house. Often, bottles or other artifacts were thrown in with the fill. The depth of the privy determined the amount of the fill required. In any case, the result was a privy filled with layers of various materials. The bottom layer being the "use" layer or "trash" layer as shown in Figure 10.

It is possible to locate these old outhouses owing to the characteristic differences in density and composition of the undisturbed earth. Because

TYPES OF PRIVIES

Construction	Shape	Location	Depth
brick	oval, round, rectangular, square	big towns and cities, behind brick buildings	not less than 6 feet deep
stone	round, square, rectangular	Limestone often used in area where stone is common.	rectangular, less than 10 feet, round holes often 20 feet or more
wood	square or rectangular	farms, small towns; may be first privy on lot	not more than 10 to 15 feet, often very shallow
barrel	round	cities and towns	8 to 12 feet

Older Privies
Figure 10

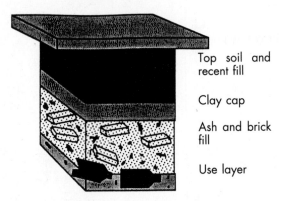

Top soil and recent fill

Clay cap

Ash and brick fill

Use layer

Older privies usually have a number of different layers.

of the manner of construction, it is fairly easy to locate them by probing the area with a metal rod or "probe."

As I mentioned earlier, your own community is a great place to begin the hunt for a privy or outhouse. A good starting point is to find an old house. Those built between 1880 and 1920 usually had at least one privy in the backyard. Try to locate a small lot with few buildings or obstructions to get in the way of your dig. First look for depressions in the ground. Since materials used to fill privy holes have a tendency to settle, a subtle depression may indicate where a septic tank, well, or privy was once located. In addition, like most household dumps, outhouses were usually located between 15 and 30 yards behind a residence or business. Another good indicator of an old privy site is an unexpected grouping of vegetation, such as bushes or trees, which flourishes above the rich fertilized ground. Privies were sometimes located near old trees for shade and privacy.

The most common privy locations were (1) directly outside the back door, (2) along a property line, (3) in one of the back corners or centered near the back property line and (4) the middle of the yard. Figure 11 graphically depicts patterns of typical outhouse locations.

Now that you've located a privy (with luck it's full of great bottles), it's time to get down and dirty and open up the hole. The approximate dimensions of the hole can usually be determined with your probe. If you know, or even think, that the hole is deeper than you are tall, it is extremely important to avoid a cave-in by opening up the entire hole. Never attempt to dig only a portion of the lined area in the hopes of getting to the trash layer quicker. Remember that the fill is looser than the surrounding ground and could come down on you. Also, always dig to the bottom and check the corners carefully. Privies were occasionally cleaned out but very often the unlucky person stuck with the job missed bottles and artifacts in the corners or on the sides. If you are not sure whether you've hit the bottom, check with the probe. It's easier to determine if you can feel the fill below what you may think is the bottom. In brick- and stone-lined holes, if the wall keeps going down, you are not on the bottom. Quite often it is difficult to date a privy without the use of detailed and accurate maps.

But it is possible to determine the age of the privy by the type and age of items found in the hole. The table on page 38 lists some types of bottles you might find in a dig and shows how their age relates to the age of the privy.

While finding a prized bottle is great, digging and refilling the hole can be hard work and very tiring. To help make this chore easier, lay a tarp on the ground surrounding the hole and as you dig, shovel the dirt onto the tarp. Then shovel the dirt off the tarp and fill 5-gallon plastic

John Gautreaux, Schriever, LA, showing off the bottles from the "wet privy" in New Orleans, LA.

Typical Privy Configurations
Figure 11

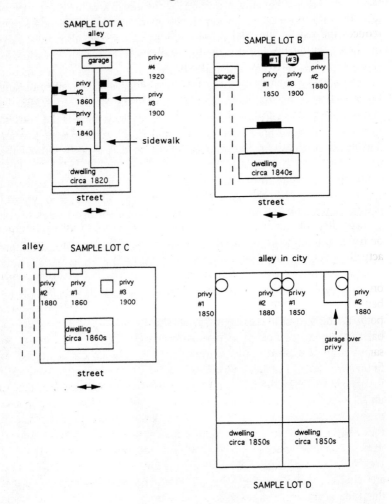

buckets. The first benefit of this method is the time and energy you'll save filling the hole. The second benefit, and maybe the biggest, is that you'll leave no mess. This becomes important for building a relationship with the property owner. The less mess the more likely you'll get permission to dig again. Also, your dig will be safer and easier if you use a walk board. Take an 8-foot-long 2 × 8 plank and place it over the hole. The digger, who is standing on the board pulling up buckets of dirt (let's all take turns), can do so without hitting the sides. This also reduces the risk of the bucket man falling in or caving in a portion of the hole. Setting up a tripod with a pulley over the hole will help to save time and prevent strain on the back.

The few short paragraphs I've presented are really just an outline of privy/outhouse digging. There are two publications that discuss the subject in greater detail, and people interested in privy/outhouse digging should locate them: *The Secrets of Privy Digging* by John Odell and *Privy Digging 101* by Mark Churchill. Information on how to purchase both of these fine publications can be found in the Bibliography. Now, let's have some "outhouse" fun.

The Probe

Regardless of whether you are digging in outhouses, old town dumps, or beneath a structure, a probe is an essential tool. The basic probe is actually a very simple device as shown in Figure 12.

It is usually 5 to 6 feet in length (the right length for you depends on your height; a taller person may find that a longer probe will work better), with a handle made out of hollow or solid pipe tapered to a point at the end so it's easier to penetrate the ground. Also, welding a ball bearing on the end of the rod will serve as a help in collecting soil samples. As discussed earlier, examining the soil samples is critical to finding privies. To make your probing a bit easier, add some weight to the handle by filling the pipe with lead or welding a solid steel bar directly under the handle. The additional weight will reduce the effort needed to sink the probe. While probing, press down slowly and try to feel for differences in the consistency of the soil. Unless you are probing into sand, you should reach a point at which it becomes difficult to push, a natural bottom. If you find you can probe deeper in an adjacent spot, you may have found an outhouse. When this happens, pull out the probe and plunge it in again, this time at an angle to see if you feel a brick or wood line. After some practice, you'll be able to determine what type of material you are hitting. Glass, brick, crockery, and rocks all have their own distinctive sound and feel. While there are a number of places where you can purchase probes, you might want to have one custom made to conform to your body height and weight for more comfortable use.

DATING DIGGING SITES BY THE BOTTLES YOU FIND

Material	1920+	1900–19	1880–1900	1860–80	1840–60	Pre–1840
crown tops	yes	yes	no	no	no	no
screw tops	yes	yes	no	no	no	no
aqua glass	yes	some	yes	yes	yes	yes
clear glass	all	most	some	some	some	some
ground lip fruit jar	no	rare	yes	yes	rare	no
hinge mold	no	no	no	yes	yes	no
pontiled	no	no	no	yes	yes	yes
free blown	no	no	no	no	no	yes
historical flasks	no	no	no	yes	yes	yes
stoneware (crockery)	no	no	yes	yes	yes	yes

Bottle Probe
Figure 12

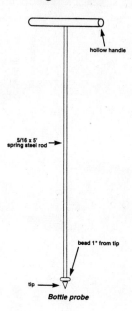

hollow handle

5/16 x 5'
spring steel rod

bead 1" from tip

tip

Bottle probe

Digging Equipment and Tools

When I first started digging, I took only a shovel and my luck. After a few broken bottles, I learned I was doing things the hard way. Since then, I've refined my list of tools and equipment. The following list includes those items that I've found useful; they are often recommended by other veteran diggers as well.

GENERAL DIGGING EQUIPMENT
- probe
- long-handled shovel
- short-handled shovel
- long-handled potato rake
- small hand rake
- old table knives
- old spoons

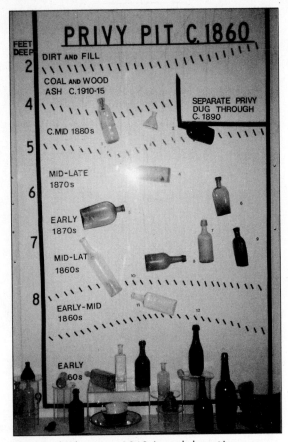

Privy pit display circa 1860 (actual dug pit),
National Bottle Museum, Ballston, Spa, New York.

- hard- and soft-bristle brushes
- gloves, boots, eye protection, hat, and durable clothing
- insect repellent, snakebite kit, first-aid kit
- extra water
- dirt sifter (for coins or other items,
     a 2 × 2-foot wooden frame with chicken wire)
- hunting knife
- boxes for packing and storing bottles

PRIVY/OUTHOUSE DIGGING EQUIPMENT
- long-handled shovel
- 5-foot probe
- slam probe*
- pick
- root cutters
- short-handled scratcher*
- 1-inch × 15-foot or more rope with clip
- tripod with pulley*
- walk board
- short-handled shovel
- 10-foot probes*
- posthole digger
- pry bar
- ax
- 5-gallon buckets
- heavy tarps
- hardhat and gloves

*Indicates optional item.

General Rules and Helpful Hints

I know I said there were no rules, but there is something you should always do: Always be responsible and ask for permission to dig. As a safety precaution, do not leave any holes open overnight. Do not damage shrugs, trees, or flowers unless the owner approves. When the digging is complete, always leave the site looking better than it was when you started. I can't stress this enough. That means filling in all holes and raking over the area. Remove your trash as well as trash left by previous prospectors or others. Always offer to give the owner some of the bottles. They may not want any, but they will appreciate the gesture. If you adhere to these few rules, the community or owner will thank you and future bottle diggers will be welcomed.

Try not to go out on a dig alone. But if you do be sure to tell someone where you're going and for how long you expect to be gone. When digging an outhouse, my recommendation is to go with no fewer than three people.

When you start to dig, don't be discouraged if you don't find any bottles. If you unearth other objects such as coins, broken dishes, or bottle tops, continue to dig deeper and in a wider circle. If you don't find any bottles, move to another spot. Always work from the edge to the center of the hole. Don't get discouraged! Even the very best have come home with empty bags and boxes, but never without the memory of a good time.

When you do find a bottle, stop your digging and remove the surrounding dirt a little at a time with a small tool, brush, or spoon. Handle the bottle very carefully since old bottles are very fragile.

Now that you know how to do it, what are you waiting for? Grab those tools, get those maps, and get started making the discoveries of a lifetime.

I first met David Finnern in 1994 while giving a talk to the California Wreck Divers Club following the publication of the First Edition of this book.

David first entered the undersea realm in 1962 at the age of 12 and had built his first underwater camera at age 15. He soon found himself spending most of his free time searching the ocean depths for sunken treasures, and his explorations have led to the discovery of a number of shipwrecks and lost ports. He has invented and patented underwater equipment, been a diving supervisor on both underwater salvage and mining endeavors, and is a former President of the California Wreck Diver, Inc. and the Adventurers Club. As an award winning writer, David has published more than 150 articles on underwater explorations and has authored several books, including the critically acclaimed Passage Through Deep Waters *and* The Sport Diver's Guide to Sunken Treasure. *His work has been translated into more that forty languages and published in more than sixty countries.*

I feel honored that David has taken the time to tell us about the fun and excitement of Diving for Bottles.

The oceans, lakes and rivers of the world could be considered the greatest depositories of the past. They conceal literally countless items either lost or discarded by previous generations who lived far differently than we do today. Water, however, can be a formidable adversary against exploration and discovery, and it by no means provides for a perfect and permanent time capsule. Few manmade items can withstand the constant movement of flowing liquid, or the barrage of chemical and biological attacks found in the sea.

Although glass is one the most delicate of all artifacts lost to the depths, it is still considered a relatively common underwater discovery. In past centuries, water was considered to be a universal dumping ground. While one may question the intelligence of this, the practice is of considerable benefit to the bottle diver. Any beach, whether at a lake, river or the ocean, is a possible collection site for antique bottles. The age of the beach, however, is all-important.

If a beach has been in use for many years, chances are the local residents have thrown countless bottles into the water after consuming the contents. Most lakes, rivers and oceans also have specific areas which have been used as trash dumps. The location of these areas has often been obscured by time, but a little common sense goes a long way in finding such a site. If an old house is located on a river, chances are the past inhabitants dumped their trash directly in front of the house. The same is true for ports and landings. Although there were usually strict rules about dumping trash and ballast in harbors for fear of lessening the water's depth, it would appear the laws were largely ignored by both ships' crews and dock workers.

Antiquated resorts located on the waterfront are another possible site for bottles. The resort's staff had the choice to haul the trash away or throw it in the water, and there's little doubt which choice was made.

Research is the key to finding these older sites. One of the most obvious and beneficial resources is local senior citizens. Many seniors can relate stories of family picnics or summer lifeguard jobs they had long ago which can lead directly to sites which may or may not still be in use. Newspapers are another invaluable source. Most libraries have older newspapers on microfilm. It's a fascinating process to research old headlines about Fourth of July and other celebrations which were held at a nearby swimming hole. Newspapers can also lead to other possible sites, such as amusement parks which had one time been perched over the water on a pier.

Old maps are another source of information. Antiquated road and insurance maps can reveal countless details about schools, fairgrounds, saloons and other structures which had once been near or over the water.

While diving for bottles can be fun and lucrative, it can also be potentially hazardous. Like shipwreck or any type of salvage diving, one dives where the treasures are, not necessarily where the best diving is to be found. Thus, limited visibility, currents, boat traffic and underwater obstructions can be formidable hazards commonly encountered. As with all diving endeavors, safety and diving within one's own skill level and education is a must.

Diving conditions can vary a great deal in bottle diving. Older bottles may be found, for example, in a relatively warm, shallow and clear lake where only a mask, fins and snorkel are required. However, as soon as the water depth drops below that of safe free diving, one must strap on a tank and regulator, which requires a minimum of basic scuba certification from a recognized agency.

A common misconception, however, is that a basic scuba class prepares a diver for all underwater conditions and possibilities. It does not. Searching for lost bottles can lead a diver into countless environments. Limited visibility and deep diving are just two examples of underwater exploration which require advanced and specialty certifications, as well as experience, before one can safely venture into these realms.

Unlike most treasures found underwater, the majority of bottles and glassware were not inadvertently lost, but purposefully discarded. This can make them quite plentiful in some areas. Considering the thrill of discovering a piece of history and the price tag commonly associated with antique glass, it might be worth the effort to explore a few of these areas, which may very well be near your home. Since some regions have laws forbidding diving or collecting in certain areas, be sure to do the legal research before making the dive.

Rivers

There are many underwater bottle sites that qualify as ugly diving environments, but it's my experience that rivers have just about the worst conditions one can plunge into. The following story describes one of my early river dives and is featured in my book *The Sport Diver's Guide To Sunken Treasure.*

Steve, Mike and I stood on the rock levee above the brackish river. They were locked in a conversation regarding the dive plan while I scanned the levee for a relatively smooth path down to the water's edge. Mike, with his head still turned away from the river and discussing the dive, suddenly stepped off the road and plowed his way downward through the brush-covered rocks. "So this is river diving," I mumbled to myself.

As Steve followed Mike's lead I resigned myself to pathlessness and took the mighty step off the road and half-hiked, half-tumbled my way to the river's edge. As I made a perfect though unintentional giant stride into the water, Steve's voice reverberated, "Now you've got it!"

I smiled, sort of, then double-checked the compass bearings written on my slate and let the air hiss from my BC to begin descent. My first observation was visibility was limited to two feet which, according to my comrades, was exceptionally good.

I followed the contour of the levee downward and turned on my light at about 15 feet. At 20 feet, the light became a necessity as the millions of particles suspended above absorbed and reflected most of the sun's rays.

The bottom suddenly leveled out at 25 feet and immediately my eyes caught a glimpse of the reason we were diving here; bottles and pots blanketed the mud. I picked up a few and a mud cloud bellowed upward reducing visibility to zero. I checked my compass but to no avail; I could see nothing. I swam a few feet, checked it again and continued outward from the bank. I was looking for a deeper channel not a mud bank.

Suddenly the bottom disappeared. How does one lose the bottom, I thought. Had I inadvertently ascended? I backtracked a little and discovered a vertical mud wall disappearing into the depths. I had been warned about these walls. They can be firm or dangerously soft and it is imperative to check before following them down. I ran my hand along the edge then into the wall. It was penetrable yet seemed firm enough. I free fell along the wall and into the blackness until at 40 feet I hit the river's bottom.

I sat motionless for just a minute allowing the mud to clear from my landing when suddenly a massive, shadowy skeleton loomed before my eyes. Instinctively, my body retreated until my brain finally recognized a pine tree and not a dead Goliath. Is this fun or what?

I moved slightly away from the tree and mud cliff and scanned the light's eerie beam before me. They were everywhere! Bottles thrown overboard from a landing which had been abandoned over 100 years ago. I was literally surrounded by history, items left untouched until my visit.

It's easy to understand why rivers are formidable adversaries when it comes to diving. There is the current to contend with, and a plethora of obstructions (I have found everything from cars and trucks to washing machines in rivers). There are trees and steel cables and, of course, discarded fishing and anchor line. There are rocks and mud walls which can dislodge at any time, and bottoms of silt so soft and mushy that one merely slows down upon contact. But it would seem the one problematic factor that supersedes all others is the poor visibility. Oftentimes, visibility is limited to a mere six inches. As one dives deeper, it becomes extremely dark, until at about 30 feet it is pitch black and the only comforting reference point becomes a tiny ray from an underwater flashlight.

When diving in such limited conditions it's just about impossible to know which way the levee or bank is once submerged. Even the current can reverse, affected by ocean tides 100 or more miles away, magnifying any confusion about direction. Therefore, only experienced and qualified divers should attempt river exploration. It's also imperative to take compass bearings or connect a diving reel to the bank prior to descending just to make sure you can find your way home.

With all this to contend with one might very well ask, why dive a river? There are two answers. First, no one else wants to dive rivers because they're so ugly. Secondly, that leaves just about everything lost on the bottom undisturbed.

For divers, there are two distinct possible sites for bottle hunting: dumps and landings. Some of these sites are readily recognizable from visible debris, such as exposed pilings. Others have been obscured by time and only research will reveal the correct clues for discovery. Depending on past activity, river bottoms can be literally blanketed with objects, including glassware. I have dived a few sites where it is difficult to see the bottom for all the discarded items.

Lakes

Generally, lakes are fairly easy to explore underwater. Probably the most common bottle discoveries in lakes are the result of an isolated case of littering; a fisherman many years ago finished his beer and simply cast the bottle into the water. With this in mind, the first place to look is in the very coves and fishing spots that are still in use today. While there may be numerous remnants from modern litterbugs, there may be some evidence of the past as well. Like fishing spots, older swimming holes are another good place for bottle hunting. Research can also lead to other sites. For example, small communities, located on the water's edge most certainly indicate vibrant activity took place just offshore.

Research can also point you to the location of resorts that used to dot the lake's shoreline. These can be particularly productive bottle diving

Diver with bottles taken out of a lake.

sites. My companions and I once searched for just such a place on a small mountain lake. We knew it existed from old newspaper accounts and even had a photo of the structures that stood in the 1890s.

We began our exploration in the most obvious area: the site of a current resort community. But though we were armed with evidence, we had to make several dives before we discovered the right location. It wasn't until we explored about a quarter of the lake that the first few clues began to emerge. At first, it was merely a few bottles. As I entered the water for the last dive of the day, I landed directly on top the remains of a crumbling rowboat, the exact type of rowboat that was in our old photograph. The next day's dives produced numerous bottles and jars from the era. There was no doubt that there was a large logging or mining camp in the area, proving that lakes can, indeed, be lucrative areas to dive for bottles.

While no obvious remnants of a port may exist on land, debris usually litters the lake bottom at any landing site. Pilings, or stumps of pilings, are telltale signs that a landing once existed. While there is no secret to diving an old landing, it may have obstructions and is potentially hazardous. Especially if water visibility is limited. I once explored a landing that ended in a massive pile of railroad tracks. This was no hazard since visibility was excellent and I saw the obstacles to be avoided. But in

Diver underwater (lake) after finding a bottle.

lesser conditions, it would have been easy to wander unknowingly into the mess, which would have been a serious and possibly dangerous blunder.

Keep in mind that ascent rates and decompression schedules can be dramatically altered because of altitude. Thus, appropriate calculations and adjustments are a must when diving mountain lakes.

Oceans

Like lakes and rivers, the oceans of the world have their share of both landings and trash dumps. But they may be located farther from the shoreline than inland sites. Some landings consisted of piers that extended a mile or more out to sea to avoid interference from surf. And it wasn't unusual for ships to dump their trash several miles out to sea.

Various whiskey, beer, bitters, and ale bottles taken from a lake.

Various medicine, ink, fruit jar, and glass containers taken from a lake.

Variety of whiskey, beer, and bitters bottles taken from a lake.

Steamship china is certainly one of the more exciting possibilities found at ocean landings. (Some types of steamship china may also be found at freshwater sites). To me, there is simply nothing more energizing than discovering a piece of china that can be identified with a specific time and place. And some of the steamship logo designs are spectacular indeed.

Diving for antique glass in the ocean can be a relatively simple endeavor since many objects lie exposed. However, this exposure can be deceptive. Bottles can travel great distances over the years, especially in areas where surge and currents are prevalent. And for some reason, one bottle can end up resting in plain view above the sand while another of the same vintage will be deeply buried. Due to this phenomenon, it is wise to set a search pattern using a compass or a diving reel to search the area for the less conspicuous bottles.

Particular attention must be paid to the immediate areas around rocks and pilings when searching for bottles entombed beneath the sand. Bottles rolling across the bottom may very well become lodged next to an immovable obstruction. One easy way to search for these buried bottles is with a probe. However, a probe is of little help in these areas, where a little sand fanning is a required procedure.

Regardless of where you're diving, identifying a particular find can be difficult. Thus, it is extremely important to treat all finds carefully. Generally, it can be determined whether or not it's an antique by simply inspecting the bottle for imperfections. It's amazing how crudely manufactured many early bottles were. The base is often uneven. Bubbles are usually present in the glass and even the neck can be crooked. The top can also be a telltale sign of age. The seam along the sides of early bottles does not extend over the top because it was applied independently.

Generally, color can be another sign of a bottle's age. Prior to 1860, iron slag was used in bottle manufacturing giving the glass a dark olive green color which has become known as "black glass." Common colors of bottles from 1860-1900 include aqua, cobalt, brown, green and purple. This latter color can be particularly beautiful, although it was not the original color intended by the manufacturers. The iron naturally found in sand caused the glass to become green or blue during the manufacturing process. Manganese was commonly used to counteract this phenomenon and bring the glass to clear. But when the manganese is exposed to ultraviolet rays for any length of time, the clear glass will turn to a deep and striking purple color.

Exploring underwater for antique glass is not only fun and lucrative, but a voyage into the past. And perhaps that subtle connection with generations of a different era is the real discovery.

Bottle Handling

While selling my bottles and listening to buyers at various shows, I am inevitably asked questions about cleaning, handling, and storing old bottles. Some collectors believe that cleaning a bottle diminishes its collectible value and desirability. Leaving a bottle in its natural state, as it was found, can be special. Others prefer to remove as much dirt and residue as possible. The choice rests with the owner. The following information will provide some help with how to clean, store, and take care of those special finds.

Bottle Cleaning

First off, never attempt to clean your new find in the field. In the excitement of the moment, it's easy to break the bottle or otherwise damage the embossing. With the exception of soda and ale bottles, glass bottles manufactured prior to 1875 usually have very thin walls. But even the bottles with thicker walls should be handled very carefully. The first step is to remove as much loose dirt, sand, or other particles as possible with a brush or a quick warm water rinse. Then, using a warm water solution and bleach (stir the mixture first), soak the bottles for a number of days (depending upon the amount of caked on dirt). This should remove most of the excess grime. Other experienced collectors use cleaning mixtures of straight ammonia, kerosene, lime-a-away, and chlorine borax bleach. Do not use mixtures that are not recommended for cleaning glass.

After soaking, clean bottles with a bottle brush, steel wool, an old toothbrush, or any semi-stiff brush. At this point, you may want to soak the bottles again, this time in lukewarm water to remove any traces of cleaning materials. Either let the bottles air-dry or dry them with a soft towel. If the bottle has a label, the work will become more painstaking since soaking is not a cleaning option.

One last note: do not clean your bottles in a dishwasher. While the hot water will produce a very clean bottle, the extreme heat could crack or even shatter fragile old bottles. A better option is a specialist who will clean your rare bottles with special tumbling machines. These machines, which leave the bottle with a clean, polished look, can also be purchased for personal use.

Bottle Display

Now that you have clean, beautiful bottles, display them to their best advantage. My advice is to arrange your bottles in a cabinet rather than on wall shelving or randomly around the house. While the last two options are more decorative, they also leave the bottles more susceptible to damage. When choosing a cabinet, try to find one with glass sides, which will provide more light and better viewing. As an added touch, a light fixture sets off your collection beautifully. If you still desire a wall shelving arrangement, make sure the shelf is approximately 7" wide with a front lip for added protection. This can be accomplished with round molding. Also, after the bottle is placed in its spot, draw an outline around the base of the bottle and then drill four 1/4" holes just outside that outline for pegs. These pegs will provide further stability for the bottle. If you have picked up any other goodies from your digging like coins or gambling chips, scatter them around the bottles for a little western flavor.

Bottle Protection

Because of earthquake activity, especially in Northern and Southern California, bottle collectors across the country have taken added steps to protect their valuable pieces.

Since most of us have our collections in some type of display cabinet, it's important to know how to best secure it. First, fasten the cabinet to the wall studs with brackets and bolts. If you are working with dry wall and it's not possible to secure the cabinet to a stud, butterfly bolts will provide a tight hold. Always secure the cabinet at both the top and bottom for extra protection.

Next, lock or latch the cabinet doors. This will prevent the doors from flying open. If your cabinet has glass shelves, be sure to not overload them with too many bottles. In an earthquake, the glass shelving can break under the stress of excess weight.

Finally, it's important to secure the bottles to the shelves with some type of adhesive, wax, or double sided tape. There are a number of adhesives available at local home improvement centers and hardware stores. One of the newest and most commonly used adhesives is called Quake Hold. This substance, which come in a wax, putty, and gel, is similar to the wax product used by museums to secure their art work, sculptures, and various glass pieces. In fact, Quake Hold itself is now used extensively by numerous museums, but is readily available to the general public at many home improvement stores and antique shops.

Bottle Storage

For those bottles you've chosen not to display, the best method for storing them is to place them in empty liquor boxes with cardboard dividers (which prevent bottles from knocking into each other). As added protection, you might want to wrap the individual bottles in paper.

Record Keeping

Last but not least, it's a good idea to keep records of your collection. Use index cards detailing where the bottle was found or purchased, including the dealer's name and price you paid. Also, assign a catalog number to each bottle, record it on the card, and then make an index. Many collectors keep records with the help of a photocopy machine. If the bottle has embossing or a label, put the bottle on the machine and make a copy of it. Then, type all the pertinent information on the back of the image and put it in a binder. When it comes to trading and selling, your record-keeping will be invaluable.

Old Bottles
(Pre-1900)

Old Bottles: Pre– 1900

T he bottles listed in this section have been broken down into individual categories by physical type and/or by the original contents of the bottle. For most categories, the trade names can be found in alphabetical order if they exist. Note that in the case of certain early bottles, such as flasks, a trade name does not appear on the bottle. These bottles have been listed according to the embossing or other identification on the bottle itself.

Since it is impossible to list every bottle available, I've tried to provide a good cross section of bottles in various price ranges and categories rather than listing only the rarest or most collectible pieces.

The pricing shown reflects the value of the particular bottle listed. Similar bottles could have values higher or lower than the items specifically listed in this book. This listing will still provide a good starting point for determining a price range.

Ale and Gin

Since ale and gin bottles are almost identical in style and similar in other ways, it becomes difficult to determine what the bottle originally contained unless information is provided on the bottle itself. Ale bottles should not be confused with beer bottles, a common mistake because of the similarities in shape.

Ale was a popular beverage at a time when available wines were not as palatable. Even the very best ale was not expensive to make or buy so it's easy to understand the demand for it. The bottles used by colonial ale makers were made of pottery and imported from England. When searching out these bottles, keep in mind that the oldest ones had a matte or unglazed surface.

In the seventeenth century, a Dutch physician named Francesco De La Bor prepared gin as a medical compound for the treatment of kidney disease. While its effectiveness in purifying the blood was questionable, gin drinking became very popular. It became so popular that many chemists decided to go into the gin-brewing business full-time to meet the growing demand. During the nineteenth century, gin consumption in America increased at a steady rate.

The design of the gin bottle, which has a squat body, facilitated packing in cases by preventing shifting and possible damage in shipping. The first case bottles had very short necks and were octagonal. Designs that came later featured longer necks. Bottles with tapered collars are dated to the nineteenth century. Case bottles vary in size from a half pint to multiple gallons. The early bottles were crudely made and have distinct pontil scars.

A/XXX/Cream Ale/Nashville Tenn/This Bottle Is Never Sold—McCormack/and/McKee
Amber, 9 in., Quart, smooth base, applied double collar
mouth $300–400
American 1875–1885

African T CO—(Motif of Serval Cat) Serval
Yellowish Olive Green, 8½ in., smooth base, applied
mouth $50–70
Dutch 1875–1890

A. Van Hoboken & Co/Rotterdam (Sealed Case Gin "AH" on Seal)
Olive Green, 11⅛ in., smooth base, applied mouth...................$70–100
Dutch 1875–1890

Beste Schiedammer Genever de Wildeman Fabriek Van Levert & Co. Te Amsterdam
Medium Olive Amber, 11¾ in., smooth base, applied
mouth $80–100
Dutch 1870–1890

Booth & Sedgwick's—London—Cordial Gin
Yellowish Olive Green, 10 in., pontil base, applied mouth........$75–100
English 1880–1890

Case gin bottles, African, 1885, $65–$100.

Bouvier's/Buchu Gin
Clear Glass, 11¾ in., smooth base, tooled mouth......................$95–110
American 1900–1910

Champion/P & C/Scotch Ale
Golden Yellow Amber, 7 in., smooth base, applied mouth..........$70–90
American 1885–1890

Clan Ivor Whisky/Registered/Bottled Only/by/Henry Mitchell & Cop/Limited/Cape Hill/Birmingham—Case Gin
Yellow Olive, 10 in., smooth base, applied mouth......................$80–100
English 1870–1890

Cream/Ale/Templeton/Louisville
Deep Red Amber, Quart, smooth base, applied double collar
mouth $125–150
American 1865–1875

Daniel Visser & Zonen/Schiedam, Genuine Hollands Geneva
Olive Green, 9 in., smooth base, applied mouth..........................$60–90
Dutch 1875–1890

Dekuyper's Square Face—Who Dekuyper Nightly Takes/Soundly Sleeps and Fit Awakes
Olive Green, 9½ in., smooth base, applied mouth.......................$60–90
Dutch 1880–1910

Demott's Porter/& Ale
Light Blue Green, 7½ in., iron pontil, applied mouth $30–50
American 1880–1900

E.Kinderlen Rotterdam, Genuine Holland Freebooter Geneva Kinderlen, Steam Distiller Comy. Established 1860 Delfshaven Near Schiedam
Olive Green, 12 in., smooth base, applied mouth.........................$75–90
Dutch 1875–1890

Erven L. Bols/Het Lootsje/Amsterdam—Sealed Pinch Side Case Gin
Medium Yellowish Olive Green, 10¼ in., smooth base, applied
sloping collar mouth $350–500
Dutch 1880–1890

Geneva, F. Nolet, Schiedam—Case Gin
Medium Olive Green, 5½ in., smooth base, tooled mouth..........$60–80
Dutch 1800–1880

Geneva, F. Nolet, Schiedam—Case Gin
Medium Olive Green, 9⅜ in., pontil base, applied mouth $70–90
Dutch 1800–1880

HdB & C (On Applied Seal)—Case Gin
Olive Green, 6⅜ in., smooth base, applied mouth......................$60–85
Dutch 1875–1890

Herman Jansen/Schiedam/Holland (on Applied Seal)
Yellowish Olive Green, 10⅝ in., smooth base, applied
mouth $80–125
Dutch 1875–1890

Hoytema & Co—Case Gin
Medium Olive Amber, 8⅝ in., smooth base, applied mouth.......$40–70
Dutch 1870–1890

HZS—Applied Seal Case Gin
Moss Green, 11½ in., smooth base, applied mouth....................$50–75
Dutch 1885–1895

Case gin bottles, V. Hoytema & C, 1885, $85–$125.

A.M. Bininger & Co.,
No. 19 Broad St., N.Y.,
Old London Dock Gin, 1885,
$225–$325.

JDKZ—This Bottle Is The/John De Kuyper & Son/Rotterdam
Clear, 7 in., smooth base, tooled mouth......................................$50–75
Dutch 1880–1900

John Ryan/XXX Porter & Ale Philada
Deep Cobalt Blue, 6⅞ in., iron pontil, applied mouth $150–250
American 1845–1855

**Juniper/Leaf Gin—Warning/This Bottle Is the Property of Theodore
Netter/(Contents Only Sold) Any Peson or Persons Using the Name
Juniper Leaf Gin Refilling or Selling This Bottle Will Be Prosecuted
Under Patent Righs. Theodore Netter—Case Gin**
Medium Amber, 10½ in., smooth base, tooled mouth.............$175–200
American 1880–1900

Knickerbocker/Gin Company N.Y.
Deep Teal Blue Green, 5⅞ in., smooth base, applied mouth $125–200
American 1875–1885

Club house gin, London Jockey, 1865–1875, $300–$400.

L. Meigs (Embossed Key) Antwerp—Sealed Case Gin
Yellowish Olive Amber, 7⅜ in., smooth base, applied mouth and seal..$50–100
Dutch 1885–1895

Levert & Schudel/Haarlem—Case Gin
Aqua, 5½ in., smooth base, applied mouth..................................$60–85
Dutch 1875–1890

Levert & Schudel/Haarlem—Case Gin
Medium Green, 5⅝ in., smooth base, tooled mouth....................$40–70
Dutch 1880–1900

Lighthouse Echte Jenever Holland Gin, Sole Agents for the United States, the Ginter Co., Boston, Mass.
Grass Green, 10¾ in., smooth base, tooled mouth.....................$80–125
American 1885–1895

M. Keane XXX Ale

Medium Cobalt Blue, 9 in., smooth base, applied sloping double collar mouth $400–500
American 1865–1875 (Very Rare, less than five known examples)

Mullier/Ra Doval—Wide Mouth Case Gin

Smoky Clear Glass, 12¾ in., pontil base, flared mouth...........$325–425
European 1855–1875

P. Loopuyt & Co./Distillrs/Schiedam

Olive Green, 9½ in., smooth base, applied mouth......................$60–90
Dutch 1880–1910

Philadelphia/XXX/Porter & Ale (Five Pointed Star)

Deep Yellowish Olive Green, 6¾ in., smooth base, applied blob type mouth $70–90
American 1855–1865

W.C. Peacock & Co.,
Honolulu, HI, 1875–1895,
$750–$1200.

Royal/Iain/Batavia
Medium Yellow Green, 11¾ in., smooth base, applied
mouth $125–175
Dutch 1875–1890

Rye Malt/Gin (Inside Circle Around a Crown) H.H.S. & Co. (Inside Crown)—Henry h. Shufeldt & Co.
Golden Yellow Amber, 9⅝ in., smooth base, applied mouth.....$80–100
American 1870–1890

S.A. Maas/Schiedam—Sealed Case Gin
Yellowish Olive Amber, 9⅛ in., smooth base, applied
mouth $50–100
Dutch 1885–1985

Silver Overlay Back Bar Bottle, Overlay Decoration and the Word "Gin"—Case Gin
Olive Amber, 9½ in., "A" on smooth base, applied mouth $200–300
Dutch 1880–1900

Tapan Zee Holland Gin Distilled by the Fleischmann Co. Peekskill, N.Y. (Label)
Deep Olive Green, 10⅛ in., smooth base, tooled mouth...........$70–100
American 1880–1900

Van Drukker Brand Holland Gin
Olive Green, 10¼ in., smooth base, applied mouth.....................$60–90
Dutch 1875–1890

Visser's Grey Stallion Geneva Oldest Distillery Established 1714 Schiedam
Olive Green, 9 in., smooth base, applied mouth..........................$60–85
Dutch 1875–1890

White/Lily—Applied Seal Case Gin
Clear, 11⅛ in., smooth base, tooled mouth $70–90
Dutch 1880–1890

W.S.C./Club House Gin
Yellowish Olive Green, 9¼ in., smooth base, applied
mouth $300–400
American 1860–1875

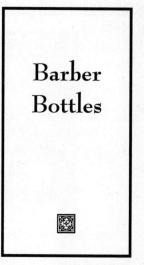

Barber Bottles

Starting in the mid-1860s and continuing to 1920, barbers in America used colorful decorated bottles filled with various tonics and colognes. The finish of these unique and colorful pieces originated when the Pure Food and Drug Act of 1907 restricted the use of alcohol-based ingredients in unlabeled or refillable containers.

Very early examples will have rough pontil scars with various types of ornamentation such as fancy pressed designs, paintings, and labels under glass. The bottles were usually fit with a cork, metal, or porcelain-type closure.

A. Winkel Sr. Bay Rum
Milk Glass with multicolored enamel decoration, smooth base (W. T. & Co.), ground lip...$400–500
American 1885–1925

Barber Bottle
Teal Blue Melon, 8½ in., smooth base, tooled mouth $80–125
American 1885–1925

Barber Bottle
Deep Cobalt Blue with Orange and White Enamel Floral
decoration...$75–120
American 1885–1925

Barber Bottle
Cobalt Blue, 7⅞ in., smooth base, sheared lip.........................$75–150
American 1885–1925

American barber bottles, 1880–1910, $100–$300 (each).

Barber Bottle
Cobalt Blue with White enamel, Mary Gregory, 8 in., pontil base,
rolled lip...$200–300
American 1885–1925

Barber Bottle
Art Glass, Clear with applied Ruby Crackle Pattern, 7¾ in., smooth
base, polished lip $150–250
American 1885–1925

Barber Bottle
Turquoise Blue, Hobnail-Pattern, 7 in., pontil, rolled lip $80–120
American 1885–1925

Barber Bottle
Opalescent Clear Glass, 7 in., melon sided, smooth base, rolled
lip $100–125
American 1895–1925

Barber Bottle
Opalescent Clear Glass, 8¼ in., Spanish Lace Pattern, pontil, rolled
lip $100–150
American 1885–1925

Barber Bottle
Clear Glass with Pink and White alternating Swirl Pattern, pontil,
rolled lip...$95–125
American 1885–1925

Barber Bottle
Frosted Turquoise Blue, 8⅞ in., smooth base, polished lip.......$80–120
American 1890–1925

Barber Bottle
Green, 7¼ in., smooth base, tooled lip $30–50
American 1885–1925

Barber Bottle
Milk Glass with Multicolored Cherub decoration, 7⅞ in., pontil,
sheared lip..$250–350
American 1885–1925

Barber Bottle
Deep Grass Green, 6¾ in., rib-pattern, smooth base, sheared lip....$100–150
American 1885–1920

Barber Bottle
Medium Purple Amethyst, 7⅛ in., rib-pattern, pontil, sheared
lip...$125–150
American 1885–1920

Barber bottle (Mary Gregory Type "Fountain") $500–$700;
Barber bottle (Cologne) $150–$250; Paper shaving vase,
$2500–$3500; Barber bottle (Bay Rum) $300–$400; Barber
bottle $300–$500. All circa 1885–1925.

Barber bottle $250–$350; Barber bottle $1200–$1800; Barber bottle (Mary Gregory Cameo Style) $200–$300; Barber bottle, $200–$300; Barber bottle, $200–$300. All circa 1885–1925.

C.F. Hawman Bay Rum
Milk Glass with multicolored enamel decoration, 9½ in., smooth base (W. T. & Co.), ground lip...$350–450
American 1885–1925

Corner's Quinine Dandruff Cure Buffalo, NY
Clear Glass, 7 in., smooth base, tooled lip $100–125
American 1900–1920

DeLoney's Hair, Scalp and Face Tonic Contains 43% Grain Alcohol Deloney & Co. Hammond, Ind.
Clear Glass, 7½ in., smooth base, tooled lip................................$45–65
American 1920–1935

E.S.N. (Label under Glass)
Clear Glass with Multicolored Label, smooth base (W. T. & Co.), ground lip...$275–325
American 1885–1925

Hair Oil D.V. Sledge Propr.
Clear Glass, 7¾ in., smooth base, tooled mouth......................$ 75–125
American 1890–1925

J.N. Hogarth Bay Rum
Milk Glass with Multicolored Floral decoration, smooth base (W. T. &
Co.), ground lip $200–300
American 1885–1920

Jas. Wolfinger Tonic
Milk Glass with Multicolored Enamel decoration, smooth base (W. T.
& Co.), ground lip..$200–300
American 1885–1920

KDX Koken Companies St. Louis, Mo (Original Crown Stopper & Label)
Black Glass, 8⅛ in., smooth base, tooled mouth $125–150
American 1890–1920

**Levarn's Golden Wash Shampoo Manufactured by the Mettowee
Toilet Specialty Co. Granville, New York (Label under Glass)**
Clear Glass, 7½ in., smooth base, tooled lip...............................$45–60
American 1920–1935

Lucky Tiger for Hair and Scalp Kansas City, Mo (Label)
Clear Glass, 8¼ in., smooth base, tooled lip...............................$50–70
American 1910–1925

N. Wapler/N.Y.
Green, 7¼ in., smooth base, tooled lip $50–70
American 1885–1920

Pompeian Hair Massage Does Remove Dandruff (Label under Glass)
Clear Glass, 8⅛ in., smooth base, rolled lip.............................$125–150
American 1920–1930

**Property/of/Lucky/Tiger/Remedy/Co./Kansas/City/Mo., For Dandruff
and Eczema Lucky Tiger, Lucky Tiger Femedy Co. Kansas City, Mo**
Clear Glass, 8¾ in., smooth base, tooled mouth......................$150–200
American 1900–1925

**Reliable Trade Mark Brand Twin Action Shampoo Reliable Barber
Supply Company Pittsburgh, Pa**
Milk Glass, 6⅞ in., smooth base, rolled lip..................................$60–90
American 1910–1930

**Stewarts Perfection Shaving Lotion Godrich Gamble Company St.
Paul, Minn**
Clear Glass, 7¾ in., smooth base, rolled lip.................................$15–25
American 1890–1930

Fitch's Dandruff Remover Shampoo, 1900–1925, $25–$35.

T. Noonan & Co/Barber Supplies/Boston, Mass
Clear Glass, 8⅜ in., smooth base, tooled mouth.......................$80–100
American 1885–1915

T. Noonan & Co/Barber Supplies/Boston, Mass
Clear Glass, 10¼ in., smooth base, tooled mouth.....................$80–120
American 1885–1910

The Fitch Ideal Dandruff Remover (Label), This Bottle Is Loaned by the Fitch Dandruff Cure Co. (Embossed)
Clear Glass, 7⅞ in., smooth base, tooled mouth......................$150–250
American 1900–1920

The N.S.W. Barbers Supply House/C&A
Red Amber with overall Quilt pattern, 6⅛ in., smooth base (Bottle Made In USA), tooled mouth $100–125
Australian 1890–1910

Tonique De Luxe Koken Companies St. Louis, Mo
Black Glass, 8⅛ in., smooth base, tooled mouth $125–150
American 1890–1920

Beer Bottles

Attempting to find an American beer bottle made before the mid-nineteenth century is a difficult task, since up until that time most of the bottles used for beer and spirits were imported. The majority of these imported bottles were black glass pontiled bottles made in three-piece molds and rarely embossed. There are four types of early beer bottles: the porter, which is the most common, was used from 1820 to 1920; the ale from 1845 to 1850; the early lager used from 1847 to 1850 (rare), and the late lager from 1850 to 1860.

In spite of the large amounts of beer consumed in America before 1860, beer bottles were very rare and all have pontiled bases. Most of the beer manufactured during this time was distributed and dispensed from wooden barrels, or kegs, and sold to local taverns and private bottlers. Collectors often ask why the various breweries did not bottle the beer they manufactured. During the Civil War, the federal government placed a special tax, which was levied by the barrel, on all brewed beverages. This taxing system prevented the brewery from making the beer and bottling it in the same building. Selling the beer to taverns and private bottlers was much simpler than erecting another building just for bottling. This entire process changed after 1890 when the federal government revised the law to allow breweries to bottle the beer straight from the beer lines. The following list reflects the age and rarity of beer bottles made between 1860 and 1940.

Year	Rare	Scarce	Semi-common	Common
1860–1870	X			
1870–1880		X		
1880–1890			X	
1890–1930				X

Embossed bottles marked "ale" or "porter" were first manufactured between 1850 and 1860. In the late 1860s, the breweries began to emboss their bottles with names and promotional messages. This practice continued into the twentieth century. It is interesting to note that Pennsylvania breweries made most of the beer bottles during the second half of the nineteenth century. By 1890, beer was readily available in bottles around most of the country.

The first bottles used for beer in the United States were made of pottery, not glass. Glass did not become widely used until after the Civil War (1865). A wholesaler for Adolphus Busch named C. Conrad sold the original Budweiser beer from 1877 to 1890. The Budweiser name was a trademark of C. Conrad, but in 1891, it was sold to the Anheuser-Busch Brewing Association. Up until the 1870s, beer bottles were sealed with cork stoppers. Late in the nineteenth century the lighting stopper was invented. It proved a convenient way of sealing and resealing blob-top bottles. In 1891, corks were replaced with the "Crown Cork Closure," invented by William Painter. This made use of a thin slice of cork within a tight-fitting metal cap. Once these were removed, they couldn't be used again.

Up until the mid-1930s, beer came in green glass bottles. After Prohibition, brown glass came into use since it was thought to filter damaging rays of the sun and to preserve freshness.

Ainslie/Leeds/Street/Brewery/Liverpool (Embossed)
Olive Amber, 8¾ in., pontil base, applied mouth....................$400–600
English 1790–1810

Alexander's Excelsior Beer
Pale Greenish Aqua, 7½ in., smooth base, tooled mouth $15–25
American 1880–1890

Aug.J.Lang (Monogram) San Francisco
Medium Yellowish Amber, 5½ in., smooth base, tooled lip $250–350
American 1880–1900 (Extremely Rare—only 3 or 4 known pieces)

A. W. Kenison Co., Auburn, Cal
Medium Amber, 11¾ in., smooth base, applied top....................$30–40
American 1880–1890

Bay View Brewing Co. Seattle, Wash—Not to Be Sold
Medium Olive Green, 11¾ in., smooth base, applied
mouth $125–175
American 1880–1890

N. Kessler Brewery, Helena, MT., 1880–1895, $15–$20 (each).

Barner and Riebe Bottler's, Redding Cal
Amber, 11¼ in., smooth base, crown top $30–60
American 1890–1900 (very rare)

Bosch Lake—Linden Mich.
Light Amber, 7¼ in., smooth base, tooled top.............................$30–60
American 1880–1890

This Bottle/Buffalo Br'g Co/Sacramento/Not to Be Sold
Red Amber, 12⅛ in., smooth base, applied mouth..................$250–350
American 1890–1920

C. Conrad & Co's/Original/Budweiser/U.S. Patent No 6376
Aqua, 9¼ in., smooth base, applied mouth..............................$90–140
American 1880–1890 (rare in this size)

C. Conrad & Co's/ Original/Budweiser/U.S. Patent No 6376
Aqua, 12 in., smooth base, applied mouth $100–150
American 1880–1890

California Bottling Co. S.F.
Light Amber, 10¾ in., smooth base, applied top........................$30–60
American 1880–1890

Calumet Brewing Co., Calumet Mich
Amber, 11¾ in., smooth base, applied mouth $70–120
American 1880–1890

Cascase Lager S.F. Cal
Amber, 11¼ in., smooth base, tooled top $30–50
American 1880–1890

C.J. Vath & Co., San Jose
Amber, 11½ in., smooth base, tooled top $30–60
American 1880–1890

C. Thomas Truckee
Olive Green, 7¼ in., smooth base, tooled top split, four piece
mold $1000–2000
American 1877–1890 (rare—less than 6 known pieces)

Valley Brew Lager Beer,
El Dorado Brewing Co., Stockton, CA,
1885–1895, $25–$35.

Christian Moerlein Brewing Cincinnati, O
Amber, 7½ in., smooth base, crown top $20–30
American 1880–1890

Consolidated Milwaukee Beer Agency Helena, Mont
Amber, 7¼ in., smooth base, tooled top $50–100
American 1880–1890

Dr. Cronk's Beer
Bright Yellow Green, 12–sided, pontiled, tooled lip $2000–3500
American 1850–1865

E.Wagner/Manchester/N.H.
Amber, 8½ in., smooth base, tooled mouth $15–20
American 1880–1920

Gambrinus Brewing Co / G.B. Co./Portland, Or.
Amber, 11¼ in., smooth base (S.B. & G CO), tooled mouth $40–60
American 1880–1900

Germania Bottling House D. Nashan, Manager Boston
Aqua, 7¼ in., smooth base, applied top with wire bail seal........$30–60
American 1880–1890

Gray's Bro. Stout Phila
Medium Olive Amber, 6⅞ in., pontil base, applied seal..........$100–150
American 1820–1830

Gold Edge Bottling Works J.F. Deininger Vallejo
Golden Amber, 7¾ in., smooth base, applied top......................$60–120
American 1875–1890 (Extremely Rare)

G.W. Hoxie's Premium Beer
Emerald Green, 6½ in., smooth base, applied sloping collar
mouth $175–225
American 1855–1865

Gustave Gnauck Benicia Brewery, Benicia, Cal
Amber, 7¼ in., smooth base, tooled top, four mold split........$200–300
American 1880–1890

Hansen & Kohler Oakland Cal.
Amber, 11¼ in., four-piece mold, smooth base, tooled top $30–60
American 1880–1890 (Scarce)

Great Falls Select, $7–$10; Great Falls Select, $10–$15;
Highlander Beer, Missoula, MT., $5–$7; Highlander Premium
Beer, $5–$7. All circa 1930–1935.

Henry Braun/Beer Bottling/Oakland, Cal.
Amber, 7¾ in., smooth base, tooled mouth..............................$80–120
American 1880–1900

Honolulu/Brewing Co./Honolulu, H.T.
Aqua, 12 in., smooth base, tooled mouth................................$100–150
American 1880–1900

J. Gahm & Son/Boston
Aqua, 7¾ in., smooth base, tooled mouth $15–20
American 1880–1920

**J.J. Hottenstine & Bro/Allentown/Penna—This Bottle Is/Not To Be
Sold**
Deep Cobalt Blue, 6¾ in., smooth base, applied mouth..........$125–175
American 1855–1865

**J.J. Hottenstine & Bro/Allentown/Penna—This Bottle Belongs To/J.J.
Hottenstine/& Bro.**
Deep Cobalt Blue, 9⅜ in., smooth base, applied mouth......$1000–1500
American 1870–1880 (Original lightning style closure)

Jamica Champagne Beer S.F. D. L. Fonseca & Co.
Blue, 7¼ in., smooth base, blob top..$300–800
American 1885–1886

John Houb Sacramento Cal. (Monogram)
Amber, 11¼ in., smooth base, crown top $30–50
American 1890–1910

John Lyons/Wholesale/Dealer In/Wines & Liquors/Boston
Olive Green, 8 in., smooth base, tooled mouth...........................$15–20
American 1880–1920

Kahny & Burbacher Bottlers Redding, Cal
Amber, 7½ in., smooth base, tooled top, three piece mold.........$50–80
American 1875–1890

Lammers Denver, Colorado
Aqua, 7¾, smooth base, tooled top $30–40
American 1880–1890

Fredericksburg Brewery, Lager Beer, Oakland Bottling Co., 1880–1895, $30–$40.

Mokelumne Hill Brewery Lagomarsino
Amber, 11 in., smooth base, tooled lip.....................................$120–160
American 1880–1900

Phoenix Bott'g/Phila/This Bottle/Not To Be Sold (On Applied Seal)
Olive Green, 9⅜ in., smooth base (This Bottle Not To Be Sold),
applied mouth...$300–400
American 1885–1895 (original lightning style closure)

Phoenix/13oz. Trade(Motif of Eagle)Mark /Bottling Works Buffalo N/Y
Amber, 9½ in., smooth base, tooled mouth...............................$90–125
American 1880–1920

**Robert Portner/Brewing Co./Trade/Tivoll/ Mark (Inside Diamond)/
Alexandria, Va—This Bottle/Not To/Be Sold**
Olive Green, 9⅜ in., smooth base, applied blob type
mouth $100–150

S. Fulford (Motif Of Lion) Manchester
Amber, 8 in., smooth base, tooled mouth....................................$15–20
American 1880–1920

S & H Chicago
Yellow Olive, 11½ in., smooth base (A. & D.H.C.) on reverse at
base, applied mouth...$600–800
American 1865–1875 (rare Chicago beer)

Schlitz Milwaukee Beer Nadeau 7 Waller Agts.Portland
Amber, 7½ in., smooth base, tooled top $80–120
American 1880–1890

Sierra Bottling Co. Ieland's Best, Jamestown, Cal
Dark Amber, 9¾, smooth base, applied top..................................$30–60
American 1875–1890

The F.W.Cook/Brewing Co/Evansville, Ind.
Amber, 8⅛ in., smooth base, tooled mouth................................$10–15
American 1880–1920

**The George Bechtel Brewing Co. (Motif of Soldier Carrying an
American Flag with the Word) Excelsior/Bottle at Brewery/Stapleton/
Staten Island—This Bottle/Not To Be Sold**
Amber, 9½ in., smooth base, tooled mouth...............................$85–100
American 1880–1920

The John Hauck/Brewing Co. Cincinnati, O.
Amber, 8 in., smooth base, tooled mouth.....................................$15–20
American 1880–1920

The Phoenix Brewery Co., Victoria B.C.
Dark Olive Green, 10¾ in., pontil base, applied top.................$50–120
American 1880–1890

The Springfield Brewing/Co./Springfield/Mass.
Amber, 7¾ in., smooth base, tooled mouth $15–20
American 1880–1920

The/Tip Top, The Tip Top/Larger Beer
Aqua, 7 in., smooth base, applied blob top................................$20–30
American 1890–1910

John Wieland's, Export Beer, S. F., 1885–1895, $30–$40.

Tiffany & Allen/Spruce Beer/Washington & Mrket/Cor/Fair & / Washington/St./Paterson/N.J
Deep Cobalt Blue, 7¾ in., smooth base, applied mouth........$800–1000
American 1870–1880

Tivoli Brewing Co., Registered Detroit Mich
Amber, 11¼ in., smooth base, tooled top $30–50
American 1880–1890

Tweedie Red Hand San Francisco
Olive Green, 11¾ in., smooth base, applied top......................$300–500
American 1880–1890

U.S. Bottling Co., John Fauser & Co., S.F. Cal
Dark Amber, 9¼ in., smooth base, applied top with original wire
bail..$40–80
American 1880–1890

West End Brewing Co./Utica, N.Y. (Monogram)
Amber, 9¾ in., smooth base, tooled mouth $10–15
American 1880–1920

Wonder Bottling Co. W. Noethig Sacramento, Cal.
Amber, 10¾ in., smooth base, tooled top, four piece mold $50–100
American 1880–1890

Wreden's Lager Oakland
Amber, 11¼ in., smooth base, tooled top $30–50
American 1890–1900 (Scarce)

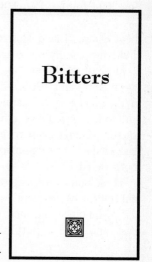

Bitters

When looking at antique bottles as collectibles, bitters bottles have long been favorites. Because of their unique form, bitters bottles were saved in large numbers, giving the collector of today some great opportunities to build very special collections.

Bitters, which originated in England, is a type of medicine made from roots or herbs named for their bitter taste. During the eighteenth century, bitters were added to water, ale, or spirits with the intent of curing all types of ailments. Because of the pretense that these mixtures had some medicinal value, bitters became very popular in America, since Colonists could import them from England without paying the liquor tax. While most bitters had a low alcohol content, some brands were labeled as high as 120 proof, higher than most hard liquor available at the time. As physicians became convinced bitters did have some type of healing value, the drink became socially acceptable. This thought process promoted sales to people who normally weren't liquor drinkers and also provided upstanding citizens a good excuse for having liquor in the home (for medicinal purposes, of course).

The best known among the physicians who made their own bitters for patients was Dr. Jacob Hostetter. After his retirement in 1853, he gave permission to his son David to manufacture it commercially. Hostetters Bitters was known for its colorful and dramatic advertisements. While Hostetters said it wouldn't cure everything, the list of ailments it claimed to alleviate with regular use covered most everything: indigestion, diarrhea, dysentery, chills, fever, liver ailments, and pains and weakness that came with old age (at that time, a euphemism for impotence). Despite these claims, David Hostetter died in 1888 from kidney failure, which could supposedly be cured by his bitters.

Most of the bitters bottles, over 1,000 types, were manufactured between 1860 and 1905. The more unique shapes, called "figurals," were in the likenesses of cannons, drums, pigs, fish, and ears of corn. In addition, a variety of other forms produced bottles that were round, square, rectangular, barreled-shaped, gin-bottle-shaped, twelve-sided, and flask-shaped. The embossed varieties are the most collectible, older, and more valuable.

These bottles were most commonly amber (pale golden yellow to dark amber-brown), frequently aqua (light blue), and sometimes green or clear glass. The rarest and most collectible colors are dark blue, amethyst, milk glass, and puce (a purplish brown).

American Life Bitters—P.E. Iler, Manufacturer, Tiffin, Ohio
Medium Yellowish Amber, 9 in., smooth base, applied
mouth $3000–4000
American 1870–1875

Angelica Bitters or Poor Man's Tonic, Geo. H. Fickardt, Circleville, Ohio
Bluish Aqua, 7¾ in., smooth base, tooled mouth $140–180
American 1890–1910 (rare)

Augauer Bitters—Augauer Bitters Co. Chicago
Green, 8 in., smooth base, tooled mouth......................................$30–60
American 1850–1860

Big Bill Best Bitters
Medium Amber, 12 in., smooth base, tooled mouth................$140–180
American 1900–1910

Brady's Family Bitters
Golden Amber, 9½ in., smooth base, applied sloping collar
mouth $100–150
American 1875–1885

Brown's Castilian
Amber, 11⅛ in., smooth base, applied mouth $125–150
American 1865–1875

Brown's Celebrated Indian Herb Bitters—Patented 1868
Yellow Olive, 12⅛ in., smooth base, rolled lip $2800–3800
American 1868–1875

B.T. 1865 S.C., Smith's, Druid Bitters
Deep Cherry Puce, 9½ in., Barrel, smooth base, applied disc
mouth $800–1200
American 1860–1870 (Scarce)

Burkhart's Homestead Bitters—Fond du Lac, Wis
Medium Amber, 9¼ in., smooth base, tooled mouth...............$200–250
American 1885–1895

Celery Bitters—S.CTY.W. Co. (Around Shoulder)—Steuben County Wine Co. Chicago
Clear, 5⅝ in., smooth base, tooled lip...$40–60
American 1865–1875

Chas. Nichols Jr. & Props., Lowell Mass, Dr. Chandler's Jamaica Ginger Root Bitter's
Medium Yellow Green, 9¾ in., smooth base, applied double collar
mouth $8000–12000
American 1865–1875 (rare—only three known examples)

Old Homestead Wild Cherry
Bitters, 1855–1865, $175–$250.

Cole Bros Vegetable Bitters—C.L., Cole Prop'r—Binghamton, N.Y.
Amber, 7⅞ in., smooth base, tooled mouth $60–80
American 1840–1855

Curtis—Cordial—Calisaya—the Great-Stomach Bitters 1866 CCC 1900
Deep Amber, 11½ in., smooth base, applied mouth............$1000–1500
American 1875–1885

Dr. B. Olen's Life Bitters—New York—Price 50 Cts
Aqua, 5 in., pontil base, flared lip $350–450
American 1825–1840

Dr. B. H. Kauffman Stomach Bitters—Lancaster PA
Blue Green, 9¼ in., iron pontil, applied sloping double collar
mouth $3500–5500
American 1845–1855 (rare—only three known examples)

Dr. Bell's Blood Purifying Bitters, the Great English Remedy
Yellowish Amber, 9⅜ in., smooth base, applied mouth...........$125–150
English 1865–1875

Dr. Hardmann's—Good Samaritan Stomach Bitters
Golden Yellow Amber, 9¼ in., smooth base, applied sloping collar
mouth $350–450
American 1875–1885

Dr. Herbert John's—Indian Bitters—Great Indian Discoveries
Amber, 8½ in., smooth base, tooled mouth.............................$100–150
American 1880–1895

Dr. Hoofland's German Bitters—Liver Complaing—Dyspepsia & C—C.M. Jackson, Philadelphia
Deep Bluish Aqua, 8 in., smooth base, applied mouth $30–60
American 1855–1865

Dr. J.R.B. McClintock's Dandelion (Monogram) Bitters, Philadelphia
Aqua, 8⅛ in., smooth base, tooled mouth $80–120
American 1880–1890 (rare)

Dr. Lamot's—Botanic Bitters
Medium Amber, 8⅝ in., smooth base, tooled mouth...............$175–275
American 1880–1890 (Rare)

Dr. Langley's Root & Herb Bitters
Orange Amber, 5¾ in., smooth base, applied mouth $80–120
American 1860–1870

Dr. Loew's Celebrated Stomach Bitters & Nerve Tonic—The Loew & Sons Co. Cleveland, O
Deep Yellowish Olive Green, 9¼ in., smooth base, tooled
mouth $200–300
American 1890–1910

Dr. Med Koch's Universal Magen Bitters (Diamond Pattern on Two Panels)
Olive Green, 8 in., smooth base, applied sloping collar
mouth $200–300
German 1870–1880

Dr. Planett's Bitters
Aqua, 9¾ in., iron pontil, applied sloping collar mouth $200–275
American 1840–1855

Dr. R.F. Hibbard's Wild Cherry Bitters
Aqua, 6⅞ in., smooth base, applied mouth..............................$125–150
American 1840–1855

Dr. Sperry's Female Strengthening Bitters, Waterbury, Ct (Label)
Clear, 9¼ in., smooth base, tooled mouth $70–90
American 1870–1880 (rare with label)

Dr. Stoughten's—National Bitters Patd, Hamburg, Pa
Amber, 10⅛ in., smooth base, applied $700–900
American 1870–1875

Dr. Zabriskie's—Jersey City—N.J.—Bitters
Clear, 6⅛ in., pontil base, flared lip..$250–300
American 1840–1855

Dingens Napoleon Cocktail Bitters, Dingen's Brothers, Buffalo N.Y.
Yellowish Olive Amber, 9½ in., Banjo Lady's Leg, smooth base, applied
mouth $3500–5500
American 1865–1875 (rare)

E. Dexter Loveridge Wahoo Bitter (Motif of Eagle with Arrow)
Amber, 10⅛ in., smooth base, applied sloping collar
mouth $375–500
American 1860–1880

E.J. Rose's Magador Bitters for Stomach, Kidney & Liver—Superior Tonic Cathartic and Blood Purifier
Amber, 8¾ in., smooth base, tooled mouth..................................$40–60
American 1860–1880

G.C. Blake's, Anti. Despeptic, Bitters
Aqua, 7 in., iron pontil, applied mouth....................................$700–900
American 1840–1855

G.C. Segur's Golden Seal Bitters—Springfield, Mass
Aqua, 8¼ in., open pontil, applied sloping collar mouth........$175–275
American 1845–1855

Grer's Eclipse Bitters
Amber, 8¾ in., smooth base, applied sloping collar mouth $80–120
American 1875–1885

Herkules Bitter, AC (Monogram) 1 Quart
Bright Yellow Green, 7¼ in., smooth base, tooled lip..........$1500–2200
American 1900–1910

Hertrich's Gesundheits Bitter, Hans, Hertrich Hof, Erfinder U Allein Destillateur—Gesetzuch Geschultzi
Deep Olive Green, 11½ in., smooth base, applied double collar
mouth $500–700
American 1870–1880

Hi-Hi Bitters—Hi-Hi Bitters Co., Rock Island Ill
Amber, 9⅝ in., smooth base, applied double collar mouth.........$60–80
American 1840–1855

Holtzermann's Patent Stomach Bitters (Label)
Medium Amber, 9¾ in., smooth base, tooled mouth...............$275–375
American 1875–1890

Hutchings—Dyspersia Bitters—New York
Aqua, 9½ in., iron pontil, applied sloping collar mouth $70–90
American 1840–1855

Dr. C.W. Robacks Stomach Bitters, Cincinnati, OH, 1860–1870, $500–$600; National Bitters, 1867–1875, $700–$1000; Holtzermann's Patent Stomach Bitters, 1855–1870, $1500–$2000; S.T. Drake's 1860 Plantation X Bitters, patented 1862, 1862–1870, $1500–$2000.

I. Newton's Jaundice Bitters—Norwich Vt.
Aqua, 6¾ in., open pontil, rolled lip.......................................$200–300
American 1840–1855 (extremely rare)

Jackson's Stonewall Bitters (Motif of Stone Wall)—Quinlin—Bros & Co—St. Louis—Mo
Medium Golden Amber, 9½ in., smooth base, applied sloping collar mouth $2800–3800
American 1865–1875

J.F.L. Capitol Bitters
Golden Amber, 9¼ in., iron pontil, applied double collar mouth $200–300
American 1860–1870

Jno. Moffat—Phoenix Bitters—New York—Price $1
Yellow Amber with Olive tone, 5⅝ in., pontil base, applied
mouth $500–700
American 1830–1845

Joel Whary's Herb Bitters
Medium Amber, 9⅛ in., smooth base, tooled mouth...............$150–250
American 1885–1895

John Roots Bitters—1834 Buffalo, N.Y.
Medium Blue Green, 10 in., smooth base, applied mouth.......$400–700
American 1865–1875

**John W. Steele's Niagara Star Bitters (Motif of Eagle)—John W.
Steele's—Niagara (Motif of Star) Bitters—1864**
Medium Amber, 10 in., smooth base, applied mouth $175–225
American 1865–1875

**Jones Universal Stomach Bitters—Manufactured by C.O. Jones & Co.
Williamsport, Penn**
Amber, 9 in., smooth base, applied sloping collar mouth........$175–275
American 1870–1880

Kagy's Superior Stomach Bitters
Deep Amber, 9½ in., smooth base, applied sloping collar
mouth $200–300
American 1870–1880

Anna Pottery Pig, 1882, $3500–$4500; Suffolk Bitters, Philbrook &
Tucker, Boston, 1865–1875, $600–$700; Berkshire Bitters,
Annan. & Co., Cincinnati, OH. 1865–1875, $1000–$1500.

Kantorowicz 1823–1923 (On Two Sides) (Laurel Wreath and Flower Basket)
Clear, 9 in., smooth base, tooled mouth.....................................$125–150
American 1845–1855

Kelley's Old Cabin Bitters—Patented 1863
Deep Amber, 9¼ in., smooth base, applied sloping collar
mouth $1200–1600
American 1863–1870

Kimball's Jaundice—Bitters—Troy, N.Y.
Yellowish olive amber, 7 in., iron pontil, applied sloping collar
mouth $375–450
American 1845–1855

Knapps—Health, Restorative Bitters N.Y.
Aqua, 8⅛ in., pontil base, applied sloping collar mouth $300–400
American 1845–1855

Lediard's—O.K. Plantation—Bitters 1840
Medium Yellowish Amber, 10⅛ in., smooth base, applied sloping
collar mouth $900–1400
American 1870–1880

Life of Man Bitters—C. Gates & Co.
Olive Green, 8 in., smooth base, tooled mouth............................$30–50
American 1865–1875

Litthauer Stomch Bitters, Invented 1864 by Josef Loewenthal Berlin
Milk glass, 9½ in., smooth base, applied mouth......................$250–350
American 1895–1905

London—Wryghte's Bitters—London
Olive Green, 5¾ in., pontil base, applied mouth......................$350–450
English 1860–1870

Marshall's Bitters—The Best Laxative and Blood Purifier
Amber, 8¾ in., smooth base, tooled mouth $40–60
American 1860–1880

McConnon's Stomach Bitters, McConnon & Company Winona, Minn
Medium Amber, 9⅛ in., smooth base, tooled mouth...............$200–300
American 1880–1890

Unembossed Bitters barrel, 1855–1865, $700–$1000;
S & H Chicago, 1865–1875, $600–$700 (Beer); Dingens
Napoleon Cocktail Bitters, 1865, $3500–$5000;
Hopatkong Whiskey, 1875–1885, $500–$700;
McKeever's Army Bitters, 1865–1875, $1500–$2000.

McKeever's Army Bitters
Amber, 10½ in., smooth base, applied sloping collar
mouth $1400–1800
American 1865–1875

Mishler's Herb Bitters—Tablespoon Graduation—Mishler Herb Bitter Co.
Yellow with Amber tone, 9¼ in., smooth base (Stoeckel's Grad Pat
Feb 6'66), applied double collar mouth $80–120
American 1866–1875

Morning (Five-Pointed Star) Bitters, Inceptum
Golden Amber, 12⅜ in., iron pontil, applied sloping collar
mouth $200–300
American 1865–1875

Moulton's Oloroso Bitters Trade (Motif of Pineapple) Mark
Aqua, 11¼ in., smooth base, applied double collar
mouth $250–350
American 1860–1870

Damiana Bitters, 1877–1910,
$30–$60.

New York Hop Bitters Company (Motif of American Flag)
Deep Aqua, 9⅞ in., smooth base, applied sloping collar mouth......$175–250
American 1870–1880

Nibol Kidney and Liver Bitters—the Best Tonic, Laxative & Blood Purifier
Amber, 9½ in., smooth base, tooled mouth............................$100–175
American 1890–1900

No. 3 Dr. Saylor's German Rheuma Stomach Herb Bitters—Arcanum, Dr. G.S. Engler Propr, Bethlehem, Pa
Amber, 8¾ in., smooth base, tooled mouth............................$350–550
American 1880–1890 (extremely rare)

Old Dr. Townsend's Celebrated Stomach Bitters
Yellowish Amber, 8⅝ in., pontil base, applied mouth, applied
handles..$8000–12000
American 1860–1870

Old Homestead Wild Cherry Bitters—Patent
Golden Amber, 9⅚ in., applied sloping collar mouth..............$150–200
American 1865–1875

Orruro—Bitters
Oliver Green, 10¾ in., smooth base, applied mouth...................$20–50
American 1875–1885

Palmer's Tonic—Bitters—Andrus & Palmer, Sole Proprietor & Manufacturers (Motif of Eagle)
Emerald Green, 10¼ in., smooth base, applied sloping collar
mouth $4000–6000
American 1865–1875

P & D.H. Co. (Monogram)
Yellow with Olive tone, 10⅛ in., smooth base (Sazerac Aromatic
Bitters), applied mouth...$175–275
American 1870–1880 (scarce in this size)

Professor B.E. Mann's—Oriental Stomach Bitters—Patented
Medium Amber, 9⅞ in., smooth base, applied sloping collar
mouth $800–1400
American 1865–1875

Red Jacket Bitters—Monheimer & Co.
Medium Amber, 9⅝ in., smooth base, tooled mouth...............$125–150
American 1885–1895

Reed's Bitters—Reed's Bitters
Medium Amber, 12⅜ in., Lady's leg, smooth base, applied double
collar mouth $225–300
American 1870–1880

Rex Kidney and Liver Bitter—the Best Laxative and Blood Purifier
Golden Yellow Amber, 6¾ in., smooth base, tooled mouth $150–250
American 1890–1910 (rare in this size)

Royal Italian Bitters, Registered (Motif of Shield, Crown, Spears, and Drapery) Trade Mark, A.M. Gianelli, Genova
Pinkish Amethyst, 13¼ in., smooth base, applied disc mouth $500–700
American 1880–1895

Rosswinkle's Crown Bitters
Golden Yellow Amber, 9 in., smooth base, applied sloping collar
mouth $275–375
American 1875–1885

Russian—Imperial—Tonic Bitters
Bluish Aqua, 9⅝ in., smooth base, applied mouth $1000–1500
American 1865–1875 (rare)

Sanborn Kidney and Liver Vegetable Laxative Bitters
Amber, 9⅝ in., smooth base, applied sloping double collar
mouth $60–80
American 1840–1855

San Joaquin Wine Bitters
Amber, 9⅞ in., smooth base, applied sloping double collar
mouth $275–375
American 1870–1880

Lash's Bitters Co., 1908–1917,
$75–$100.

Schroeder's Bitters, Louisville, Ky.
Amber, 12⅛ in., Lady's leg, smooth base, applied mouth $175–275
American 1865–1870 (rare)

Simon's Centenial Bitters—Trade Mark (Figural of George Washington
Aqua, 10 in., smooth base, applied mouth $500–700
American 1870–1880

Simon's Prussian Vegetable Bitters
Medium Amber, 10 in., smooth base, applied sloping collar
mouth $250–350
American 1875–1885

S.O. Richardson's—Bitters—South Reading Mass
Deep Aqua, 6¾ in., iron pontil, applied mouth.........................$80–120
American 1845–1855

S & S Bitters, Der Doktor
Amber, 9⅜ in., smooth base, tooled mouth.............................$150–200
American 1885–1900

Suffolk Bitters, Philbrook & Tucker, Boston
Medium Amber, Pig, 10 in. Long, smooth base, applied double
collar mouth..$500–700
American 1865–1875

Thads. Waterman (Warsaw) Stomach Bitters
Amber, 10 in., 8–sided smooth base, applied sloping collar
mouth $1500–2200
American 1865–1875 (rare—only three known to exist)

The Great Universal Compound Stomach Bitters Patented 1870— Professor Geo. J. Byrne, New York
Yellow with Olive tone, 10¾ in., smooth base, applied
mouth $2800–3800
American 1870–1875

Tyler's Standard American Bitters
Root Beer Amber, 9⅜ in., smooth base, applied sloping collar
mouth $150–200
American 1870–1880

Dr. Henley's Wild Grape Root, IXL,
Bitters, 1868–1893, $75–$150.

**TT & CO.—Hop Bitters—1884 (Design in Diamond Trade Mark)
Gipps Land Hop Bitters Co.**
Pale Green, 9⅜ in., smooth base, applied sloping collar mouth......$40–60
American 1860–1880

Ulmer's Mountain Ash Bitters—New German—Remedy
Aqua, 7 in., pontil base, applied sloping collar mouth...........$800–1200
American 1840–1855 (Rare)

Wahoo & Calisaya Bitters, Jacob Pinkerton—I.M.—O.K. Y!!—Y!!!
Medium Amber, 10⅛ in., smooth base, applied sloping collar
mouth $400–600
American 1860–1880

Wallace Tonic Stomach Bitters—Geo Powell & Co. Chicago, Ill
Medium Amber, 9 in., smooth base, applied sloping collar
mouth $80–120
American 1870–1880

White's Stomach Bitters
Golden Amber, 9½ in., smooth base, applied sloping collar
mouth $150–200
American 1875–1885

Wolpert's Premium Bitters, the R. Brand Co., Toledo, O (Label)
Clear, 10 in., smooth base, tooled lip...$40–60
American 1865–1875

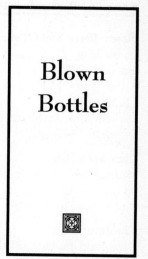

Blown Bottles

As mentioned earlier, free-blown bottles, also called simply blown bottles, were made without the use of molds and were shaped by the glassblower. It is difficult to attach ages and origins to them, since many were produced in Europe and the United States for a long time before records were kept.

Another type of blown bottle, the blown three-mold, was formed in a three-piece mold. These bottles were manufactured between 1820 and 1840 in Europe and the United States, and it is quite difficult to distinguish bottles from different sides of the Atlantic. Since blown three-mold and pressed three-mold are similar, it is important to know how to differentiate between them. With blown glass, the mold impression can be felt on the inside, while pressed glass impression can only be felt on the outside. Most blown three-mold bottles came in amethyst (purple), sapphire blue, and a variety of greens.

Black Glass Freeblown Spirits Bottle
Deep Yellow Olive, 11¼ in., pontil, sheared mouth $350–650
English 1750–1780 (rare size)

Blown Decanter
Clear Glass, 7⅞ in., pontil, tooled mouth $400–600
Norwegian 1830–1840

Blown Three Mold Decanter
Medium Olive Green, 8¼ in., pontil base, applied double collar
mouth $2500–3500
American 1820–1830 (scarce)

Blown Three Mold Toilet Water Bottle
Cobalt Blue, 5⅜ in., pontil base, flared lip...............................$175–275
American 1825–1835

Chestnut Flask
Medium Pink Amethyst, 6¼ in., pontil, sheared lip $100–150
European 1840–1870

Chestnut Flask
Medium Amber, 24 rib-pattern swirled to left, 5 in., pontil, sheared
lip $200–300
American 1820–1835

Chestnut Flask
Deep Sapphire Blue, 20 rib-pattern swirled to right, pontil, flared
lip $500–700
American 1820–1835

Club Bottle
Aqua, 8¾ in., pontil, applied sloping collar mouth $50–70
American 1845–1855

Club Bottle
Bluish Aqua, 24 Rib-pattern swirled to right, 8⅞ in., pontil, applied
mouth $150–200
American 1820–1835

Freeblown Chestnut Bottle
Yellow Olive, 7⅞ in., pontil, tooled sloping collared
mouth $150–300
American 1800–1830

Freeblown Chestnut Bottle
Yellow Olive, 6¾ in., pontil, outward rolled mouth $150–300
American 1783–1830

Freeblown Chestnut Bottle
Light Yellow Olive, 5⅝ in., pontil, crudely rolled mouth $125–250
American 1783–1830

Freeblown Jar
Yellowish Olive, 6½ in., pontil, sheared mouth $300–600
American 1815–1840 (Willington Glass Works)

Freeblown Nailsea Jar
Milk Glass with Red loopings, 6½ in., pontil, tooled
mouth $200–350
American 1800–1840

Large Freeblown Demijohn
Yellowish Olive Green, 17 in., pontil, applied sloping collared
mouth $100–200
American 1815–1840

Large Freeblown Demijohn
Medium Yellowish Olive, 21 in., pontil, applied sloping collared
mouth $100–200
American 1815–1840 (three part mold)

Large Globular Freeblown Bottle
Yellowish Olive, 10¾ in., pontil, tooled mouth $200–400
American 1783–1830

Globular Freeblow Bottle
Deep Yellow Olive, 10 in., pontil, sheared mouth...................$200–400
American 1783–1830

Miniature Freeblown Demijohn Bottle
Medium Yellow Green, 3½ in., pontil, sheared mouth.............$50–100
American 1800–1830

Miniature Midwestern Globular Bottle
Medium Golden Amber, 3¼ in., pontil, rolled lip $600–800
American 1820–1835 (Zanesville)

Selection of globular bottles, 1770–1820, $450–$1200 (each).

Selection of Nailsea flasks and bottles, 1850–1880, $80–$200 (each).

Miniature Midwestern Globular Bottle

Bluish Aqua, 3⅜ in., pontil, rolled lip...$50–70
American 1820–1835 (Zanesville)

Miniature New England Globular Bottle

Golden Amber with Multicolored enamel floral decoration, 3⅞ in.,
pontil, rolled lip $700–900
American 1820–1835

Nailsea "Ball" Decanter

Deep Colbalt Blue, 7⅛ in., smooth base, ground and polished
lip $700–900
English 1870–1890 (very rare)

Nailsea Gemel Flask

Clear Glass with red and white loop pattern, 11 in., pontil, sheared
lip ....$ 60–80
English 1850–1880

Nailsea Flask

Deep Colbalt Blue, 8¼ in., pontil, tooled mouth....................$250–350
English 1870–1890

Nailsea Flask
Deep Amber with White Looping, 4⅝ in., pontil, sheared lip $200–300
English 1850–1870

Nailsea Flask
Medium Olive Green, 6½ in., pontil, sheared lip $175–225
English 1850–1870

Pitkin Flask
Yellowish Tobacco Amber, 5⅞ in., pontil, sheared lip.............$250–325
American 1820–1830

Pitkin Flask
Root Beer Amber, 6 in., pontil, sheared lip $300–400
American 1800–1820

Three Mold Condiment Bottle
Clear Glass, 4¼ in., pontil, ground lip...$70–90
American 1820–1835

Three Mold Decanter
Medium Olive Green, 10 in., smooth base, applied sloping double collar mouth $2500–3500
American 1810–1830 (Keene, New Hampshire Glassworks)

Three Mold Decanter
Clear Glass, 6⅞ in., pontil, flared lip $100–125
American 1815–1825

Zanesville Swirl Bottle
Deep Amber, 7⅞ in., pontil, rolled lip......................................$350–450
American 1820–1830

Cosmetic Bottles

This category includes those bottles that originally contained products to improve personal appearances, including treatments for skin, teeth, scalp (hair grooming and restoring agents), and perfumes. The most popular of these are the hair and perfume bottles.

Hair bottles are popular as collectible items because of their distinctive colors, such as amethyst and various shades of blue. The main producer of American-made perfume bottles in the eighteenth century was Casper Wistar, whose clients included Martha Washington. Another major manufacturer of that time was Henry William Stiegel. While most of Wistar's bottles were plain, Stiegel's were decorative and are more appealing to collectors.

In the 1840s, Solon Palmer started to manufacture and sell perfumes. By 1879, his products were being sold in drugstores around the country. Today, Palmer bottles are sought after for their brilliant emerald green color.

A. H. Brown Hair Specialist, Southampton
Cobalt Blue, 6⅛ in., smooth base, tooled lip $35–60
English 1880–1900

Aubry Sisters
Milk glass, 1 in., smooth base (Pat Aug 22, 1911) ABM lip........$15–20
American 1911–1925

Boswell & Warner Colorific (Hair Dye—New York)
Cobalt Blue, 5½ in., smooth base, tooled top $30–50
American 1880–1890

Phalon Perfumer N.Y.,
1859–1863, $50–$100.

Bruno Court Parfumeur
Green, 5½ in., smooth base, Gold neck, ABM lip $10–15
American 1910–1920

Catalan Hair Renewer
Cobalt Blue, 5¼ in., smooth base, tooled lip $40–60
American 1880–1890

Clark's Hair Gloria Philadelphia
Medium Golden Amber, 7⅞ in., smooth base, tooled mouth......$50–75
American 1880–1900

Cologne Bottle
Power Blue Milk glass, 11-sided, 2⅝ in., pontil base, tooled flared
lip $100–150
American 1865–1880

Cologne Bottle
Milk glass with beaded flute pattern, 8 in., smooth base, tooled
lip $100–125
American 1865–1880

Cologne Bottle
Power Blue glass, 9⅜ in., pontil base, rolled lip $140–180
American 1865–1875

Cologne Bottle
Deep Cobalt blue, 9⅞ in., Flute Pattern, pontil base (Registered 30
May 1850), applied mouth $100–150
English 1850–1860

Cologne Bottle
Deep Cobalt Blue, 9⅞ in., Diamond Pattern, pontil base (Registered 30
May 1850), applied mouth $100–150
English 1850–1860

C. W. Hutchins Perfumer, New York
Clear, 3¼ in., smooth base, ABM lip...$5–10
American 1905–1920

The Original Balm of Thousand
Flowers, Jules Hauel Philada.,
1840–1850, $50–$100.

Dr. Koch's Toilet Articles, Winona Minn
Clear, 5¼ in., smooth base, ring top $8–10
American 1900–1930

Dr. Tebbett's Physiological Hair Regenerator
Medium Amethyst, 7⅝ in., smooth base, applied mouth $200–300
American 1865–1870

E.N. Lightner & Co. E.N.L. & Co. (Monogram), Detroit Mich—Label under Glass—Lightner's White Rose Perfume
Clear, 6⅜ in., smooth base, tooled mouth $300–400
American 1885–1900

Fancy Cologne Bottle (Embossed Dancing Indians)
Aqua, 4⅞ in., open pontil, rolled lip $125–175
American 1845–1855

Florida Water, Davis Bro's San Francisco
Aqua, 9¼ in., smooth base, tooled lip $70–90
American 1865–1875

Florida Water Bottle (Label—Lady Grey Florida Water, Lady Grey Perfumery Co. Boston, Mass, U.S.A.)
Aqua, 8⅞ in., smooth base, tooled mouth $30–60
American 1870–1900

Florida Water Bottle (Label—Florida Water R.H. White Co. Boston, Mass)
Aqua, 9¼ in., smooth base, applied mouth $30–60
American 1870–1900

Harrison's Columbian Perfumery
Clear glass with pink tone, 2⅝ in., smooth base, ground lip $175–225
American 1850–1860 (Manufactured by same company—Harrison's Columbian Ink)

Harry D. Harber's Magic Hair Coloring
Sapphire Blue, 7⅛ in., smooth base, tooled lip $30–50
English 1875–1895

Hessig-Ellis Chemist, Memphis Tenn
Clear, 6½ in., smooth base, ABM lip, Q Ban For The Hair (on back) $10–15
American 1900–1930

Holt's Nickel Cologne (In a Sunken Front Panel)
Clear, 2⅞ in., smooth base, ABM lip..$5–10
American 1900–1925

Hubbard, Harriet, Ayer N.Y. (In a Square with Monogram, 3¾ Ounces on the Trunk)
Clear, 4¾ in., smooth base, square screw top................................$7–10
American 1910–1930

Hunt & Co. Perfumery Philada
Opalescent Milk glass, 4¾ in., smooth base, tooled lip...........$150–200
American 1855–1865 (rare)

J.L. Giofray & Co. Hair Renovator, Rockland Me
Medium Red Amber, 7⅝ in., smooth base, applied double collar
mouth $400–600
American 1850–1860

Kranks Cold Cream
Milk glass, 2¾ in. jar, smooth base, screw top $5–10
American 1910–1930

Lightner's Heliotrope Perfumes (Lightning on Back—L.E.N. & Co. Detroit Mich
Milk glass, 6½ in., smooth base, tooled top................................$75–100
American 1890–1910

Magna Toilet Cream C.J. Countie & Co. Chemists Boston U.S.A., an Exquisite Communion of Rare Blossoms, a Dainty Luxury for the Skin
Milk Glass, 2¾ in., smooth base, smooth top with lid............$150–250
American 1885–1900

Melanine Hair Tonic, Dodge Brothers
Deep Purple Amethyst, 7⅜ in., smooth base, applied double collar
mouth $400–600
American 1855–1865

Mrs. S.A. Allen's World Hair Restorer New York
Golden Amber, 7½ in., smooth base, applied top......................$70–120
American 1880–1890

Seahorse scent bottle, 1840–1855, $150–$175; Sunburst scent bottle, 1850–1860, $300–$400; Fancy cologne bottle, 1840–1860, $200–$300; Sunburst scent bottle, 1855–1865, $250–$350; Fancy scent bottle, 1850–1860, $400–$600.

Paris Perfume Co., Jersey City, N.J. Guaranteed Full 2 oz
Clear, 6 in., smooth base, ring top $7–10
American 1900–1930

Prepared by N. Smith Prentiss, Espirit De____New York
Aqua, 5½ in., open pontil, flared lip.......................................$100–125
American 1845–1855

Price's Soap Company Limited
Cobalt Blue, 6 in., smooth base, applied top................................$30–50
English 1875–1895

Professor Benbow Specialist for the Hair, 26 Grand Parade
Deep Cobalt, 6¼ in., smooth base, tooled lip.............................$40–60
American 1845–1855

Professor Woods Hair Restorative Depots, St. Louis & New York
Aqua, 6⅞ in., open pontil, applied sloping collar mouth............$40–60
American 1845–1855

Reed, Carnrick & Adndrus N.Y.
Clear, 8⅞ in., smooth base, tooled mouth $35–55
American 1870–1900

Dr. T.J. Monroe's Hair Renovator, 1845–1855, $4000–$6000.

Ricksecker Sweet Clover Cologne N.Y.
Multicolored Milk glass, 8½ in., smooth base, polished lip.....$275–375
American 1885–1910

S. Barrow Evans, Hair Restorer
Light Cobalt Blue, 6 in., smooth base, tooled lip.........................$40–60
American 1880–1890

Sandwich Cologne
Deep Cobalt Blue, Polygonal, 4¾ in., smooth base, rolled lip.....$250–350
American 1865–1880 (Scarce—Color)

St. Clair's Hair Lotion
Deep Blue, 6½ in., smooth base, applied top.............................$50–100
American 1890–1900

Sunburst Scent Bottle
Clear glass, 2¾ in., pontil base, tooled lip.................................$90–140
American 1865–1880

Swan & Co Cologne Bottle—Label (N. Carrington's Best Quality Bay Water, Boston, Mass)
Clear, 11⅛ in., smooth base, rolled lip....................................$275–375
American 1870–1880

The Mexican Hair Renewer
Deep Cobalt Blue, 7¼ in., smooth base, tooled mouth...............$50–75
American 1880–1890

Truman's Nusery Lotion
Cobalt Blue, 5¼ in., smooth base, tooled lip $40–70
American 1880–1890

**U—Rar—Dos for the Complexion Woodward Clarke & Co.
Portland Oregon**
Cobalt Blue, 5 in., smooth base, tooled top...................................$30–50
American 1900

W.C. Monogomery's Hair Restorer, Philad
Black Amethyst, 7⅝ in., smooth base, applied double collar
mouth $275–375
American 1865–1875 (rare)

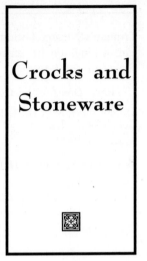

Crocks and Stoneware

While crocks are made of pottery and not glass, many bottle collectors also have crock collections since crocks have been found wherever bottles are buried. Crock containers were manufactured in America as early as 1641 and were used extensively in the sale of retail products during the nineteenth and early twentieth centuries. Miniature stoneware jugs were often used for advertising as were some stoneware canning jars. Store owners favored crocks since they kept beverages cooler and extended the shelf life of certain products. Crocks appeal to collectors because of their interesting shapes, painted and stenciled decorations, lustrous finishes, and folk art value.

In the late 1800s, the discovery of microbes in disease-causing bacteria prompted many medicine makers to seize a profitable if unethical opportunity. An undocumented number of fraudulent cures were pushed on gullible and unsuspecting customers. The most infamous of these so-called cures were produced and sold in pottery containers by William Radam. He was given a patent for his "Microbe Killer" in 1886 and stayed in business until 1907, when the Pure Food and Drug Act ended his scheme. His "cure" was nothing but watered-down wine (wine comprised only 1 percent of the total contents).

With the invention of the automatic bottle machine in 1903, glass bottles became cheaper to make and hence more common. The production and use of pottery crocks and containers began a steady decline.

Three Gallon Stoneware Jug—A.K. Vballard, Burlington, Vt. 3
Grayish with cobalt slip Cluster of Grapes, 15¾ in., applied
handle $300–400
American 1880–1895

Two Gallon Stoneware Crock—A. Plaisted & Co. Gardiner Me 2, Bird on a Branch
Grayish Tan with cobalt slip, 10¾ in., applied handle $275–350
American 1860–1875

Stoneware Jug—Beat It for Hesselschwerdt's and Save the Difference Kalona Iowa
Grayish white, 3 in. $60–80
American 1890–1910

Stoneware Jug—B.J. Semmes & Co 256 Second St. Memphis, Tenn
Cream, 8⅜ in., applied handle..$80–120
American 1885–1890

Stoneware Advertising Jug—Bozo Radovich, 48 W. San Fernando St., San Jose, Cal
Cream with dark Brown glaze, 7¼ in. $200–300
American 1890–1910 (Rare)

Stoneware Jug—Burd & Gordon, Trenton, N.J.
Cream with Brown glaze, 7 in. $70–90
American 1890–1910

Saltglaze stoneware jug, Casey Bros. Scranton, Pa., 1880–1900, $175–$225; Saltglaze stoneware cooler, Ice Water, 1880–1895, $400–$600; Saltglaze stoneware pitcher, 1870–1890, $500–$800.

Riechers Bros., Wholesale and Retail, General Merchandise, Ingomar, Mont., 1875–1900, $400–$500.

Two Gallon Saltglazed Stoneware Crock—Burger Bro's & Co. Rochester N.Y.
Grayish Tan with cobalt slip floral decoration, 9⅛ in., applied handle $200–300
American 1865–1885

Saltglaze Stoneware Jug—B.W. Parrington 3 Elmira, N.Y., Casey Bros. Scranton Pa.
Gray, 15 in., handled $175–225
American 1880–1900

Stoneware Scratch Jug—Compliments of Peter Koch, 32 Lowry St., Allegheny Pa.
Tan, 7⅜ in., applied handles $125–150
American 1880–1910

Saltglaze Stoneware Crock—Cooper & Poser, Maysville, Ky.
Dark grayish brown, 8 in. $140–180
American 1870–1890

Two Gallon Stoneware Jug—Cowden & Wilcox Harrisurg, Pa. 2
Gray with cobalt slip flower decoration, 13 in., applied handle.......$200–275
American 1875–1890

Gus Olson's Liquor Store,
Livingston, Mont., 1875–1900,
$250–$450.

Ovoid Stoneware—D. Goodale
Reddish Brown, 11 in., handled...$80–140
American 1820–1830

Saltglaze Stoneware Jug—E.E. Hall & Co./17th Blackstone St/Boston
Gray, 9½ in. $120–160
American 1880–1890

One Gallon Stoneware Crock—E. Selby & Co. Hudson N.Y.
Gray with cobalt slip decoration, 6⅞ in., applied handles.......$150–200
American 1860–1870

Stoneware Crock—Frederick Nolte Fancy Groceries, 2503 Chapline St. Wheeling W. Va
Dark Gray, 9¾ in. $150–250
American 1875–1895

Stoneware Crock—G.E. McKeever & Co. Stoneware Detroit Mich.
Grayish White, 5¼ in. $60–80
American 1890–1910

Stoneware Crock—Hamilton & Jones Manufacturers Greensboro Pa.
Dark Gray with cobalt slip stenciled decoration, 9⅞ in. $100–150
American 1876–1895

Stoneware Commemorative Mug—High Rock Spring Discovered by the Indians in 1767 at Saratoga Springs, N.Y.
Cream with brown, green, and black glaze, 4¾ in., Germany and
436/7 on base...$50–70
American 1890–1910

Two Gallon Stoneware Jug—James Ryan Pittston Pa 2, B Granahan Pittston Pa
Gray Glaze, 13 in., applied handle...$150–225
American 1875–1895

Stoneware Crock—J.H. Drury & Co. Newport, R.I.
Grayish White, 5¼ in. $60–80
American 1885–1900

One Gallon Stoneware Jug—J.S. Taft & Co. Keene N.H.
Gray with cobalt slip leaf decoration, 10¾ in., applied
handle...$175–225
American 1870–1880

One Gallon Stoneware Jug—McCusker & Son 28 & 30 St. Troy, N.Y.
Gray with dark cobalt slip lettering, 9⅝ in. $120–140
American 1860–1895

Martin Pickling Company,
Billings, Montana, 1875–1900,
$200–$300.

Saltglaze Stoneware Crock—Paul Cushman
Gray, 10 in., applied double handles $600–800
American 1805–1815

One Gallon Stoneware Jug—Pure Old Liquor from J.H. Kearns, Pro. Sunny Side Saloon, Lebanon, Ky.
Cream with black transfer, 10½ in. $95–125
American 1880–1910

Three Gallon Stoneware Jug—R.G. Smalley & C. No. 18 Blackstone St. Boston (Above a Swan)
Dark Gray, 15¼ in., applied handle $250–350
American 1875–1890

Stoneware Advertising Jug—S.T. Suit/Suitland, Md./Little Brown Jug/ The Whiskey in This Jug/Was Made 1809/and Jugged by Me/1880
Brown, 7¼ in. $250–350
American 1890–1895

One Gallon Stoneware Crock—Sysan Bros. Stoneware Somerset Mass
Gray, 7¼ in., applied handles..$175–225
American 1880–1895

Miniature Stoneware Jug—The Woodward Co., Roanoke Va Jug Trade & Spe???
Cream, 3⅛ in., applied handles $100–150
American 1880–1900

Stoneware Advertising Jug—The Yellowstone, 22 Montgomery St. S.F., Twomey & Miholovich Inside a Neck Medallion
Cream top with dark brown glaze bottom, 6¾ in. $200–300
American 1890–1910

Saltglaze Stoneware Jug—True—Fruit Fountain Syrups, J. Hungerford Smith Co., Rochester, N.Y.
Gray, 12¼ in. $100–150
American 1890–1910

Stoneware Crock—W.D. Cooper & Bro, No. 6, Diamond, Pittsburgh
Gray with cobalt slip decoration, 9⅞ in. $100–150
American 1880–1895

Sample of my $2.00 Whiskey, M.D., Beer, Delta, LA, 1890–1910,
$100–$150; Belle Meade Mercantile Co's, 1890–1910, $100–$150;
Morris & Dickson Co., 1890–1910, $70–$90; 15th Annual Reunion,
Confederate Veterans, June, 1906, 1880–1910, $400–$600; Merry
Christmas, The Casper Company Incorporated, Roanoke, VA,
1890–1910, $150–$275. (All miniature advertising jugs.)

Stoneware Crock—Weyman & Bro, Pittsburgh, Pa.
Light Gray with cobalt decoration, 9½ in. $100–125
American 1880–1895

**Four Gallon Saltglaze Stoneware Crock—WM.E. Warner West Troy
(NY) 4**
Grayish with cobalt floral decoration, 10⅞ in., applied handles......$150–200
American 1845–1870

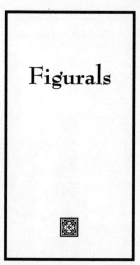

Figurals

Figural bottles were produced in large numbers in the late nineteenth and early twentieth centuries. These whimsical bottles were made in the shapes of animals, people, boots, and books, among other things. They came in a wide variety of colors and sizes and were quite popular among the very rich and the aristocrats of the time.

Atterbury Duck
Milk glass, 11⅝ in., smooth base, ground lip $350–450
American 1871–1880

Automobile
Clear glass, 5½ in. long, smooth base, tooled lip. $35–45
American 1890–1910

Bear Bottle
Clear glass, 4 in., smooth base (G.F. Knapp/Philada), tooled lip......$70–90
American 1880–1900

Bear Reading Book
Aqua, 4⅝ in., smooth base, tooled lip..$20–30
American 1890–1910

Billy Club
Clear glass, 10½ in. $30–50
American 1895–1915

Figural fountain bottle, 1885–1910, $300–$400; Figural madam bottle, 1890–1915, $800–$1000; Statue of Liberty jar, 1886–18980, $40–$60; D.D. Alsace-Depose figural bottle, 1885–1910, $400–$600; Figural Indian maiden, 1885–1915, $150–$250; Figural nightstick, 1885–1910, $100–$125; Saltglaze pottery pig, 1880–1895, $500–$900.

Child with Rattle
Aqua, 4⅞ in., smooth base, tooled lip..$20–30
American 1895–1915

Clock
Clear glass, 3⅛ in., smooth base, tooled lip................................$35–45
American 1890–1915

Clown
Frosted sun clear glass, 12⅞ in., pontil, ground lip $100–150
European 1890–1910

Crying Baby
Clear glass, 6 in., smooth base, tooled mouth............................$25–40
American 1890–1910

Ear of Corn
Clear glass, 10¾ in., smooth base, tooled mouth.......................$80–120
American 1880–1910

Fancy Shoe
Frosted Clear Glass, 10¾ in. long, pontil, tooled mouth...........$80–100
French 1880–1910

Figural Hand
Clear glass, 5½ in. long, smooth base, tooled lip $20–30
American 1890–1910

Fisherman
Clear glass, 13 in. $35–45
American 1890–1910

Fox Reading a Book
Clear glass, 3⅛ in., smooth base, tooled lip................................$35–45
European 1890–1915

Hand Holding Bottle
Light Cornflower, 9⅝ in., pontil, tooled mouth.......................$100–150
French 1890–1910

Hand Holding Dagger
Deep Cobalt Blue, 14¼ in., pontil, tooled mouth....................$350–450
English 1890–1910

Hand Holding Dagger
Frosted Turquoise, 11¼ in., pontil, tooled mouth...................$175–225
French 1880–1900

Hand Holding Dagger
Green, 14½ in., smooth base, ABM lip......................................$125–150
French 1910–1920

Hessian Soldier
Clear glass, 7⅜ in., smooth base, tooled lip................................$40–60
American 1890–1915

Jester and Dog
Clear glass, 6¾ in., smooth base, tooled lip................................$40–60
American 1890–1915

Kettle (Candy Container)
Clear glass, 4 in. $20–30
American 1910–1935

La Tsarine Bonbon Jar, La Tsarine/Bonbons/John Avernier
Milk glass, 3⅛ in. $175–225
French 1895–1910

Log Cabin—Smokine/Imported and Bottled/By/
Alfred Andresen & Co/The Western Importers/Minneapolis, Minn/
And/Winipeg. Man
Reddish-Amber, 6¾ in., smooth base, tooled mouth. $175–275
American 1890–1900

Man in Hat
Clear glass, 7½ in., smooth base, tooled lip..............................$40–60
American 1890–1910

Man on Barrel
Clear glass, 4⅞ in., smooth base, tooled lip...............................$20–30
American 1890–1910

Military Style Cap (Candy Container)
Clear glass, 2 in. $20–30
American 1910–1935

Napoleon Bottle
Frosted clear glass, 15 in., pontil, ground lip.........................$150–200
French 1890–1910

Owl Bottle
Clear glass, 5⅝ in. $30–50
American 1880–1910

Peacock Bottle
Clear glass, 4¼ in., smooth base, tooled lip..............................$20–30
American 1895–1915

Pipe
Clear glass, 8¼ in., ground lip..$30–50
American 1890–1910

Policeman
Cobalt Blue, 18⅝ in., smooth base $175–250
French 1905–1930

Poodle
Clear glass, 3¼ in., smooth base, tooled lip $15–25
American 1890–1915

Rabbit Bottle
Clear glass, 9 in., smooth base, tooled mouth. $80–100
European 1880–1910

Revolver
Straw Yellow, 7⅝ in. $30–50
American 1895–1915

Revolver (Diamond Revolver—On Back of Handle)
Amber, 8 in. long, ground lip. $125–150
American 1890–1910

Seated Monkey
Clear sun-colored amethyst, 4⅝ in., smooth base, tooled lip $80–120
American 1890–1910

Soldier
Clear glass, 11⅜ in. $35–45
American 1895–1915

Standing Pig
Clear glass, 7⅛ in., ground lip $175–275
French 1885–1910 (rare—French bon-bon jar)

Wheelbarrow (Candy Container)
Clear glass, 3 in. $20–30
American 1910–1935

Wiseman or Arabian Bonbon Jar
Frosted clear glass, 11⅛ in., ground base opening $175–225
French 1890–1915

Woman with a Basket
Pale Green, 13¾ in. $35–45
American 1895–1915

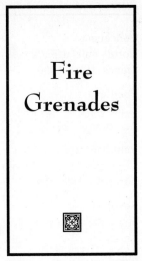

Fire Grenades

Fire grenades are a highly prized item among bottle collectors and represent one of the first modern improvements in fire fighting.

A fire grenade is a bottle about the size of a baseball that was filled with water. Its use was simple. When thrown into a fire, it would break and spread its contents, hopefully extinguishing the flames.

The first American patent on a fire grenade was issued in 1863 to Alanson Crane of Fortress Monroe, Virginia. The best-known manufacturer of these highly specialized bottles was the Halden Fire Extinguisher Company in Chicago, which was awarded a patent in August 1871.

These grenades were manufactured in large numbers by companies with names as unique as the bottles themselves: Dash-Out, Diamond, Harkness Fire Destroyer, Hazelton's High Pressure Chemical Firekeg, Magic Fire, and Y-Burn. The fire grenade became obsolete with the invention of the fire extinguisher in 1905. Many of these grenades can still be found with the original closures, contents, and labels.

American Fire Extinguisher Co. Hand Grenade
Clear glass pint, 6¼ in., smooth footed base, smooth lip........$350–450
American 1885–1895

Barnum's Hand Fire Ext. Patent June 26, 1869 Diamond (With Original Label) G.H. Downing 213 West 50th Street N.Y.
Yellow Amber, smooth base, tooled mouth (with sealer and cork) $200–300
American 1869–1885

C.& N—W. Ry (Railroad Fire Grenade—Chicago and Northwestern Railroad)

Clear glass cylinder, 17¾ in., smooth base, sheared lip............$80–100
American 1880–1900

California Fire Extinguisher—Picture of Walking Bear

Amber, smooth base, applied single roll collar $3000–4000
American 1870–1875 (original contents and partial label)

Fire Grenade, Grenade Unic Extinctrice

Medium Orange Amber, 5½ in., smooth base, ground lip $275–375
French 1880–1895

Fire Grenade, Grenade Unic Extinctrice

Yellow Orange Amber, 5⅝ in., smooth base, ground lip.........$275–375
French 1880–1895

Flagg's Fire Extinguisher—Pat'd Aug. 4, 1868

Orange Amber, 5⅞ in., smooth base, ground lip..................$800–1000
American 1870–1885

Grenades du Progres—Grenades Extingtives

Yellow with Orange Amber tone, 5⅛ in., pontil, tooled mouth $400–600
French 1875–1890

California Fire Extinguisher
(embossed California bear)
$6000–$7500 (amber).

Flagg's Fire Extinguisher, Pat'd Aug. 4, 1868, 1870–1885,
$700–$800; Healy's Hand Fire Extinguisher, 1880–1890,
$700–$900; Fire Grenade, Universal Fire Extinguisher,
1880–1890, $500–$600; Fire Grenade, 1880–1890,
$200–$300.

Grenade L'urbaine
Yellow with Amber tone pint, 6½ in., smooth base, ground
lip $300–500
French 1880–1895

Harden Start Hand Grenade (Star)—Fire Extinguisher
Cobalt Blue pint, 6¾ in., smooth base, ground lip.................$140–180
English 1880–1890

Hayward's Hand Fire Grenade—S.F. Hayward 407 Broadway N.Y—Patented Aug. 8 1871
Medium Yellowish Amber pint, 6¼ in., smooth base, tooled
mouth $250–325
American 1871–1885

Hayward's Hand Fire Grenade—S.F. Hayward 407 Broadway N.Y. Patented Aug. 8 1871
Light Smoky Sapphire pint, 6⅛ in., smooth base, tooled
mouth $400–600
American 1871–1885

Little Giant Fire Extinguisher, pint, $2500 (aqua).

Harden flat star pints, (L) French $350; (R) English $350 (cobalt blue).

H.S.N. Diamond quart, $2000 (amber).

Healy's Hand Fire Extinguisher
Yellow Amber, 11¾ in., smooth base, applied mouth $700–900
American 1880–1890 (cone form)

Hns (Monogram)
Light to Medium Straw Yellow Quart, 7⅛ in., smooth base, ground
lip $140–180
American 1880–1890

Ira Pain's Filled Ball Pat. Oct. 23. 1877
Golden Amber, 3 in., smooth base, tooled mouth.....................$100–200
American 1877–1895

Magic Fire Extinguisher Co.
Yellow Amber pint, 6¼ in., smooth base, ground lip..............$375–450
American 1875–1890 (Scarce)

Miniature Fire Grenade/Figural Bottle—Fire Dep't/Throw/Into Fire, Copyright 1927/Fred Adams/Advertising/Phila.Pa
Clear Glass, 4⅜ in., smooth base, tooled mouth.....................$140–180
American 1927

P.R.R. (Pennsylvania Railroad)
Clear glass, 7¼ in., smooth base, tooled mouth.......................$500–700
American 1880–1895

Healy's Hand Fire Extinguisher,
quart, $1000 (amber).

P.R.R. (Pennsylvania Railroad)
Light Aqua glass, 7 in., smooth base, tooled mouth...............$800–1200
American 1880–1895

Prevoyante Extingeur Grenade
Orange Amber pint, 5⅝ in., smooth base, ground lip.............$350–450
French 1880–1890

Rockford/Kalamazoo/Automatic And/Hand Fire Extinguisher/Patent Applied for
Medium Cobalt Blue, 11 in., smooth base, ground lip.............$375–475
American 1890–1910

Sinclair Hand Grenade 13 Eldon St. London
Medium Cobalt Blue, 7⅛ in., smooth base, tooled mouth $175–250
English 1880–1890

Star Fire Extinguisher
Sapphire Blue, 7¼ in., smooth base, tooled mouth $100–150
American 1878–1885

Hayward's Diamond Panal pint,
$450–$460 (cornflower blue).

English Fire Grenade,
"Merryweather London" pint,
$1000–$1200 (amber).

German Fire Grenade,
"Eberhardt" 1-½ quart,
$1500–$2000 (light amber).

French Fire Grenade,
"V. Fournier" pint, $1500–$2000
(ice blue).

Argentinian "Hand Grenade Shaped" quart, $500–$750 (aqua).

Star Fire Extinguisher
Turquoise, 7¼ in., smooth base, tooled mouth $40–80
American 1875–1885

Systeme/Labbe—Grenade/Extingteur—L'incombustibilite
Yellow Topaz, 5½ in., smooth base, ground lip $400–600
French 1875–1895

Systeme Labbe—Grenade Extingteur—L'incombustibilite—Paris
Medium Orange Amber, 5¾ in., smooth base, ground lip $375–475
French 1880–1900

The Imperial
Clear glass, 6½ in., smooth base, tooled mouth $300–400
English 1890–1910

Universal Fire Extinguisher
Medium Sapphire Blue, 7 in., pontil, tooled mouth $600–800
English 1880–1890

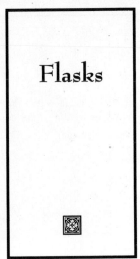

Flasks

Flasks have become a most popular and prized item among collectors owing to the variety of decorative, historical, and pictoral detail featured on many pieces. The outstanding colors have had a major effect on the value of these pieces, more so than with most other collectible bottles.

Early history documents that American flasks were first manufactured by the Pitkin Glasshouse in Connecticut around 1815, and quickly spread to other glasshouses around the country. Early flasks were free-blown and represent some of the better craftsmanship with more intricate designs. By 1850, approximately 400 designs had been used that produced black graphite pontil marks. The pontils were coated with powdered iron, which allowed the flasks' bottoms to break away without damaging the glass. The flasks made between 1850 and 1870 had no such markings because of the widespread use of the newly invented snap-case.

Since flasks were designed to be refilled with whiskey or other spirits, more time and effort was expended in the manufacturing process than for most other types of bottles. Flasks soon became a popular item for use with all types of causes and promotions. Mottos were frequently embossed on flasks and included a number of patriotic sayings and slogans. One of the more controversial flasks was the Masonic flask, which bore the order's emblem on one side and the American eagle on the other. Public feelings were high against this representation but the controversy soon passed. Masonic flasks are now a specialty item for collectors.

Also highly collectible are the Pitkin-type flasks, named for the Pitkin Glassworks where they were exclusively manufactured. While Pitkin-type flasks and ink bottles are common, the bottles, jugs, and jars are very rare. German Pitkin flasks are heavier and straight-ribbed, while the American pattern is swirled or broken-ribbed with unusual colors such as dark blue.

The George Washington depiction was a popular face on flasks, as were the candidates for the presidential elections of 1824 and 1828. These promoted the likenesses of Andrew Jackson and John Quincy Adams. Events of the time also were reflected on these flasks.

Because of the use of flasks for the promotion of various political and special interest agendas, they represented a major historical record of the people and events of those times.

Acorns and Leaves—Rampant Lions and Shield
Deep Cobalt Blue, Pint, pontil base, sheared lip..........................$75–100
American 1860–1880

Albany Glass Works—Bust of Washington—Albany—N.Y.—Ship
Bluish Aqua, Pint, pontil base, applied double collar
mouth $140–180
American 1825–1835

All Seeing Eye Inside Star—Ad—Bent Arm Inside Star—Grja
Medium Yellowish Olive Amber, Pint, open pontil, sheared lip $140–180
American 1820–1830

Baltimore—Anchor—Glass Works (in Banner)—Sheaf of Wheat
Deep Amber, Quart, smooth base, applied mouth....................$500–700
American 1865–1875 (rare—color)

Baltimore Glass Works—Anchor—Eagle, Resurgam
Medium Yellowish Green, Pint, smooth base, applied sloping collar
mouth $1500–3000
American 1860–1870 (extremely rare—Baltimore Glass Works)

Baltimore Glass Works and Anchor—Sheaf of Rye
Sapphire Blue, Calabash Quart, pontil base, applied double collar
mouth $1500–3000
American 1845–1860 (rare—Baltimore Glass Works)

Boar's Head—Deer Historical Flask
Purple Amethyst, Half-pint, pontil base, tooled flared
mouth $200–400
Germany 1850–1860

Boy with Dog Carrying Bird—Girl with Bundle
Amethyst, Half-pint, pontil base, sheared lip $40–120
European 1840–1850

Bridgeton New Jersey—Bust of Washington—Eagle—T.W.D.
Greenish Aqua, Quart, pontil base, sheared lip $200–300
American 1820–1830

Bust of Byron—Bust of Scott
Medium Olive Green, Half-pint, pontil base, sheared lip $175–250
American 1820–1830

Bust of Franklin—Bust of Franklin
Pale Greenish Aqua, Quart, pontil base, sheared lip.................$200–250
American 1820–1825

Chapman with Banjo Player and Dancing Sailor
Bluish Aqua, Half-pint, open pontil, sheared lip.........................$80–130
American 1860–1870 (rare)

Cluster of Grapes—Lion and Shield
Deep Cobalt Blue, Pint, pontil base, sheared lip........................$75–100
American 1860–1880

Columbia—Kensington—Eagle—Union Co.
Bluish Aqua, Pint, pontil base, sheared lip................................$500–700
American 1820–1830

Columbia with Liberty Cap—Kensington—Eagle—Union Co.
Bluish Aqua, pint, pontil base, sheared lip $125–150
American 1825–1835

Corn for the World Baltimore
Copper—Puce, Quart, open pontil, applied top $400–700
American 1845–1855

Cornucopia—Lancaster Glassworks N.Y.—Urn
Bluish Aqua, Pint, pontil base, sheared lip................................$125–150
American 1825–1835

Corset Waist Scroll Flask
Bluish Aqua, Pint, pontil base, sheared lip................................$500–700
American 1845–1855 (scarce)

Cross—Goblet
Pale Aqua, Half-pint, pontil base, sheared lip $400–600
American 1835–1845

Double Eagle Historical Flask
Sapphire Blue, Pint, smooth base, applied mouth with
ring $600–1200
American 1860–1880

Eagle—A. & D.H.C. (Motif of Woman Riding Bicycle)
Aqua, Pint, smooth base, applied mouth $175–250
American 1865–1875

Eagle—Coffin & Hay (Motif of Furled Flag) Hammonton
Pale Green, Quart, pontil base, sheared lip..............................$175–225
American 1825–1835

Eagle—Farley & Taylor, Richmond.Ky
Dark Golden Amber, 2½ Quart, iron pontil, sheared
mouth $4000–8000
American 1850–1855 (extremely rare)

Eagle—Furled Flag—For Our Country
Chocolate Tobacco Amber, Pint, pontil base, sheared lip.....$3500–4500
American 1825–1835 (rare—color)

Cross Inside Laurel Wreath-Crossed Guns and Arrow, 1850–1880,
$200–$250; Hunter-Grape Vine, 1850–1880, $200–$250; Hunter
Holding Rabbit, Laurel Wreath, 1850–1880, $150–$200; Grape Vine-
Grape Vine, 1850–1880, $150–$200; Hunter-Laurel Wreath,
1850–1880, $150–$200; Cluster of Grapes-Cluster of Grapes,
1850–1880, $150–$200.

Eagle-Eagle, 1825–1835, $500–$700; Eagle-Eagle, 1825–1835,
$1500–$2000; Jenny Lind-Bust of Jenny Lind-Glasshouse,
1855–1860, $500–$600; Eagle-Eagle, 1825–1835, $1000–$1300;
Eagle-Eagle, 1830–1840, $2000–$2500.

Eagle—J.K.B.—Masonic Arch
Yellowish Topaz, Pint, pontil base, rolled mouth..................$2800–3800
American 1815–1825 (rare in this color)

Eagle—Louisville—Ky—Glass Works Historical Flask
Golden Amber, Half-pint, smooth base, applied round collar
mouth $400–800
American 1855–1860

Eagle—Lyre
Deep Aqua, Pint, pontil base, sheared lip $600–900
American 1825–1840

Eagle—Morning Glory
Deep Bluish Aqua, Pint, open pontil, applied double collar
mouth $600–800
American 1825–1835 (scarce)

Eagle on Laurel Wreath
Golden Yellow—Half-pint, smooth base, applied mouth..........$200–300
American 1855–1870

Eagle with Shield—Flag—for Our Country
Amber, Pint, pontil base, sheared lip $1400–1800
American 1825–1835 (rare)

Union with clasped hands and shield-flying eagle with banner and shield on reverse, 1855–1870, $50–$100.

Eagle—Zanesville—Ohio—Eagle
Bluish Aqua, Pint, smooth base, applied mouth $200–300
American 1855–1870

Eripuit Coleo Fulmen Sceptrumque Tryannis—Benjamin Franklin—Bust of Franklin—Kensington Glass Works, Philadelphia—T.W. Dyott, M.D.—Bust of Dyott
Pale Aqua, Quart, pontil base, sheared lip $200–300
American 1825–1835

Fells—Bust of Washington—Point Monument—Balto
Medium Pink Amethyst, Pint, pontil base, tooled lip $800–1200
American 1825–1835 (extremely rare)

Flora Temple (Motif of Horse) Harness Trot 219¾, Oct.15, 1859
Deep Burgundy Puce, Quart, smooth base, applied mouth $200–300
American 1859

Flora Temple (Motif of Horse) Harness Trot 219¾
Medium Blue Green, Pint, smooth base, applied mouth $500–800
American 1859

General Lafayette—T.W.D. Eagle Portrait Flask
Pale Aquamarine, pint, pontil base, sheared mouth..................$200–400
American 1820–1838

J.H. Cutter Old Bourbon,
E. Martin & Co., Sole Agents,
1871–1879, $500–$700.

Grape Vine—Grape Vine
Cobalt Blue, Half-pint, pontil base, flared lip $250–350
European 1850–1880

Horseman—Hound
Aqua, Pint, smooth base, applied double collar mouth $80–120
American 1860–1870

Hunter—Laurel Wreath
Deep Cobalt Blue, Pint, smooth base, sheared lip $275–375
European 1850–1880

Hunter Holding Rabbit—Laurel Wreath
Deep Cobalt Blue, Half-pint, pontil base, sheared lip...............$275–375
European 1850–1880

Hunter—Seated Bear
Deep Cobalt Blue, pint, polished pontil, flared lip $100–140
European 1880–1920

J.F.T. and Co. Philad.
Light Amber, 26 Molded rims, applied handle, open pontil, double
rolled top...$300–600
American 1840–1850

Louis Taussig & Co.,
26 & 28 Main St., S.F.,
1881–1883, $200–$400.

Jenny Lind—Bust of Jenny Lind— Glass (Motif of 6–pointed Star) Factory—Glasshouse
Deep Aqua, Calabash, open pontil, applied sloping collar mouth......$80–120
American 1850–1860

Jenny Lind—Bust of Jenny Lind—Glass Works—Glasshouse—S. Huffsey
Aqua, Calabash, pontil base, applied sloping collar mouth..........$70–90
American 1850–1860

Jenny Lind—Bust of Jenny Lind—Millfora G. Works—Glass Works
Aqua, Calabash, pontil base, applied sloping collar mouth......$140–180
American 1855–1865 (scarce)

Lafayette—DeWitt Clinton Portrait Flask
Yellowish Olive, Half-pint, pontil base, sheared mouth..........$700–1400
American 1824–1825

Liberty Cap—Eagle—B & W
Aqua, Pint, pontil base, sheared lip..$250–350
American 1825–1835

Liberty—Eagle—Willington Glass Co—West Willington—Conn
Olive Green, Pint, smooth base, applied sloping collar mouth......$80–120
American 1855–1870

E. Brown Wine & Spirit Merchant,
New Westminster B.C.,
1871–1886, $100–$300.

Lockport. Glass. Works—Washington—Washington Portrait Flask
Bluish Aqua, Quart, Pontil base, applied double collar mouth.....$400–800
American 1843–1860

Louis Kossuth—Bust of Kossuth—Frigate—U.S. Steam Frigate—Mississippi—S. Hufsey
Bluish Aqua, Calabash, iron pontil base (P.H. DOFLEIN—MOULD
MAKER—NTH ST. ST. 84), applied sloping collar mouth.......$250–350
American 1855–1865

Major—Bust of Ringgold—Ringgold—Bust of Ringold—Rought Ready
Medium Blue Green, Pint, pontil base, sheared lip..............$1800–2800
American 1825–1835 (extremely rare)

Masonic Arch—Frigate—Franklin
Pale Green, Pint, pontil base, sheared lip.................................$500–700
American 1825–1835

Masonic—T.W.D. Eagle Historical Flask
Aquamarine, Pint, pontil base, sheared lip..............................$125–250
American 1820–1830

Murdock & Coassel—Zanesville Ohio
Deep Greenish Aqua, Pint, pontil base, sheared lip..............$1000–1600
American 1825–1835

Ravenna Glass Works
Yellow Olive, Pint, smooth base, applied mouth $1000–1500
American 1855–1865 (extremely rare)

Sailboat and Bridgeton New Jersey
Light Aqua, Pint, open pontil, sheared lip $70–130
American 1855–1865

Scroll Flask
Medium Yellowish, Half-pint, pontil base, sheared lip..........$1000–1800
American 1835–1845 (scarce)

Scroll Flask
Deep Olive Green, Pint, pontil base, sheared lip.....................$500–700
American 1845–1855

Scroll Flask
Bluish Aqua, Half-gallon, open pontil, sheared lip...................$350–450
American 1845–1855

Sheaf of Wheat—Pitchfork and Rake (Five Pointed Star)
Medium Green, Pint, open pontil base, applied double lip......$500–800
American 1850–1860

**Sheaf of Wheat—Pitchfork and Rake—Westford Glass Col.
Westford Conn.**
Olive Amber, Pint, smooth base, applied double collar mouth....$100–150
American 1850–1860

Selection of "The Father of His Country-Bust of Washington" flasks, 1850–1860, $150–$800 (each).

Sheaf of Wheat—Star
Yellowish Green, Half-pint, pontil base, sheared lip $1200–1800
American 1850–1860

Sheaf of Wheat—Star
Amber, Handled Calabash, iron pontil, applied mouth and
handle $350–450
American 1855–1870

Ship and Albany Glassworks
Aqua Marine, Pint, open pontil, applied tapered top $100–200
American 1855–1870

Sloop—Star
Light Blue Green, Half-pint, pontil base, sheared base $200–300
American 1825–1835

Soldier, Balt. Md—Dancer
Yellow Olive, Pint, smooth base, applied mouth $700–1000
American 1860–1870 (rare in this color)

Soldier—Dancer
Aquamarine, Pint, pontil base, sheared mouth.........................$100–200
American 1840–1860

Soldier—Deer on Hilltop Behind Cabin
Deep Cobalt Blue, pontil base, wide flared lip.........................$175–250
European 1860–1890

Soldier—Fanny Essler Pictorical Flask
Yellow Amber, Pint, smooth base, applied collar mouth $500–1000
American 1860–1870 (Maryland Glass Works)

Spruance, Stanley & Co. 410 Front St. S.F.
Dark Amber, Pint, smooth base, tooled top..............................$400–600
American 1880–1885 (scarce)

Stag—Tree Stump w/Rifle, Hunting Horn, Bag and Sun with Rays
Amethyst, Half-pint, solid rod pontil, sheared lip......................$70–120
American 1850–1860

Stoneware Double Eagle Flask
Light Brown Pottery, Half-pint, ...$80–120
American 1890–1920

Success to the Railroad—Horse Pulling Cart
Yellow Amber, Pint, open pontil, sheared lip $175–250
American 1825–1835

Summer Tree—Summer Tree
Aqua Marine, Pint, smooth base, applied double collar
mouth $100–200
American 1860–1880

Sunburst Flask
Moss Green, Half-pint, pontil base, sheared lip $500–700
American 1810–1820

The Father of His Country—Bust of Washington—a Little More Grape Captain Bragg—Bust of Taylor
Light Teal Blue, Quart, pontil base, sheared lip........................$275–375
American 1849–1860 (scarce)

The Great Western Hunter—Stag Historical Flask
Aquamarine, Pint, smooth base, applied mouth with ring $200–400
American 1860–1870 (rare)

Traveler's (Stylized Duck) Companion—Lockport (Beaded Star) Glas—Works Bottle
Blue Green, Pint, smooth base, applied round collar mouth $1200–2400
American 1860–1870

Eagle-Lyre, 1825–1840, $600–$900; Corn for the World-Ear of Corn Monument-Baltimore, 1845–1865, $800–$1200; Eagle-Cornucopia, 1825–1835, $2500–$3500; Corn for the World-Ear of Corn, 1845–1865, $600–$1000; Bust of Jenny Lind-Lyre, 1855–1860, $800–$1200.

Union—Clasped Hands—F.A. & Co—Cannon
Aqua, Pint, smooth base, applied mouth $175–275
American 1865–1875 (scarce)

Union—Clasped Hands—L.F. & Co—Eagle—Pittsburgh Pa
Amber, Pint, smooth base, applied mouth $275–375
American 1865–1870

Washington—Bust of Washington—Bridgeton New Jersey—Bust of Taylor
Medium Bluish Green, Pint, pontil base, sheared lip...............$500–700
American 1825–1835

Waterford Clasped Hands—Eagle with Banner
Yellow with Olive tone, Quart, smooth base, applied square collar
mouth $700–900
American 1860–1870 (Scarce Mold—Extremely Rare color)

Where Liberty Dwells There Is My Country—Benjamin Franklin—Bust of Franklin—Dyotville Glass Works Philadelphia—T.W. Dyott, M.D.—Bust of Dyott
Aqua, Pint, pontil base, sheared lip...$175–275
American 1820–1830

Yerba Buena—Bitters Flask
Reddish Amber, 9⅞ in., smooth base, tooled sloping collar
mouth $60–120
American 1880–1890

Zanesville—Eagle—Ohio—J. Shepard & Co—Masonic Arch
Yellowish Amber, Pint, pontil base, sheared lip.......................$500–700
American 1825–1835

10–Diamond Pattern Chestnut Flask
Golden Amber, 4½ in., pontil base, sheared lip...................$1000–1700
American 1820–1830

10–Diamond Pattern Chestnut Flask
Yellow with Olive tone, 5½ in., pontil base, sheared lip.....$2800–3800
American 1820–1830

Food and Pickle Bottles

Food bottles are one of the largest and most diverse categories in the field of collectible bottles. They were made for the commercial sale of a wide variety of food products excluding beverages except milk. Food bottles are an ideal specialty for the beginning collector since as a group they are so readily available. Many collectors are attracted to food bottles for their historical value. Nineteenth- and early twentieth-century magazines and newspapers contained so many illustrated advertisements for food products that many collectors keep scrapbooks of ads as an aid to dating and pricing the bottles.

Prior to the introduction of bottling, food could not to be transported long distances or kept for long periods of time on account of spoilage. The bottling of foodstuffs revolutionized the industry and began a new chapter in American business merchandising and distribution. With the glass bottle producers were able to use portion packaging, save labor, and sell from long distances.

Suddenly local producers faced competition from great distances and many interesting bottles were created specifically to distinguish them from others. Pepper sauce bottles, for instance, were made in the shape of Gothic cathedrals with arches and windows (green and clear); mustard jars and chili sauce bottles had unique embossing; cooking oil bottles were made tall and slim, and pickle bottles had large mouths. The pickle bottle is one of the largest of the food bottles, with a wide mouth and a square or cylindrical shape. While the pickle bottles were often unique in shape and design, their colors were almost exclusively aqua, although occasionally you will find a multicolored piece. When looking through ghost town dumps and digging behind older pioneer homes, you are sure to find them in great numbers since pickles were a common and well-liked food, especially in the mining communities.

Two of the more common food bottles are the Worcestershire sauce bottles distributed by Lea & Perrins and the Heinz sauce bottles. The Worcestershire sauce in the green bottle was in high demand during the nineteenth century and is quite common. Henry J. Heinz introduced his sauces in 1869 with the bottling of horseradish but didn't begin bottling ketchup until 1889.

Acker's/Select/Tea/Finley Acker & Co/Tea Specialists/Philadelphia/ U.S.A.(Motif of Tea Leaf) Finley Acker & Co/A/HG/Registered(Motif of Man Riding an Elephant)

Bright Yellow Green, 11⅛ in., smooth base, smooth lip..........$300–400
American 1910–1920

A. Kemp New York(Pickle Jar)

Aqua, 5½ in., smooth base, smooth lip.......................................$15–20
American 1860–1925

Albany Glass Works(Cathedral Pickle Jar)

Aqua, 8⅝ in., iron pontil, rolled lip..$500–800
American 1850–1860(Extremely Rare)

Apple Juice Vinegar,
S.R. Buford & Co., Fine Groceries,
Virginia City, Mont, 1880–1895,
$25–$35.

Golden Gate Brand Gherkins,
Fisher Packing Co., San Francisco,
1900–1920, $35–$65.

Mount's Pickles,
The Mount Pickle Co.,
Salt Lake City, Utah,
1900–1920, $40–$55.

Anchor Pickle and Vinegar Works(Pickle Jar)
Deep Bluish Aqua, 8 in., smooth base (H.N. & Co.), applied
mouth $60–80
American 1880–1890

Arrow Brand Pickles, J.J. Wilson Chicago (Pickle Jar)
Yellow with Amber, 8⅝ in., tooled mouth $100–150
American 1880–1900

B & C (Mustard Jar)
Aqua, smooth base, tooled lip $25–35
American 1870–1880

**Base Ball Brand Dill Pickles—Packed for Jageman-Bode Co.
Springfield, Ill.**
Aqua, 9½ in., smooth base, smooth base $15–20
American 1860–1925

Bastine & Co Pure Flavoring Extracts New York
Deep Teal Green, 9¾ in., smooth base, tooled mouth..............$80–120
American 1890–1900

Cathedral Pickle Jar
Medium Apple Green, 10⅞ in., smooth base, applied
mouth $250–350
American 1855–1865

C.D. Brooks/Boston
Amber, 9½ in., smooth base, applied mouth $60–90
American 1885–1900

Challenge Mills Brand Pepper Sauce 534 Washington St. New York
Aqua, 8¼ in., smooth base, tooled mouth $70–90
American 1880–1895

E.H.V.B./N.Y. (Cathedral Pickle Jar)
Light Green, 6–sided, 9 in., iron pontil, applied mouth $350–500
American 1855–1865

Cathedral pickle, 1860–1880,
$150–$250.

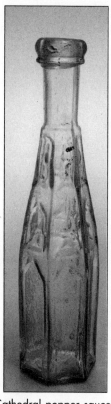

Cathedral pepper sauce
bottle, 1870–1880,
$100–$200.

Cathedral pepper sauce
bottle, 1870–1880,
$50–$75.

E.R. Durkee & Co. New York (Pepper Sauce)
Amber, 8 in., smooth base, tooled mouth.....................................$25–40
American 1865–1885

E.T. Cowdrey & Co./Boston
Amber, 7⅝ in., smooth base, applied mouth $60–90
American 1885–1900

Felton Grimwade & Crickford Ltd. (Sauce Bottle)
Deep Cobalt Blue, 8¼ in., smooth base, tooled mouth $40–60
Australian 1880–1910

F.H. Faulding & Co. Perth (Sauce Bottle)
Deep Cobalt Blue, 8¼ in., smooth base, tooled mouth $40–60
Australian 1880–1910

G.P. Sanborn & Son/Union (Inside Shield and Star) Boston Pickle
Golden Yellow Amber, 5⅛ in., smooth base, ground lip.........$140–180
American 1890–1900

Globe Tobacco Company Detroit (Cigar Jar)
Yellow with Amber tone, 7⅛ in., smooth base, ground lip.........$60–90
American 1895–1915

H.G. Hotchkiss Lyons N.Y.—Oil of Spearmint Manufactured by H.G. Hotchkiss Lyons Wayne County, N.Y.
Cobalt Blue, 8¾ in., smooth base, tooled mouth....................$100–150
American 1880–1895

H.J. Heinz Co/Patd, Heinz Fresh Cucumber Pickle (Label)
Clear glass quart, smooth base, ABM lip......................................$40–60
American 1925–1935

Peach Cordial,
Lyons' California Glace Fruit Co.,
San Francisco, Cal, 1890–1920,
$15–$25.

California Home Brand,
Worcestershire Sauce,
San Francisco, 1880–1910, $10–$15.

Heinz's Trieste Mustard, hand blown in Heinz glass factory, Sharpsburg, PA, 1885–1910, $75–$125.

H.J. Heinz Co/Patd, Heinz Apple Buter (Label)
Clear glass quart, smooth base, ABM lip......................................$40–60
American 1925–1935

H.J. Heinz Co.—Pittsburgh, PA—Heinz India Relish
Clear, 6¼ in., smooth base, tooled lip...$60–80
American 1925–1935

H.J. Heinz Co.—Pittsburgh, PA—Heinz Bulk Cross Cut Sweet Pickles
Aqua, 7⅝ in., smooth base, ABM lip..$60–80
American 1925–1935

H.J. Neuhauser (Mustard)
Olive, 5 in., pontil, rolled lip $125–150
American 1850–1860 (scarce mustard)

Holman's/Baking Powder/Buffalo. N.Y.
Light Blue Green, 5¾ in., smooth base, tooled mouth $80–120
American 1880–1890

Licorice/Y & S(Monogram)/Lozenges
Clear glass, 9¼ in., smooth base (Adiams Patent), ground lip $80–120
American 1880–1900

Heinz's Preserved Sweet Pickles,
hand blown in Heinz glass factory,
Sharpsburg, PA, 1893–1905,
$55–$100.

M.B. Espy Philada (Pickle Jar)
Aqua, 11⅝ in., iron pontil, rolled lip $300–400
American 1850–1860

McCollick & Co. New York (Pickle Jar)
Teal Blue pint, 8⅝ in., iron pontil, rolled lip...........................$500–800
American 1850–1860

Pepper Sauce Derby Brand Glaser, Crandell Co., Chicago Ill
Clear glass, 8¼ in., smooth base, tooled mouth..........................$70–90
American 1880–1895

Pickle Jar
Deep Greenish Aqua, 10⅝ in., large iron pontil, rolled lip $250–350
American 1855–1865 (Scarce)

Pioneer Pickle Works, Sacramento, Cal (Pickle Jar)
Bluish Aqua, 10¾ in., smooth base, rolled lip $75–125
American 1880–1890

Planters Peanuts (Counter Top Jar)
Clear glass, 12¼ in., smooth base...$150–200
American 1920–1940

Heinz's Tabasco Pepper Sauce,
hand blown in Heinz glass factory,
Sharpsburg, PA, 1880–1899,
$65–$100.

Pure Horse Radish, R.D. Bisbee, Chesterfield, Mass
Light Cornflower Blue, 7⅛ in., smooth base, tooled lip $60–90
American 1875–1885

R & F. Atmore (Cathedral Pickle Jar)
Bluish Aqua, 11½ in., pontil base, applied mouth...................$200–300
American 1865–1875

**Siphon Kumysgen Bottle/For Preparing/Kumyss from Kumysgen
(Inside Cross and Crescent Moon) Reed & Carnrick**
Deep Cobalt Blue, 8⅝ in., smooth base, tooled mouth $125–150
American 1890–1900

**Skilton Foote & Co. S/Trade (Motif of Monument) Mark/Bunker Hill
Pickles, Onions, from Skilton, Foote & Co., Bunker Hill Pickles**
Yellow Olive, 7⅜ in., smooth base, tooled mouth $150–200
American 1870–1885

Spanish Peppersauce, The Columbia Preserving Works Chicago
Aqua, 9½ in., smooth base, smooth lip..$15–25
American 1860–1925

Heinz's Keystone Ketchup,
produced in Heinz glass factory,
Sharpsburg, PA 1889–1913,
$35–$45.

Heinz's Table Sauce, hand blown
in Heinz's glass factory,
Sharpsburg, PA, 1895–1910,
$45–$65.

Stoddard 'Cloverleaf' Pickle Bottle
Reddish Amber, 8¼ in., smooth base, rolled lip......................$300–400
American 1860–1875

T.A. Bryan & Co's/Perfection/Tomato Sauce/Baltimore, Md
Amber, 8⅜ in., smooth base, tooled sloping collar mouth......$175–225
American 1885–1895 (scarce)

This Trade Mark Registered/Maple Sap and Boiled Cider Vinegar/ The C.I. Co. L'T'D, East Rindge, N.H.
Cobalt Blue, 11¼ in., smooth base, applied mouth.................$700–900
American 1880–1895

64oz William-Underwood & Company Boston (Pickle Jar)
Aqua, 12½ in., iron pontil, rolled lip $250–350
American 1850–1860

Wells-Miller & Provost
Deep Aqua, 11⅝ in., iron pontil, applied mouth.....................$140–180
American 1850–1860

W.F. & Co. (Mustard Jar)
Aqua, smooth base, tooled lip $25–35
American 1870–1880

W.K. Lewis & Co. Boston (Pickle Jar)
Deep Bluish Aqua, 10½ in., iron pontil, applied mouth..........$250–350
American 1850–1860

W.M. Numsen & Sons Baltimore (Pickle Jar)
Yellow Green, 9¼ in., pontil, rolled lip....................................$375–475
American 1850–1860

W.S. Kimball & Co. (Cigar Jar)
Golden Yellow amber, 5⅞ in., smooth base, ground lip............ $60–90
American 1890–1915

Heinz's Mince Meat, hand blown
in Heinz glass factory, Sharpsburg,
PA, 1893–1905, $35–$55.

Fruit Jars

Unlike food bottles, fruit jars were sold empty for use in home preservation of many different types of food. The use of fruit jars was predominant in the 1800s, when food-stuffs were not available prepackaged and home canning was the only option. Though fruit jars carry no product or advertising, they aren't necessarily common or plain since the bottle manufacturers' name is usually embossed in large lettering along with the patent date. The manufacturer whose advertising campaign gave fruit jars their name was Thomas W. Dyott, who was in the market early, selling fruit jars by 1829.

With respect to closures, the most common of those used in the first fifty years was a cork sealed with wax. In 1855, an inverted saucerlike lid was invented that could be inserted into the jar to provide an airtight seal. The Hero Glassworks invented the glass lid in 1856 and improved upon it in 1858 with a zinc lid invented by John Landis Mason, who also produced fruit jars. Because the medical profession warned that zinc could be harmful, Hero Glassworks developed a glass lid for the Mason jar in 1868. Mason eventually transferred his patent rights to the Consolidated Fruit Jar Company, which let the patent expire. In 1880, the Ball Brothers began distributing Mason jars, and in 1898 the use of a semiautomatic bottle machine increased the output of the Mason jar until the automatic machine was invented in 1903.

Fruit jars come in a wide variety of sizes and colors, commonly aqua and clear. It's more difficult to find blues, ambers, blacks, milk glass, greens, and purples.

A. & D.H. Chambers, Union Fruit Jar, Pittsburgh, Pa, D/G/ Co. (Monogram)
Aqua, Quart, pint, smooth base...$55–65
American 1850–1900

A.G. Smalley & Co. Boston Mass
Amber, Quart, smooth base, ground lip..$70–80
American 1865–1885

A. Stone & Co., Philada, Manufactured By Cunninghams & Co. Pittsburgh Pa
Deep Bluish Aqua, Pint, iron pontil, applied groove ring.....$1000–1500
American 1855–1865

Acme, L.G. Co. (Around Star), Trade Mark, 1893–Mason's Patent, Nov 30th 1858
Aqua, Pint, smooth base, ground lip...$150–200
American 1893–1900

Acme, L.G. Co. (Around Star), Trade Mark, 1893–Mason's Patent, Nov 30th 1858
Aqua, Quart, smooth base, ground lip.......................................$150–200
American 1893–1900

Acme, L.G. Co. (Around Star), Trade Mark, 1893–Mason's Patent, Nov 30th 1858
Aqua, Half-gallon, smooth base, ground lip..............................$150–200
American 1893–1900

American (Motif of Eagle with Flag) Fruit Jar
Pale Green, Half-gallon, smooth base, ground lip.....................$125–175
American 1885–1895

Arthur Burnham & Gilroy, 10th & Geo. Sts., Philadelphia—R. Arthur's Patent, Jany 2nd 1855
Bluish Aqua, 7¼ in., smooth base, ground lip.........................$600–800
American 1855–1860 (rare)

Atlas Mason's Patent
Light Apple green, quart, smooth base, ABM lip.........................$60–80
American 1855–1865

Atlas Strong Shoulder Mason
Deep Smoky Blue, Quart, smooth base and lip $60–80
American 1815–1925

Ball Perfect Mason
Deep Yellowish Olive Amber, Quart, smooth base and lip $55–75
American 1915–1925

Patd Feby 9th 1864, Banner, Reisd Jan 22d 1867
Deep Bluish Aqua, Quart, smooth base, ground lip $175–225
American 1867–1875

B.B.G.M. Co. (Monogram)
Bluish Aqua, Quart, smooth base, ground lip...............................$70–90
American 1890–1915

Patd March 26th 1867 B.B. Wilcox
Aqua, Quart, smooth base, ground lip...$60–80
American 1885–1890

Bee
Aqua, Half-gallon, smooth base, ground lip..............................$600–800
American 1869–1875 (rare)

Bellerjeaus Simplicity Fruit Jar, Patd Mar 31st 1868
Aqua, Quart, smooth base, ground lip.....................................$800–1200
American 1868–1870 (extremely rare)

Best
Clear, Half-gallon, smooth base, ground lip..................................$35–50
American 1890–1900

Boston Trade Dagger (Motif of Dagger)
Greenish Aqua, Quart, smooth base, ground lip.......................$140–160
Australian 1890–1900

Buckeye
Bluish Aqua, Quart, smooth base, ground lip...........................$150–200
American 1870–1885

C.D. Brooks Boston
Golden Yellow Amber, Quart, smooth base, applied mouth $40–80
American 1885–1895

Bellerjeaus Simplicity fruit jar, pat'd Mar 31, 1868, 1868–1870, $800–$1200; The Van Vliet Jar of 1881, 1881–1890, $300–$400; Bee fruit jar, 1869–1875, $600–$800; The Van Vliet Jar of 1881, 1881–1890, $275–$375; Newman's Patent Dec 20, 1859, 1859–1865, $250–$350.

Chef, Trade Mark, the Berdan Co. (Around Motif of Chef)—Pat's July 14th 1908
Aqua, pint, smooth base, ground lip..$10–20
American 1880–1895

C. K. Halle & Co, 121 Water St. Cleveland, O.
Aqua, Quart, smooth base, applied mouth...............................$120–140
American 1870–1885

Clark Fruit Jar Co., Cleveland, O.
Aqua, Quart, smooth base, ground lip..$60–80
American 1885–1895

Clark's Peerless
Aqua, pint, smooth base, ground lip..$10–20
American 1860–1890

Colburn's Fountain Stopple Jar
Aqua, Quart, smooth base, applied mouth...............................$275–375
American 1875–1890 (rare)

Triumph No. 1, 1865–1880, $450–$550; Mason's
Patent Nov. 30th 1858, 1870–1880, $250–$350;
Mason's Patent Nov 30th 1858, 1880–18980, $50–$90;
Mason's Patent Nov. 30th 1858, 1880–1890,
$65–$100.

Common Sense Jar—Gregory's Patent, Aug 17th 1869
Aqua, Quart, smooth base, applied mouth............................$1000–1500
American 1870–1880 (scarce)

Crown (Motif of Crown) Imperial Pt.
Aqua, Quart, smooth base, ground lip...$7–10
American 1885–1895

Crystal Jar
Clear, Quart, smooth base, ground lip..$25–35
American 1880–1895

Cunningham & Co Pittsburgh Pa
Blue, Pint, red iron pontil, applied mouth................................$300–400
American 1855–1865

Dexter
Aqua, Midget, smooth base, ground lip $200–300
American 1875–1890(Rare)

Dillon & Co. Fairmount, Ind.
Light Emerald Green, Half-Gallon, smooth base, applied wax seal
ring $150–250
American 1880–1890

A. Stone & Co. Philada, 1860–1870, $150–$200; Indicator, 1875–1885, $600–$800; Western Pride Patented June 22, 1875, 1875–1880, $100–$150; Triumph No. 1, 1865–1880, $450–$550; The Puritan-L.S. Co., 1880–1890, $200–$250.

Patd Dec 28th 1858, Eagle, Reisd June 16th 1868
Aqua, Quart, smooth base, applied groove ring..........................$80–100
American 1870–1875

Eagle
Aqua, Quart, smooth base, applied mouth.................................$80–120
American 1875–1885

Empire
Blue, Quart, smooth base, applied mouth................................$275–375
American 1860–1865 (very rare and early jar)

Eureka, 17, Patd Dec 27th 1864
Aqua, Half-Gallon, smooth base, ground lip................................$40–60
American 1865–1870

F. & J. Bodine Philada
Aqua, Quart, smooth base, ground lip......................................$80–100
American 1870–1880

Farrar's Patne Self Sealing Jar 1893
Brown Glaze pottery, Half-gallon, smooth base.........................$250–350
Canadian 1893–1900 (scarce)

Geo. D. Brown & Co.
Clear, Pint, smooth base, ground lip...$50–70
American 1882–1895

The Canton Electric Fruit Jar, 1870–1900, $2500–$5000; Air Tight Fruit
Jar, 1850–1860, $8,000–$16,000; "W" Fruit Jar, 1860–1880,
$700–$1400; Mason's Patent Nov. 30th 1858-H G Co Fruit Jar (dense/
amber/black), 1870–1890, $4000–$8000; Mason's Patent Nov. 30th 58
Fruit Jar, 1870–1890, $1200–$2400.

Globe
Golden Yellow Amber, Quart, smooth base, ground lip...............$60–90
American 1885–1895

Griffin's Patent Oct. 7 1862
Aqua, Quart, smooth base, ground lip..$80–120
American 1862–1870

Griffin's Patent Oct. 7 1862
Bluish Aqua, Half-gallon, smooth base, ground lip...................$150–250
American 1862–1870

Haines's Improved March 1st 1870
Aqua, Quart, smooth base, applied mouth.................................$80–100
American 1870–1875

H.W. Pettit Westville, N.J.
Clear, Quart, smooth base, ABM lip...$10–20
American 1880–1900

Helme's Railroad, Mills
Amber, Quart, smooth base, ground lip...$70–80
American 1880–1900

Granger—Ground Lip, Cohansey
Closure, $800 (only 2 known), aqua.

Commodore (bulbous shape), Applied
Lip, Metal Doane's Nov.7,1865,
Patent Stopper with thumbscrew,
$1500, aqua.

Illinois Pacific Glass Co.
Clear, Quart, smooth base(S.F. CAL.) ground lip.........................$25–30
American 1880–1900

Improved Everlasting Jar
Smoky clear, Quart, smooth base, ground lip..............................$25–30
American 1885–1890

Indicator
Aqua, Quart, smooth base, ground lip.....................................$600–800
American 1875–1885

J.P. Smithl Son & Co.—Pittsburgh, Pa
Deep Aqua, Quart, smooth base, applied groove ring..................$30–40
American 1875–1895

Johnson & Johnson, New York
Deep Cobalt Blue, Quart, smooth base, ground lip..................$250–300
American 1900–1915

L & W
Aqua, Quart, smooth base, applied mouth....................................$60–80
American 1875–1885

Lafayette
Aqua, Half-gallon, smooth base, applied mouth $100–150
American 1890–1900

Lightning Putnam 763, Trade Mark
Amber, Half-pint, smooth base, ground lip............................$1000–1500
American 1882–1885 (rare)

Ludlow's Patent, June 28 1859
Deep Green Aqua, Half-Gallon, smooth base, ground lip.........$150–170
American 1859–1865

Magic Fruit Jar, Wm McCully & Co, Pittsburgh Pa, Sole Proprietors, No 4–Patented by R.M. Dalby, June 6th 1856
Amber, Quart, smooth base, ground lip....................................$125–175
American 1866–1870

Mansfield
Clear, Quart, smooth base (Mansfield Glass W'k's., Knowlton's May 03) ABM lip $275–375
American 1903–1910

Mason's, C.F.J.Co. (Monogram) Ptent, Nov 30th 1858
Light Yellow Olive, Quart, smooth base, ground lip $70–90
American 1870–1880

Mason's/Patent/Nov 30th (Cross)
Aqua, Quart, smooth base (Pat Nov 26 67), ground lip..............$60–70
American 1880–1890

Pogue Bridgeton N.J., $5000; Improved Standard—April 17th 1888, Ground Lip, Tin Lid, $1500; A.P. Brayton, $2500; Webster's Patent Feb. 16, 1864, $2750; all aqua.

Mason's Patent Nov 30th 1858—Cjfco (Monogram)
Light Apple Green, Half-gallon, smooth base, ground lip $50–90
American 1880–1890

Mason's Patent Nov 30th 1858—Dupont (In Circle)
Light Apple Green, Half-gallon, smooth base, ground lip $200–300
American 1880–1890

Mason's (Keystone in Circle) Patent Nov. 30th 1858
Amber, Half-gallon, smooth base, ground lip..........................$400–600
American 1870–1880

Millville, Atmosphric Fruit Jar—Whitall's Patent, June 18th 1861
Bluish Aqua, Quart, smooth base, applied groove ring.................$60–80
American 1865–1870

Millville/ W.T. Co. (Monogram) Improved
Aqua, Quart, smooth base, ground lip.......................................$25–35
American 1880–1900

Moore's Patent Dec 30 1867
Aqua, Quart, smooth base, ground lip.......................................$40–60
American 1880–1895

Mrs. G.E. Haller Patd. Feb 25. 73
Aqua, Half-gallon, smooth base, applied mouth with internal screw
threads...$60–80
American 1873–1880

Myers Test Jar
Deep Bluish Aqua, Quart, smooth base, ground lip $70–90
American 1869–1875

Newman's Patent Dec 20th 1859
Deep Bluish Aqua, Quart, smooth base, ground lip $250–350
American 1859–1865

Protector
Aqua, Quart, smooth base, ground lip.......................................$40–60
American 1880–1895

Potter & Bodine Air-Tight Fruit Jar, Philada-Patented April 13th 1858
Aqua, Half-gallon, smooth base, groove ring............................$175–250
American 1860–1865

Put on Rubber Before Filling, Mrs. S.T. Rorer's, Star & Crescent (Motif of Star and Crescent Moon), Self Sealing Jar
Aqua, Quart, smooth base, ground lip......................................$300–400
American 1875–1885

S. McKee & Co.
Aqua, Quart, smooth base, applied groove ring...........................$60–80
American 1875–1895

Safety Valve, Patd May 21 1895, Ah (Monogram)
Aqua, Half-gallon, smooth base, ground lip.................................$40–60
American 1880–1890

Safety Valve, Patd May 21 1895, Hc (Over Triangle)
Deep Bluish Aqua, Half-gallon, smooth base, ground lip.............$70–90
American 1875–1890

San Francisco Glass Works
Bluish Aqua, Quart, smooth base, applied groove ring.............$300–400
American 1875–1895 (rare)

Sun (Inside Circle with Radiating Lines) Trade Mark
Aqua, Quart, smooth base (J.P. Barstow), ground lip...................$70–90
American 1890–1895

Standard
Bluish Aqua, Half-gallon, smooth base, applied groove ring........$55–85
American 1880–1890

Star Glass Co.
Pale Citron, Quart, smooth base, applied groove ring.................$50–70
American 1875–1895

Stevens Tin Top, Patd July 17, 1873
Aqua, Quart, smooth base (S.K. & Co. Around N within star),
applied groove ring..$70–90
American 1875–1895

Eagle—Glass Lid, Smooth lip, quart, $250, aqua.

Stoneware Canning Jar
Grayish Pottery, smooth base (Glass Bros. Co. London, Ont.) $140–180
Canadian 1890–1910

The American A.N.G. Co. (Monogram) Porcelain Lined, Dexter Fruit Jar
Aqua, Quart, smooth base, ground lip $175–225
American 1870–1885

The Ball Pat Apl'd for
Aqua, quart, smooth base, ground lip $275–375
American 1899–1900

The Champion, Pat. Aug. 31, 1869
Aqua, Half-gallon, smooth base, sheared and ground lip $150–250
American 1869–1875

Trade Mark, the Dandy
Amber, Quart, smooth base (Gilberds), ground lip $125–150
American 1885–1890

The Eclipse
Bluish Aqua, Quart, smooth base, applied groove ring.................$70–90
American 1875–1895 (scarce)

The King, Pat. Nov. 2. 1860
Aqua, Quart, smooth base, ground lip $200–300
American 1860–1870

The Marion Jar, Mason's Patent, Nov 30th, 1858
Blue Green, Half-gallon, smooth base, ground lip $35–50
American 1880–1890

The Mason Jar of 1858/Trade Mark
Aqua, Quart, smooth base, ground lip $125–150
American 1880–1890

The Model Jar, Patd, Aug. 27 1867, Rochester. N.Y.
Bluish Aqua, Quart, smooth base, ground lip...........................$200–300
American 1867–1875

The Pearl
Aqua, Quart, smooth base (Patd Dec 17 61 Reis Sep 1 68/Patd Nov
26/Aug 23 70 Feb 7 77) ground lip $25–35
American 1860–1880

The Penn
Aqua, Quart, smooth base (Beck Phillips & Co Pitts. Pa), applied
groove ring $80–120
American 1875–1895

Hartell's Glass Air-Tight Cover,
Patented Oct. 19, 1858, Ground
Lip, pint, $2000, black purple.

The Salem Jar
Aqua, Half-gallon, smooth base (Pat Applied For) ground
lip $800–1200
American 1870–1880

The Schaffer Jar, Rochester, N.Y.
Aqua, Half-gallon, smooth base, ground lip..............................$250–350
American 1880–1885

The Wide Mouth Telephone Jar
Clear, Pint, smooth base, ground lip...$10–20
American 1880–1890

Triumph No. 1
Deep Bluish Aqua, Quart, smooth base, ground lip $450–550
American 1865–1880

Patd Feb. 9th 1864, W.W. Lyman (Two Stars) Reisd Jan. 22n 1867
Aqua, Quart, smooth base, ground lip $35–45
American 1867–1870

Winslow Jar
Aqua, Half-gallon, smooth base, ground lip.................................$70–90
American 1880–1890

Patd Feby 9th 1864, Victory, 1, Reisd June 22nd 1867
Aqua, Quart, smooth base, ground lip $50–70
American 1867–1875

Hutchinson Bottles

The Hutchinson bottle was developed in the late 1870s by Charles A. Hutchinson. What is most interesting about his development is that the stopper, and not the bottle itself, differentiated the design from others. The stopper, which Hutchinson patented in 1879, was intended as an improvement to cork stoppers since they eventually shrank and allowed air to seep into the bottle.

The new stopper consisted of a rubber disk that was held between two metal plates attached to a spring stem. The stem was in the form of a figure eight, with the upper loop larger than the lower to prevent the stem from falling into the bottle. The lower loop could pass through the bottle's neck and push down the disk to permit the filling or pouring of the bottle's contents. A refilled bottle was sealed by pulling the disk up to the bottle's shoulder, where it made a tight fit. When opened, the spring was hit, which made a popping sound. Thus, the Hutchinson bottle was the source of the phrase "pop bottle" and the story behind how carbonated drinks came to be known as "pop."

Hutchinson stopped producing bottles in 1912, when warnings about metal poisoning were issued. As collectibles, Hutchinson bottles rank high on the curiosity and price scales, but pricing varies quite sharply by geographical location, compared to the relatively stable prices of most other bottles.

Hutchinson bottles carry abbreviations of which the following three are the most common:

tbntbs—"This bottle not to be sold"
TBMBR—"This bottle must be returned"
TBINS—"This bottle is not sold"

A. Ludwig Napa
Greenish Aqua, 6⅞ in., smooth base, tooled mouth....................$70–90
American 1890–1910

Ardmore Bottling Works, Ardmore, I.T.
Bluish Aqua, 6⅝ in., smooth base, tooled mouth.......................$35–45
American 1890–1910

Atlanta Consolidated Bottling Co.
Bluish Aqua, 7⅝ in., smooth base, tooled mouth.......................$35–45
American 1890–1910

B.B.W. San Rafael
Clear, 7¼ in., smooth base, tooled top...$30–80
American 1885–1895

Bennettsville Bottling Works, Bennettsville S.C., Registered, This Bottle Not to Be Sold
Aqua, 6½ in., smooth base, tooled mouth $40–55
American 1890–1910

Bennington Bottling Co., North Bennington Vt.
Aqua, 8½ in., smooth base, tooled mouth $250–350
American 1890–1910

C. Andrae Port Huron, Michigan
Medium Blue, 6½ in., smooth base, applied top......................$200–300
American 1880–1890

C. Thomas. Truckee
Aqua, 6½ in., smooth base, tooled mouth $500–1000
American 1885–1895 (extremely rare)

C. Zuber
Aqua, 6½ in., smooth base, tooled mouth $20–30
American 1890–1895

Contents Mfgd by Trade (Motif of Eagle) Mark, Registered, Cleveland, O
Clear, 7¾ in., smooth base, tooled mouth $20–30
American 1890–1895

Sammons Bros—Jamestown,
1880–1895, $50–$100.

Comanche Bottling Works, Comanche, I.T.
Aqua, 6¾ in., smooth base, tooled mouth $250–350
American 1890–1900 (early bottle from the Indian Territory)

Crystal Spring Bottling Co. Barnet. Vt.
Clear, 6⅞ in., smooth base, tooled mouth $200–300
American 1890–1910 (rare)

Registered /Biedenharn/ Candy Co./Vicksburg, Miss
Pale Bluish Aqua, 7¼ in., smooth base (B.C. Co.) tooled blob
top $250–350
American 1890–1900

D. Fuelscher Central City Col. "This Bottle to Be Returned To"
Aqua, 6½ in., smooth base, tooled mouth $100–200
American 1880–1895 (scarce)

Distilled Soda Water Co. Of Alaska
Pale Aqua, 7¾ in., smooth base, tooled mouth.......................$300–600
American 1885–1895

Edward Feller, Canton, O
Clear, 7¾ in., smooth base, tooled mouth $20–30
American 1880–1895

Empire Soda Works, Vallejo
Aqua, 6½ in., smooth base, tooled mouth $50–100
American 1885–1895

F. Schmidt, Leadville, Colo
Aqua, 6½ in., smooth base, tooled mouth $70–120
American 1880–1895

Geo. House Little Falls, N.Y.
Aqua, 6¼ in., smooth base, blob top $30–60
American 1885–1895

H. Denhalter & Son, Salt Lake City, Ut.
Aqua, 6½ in., smooth base, tooled top......................................$50–100
American 1880–1910

H. Mailrd Lead City S.D (in Slug)
Aqua, 6½ in., smooth base, tooled mouth $50–100
American 1880–1910

Excelsior Bottling and Extract Co.,
San Diego, Cal, 1880–1895,
$65–$95.

Herve & Carbon
Aqua Green, 6¼ in., smooth base, tooled mouth.....................$100–200
American 1885–1895

Hollister & Co. Honolulu
Light Aqua, 7¼ in., smooth base, tooled mouth.......................$50–100
American 1880–1895

James Dewer, Elko Nevada.
Clear, 6½ in., smooth base, tooled mouth $750–1500
American 1892–1895 (rare)

James Ray, Savannah, Geo—Ginger Ale
Bluish Aqua, 7¼ in., smooth base, tooled mouth $200–300
American 1870–1880

J.F.I. Tucson
Aqua, 6½ in., smooth base, tooled mouth $60–120
American 1885–1890

Joseph C. Knorr Bottler Wilkes-Barre, Pennsylvania,Pa
Aqua, 7¼ in., smooth base, tooled mouth $30–80
American 1885–1895

Jurgens & Price Bottlers, Helena Mont.
Bluish Aqua, 7¼ in., smooth base, tooled mouth $50–85
American 1880–1895

Kalispell Liquor & Tobacco Co., Kalispel Mont.
Aqua, 7 in., smooth base, tooled mouth....................................$300–400
American 1890–1910 (very rare and desirable Montana soda)

Kroger Bros. Butte, M.T.
Bluish Aqua, 6½ in., smooth base, tooled mouth $50–85
American 1880–1895

Livermore Soda Works, Livermore Cala
Aqua, 6¼ in., smooth base, tooled mouth $30–50
American 1880–1895

Mansfield Bottling Works, Mansfield Ark.
Deep Emerald Green, 6½ in., smooth base, tooled mouth $40–55
American 1880–1895

Bay View Bottling Works, Seattle, Wash, 1880–1895, $40–$75;
Milwaukee Bottling Co., Spokane Falls, WT, 1880–1895, $50–$75;
Kalispell Brewing Co., 1880–1895, $25–$65; B, 1890–1895,
$50–$100.

Meridian Steam Bottling Co., Meridian, Miss
Light Amethyst, 6½ in., smooth base, tooled mouth $30–60
American 1880–1895

Mt. Hood Soda Water, Portand, Ore.
Aqua, 6½ in., smooth base, tooled mouth $40–90
American 1885–1895

No. 5 Bode
Amethyst, 7¼ in., smooth base, tooled top...............................$75–125
American 1800–1895

Oakland Bottling Co.
Aqua, 6¼ in., smooth base, tooled mouth $30–60
American 1885–1895

Pacific Soda Works, Santa Cruz
Aqua, 6¼ in., smooth base, tooled mouth $30–50
American 1885–1895

Pearson Bros. Bodie
Greenish Aqua, 7¼ in., smooth base, tooled mouth............$1200–1500
American 1880–1895 (rare—Bodie Ghost Town, California)

Pioneer Soda Works, San Franciso
Aqua, 6¼ in., smooth base, tooled mouth $30–60
American 1885–1895

Queen City Soda Works, Seattle W.T.A. Wolff
Aqua, 7¼ in., smooth base, tooled mouth $100–200
American 1885–1895 (very rare)

Sammons Bros. Jamestown
Aqua, 6¼ in., smooth base, tooled mouth, four-piece mold........$30–60
American 1875–1895 (scarce)

Seitz Bros. Easton, Pa—S
Clear, 6½ in., smooth base, tooled mouth $40–55
American 1880–1895

Standard Bottling Co. Peter Orello Prop. Silverton, Colo.
Aqua, 6¼ in., smooth base, tooled mouth $70–140
American 1877–1896

Gamer & Jacky, Phillipsburg, Mon., 1885–1895, $25–$40; Gamer &
Jacky, Phillipsburg, Mon., 1885–1895, $25–$40; Philipsburg Bottling
Works, Philipsburg, Mont, 1885–1895, $25–$35; Philipsburg Bottling
Works, Philipsburg, Mont, 1885–1895, $25–$35.

U.B. Co. Anaconda, Mont.—This Bottle is Never Sold, 1875–1895, $35–$50; American Soda Works—S.F., 1880–1895, $35–$50.

The Cripple Creek Bottling Works

Aqua, 6½ in., smooth base, tooled mouth $50–100
American 1880–1895 (scarce)

T.H.Kelly & Co./Eagle Bottle Works, Steubenville, O

Aqua, 6½ in., smooth base, tooled mouth $20–30
American 1880–1895

Beebe Taft & Co., Wardner, Idaho, Ter., 1875–1885, $45–$65; V & S, Port Towne, ND, 1880–1895, $35–$55; Lemaire, 1885–1913, $175–$350; James Dewar, Elko, Nev., 1892–1895, $900–$1300; Compton Bottling Co., CBC, Sheridan, Wyoming, 1880–1890, $850–$1200.

The Jefferson Mineral Water Co. (Motif of Hand) Chester, Pa
Aqua, 7¾ in., smooth base, tooled mouth $20–30
American 1880–1895

The Queen City Bottling Works
Aqua, 6½ in., smooth base, tooled mouth $25–35
American 1880–1895

The Salt Lake City Soda Water Co. Red Seal
Amethyst, 6¼ in., smooth base, tooled mouth...........................$50–100
American 1880–1895

Wm. A. Kearney Shamokin Pa
Deep Amber Quart, 9 in., smooth base, tooled mouth $175–250
American 1885–1895 (few in this color and size)

Zeis & Sons Redding, Cal
Aqua, 7¼ in., smooth base, tooled mouth $20–40
American 1880–1890

Ink Bottles

Ink bottles are unique because of their centuries-old history, which provides collectors today with a wider variety of designs and shapes than any other group of bottles. People often ask why a product as cheap to produce as ink was sold in such decorative bottles. While other bottles were disposed of or returned after use, the ink bottle was usually displayed openly on desks in dens, libraries, and studies. It's safe to assume that even into the late 1880s people who bought bottles considered the design of the bottle as well as the quality of its contents.

Prior to the eighteenth century, most ink was sold in brass or copper containers. The very rich would refill their gold and silver inkwells from these storage containers. Ink that was sold in glass and pottery bottles in England in the 1700s had no brand-name identification and, at best, would have a label identifying the ink and/or its manufacturer.

In 1792, the first patent for the commercial production of ink was issued in England, twenty-four years before the first American patent was issued. Molded ink bottles appeared in America around 1815 or 1816. The blown three-mold variety was in use through the late 1840s. The most common shaped ink bottle, the umbrella, is a multisided conical that can be found with both pontiled and smooth bases. One of the more collectible ink bottles is the teakettle, identified by the neck, which extends upward at an angle from the base.

As the fountain pen grew in popularity between 1885 and 1890, ink bottles gradually became less decorative.

Bank of England Ink (Cottage Ink)
Aqua, 3⅝ in., smooth base, tooled mouth $400–600
American 1880–1890 (rare)

Barne's National Ink
Clear, 9¾ in., smooth base, tooled mouth $65–90
American 1865–1875

Ben Franklin Teakettle Ink (Figural)
Aqua, 2¾ in., smooth base, sheared lip....................................$125–175
American 1880–1895

Billings Mauve Ink
Bluish Aqua, 1⅝ in., smooth base, ground lip............................$20–35
American 1890–1910

Blown Two-Mold Annular Ring Ink
Deep Forest Green, 1¾ in., pontil base, sheared lip................$300–400
American 1820–1835 (rare)

Blown Three-Mold Geometric Ink
Medium Yellowish Olive Green, 1⅞ in., pontil base, tooled disc
mouth $200–300
American 1820–1835

E. Waters, Troy N.Y., 1845–1855, $400–$600; E. Waters, Troy
N.Y., 1845–1855, $600–$800; W.E. Bonney, 1870–1880,
$500–$700; Harrison's Columbian Ink, 1845–1855,
$1400–$1800; Double Font Teakettle Ink, 1875–1895,
$250–$450.

Blown Three-Mold Geometric Ink
Deep Olive Amber (black), 1½ in., pontil base, tooled disc
mouth $125–150
American 1820–1835

Boss Patent
Pale Apple Green, 2¾ in., 6–sided open pontil, rolled lip $275–375
American 1845–1855 (rare–corset form)

Carter's Ink
Medium Green, 5⅛ in., smooth base, applied mouth with tooled
pour spout...$100–200
American 1860–1875

Carter's, 7½, Made in U.S.A.
Aqua, 2 in., smooth base, tooled lip $10–15
American 1880–1900

Carter's (Highly Graphic Label, Front & Back)
Deep Blue Green, 8 in., smooth base, applied sloping double collar
mouth with pour spout..$80–100
American 1870–1880

Carter's (Clover Ink)
Deep Cobalt Blue, 6–sided with recessed clover leaf in five panels,
smooth base, ABM lip..$100–150
American 1925–1930

Carter's—Dragon's French Copying Ink (Label)—Master Ink
Deep Amber, 9⅞ in., smooth base, tooled mouth...................$125–150
American 1890–1910

Caw's Black Fluid Ink (Master Ink)
Medium Blue Green, 6¾ in., smooth base, applied mouth..........$20–30
American 1890–1910

Chas M. Higgins & Co.
Clear, 9 in., smooth base, tooled mouth.....................................$65–90
American 1865–1875

Continental Inks & Mucilage
Clear, 2 in., smooth base, tooled lip $10–15
American 1880–1900

Cone Ink—Dessauer's,
1880–1890, $75–$150.

Davids (Turtle Ink)
Aqua, 1½ in., smooth base, tooled lip..$25–40
American 1880–1895

Diamond Ink Co., Milwaukee (on Base)
Clear, 1¼ in., smooth base, flared lip..$15–30
American 1840–1855

Dovell's Patent
Aqua, 2½ in., smooth base, tooled mouth $20–30
American 1880–1895

E.S. Curtis Chemical Ink Powder Half Gross (Label)
Clear, 4⅝ in., pontil base, flared lip...$70–90
English 1845–1855

Estes's Metropolitan
Aqua, Tee-pee form with pillar mold style vertical ribs, 6⅞ in., pontil
base, applied mouth..$1800–2500
American 1845–1855 (unique—only 1 or 2 known pieces)

Estes—N.Y.—Ink
Medium Blue Green, 8-sided, 6¼ in., open pontil, applied
mouth $700–1000
American 1845–1855 (rare)

E.Waters, Troy, N.Y.
Aqua, 3½ in., open pontil, applied mouth...............................$350–450
American 1845–1855

Farley's Ink
Yellow Amber, 8-sided, 3¾ in., open pontil, flared lip..........$800–1200
American 1845–1855

Field's Blue-Black Ink (Master Ink)
Dark Brown Pottery, 13⅛ in., smooth base, applied top...........$80–100
English 1890–1915 (oval stamp on base—Bourne Denby)

Fred D. Alling, Rochester NY
Aqua, 2¾ in., smooth, tooled lip...$10–15
American 1880–1900

Freeblown Inkwell
Deep Blue Aqua, 3⅜ in., pontil base, sheared and tooled mouth....$100–150
American 1825–1835

Government W.B. Tood's Writing Ink
Medium Blue Green, 1⅞ in., smooth base, tooled mouth...........$15–20
American 1870–1890

Haley, Made in U.S.A., Inc Co.
Aqua, 2 in., smooth base, tooled lip...$10–15
American 1880–1900

Harrison's—Columbian—Ink—Patent
Deep Sapphire Blue, 7⅛ in., open pontil, applied mouth....$1400–1800
American 1845–1855

Harrison's—Columbian—Ink—Patent
Aqua, 7¼ in., 12-sided, pontil base, applied mouth................$200–300
American 1845–1855

Hawley Ink Co., Made in U.S.A.
Aqua, 2¼ in., smooth base, tooled mouth $30–40
American 1890–1920

Higg's Ink
Aqua, 2 in., smooth base, rolled lip..$45–70
American 1875–1885 (rare)

Hohenthal Brothers & Co., Indelible Writing Ink, N.Y.
Deep Yellowish Olive Amber, 8⅞ in., Master ink, pontil base, applied
mouth with pour spout...$700–800
American 1845–1860

Hover—Phila (Umbrella Ink)
Medium Blue Green, 12–sided, 2 in., open pontil, rolled
lip $150–200
American 1845–1855

Hover—Phila (Umbrella Ink)
Medium Green with Olive tone, 2⅝ in., open pontil, flared
lip $150–250
American 1845–1855

J.A. Williamson Chemist (Motif of Books and Inkwells)
Deep Blue Green, 9½ in., smooth base, applied double collar mouth
with pour spout $125–150
American 1870–1880 (rare master ink)

J. Bourne & Son Patentees Demby Poteries Near Derby
Cream Colored Pottery, 5¼ in., smooth base, applied mouth.....$25–35
American 1850–1870

Jacobuis Pat., Nov 10,96'
Aqua, 1¼ in., smooth base, tooled lip...$15–20
American 1840–1855

James's Mason & Co.
Aqua, 8–sided, 2½ in., open pontil, rolled lip $150–200
American 1845–1855

Jaques Chemical Works Chicago
Aqua, 2½ in., smooth base, tooled mouth $15–20
American 1870–1890

Cone Ink—Unembossed, 1890–1910, $45–$60.

J.J. Butler, Cinct.,Ohio—Cone Ink
Bluish Aqua, 2⅜ in., open pontil, rolled lip.............................$140–180
American 1845–1855 (rare—embossed)

J. Sargant
Aqua, 10–sided, 3 in., open pontil, tooled lip.........................$200–300
American 1845–1855 (rare)

J.W. Pennell
Aqua, 2 in., smooth base, tooled mouth......................................$15–20
American 1870–1890

Kirkland's Writing Fluid—Poland, Ohio
Aqua, 2½ in., open pontil, rolled lip..$375–475
American 1845–1855 (rare)

Laughlin's and Bushfield Wheling, Wa.
Aqua, 8–sided, 3 in., open pontil, rolled lip.............................$140–160
American 1845–1855

Lovatt & Lovatt Notts. Langley Mill
Dark Brown Pottery, 4½ in., smooth base, applied mouth..........$25–35
American 1865–1875

M. & Co. Ltd (Embossed on All Four Shoulder Panels)
Medium Teal Blue, Cabin, 3 in., smooth base, tooled mouth......$200–300
American 1890–1900

Mason's Black Ink, Prepared at 19 North Third St., Philad'a' (Label)
Medium Blue Green, 12-sided, 1¾ in., pontil base, rolled lip.....$175–250
American 1840–1855

New England Master Ink
Yellowish Olive Amber, 9⅝ in., smooth base, applied mouth with
pour spout..$85–120
American 1855–1875

Patd Oct 31st, 1865 (Turtle Ink)
Aqua, 1⅞ in., smooth base, ground lip.......................................$25–40
American 1840–1855

Pattern Molded Ink
Clear, 24-vertical rib pattern, 1½ in., pontil base, tooled and pressed
in funnel lip $400–600
American 1810–1830 (rare)

Pitkin Ink
Deep Olive Amber, 36 Broken rib pattern swirled to left, 1½ in.,
pontil base, tooled disc mouth $80–100
American 1780–1820

Pitkin Ink
Yellowish Olive Amber, 36 Broken rib pattern swirled to left, 1⅝ in.,
pontil base, tooled disc mouth $600–800
American 1780–1820

Pitkin Ink
Deep Olive Green, 36 Broken rib pattern swirled to left, 1⅞ in., pontil
base, tooled disc mouth $700–1000
American 1780–1820

Pitkin Ink
Deep Olive Green, 1¾ in., pontil base, tooled disc
mouth $1000–1500
American 1790–1820 (rare-square form)

Premium Steel Pen Ink, Theodore Davids & Co. N.Y. (Ingloo Ink)
Aqua, 2 in., smooth base, ground lip..$20–35
American 1880–1890

S. Fine Blk. Ink
Medium Green, 3 in., open pontil, rolled lip $250–350
American 1845–1855

S. Fine Blk. Ink
Medium Green, 3⅛ in., open pontil, rolled lip........................$250–350
American 1845–1855

School House Ink, 1860–1870,
$100–$150.

Saltglaze Stoneware Inkwell
Gray Pottery, 1½ in., smooth base, rolled lip $30–45
American 1835–1875

Sandwich Type Inkwell
Clear, White and Blue Swirl Pattern, 2⅝ in., pontil base, metal
neck bank and hinged lid...$1200–1800
American 1860–1875

Sanford Patent Applied for
Aqua, 2 in., smooth base, tooled lip...$10–15
American 1880–1900

S.I./ Comp.
Aqua, 2⅛ in., barrel ink, smooth base, ground lip.......................$40–60
American 1850–1860

S.O. Dunbar, Taunton, Mass (Label—Fluid Magnesia Prepared by S.O. Dunbar Taunton, Mass.)
Aqua, 5¾ in., smooth base, applied mouth..................................$70–90
American 1855–1865

Square Ink
Power Blue Milk glass, 1¾ in., pontil base, flared lip..............$200–300
American 1810–1820 (rare)

Stafford's Ink (Master Ink)
Medium Blue Green, 7¾ in., smooth base, tooled mouth $50–75
American 1890–1910

Stafford's Ink (Master Ink)
Medium Blue Green, 9⅝ in., smooth base, applied mouth..........$50–75
American 1890–1910

Stuart Ink—Made Only by Stuart & Harrison—Toledo, Iowa
Deep Bluish Aqua, 3⅛ in., smooth base, applied mouth.........$175–275
American 1860–1870 (rare)

T. Davids & Co.,Pat Nov 7th 76
Medium Blue Green, 3⅛ in., smooth base, tooled mouth $15–20
American 1870–1890

R.F. Ink, 1870, $100–$200.

The World, J.Raynald—Figural Ink
Aqua, 2⅛ in., smooth base, tooled mouth $120–140
American 1885–1895 (scarce)

Titcomb's Ink Cin.
Light Blue, 12–sided, 2⅞ in., pontil base, rolled lip................$300–400
American 1845–1855 (rare)

Underwoods Ink
Aqua, 2½ in., smooth base, tooled mouth $20–30
American 1880–1895

Vitreous Stone Bottles J. Bourne & Son Patentees Demby Pottery Near Derby P&J.,Arnold London England
Dark Brown Pottery, 9½ in., smooth base, applied mouth..........$25–35
American 1855–1865

W.E. Bonney
Deep Cobalt Blue, 7⅝ in., smooth base, applied mouth..........$500–700
American 1870–1880

Williams Ink
Aqua, 11 in., smooth base, tooled mouth....................................$30–40
American 1890–1920

Wooden Inkwell
Wood with glass insert inkwell and painted grain finish, 2½ in., glass well is pontil base, rolled lip $125–175
American 1845–1860

W.W.W.
Aqua, 2 in., smooth base, tooled mouth.......................................$15–20
American 1870–1890

Medicine Bottles

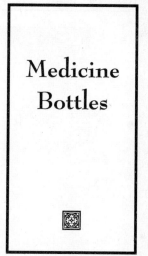

The medicine bottle group includes all pieces specifically made to hold patent medicines. Bitters bottles and cure bottles, however, are excluded from this category because the healing powers of these mixtures were very questionable.

A patent medicine was one whose formula was registered with the U.S. Patent Office, which opened in 1790. Not all medicines were patented, since the procedure required the manufacturer to reveal the medicine's contents. After the passage of the Pure Food and Drug Act of 1907, most of these patent medicine companies went out of business after they were required to list the ingredients of the contents in the bottle. The public demand quickly diminished as consumers learned that most medicines consisted of liquor diluted with water and an occasional pinch of opiates, strychnine, and arsenic. I have spent many enjoyable hours reading the labels on these bottles and wondering how anyone would survive after taking the recommended doses.

One of the oldest and most collectible medicine bottles was manufactured in England from 1723 to 1900, the embossed Turlington "Balsam of Life" bottle. The first embossed U.S. medicine bottle dates from around 1810. When searching out these bottles, always be on the lookout for embossing and original boxes. Embossed "Shaker" or "Indian" medicine bottles are very collectible and valuable. Most embossed medicines made before 1840 are clear and aqua, the embossed greens, ambers, and blues are much more collectible and valuable.

A.A. Solomons & Co—Savannah Geo.
Deep Cobalt Blue, 6⅛ in., smooth base, tooled mouth $140–160
American 1880–1900 (rare)

Cove's Pharmacy—ESTB 1876—
San Francisco, 1880–1895,
$30–$50.

A.B.L. Meyers Am—Rock Rose—New Haven
Deep Emerald Green, 9½ in., iron pontil, applied blob type
mouth $800–1400
American 1845–1855

A.J. White—the Shaker—Family Pils—Dose 2 to 4
Medium Amber, 2¼ in., smooth base, sheared lip...................$100–150
American 1890–1900

Allan's Anti-fat—Botanic Medicine Co.—Buffalo. N.Y.
Medium Sapphire Blue, 7⅝ in., smooth base, applied sloping collar
mouth $175–275
American 1870–1880

Ames Compound Concentrated Extract of Potassium
Aqua, 8¼ in., smooth base, tooled lip...$25–50
American 1880–1910

Apothecaries Hall San Francisco (Fancy Monogram)
Bluish Aqua, 5¾ in., smooth base, tooled top $30–50
American 1870–1890

Balsam of Honey
Aqua, 3⅝ in., pontil base, rolled lip...$30–40
American 1845–1855

Baker's Specific R.H. Hurd Prop. (with Picture of Uncle Sam Kneeling On Box)
Amethyst, 4¼ in., smooth base, tooled top................................$30–70
American 1875–1885

Black Gin for the Kidneys—Wm Zoeller—Pittsburgh. PA
Medium Orange Amber, 9⅛ in., smooth base, applied sloping collar mouth..$100–150
American 1870–1880

Boericke & Tafel's Triturtions
Amber, 7¾ in., smooth base, applied top $50–150
American 1880–1890

Boysen's Pharmach San-Francisco
Light Citrate, 7 in., smooth base, applied double collar mouth with wire bail..$300–700
American 1865–1875

Pure Paraffin Oil—Ziegler's Drug Store—Portland, Oregon, 1900–1920, $15–$20.

Brant's Indian Pulmonary Balsam Mt. Wallace Proprietor
Aqua, 7 in., Tubular pontil, applied top.....................................$50–120
American 1845–1855

Brown's Blood Cure—Philadelphia
Bright Green, 6¼ in., smooth base (M.B.W.—U.S.A.), tooled
mouth $100–150
American 1890–1900 (Millville Bottle Works)

Brown's Blood Treatment—Philadelphia
Medium Green, 6¼ in., smooth base (M.B.W.-U.S.A.), tooled
mouth $125–150
American 1890–1910 (Millville Bottle Works)

Burnham's Beef Wine & Iron
Aqua, 5¼ in., smooth base, tooled mouth $35–50
American 1880–1900

**By the King Royal Patent Granted to—Robt—Turlington—for His
Invented Balsam of Life—London—Jany 26 1754**
Bluish Aqua, 2⅝ in., open pontil, rolled lip...............................$80–100
American 1835–1845

C. Brinckerhoff's Health Restorative—Price $1.00—New York
Medium Olive Green, 7¼ in., pontil base, applied sloping collar
mouth $400–600
American 1845–1855

Carr Bros & Co—Druggist—Baltimore Md
Clear, 8¼ in., smooth base, tooled mouth $70–90
American 1880–1900

Carter's Ext Smart Weed Erie, Pa CSW
Light Aqua, 5¼ in., smooth base, tooled mouth..........................$20–40
American 1865–1880

Cary's Cough Cue Syrup
Aqua, 4⅞ in., smooth base, tooled mouth $8–10
American 1880–1900

Citrate of Magnesia
Medium Green, 7⅝ in., smooth base, tooled mouth....................$65–75
American 1885–1910

Derma Zema Alterative—Pfeiffer
Chemical Company, 1890–1910,
$35–$55.

Curtis Cough Cure, J.J. Mack & Co. Sole Proprietors San Francisco, Cal. C.C.C.
Light amethyst, 7 in., smooth base, tooled top..........................$50–100
American 1865–1875

C.W. Merchant, Lockport, NY
Medium Green, 5 in., open pontil, applied top..........................$60–120
American 1855–1865

C.W. Snow & Col—Druggist (Motif of Eagle and Shield with Mortar and Pestle) Syracuse N.Y.
Deep Cobalt Blue, 8¼ in., smooth base, tooled lip..................$100–150
American 1885–1895

D. Vollmer Druggist—Ft. Wayne—Ind.
Medium Cobalt Blue, 7½ in., smooth base (B.F.G. Co.), applied
mouth $175–250
American 1875–1885 (unique—only 2 or 3 known in cobalt blue in Indiana)

Deweys—Dewey's Dewferol Port, Olive Oil & Iron
Amber, 10⅛ in., smooth base, tooled lip $25–50
American 1880–1910

Dr. Barnes Ess Jamaica Ginger R. Hall & Co. Proprietors
Deep Blue Aqua, 5½ in., smooth base, applied top.....................$40–80
American 1865–1875

Dr. Birmingham's—Antibilious—Blood Purifier
Teal Blue Green, 8⅝ in., smooth base, applied mouth............$500–700
American 1865–1875

Dr. Cooper's Ethereal Oil for Deafness
Deep Bluish Aqua, 2⅝ in., open pontil, rolled lip...................$250–350
American 1840–1855 (rare)

Dr. Clark—N. York
Deep Blue Green, 9⅛ in., iron pontil, applied sloping collar
mouth $300–450
American 1845–1855

Churchill's Drugstore, Yreka, Cal,
1880–1890, $35–$45.

Dr. D. James Onic Vermifuge, 84 Chest Street, Phila
Aqua, 5 in., open pontil, applied top..$20–30
American 1855–1865

Dr. Eaton's Infantile Cordial—Church & Dupont—Sole Proprietors New York
Clear, 5 in., open pontil, applied sloping collar mouth $80–120
American 1845–1855

Dr. Eliel's Liver Regulator—South Bend, Ind.
Medium Cobalt Blue, 5³⁄₅ in., smooth base, tooled mouth $200–300
American 1885–1895

Dr. Elmore's Rheumatine—Coutaline—the Only Remedy for Rheumatic Diseases—Best Remedy for Dyspepsia & Kidney, Liver, Bladder & Blood Disorders
Medium Amber, 9³⁄₄ in., smooth base, tooled mouth...............$175–250
American 1880–1890

Dr. Geo. Clayton—Dog Remedies—Chicago
Clear, 6³⁄₄ in., smooth base, tooled mouth $70–90
American 1890–1900

Dr. H. James Cannibus Indica Craddock & Co, Proprietors Phila, Pa
Clear, 7³⁄₄ in., smooth base, tooled top.....................................$100–200
American 1855–1865

Dr. H.A. Ingham's—Nevine Pain Extract
Aqua, 4⁷⁄₈ in., pontil base, applied lip $20–30
American 1855–1865

Dr. H.B. Skinner—Boston
Medium Blue Green, 6 in., pontil base, applied mouth $700–900
American 1845–1855 (rare)

Dr. H.C. Porter & Son—Druggist—Tandy, Pa
Aqua, 5¼ in., smooth base, ABM lip..$35–70
American 1880–1900

Dr. Ham's Aromatic Invigorating Syrup
Orange Amber, 8½ in., smooth base, applied mouth $120–140
American 1875–1885

Dustin Brothers Pharmacy,
Blackfoot, Idaho, 1880–1900,
$40–$50.

Dr. Hitzfeld—Denver, Colo.—For External Use Only
Medium Cobalt Blue, 3½ in., smooth base (W.T. & Co.—U.S.A.)
tooled lip $80–100
American 1890–1915

Dr. J. Barlow Smith's Caloric Vita Oil
Clear, 5 in., smooth base, tooled top $30–70
American 1865–1880

Dr. J. Kauffman's Angeline—Hamilton, Ohio
Aqua, 7⅝ in., smooth base, tooled mouth $30–50
American 1860–1870

Dr. J. W. Bull's Cough Syrup
Aqua, 8¾ in., smooth base, tooled mouth $30–50
American 1860–1870

Dr. Lepper's Oil of Gladness, Justin Gates, Sacramento
Rich Bluish Aqua, 5 in., smooth base, applied top.....................$80–150
American 1860–1870

Dr. McBride World's Relief
Bluish Aqua, 6½ in., smooth base, applied top.........................$70–180
American 1865–1875

Dr. Mitchell
Aqua, 5⅝ in., pontil base, rolled lip..$25–50
American 1845–1855

Dr. Mitchell's Flavoring Extract, Rochester, N.Y.
Aqua, 5⅝ in., pontil base, rolled lip..$25–50
American 1845–1855

Dr. Mitchell Ox Gall & Arnica Liniment
Bluish Aqua, 4⅝ in., open pontil, rolled lip.............................$100–150
American 1845–1855 (extremely rare)

Dr. M.M. Fenner's People Remedies Fredonia, NY, USA Kidney and Backache Cure
Dark Amber, 9 in., smooth base, tooled top................................$30–60
American 1880–1895

Dr. Pareira's Italian Remedy
Aqua, 4⅛ in., pontil base, applied mouth....................................$70–90
American 1845–1855

Dr. Parker's Sons Dyspepsia Cure
Aqua, 4⅞ in., smooth base, tooled mouth $8–12
American 1880–1900

Dr. Perkins Syrup Albany
Deep Blue Green, 9⅜ in., iron pontil, applied sloping collar
mouth $1000–1500
American 1845–1855

Dr. Perkinson's Pain Killer—Balt.
Aqua, 3⅞ in., pontil base, applied lip $100–150
American 1845–1855 (rare)

Dr. Pinkham's Emmenagoogue
Aqua, 5 in., pontil base, applied lip..$20–30
American 1855–1865

Bronson & Lighthall Druggists,
Kalispell, Montana
1885–1890, $25–$35.

Dr. Urban's—Anti Bacchanalian Elixir, Louisville, Ky
Bluish Aqua, 7¼ in., pontil base, applied mouth......................$275–375
American 1845–1855

Drink Dr. Radam's Mirobe Killer (Around Shoulder)
Medium Amber, 10⅜ in., smooth base, tooled mouth.............$175–250
American 1890–1900 (scarce)

Dr. S.A. Weaver's Canker & Salt Rheum Syrup
Aqua, 9⅜ in., iron pontil, applied mouth $50–75
American 1855–1865

Dr. Sykes' Sure Cure for Catarrh
Bluish Green, 7 in., smooth base, applied top, four piece mold......$40–80
American 1865–1875

Dr. Wards's Medical Co. Winona, MN
Dark Amber, 9 in., smooth base, tooled top................................$30–60
American 1850–1860

D.S. Barnes Mexican Mustang Linament, New York
Aqua, 4 in., smooth base, sheared top...$20–30
American 1845–1855

Roberts Drug Store,
Goldfield, Nevada, 1905–1906,
$50–$100.

E.A. Buckhout's Dutch Liniment (Motif of Man)—Prepared at Machanicville—Saratoga Co. N.Y.
Deep Bluish Aqua, 4¾ in., open pontil, rolled lip...................$400–600
American 1845–1855 (scarce)

Egg Nog—Patented 1859—Put Up by the American Desiccating Co—New York
Medium Yellow Amber, 9 in., smooth base, applied mouth $500–700
American 1859–1865 (rare)

E. Quirk's—Inimitable—Essence of Tyre—for the Hair
Clear, 4 in., pontll base, wide rolled lip...................................$150–200
American 1825–1835

Eye-Lo Eye Remedy—La Porte, Ind.
Milk glass, 3½ in., smooth base, tooled lip...........................$100–125
American 1891–1910 (rare)

Fetter's (Motif of Bottle) Magnesia
Deep Green, 9⅛ in., smooth base, tooled mouth........................$60–80
American 1890–1910

From Wentz's the Place to Buy Your Drugs Gilroy, Cal
Clear, 6½ in., smooth base, tooled top..$20–30
American 1865–1875

Fulton's Diabetic Compound
Amber, 8 in., smooth base, tooled lip...$25–50
American 1880–1910

Gardiner's Liniment
Aqua, 5⅜ in., pontil base, applied mouth....................................$70–90
American 1845–1855

Gay's Compound—Extract of Canchalagua—New York
Bluish Aqua, 6¼ in., open pontil, flared lip............................$150–225
American 1845–1855 (rare)

Geo. Saunders & Co—377 Asylum St.—Hartford. Ct
Deep Cobalt Blue, 8 in., smooth base, tooled lip......................$75–100
American 1890–1900

Ginseng—Panacea
Deep Aqua, 4½ in., open pontil, rolled lip..............................$150–175
American 1845–1855

Dr. Miles' Restorative Nervine, 1890–1900, $20–$35; Phenix Sure Cure, 1890–1900, $15–$25.

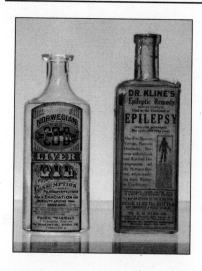

Norwegian COD Liver Oil, 1880–1895, $15–$25; Dr. Kline's Epileptic Remedy, Dr. R. H. Kline Co., 1885–1895, $20–$25.

Gleet Seven-Days—Gonorrhoea
Deep Cobalt Blue, 5 in., smooth base (M.B.W. Millville) tooled mouth $150–200
American 1890–1910 (rare)

Gogings Wild Cherry Tonic
Medium Amber, 8¾ in., smooth base, tooled mouth...............$120–140
American 1890–1900

H.A. Elliott Pharmacy, Idaho Springs, Colo
Clear, 4¼ in., smooth base, tooled top..$30–60
American 1875–1885 (scarce)

H.T. Helmbold Chemist—Philadelphia—Genuine—Extracts
Aqua, 6¼ in., open pontil, applied sloping collar mouth........$140–160
American 1845–1855

Halbert's Star Remedy—Buffalo. N.Y.
Aqua, 7¼ in., smooth base, tooled mouth $8–12
American 1880–1900

Himalaya the Kola Compound Nature's Cure for Asthma New York, Cincinatti
Amber, 7¼ in., smooth base, tooled mouth.................................$20–40
American 1880–1890

Selection of medicine bottles, 1880–1920, $10–$20 (each).

Holman's Natures Grand Restorative—J.B. Holman Prop—Boston Mass
Bluish Aqua, 6⅝ in., pontil base, applied mouth.....................$125–150
American 1845–1855 (scarce)

Hornung Apothecary, Marysville, Cal
Clear, 6 in., smooth base, tooled top...$10–20
American 1875–1885

Houcks—Vegetable—Panacea—Goodletsville, Tenn
Bluish Aqua, 7⅛ in., smooth base, applied double collar mouth $450–550
American 1855–1860

Howe & Steven—Family Dye Colors
Aqua, 6½ in., pontil base, rolled lip..$20–30
American 1855–1865

Iron Tonic—Talbot Bros.—Lawrence Mass
Deep Cobalt Blue, 7¼ in., smooth base, tooled lip...................$75–100
American 1880–1900

J. B. Wheatley's—Compound Syrup—Dallasburgh, Ky
Blue Aqua, 6 in., iron pontil, applied double collar mouth.........$70–90
American 1845–1855

J. Grout
Medium Emerald Green, 3⅛ in., pontil base, rolled lip $375–425
American 1845–1855

J. Henderson & Bros. Druggist—Pitts
Aqua, 5 in., pontil base, rolled lip $35–45
American 1845–1855

James Alternative, 84 Chest Street Phila
Aqua, 7 in., open pontil, applied top..$20–30
American 1855–1865

James Arrant Druggist—New York
Aqua, 5½ in., open pontil, applied sloping collar mouth $70–90
American 1845–1855

John Haft. Jr.—Wholesale Druggist, No 119 Wood Street—Pittsburgh, Pa
Deep Bluish Aqua, 5 in., pontil base, rolled lip...........................$35–45
American 1845–1855

J. R. Bursdall's—Arnica Liniment—New York
Bluish Aqua, 5½ in., open pontil, applied sloping collar mouth..........$70–90
American 1845–1855

Kendall's Spavin Cure
Aqua, 4⅞ in., smooth base, tooled mouth $8–10
American 1880–1900

Kodol Dyspepsia Cure—E.G. Dewitt & Co.
Clear, 8¼ in., smooth base, tooled lip...$25–50
American 1880–1910

Lippi-Blood Puriffier—Lippi Ideal Tonic
Amber, 9¼ in., smooth base, tooled lip $70–90
American 1890–1910

Log Cabin—Hops and Buchu—Remedy
Deep Amber, 10 in., smooth base (Pat Sept 6/87), applied
mouth $150–200
American 1885–1895

London
Aqua, 6 in., pontil base, rolled lip $20–30
American 1855–1865

Selection of medicine bottles, 1885–1900, $15–$25 (each).

Lord's Opaldeldoc (with Man Throwing Away Crutches)
Aqua, 5 in., smooth base, tooled top..$50–100
American 1865–1875

Lutted's S.P. Cough Drops
Clear, Log cabin on log feet, 7⅛ in., smooth base...................$125–150
American 1910–1920

Lyon's—Kathairon—New York
Aqua, 3⅝ in., pontil base, applied lip $30–40
American 1845–1855

Mack's Florida Water
Aqua, 8¾ in., smooth base, tooled top.......................................$50–100
American 1865–1875

Maguire Druggist—St. Louis. Mo
Light Green, 5¾ in., pontil base, applied sloping collar mouth.......$175–250
American 1845–1855

M.B. Roberts Vegetable Ebrocation
Light Emerald Green, 5 in., pontil base, applied sloping collar
mouth $80–100
American 1835–1855

McBurney's Kidney and Bladdar Cure, Los Angeles, Cal
Clear, 5 in., smooth base, tooled top..$20–30
American 1865–1875

Mexican Mustang Liniment
Light Green, 7¼ in., iron pontil, applied top............................$80–150
American 1845–1855

Michael Bosak Co.—Horke Vino
Medium Amber, 11½ in., smooth base, tooled mouth...............$80–100
American 1910–1920

Mitchell's—Liniment-Pittsburgh. Pa
Aqua, 4⅞ in., pontil base, rolled lip..$140–160
American 1845–1855

More's Revealed Remedy (Monogram in Shield)
Amber, 8 in., smooth base, tooled top......................................$30–50
American 1880–1890

Mrs. Winslows Soothing Syrup
Aqua, 4⅛ in., pontil base, rolled lip..$20–30
American 1855–1865

Munyon's Paw Paw
Dark Amber, 10 in., smooth base, tooled top.............................$30–70
American 1870–1885

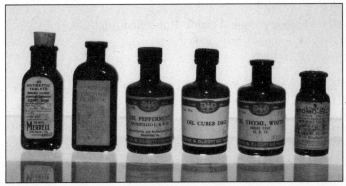

Selection of cobalt blue medicine bottles, 1895–1910, $5–$10 (each).

National Kidney & Liver Cure
Medium Amber, 9 in., smooth base, tooled mouth $120–140
American 1880–1900

N.W. Seat. MD—Negative Electric Fluid—New York
Aqua, 3¼ in., open pontil, rolled lip $35–60
American 1855–1865

Osage Indian Makes Sick People Well—Makes Weak People Strong
Medium Amber, 8⅞ in., smooth base, tooled mouth $70–90
American 1880–1900

Perry's Magnetic—Wine of Iron—Manchester
Deep Cobalt Blue, 7 in., smooth base, applied mouth $140–160
American 1870–1880

Phillip's Emulsion Cod Liver Oil New York
Dark Amber, 9 in., smooth base, tooled top $30–60
American 1865–1875

Pitt's Vital Reviver
Clear, 7⅝ in., smooth base, tooled mouth $30–50
American 1850–1860

Popular Kidney and Liver Cure Etc., H.H. Purdy Druggist, Downieville, Cal (Labeled Bottle)
Clear, 8¾ in., smooth base, tooled mouth $125–175
American 1880–1895

Powell's Pharmacy Opp. Temple Hotel Redding, Cal
Clear, 4½ in., smooth base, tooled top $20–30
American 1875–1885

Pratt's Distemper and Pink Eye Cure
Amber, 7 in., smooth base, tooled top $30–60
American 1865–1880

Primley's Iron & Wahoo Tonic—Jones & Primley Co, Elkhart. Ind
Yellowish Olive Green, 9½ in., smooth base, applied sloping collar
mouth $500–700
American 1875–1885

Prof. Deans King Catus on the Great Barbed Wire Remedy—Diney & McDaid—Trade Mark
Medium Amber, 6½ in., smooth base, tooled mouth...............$175–275
American 1885–1900

R.A. Robinson & Co—Druggists—Louisville
Deep Cobalt Blue, 7¼ in., smooth base, tooled mouth $175–250
American 1880–1900 (extremely rare)

R.P. Spence Drug Co.—Central & Andeson Sts. Knoxville, Tenn
Yellowish Green, 4⅝ in., smooth base, tooled mouth................$80–100
American 1890–1910

Regent's—Macassar Oil—for the Hair—Yibby St—London
Clear, 3½ in., pontil base, flared lip...$35–60
American 1855–1860

S.A. Palmer Druggist, Santa Cruz, Cal.
Amber, 6 in., smooth base, applied double collar mouth $30–50
American 1865–1875

Seaside Drugstore San Pedro, Cal
Clear, 5½ in., smooth base, tooled top..$30–50
American 1865–1875

S.S. Seely & Co—Morris—Otesgo County—New York
Clear, 4⅞ in., pontil base, applied lip $25–50
American 1845–1855

Selection of medicine bottles, 1885–1920, $7–$10 (each).

Shuptrine Druggist—Savannah, Ga
Teal Green, 3¾ in., smooth base (Pat.Dec,13 87–C.L.G. Co) tooled
lip $150–200
American 1890–1900

Sparks Perfect Health (Bust of Man) for Kidney & Liver
Medium Amber, 9½ in., tooled mouth....................................$150–200
American 1880–1895

Swift's Syphilitic Specific
Deep Cobalt Blue, 9⅛ in., smooth base, applied mouth..........$300–400
American 1870–1880

Stabler—Worm-Mixture
Pale Greenish Aqua, 3¾ in., open pontil, rolled lip.....................$40–60
American 1835–1850

Stanford's—Radical Cure
Cobalt Blue, 7¼ in., smooth base, applied mouth $100–150
American 1875–1885

7 Sutherland Sisters Hair Grower
Aqua, 5½ in., smooth base, tooled lip...$35–50
American 1880–1900

T. Morris Perot & Co—Druggists—Phila
Light Sapphire Blue, 4¾ in., pontil base, rolled lip $350–450
American 1844–1855

The Cure for Fits Dr. Chas. T. Price—67 William St.—New York
Clear, 8½ in., smooth base, tooled mouth $159–200
American 1880–1895

The Great—Shoshonees—Remedy of—Dr. Josephus
Deep Bluish Aqua, 6⅛ in., smooth base, tooled mouth...............$70–90
American 1875–1885

The Owl Drug Co. (Motif of Owl on Mortar and Pestle)
Tippecanoe—H.H. Warner & Co.
Deep Cobalt Blue, 9⅝ in., smooth base (W. T. & Co) tooled
mouth $300–400
American 1890–1915

Selection of amber medicine bottles, 1880–1900, $15–$20.

The Owl Drug Co. (motif of owl on mortar and pestle)
Medium Golden Amber, 6⅞ in., smooth base, tooled mouth $700–900
American 1890–1915

The Owl Drug Co. (motif of owl on mortar and pestle)
Milk Glass, 5½ in., smooth base, tooled mouth.........................$70–100
American 1890–1910

The Sherry & Iron Company, Stockton, Cal. USA, Sherry & Iron
Aqua, 11¼ in., smooth base, applied top.................................$300–500
American 1870–1890 (rare)

Trunk Bros. Denver, Colo
Clear, 5½ in., smooth base, tooled top...$20–30
American 1865–1875

Van Vleet-Mansfield Drug Co.—Manufacturing Chemist—Memphis, Tenn
Deep Cobalt Blue, 8 in., smooth base (W. T. & Co—U.S.A.) tooled
mouth $200–300
American 1890–1910 (very rare)

W.T. Wenzell, San Francisco
Deep Aqua, 5½ in., smooth base, applied top $80–150
American 1860–1880

Warner's Safe Remedies Co.
Amber, 5¼ in., smooth base, tooled mouth $35–50
American 1880–1900

We Never Sleep—Muegge—the Druggist—Baker Ore.
Yellowish Green, 5¼ in., smooth base, tooled mouth..............$100–150
American 1890–1910

Wheth & Bro Philada
Light Green, 6½ in., smooth base, tooled top............................$40–100
American 1855–1865

White's Prairie Flower Toledo, O
Deep Bluish Aqua, 7½ in., smooth base, applied top $100–200
American 1855–1865

Wm Goldstein IXL Florida Water
Aqua, 9 in., smooth base, tooled top...$50–100
American 1855–1865

Wm. H. Keith & Co—Apothecaries—San Francisco
Deep Bluish Aqua, 8½ in., smooth base, applied mouth.........$175–250
American 1855–1865 (San Franciso Dig of 1998)

Wright's India Cough Balsam
Aqua, 4⅞ in., smooth base, tooled mouth $8–10
American 1880–1900

Yerba Santa San Francisco, California (with Cross)
Aqua, 8½ in., smooth base, tooled top......................................$200–300
American 1875–1885

Youatts Gargling Oil, Comstock & Brother, New York
Bluish Aqua, 9⅛ in., smooth base, applied sloping double collar
mouth $50–75
American 1855–1865

Zollickoffer's—Anti Rheumatic—Cordial—Phila
Medium Amber, 6½ in., smooth base, tooled mouth...............$140–180
American 1875–1885

Milk Bottles

In recent years, many collectors have taken a renewed interest in collecting milk bottles. The first patent for a milk bottle was issued in January 1875 to the "Jefferson Co. Milk Assn." The bottle itself featured a tin top with a spring clamping device. The first known standard-shaped milk bottle (pre-1930) had a patent date of March 1880 and was made by the Warren Glass Works of Cumberland, Maryland. In 1884, A. V. Whiteman patented a jar with a domed tin cap to be used along with the patent of the Thatcher and Barnhart fastening device for a glass lid. There is no trace, however, of a patent for the bottle itself. Among collectors today, the Thatcher milk bottle is one of the most prized. There are several variations on the original. Very early bottles were embossed with a picture of a Quaker farmer milking his cow while seated on a stool. "Absolutely Pure Milk" is stamped into the glass on the bottle's shoulder.

An important development in the design of the milk bottle was the patent issued to H.P. and S. L. Barnhart for their methods of capping and sealing. Their invention involved the construction of a bottle mouth adapted to receive and retain a wafer disk or cap. It was eventually termed the milk bottle cap and revolutionized the milk bottling industry. Between 1900 and 1920, there were not many new patents on bottles. With the introduction of the Owens Semiautomatic and Automatic Bottle Machines, milk bottles were mass-produced. Between 1921 and 1945, the greatest number of milk bottles were manufactured and used. After 1945, square milk bottles and paper cartons were commonly used.

Of all the milk bottles, there are two types that are of particular interest to the collector. These are the "babytops," which had an embossed baby's face on the upper part of the neck, and the "cop-the-cream," which had a policeman's head and cap embossed into the neck. Both of these clear-colored bottles, along with their tin tops, are very rare and valuable.

Baby Tops
Beech Grove Dairy, Utica, NY
Quart $60

Blais Dairy, Lewiston, ME
Square Quart $65

Brookfield Dairy, Hellertown, PA
½ Pint $25

Buzzelli Sons, Niagara Falls, NY $40

Cooper Dairy, Elmer, NJ (scarce)
½ Pint $120–140

Dickson Dairy, Dickson, PA
Quart $50

Dresser Hill Farms, Charlton, MA
Quart $65

Flanders Dairy, MA
½ Pint $25

Golden Dawn Dairy, Westfield, NJ
Square Quart $45

Good-Rich Dairy Products, Mt. Carmel, PA
½ Pint $25

Highland Dairy Products, Coatsville, PA
Quart $75

Julius Anderson, Rockland, ME
Quart $50

Mirror Lake Farm, Herkimer, NY
Quart $60

Old Homestead Dairy, Windsor, VT
Quart $50

Clovis Quality Dairy—Behymer and Minnewawa, Clovis, Cal; Guard Your Health, Portland Milk Producers Assn; Clarke's, Gallup N.M., 1945–1955, $25–$35 (each).

Parkdale Dairy, Washington, NJ
Quart $60

Shaw's Dairy, Brattleboro, VT
Quart $80

Superior Dairy, Millville, NJ
Quart $140–160

Sweet's Dairy, Fredonia, NY
Quart $50

Uptown Farm, Bridgewater, MA
1 Pint... $50

Whitcombs Farm, Littleton, MA
Quart $55

Woods Dairy, Peterburg-Hopewell, VA
Square Quart $135

Cop The Cream
Blue Bell Dairy, Irvington, NJ
Pint $60

Cedar Grove Dairy, Hope, IN
Quart $90

Furman Bros., Ithaca, NY
Quart $50

Greenleaf Dairy, Petersburg, PA
Square Quart $75

Highland Dairy, Rochester, NY
Quart $50

Liberty Dairy, Huron, MI
Quart $100

Matuellas Dairy, Hazletown, PA
Quart $40

Nicks Dairy Products, Old Forge, PA
Pint $65

Randle Milk, Endicott, NY
Quart $90

State Road Dairy, Eldorado, IL
Quart $110

The Cream Whips Associated Daires, Milk Cream—Buttermilk
½ Gallon $45

Clover Leaf Dairy, Missoula,
Montana, 1955–1957, $45.

Modern Dairy, Fallon, Nevada, 1955, $65–$85.

Wakefield Dairy, Washington, D.C.
Quart $75

West End Dairy, Jeannette, PA
Quart $100

Half-Pints
Imperial Dairy Co. $8

J.A. Francisco, Caldwell, NJ $20

John Regan, Rockway Beach, LI $25

Katahoin Creamery, Caribou & Fort Fairfield,
ME(Pyroglazed) $15

Magnolia Dairy, Houston, TX $10

Mapleleaf Dairy, Cleveland, OH $10

Monticello Dairy, Charlottesville, VA $15

Mt. Desert Island Dairies, Bar Harbor, ME $20

Oakgrove Farm Co, Boston, MA $10

Peacock Dairies, Bakersfield, CA (Pyroglazed) $10

Peter Hagner, Buffalo, NY $7

Pontiac Dairy, Pontiac, MI $20

Coffee Creamers, 1890–1920, $3–$7 (each).

Reck's Milk & Cream, Pittsburg, PA $5

Sheffield Farms Co., NY $20

Somerset Dairy, Johnstown, PA $7

Stoneleidge Farm, Carmel, NY $8

Whiting Milk Co., Boston, MA $5

Square Quarts
Amador Goat Dairy, Glendale, AZ
Brown $40

Anderson's Dairy, Auburn, CA
Amber/White $12

Athens Co-Operative Creamery, Athens, GA
Orange $25

Bellview Dairy, Himrod, NY
White $15

Bixby's Dairy, Ludlow, VT
Red $8

Blue Spruce Dairy, Freehold, NJ
Blue $15

Campbell's Pioneer Dairy, Grove City, PA
Green $10

Cream-o-Land Dairy, New Brunswick, NJ
Red $25

Famous American Pioneers, Theodore Roosevelt, Twenty-Fifth President
Red, Orange, Green $25

Glass Containers Corp., Parker, PA (rare) $25

Mansfield Dairy, Stowe, VT
Green $15

Mariondale Farms, Lake Geneva, WI
Red $10

McCue's Dairy, Long Beach, CA
Red $6

Portage Coop Creamery, Portage, WI $8

R.L. Mathis Certified Milk, Decatur, Ga
Orange $10

State University of NY, Delhi Arg. & Tech Institute
Green $15

Thatcher's Dairy, Martinsburg, WV $10

The Land of Opportunity
Orange $20

Valley Dairy, Cochranton, PA
Red Pyro $5

War Slogans
America Has a Job to Do—Shamrock Dairy, Tucson, AZ
Cream Top Quart $75

Bonds Buy Bombs, Hansen Dairy, Deer Lodge, MT
Black Quart $75

Bryson's Dairy, 1930, $55; R.L.
Mathis Certified Milk, Decatur, GA
1955, $45.

Buy Bonds Today—Putnam's Dairy, Ilion, NY
Maroon Quart.. $75

Buy War Bonds, Walnut Grove Dairy, Alton, IL
Red Cream Top Quart $75

For Victory—Buy US War Bonds and Stamps
Quart $75

**For Victory—Buy United States Savings Bonds and Stamps—Nob
Hill Milk "It is Good"**
Colo. Springs, Colo $80

Keep 'Em Flying, Buy War Bonds, Melrose Dairy, Dyersburg, TN
Red Quart... $100

Keep 'Em Flying, Hoosier Dairy, Noblesville, IN
Red Quart.. $50

Let's Go! U.S.A., Walter Howe, York, PA
Orange Quart $50

Milk for Victory—Compston Bros. Dairy, Corning, CA
Black Quart $75

Revenge Pearl Harbor, Illinois Valley Sreator, Ottawa, IL
Orange Quart $75

V—For Victory—Picture of Winston Churchill, Sunshine Dairy, St. John, Newfoundland, Canada
Black & Orange Imperial Quart $250

Miscellaneous
Absolutely—Pure Milk (Man on Stool Milking Cow) The Milk Protector—H.D.T. & Co.—Potsdam—N.Y.
Clear, Quart, smooth base, tooled square collar mouth............$400–800
American 1880–1890

Chewton Dairy, Chewton, PA
Clear, Quart, smooth base, ABM lip...$60–90
American 1920–1930

Drink More—Willowdale—Farms—Milk—Nazareth, PA
Clear, Quart, smooth base, ABM lip...$50–75
American 1920–1930

E. F. Mayer—Phone—Glen'd 3887R—289 Hollenbeck St.
Amber, Quart, smooth base, ABM lip $60–90
American 1925–1930

Happy Valley Farms (Cow's Head) Rossville, Georgia—Trade Name Registered
Clear, Quart, smooth base, tooled lip...$60–90
American 1920–1930

Keystone Dairy Goat Farm, II Pa. Bridgeville, PA
Clear, Quart, smooth base, ABM lip...$40–50
American 1925–1930

Lyon Brook Dairy—Aerated—El Haynes Milk—1554 B'way Bklyn—to Be Washed and Returned
Clear, Half-pint, smooth base, tooled mouth $50–75
American 1910–1925

New-York Dairy Company (Shield) Limited—This Bottle Not to Be Bought or Sold—New-York Dairy Co—Limited
Clear, Quart, smooth base, tooled mouth $80–120
American 1905–1915

Adderholdt Bros. Creamery; Better Maid Ice Cream; 1955, $35–$45 (each).

One Quart—A.J.K. Dairy—Phoenix, Ariz
Clear, Quart, smooth base (T.Mfg. Co.), tooled mouth $60–80
American 1920–1930

Sauquoit Valley (Motif of Indian Chief) Dairy Co. Utica N.Y.—One Quart Liquid—SV (Monogram) Registered—Not Sold Wash & Return
Clear, Pattern Quart, smooth base, ABM lip $40–60
American 1920–1930

Scotia Pure Milk Co. Limited Halifax to Be Washed and Returned
Clear, Half-Gallon, smooth base, tooled mouth $50–70
Canadian 1925

T.A. Spencer—Pure—Milk & Cream—Tel. No. 198F21—Shark River—Spring Lake, N.J.
Amethyst, Quart, smooth base (T. MFG. CO) ABM lip................$40–80
American 1935

The McJunkin—Straight Dairy Co.—Buttermilk—Registered
Red Amber, ½ Gallon, smooth base, ABM lip.........................$300–400
American 1910–1920

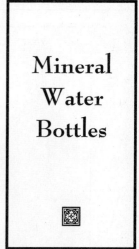

Mineral Water Bottles

The drinking of water from mineral springs was very popular for a full century, with the peak period falling between 1860 and 1900. The majority of collectible bottles were produced during these years. Although the shapes and sizes of mineral water bottles are not very creative, the lettering and design, both embossed and paper, are bold and interesting. Mineral water bottles can range in size from 7 to 14 inches. Most were cork-stopped, manufactured in a variety of colors, and embossed with the name of the glasshouse manufacturer and an eagle.

A.B.& D. Sands, New York
Deep Green, 9¼ in., smooth base, applied mouth, blown in a three-piece mold...$800–1200
American 1855–1865 (extremely rare)

A. Dearborn & Co, New York—Mineral Water, D, This Bottle Is Never Sold
Deep Cobalt Blue, 7¼ in., iron pontil, applied sloping collar mouth $100–125
American 1845–1855

A. Ritter, Mineral Water—Cincinnati—R
Light Green, 7¼ in., iron pontil, applied mouth......................$150–200
American 1845–1855

Albert Fischer, Atlantic City, N.J.
Amber, 6¾ in., smooth base, applied blob mouth.......................$40–60
American 1850–1860

Blue Lick Water Co. Ky,
1850–1855, $1500–$3000.

Alpena Magnetic Spring Co
Reddish Amber, 8¾ in., smooth base, applied double collar
mouth $400–500
American 1875–1885 (rare)

Avon Spring Water
Olive Green, 9½ in., smooth base, applied double collar
mouth $600–800
American 1865–1875

Ballston Spa Lithia Mineral Water
Emerald Green, Pint, smooth base, applied sloping double collar
mouth $75–100
American 1865–1880

Blount Springs Natural Sulphur Water—Trade Bs (monogram) Mark
Cobalt Blue, 9 in., smooth base, applied mouth.......................$175–250
American 1855–1865

Blue Lick Water, Co, Ky
Deep Blue Green, 8 in., iron pontil, applied sloping double collar
mouth $800–1200
American 1855–1865

Boothbay Medicinal Spring Water, Edward E. Race, Prop., East Boothbay, Me U.S.A.
Medium Teal Blue, 11¼ in., smooth base (E.E.Race), tooled
mouth $50–80
American 1885–1895

C. Lomax, Chicago Congress Water (Inside a Shield)
Medium Cobalt Blue, 7¼ in., iron pontil, applied blob type
mouth $100–125
American 1845–1855

Caladonia Spring, Wheelock Vt.
Medium Yellowish Amber, 9½ in., smooth base, applied sloping
double collar mouth...$200–300
American 1865–1875 (scarce)

Catell's—Superior—Mineral—Water-Salem
Sapphire Blue, 7¼ in., iron pontil, applied sloping collar
mouth $1000–1500
American 1845–1855 (rare—State of New Jersey)

California Natural Seltzer Water,
H&C with picture of bear on back,
1875–1885, $150–$250.

Jackson's Napa Soda Springs,
1870–1875, $300–$500.

Champion Spouting Spring, Saratoga Mineral Spring, C.S.S. Co., Limited Aratoga N.Y.
Deep Bluish Aqua, 7⅝ in., smooth base, applied sloping double collar mouth $125–175
American 1865–1875

Champlain Spring, Alkaline Chalybeate, Highgate, Vt.
Emerald Green, 9¾ in., smooth base, applied sloping double collar mouth $100–175
American 1870–1880

Chapman & Jose—Soda Water—Geralston
Cobalt Blue Torpedo, 9 in., smooth base, applied mouth..........$80–120
American 1845–1860

Chemung Spring Water Co., Cheung, N.Y.
Aqua, 7 in., smooth base, tooled mouth.....................................$15–30
American 1855–1865

Cherry Valley, Phosphate, Water
Aqua, 7⅜ in., smooth base, tooled mouth $15–30
American 1845–1855

Clarke & White, C, New York
Deep Emerald, 7¼ in., smooth base, applied sloping double collar mouth $50–75
American 1865–1875

Degraw, Plainfield, N.J.
Aqua, 7⅛ in., smooth base, applied blob mouth $40–60
American 1865–1875

D.J. Whelan Troy N.Y.
Aqua, 9⅜ in., smooth base, applied blob type mouth.............$100–150
American 1875–1885

Dr. Struve's—Mineral Water
Deep Yellow Olive, Half-Pint, smooth base, applied mouth.....$200–300
American 1875–1885

E.C. Stolle, North Buffalo, N.Y.
Aqua, 7½ in., smooth base, applied blob lip $125–175
American 1850–1865 (scarce)

Eureka Spring Co.—Saratoga N.Y.
Deep Yellowish Olive Green, 9 in., smooth base, applied sloping
double collar mouth...$700–900
American 1865–1875

Excelsior Spring Saratoga, N.Y.
Emerald Green, Pint, smooth base, applied sloping double collar
mouth $30–50
American 1865–1885

F. Scrader, Mineral Water, Scranton, Pa, Honesdale, Glass Works
Medium Blue Green, 7 in., iron pontil, applied blob type mouth....$250–350
American 1845–1855

Farrel & Co., Mineral Water, Evansville, I.A.—F. & Co.
Ice Blue, 7⅜ in., iron pontil, applied blob type mouth...........$140–180
American 1845–1855

Franklin Spring Mineral Water, Ballston Spa, Saratoga Co. N.Y
Deep Emerald Green, 7⅝ in., smooth base, applied sloping double collar
mouth $100–200
American 1865–1875

Frost's Magnetic Spring, Eaton Rapids Mich
Bluish Aqua, 9½ in., smooth base, applied double collar mouth.....$300–400
American 1875–1885

**Geyser Spring, Saratoga Spring, State of New York, The Saratoga,
Spouting Spring**
Bluish Aqua, 7⅝ in., smooth base, applied sloping double collar
mouth $40–60
American 1865–1875

Gettysburg Katalysine Water
Medium Emerald Green, 6⅞ in., smooth base, applied sloping
double collar mouth...$50–75
American 1865–1875

Gettsburg Katalysine Water
Medium Emerald Green, 9⅝ in., smooth base, applied sloping
double collar mouth...$70–100
American 1865–1880

G.W. Merchant, Lockport, N.Y.
Yellow Olive, 6⅞ in., smooth base, tooled mouth $20–35
American 1880–1890

H. Borgman, Mineral Water, Manufacturer, Cumberland, Md.
Deep Blue Green, 8½ in., iron pontil, applied blob type
mouth $800–1200
American 1845–1860 (rare)

Harris Lithia Water, Harris Springs
Greenish Aqua, Half-Gallon, smooth base, tooled mouth...........$80–120
American 1890–1910

Haskins Spring Co, H, Shutesbury Mass, H.S. Co.
Deep Green, 8⅜ in., smooth base (3), applied double collar
mouth $400–600
American 1885–1925 (rare saratoga bottle)

Highrock Congress Spring (Motif of Rock), C & W, Saratoga N.Y.
Olive Green, 7½ in., smooth base, applied mouth......................$15–30
American 1845–1855

Hopkins, Chalybeate, Baltimore
Medium Blue Green, Pint, smooth base, applied sloping double
collar mouth. $175–225
American 1860–1875

Natural Mineral Water, F.M.
Vallejo, 1870–1875, $200–$400.

Hulshizer & Co.—Premium Mineral Water
Emerald Green, 7½ in., iron pontil, applied mouth.................$600–900
American 1845–1855

J.A. Blaffer & Co., New Orleans
Deep Golden Amber, 6⅜ in., smooth base, applied double collar
mouth $200–300
American 1865–1875

John H. Gardner & Son, Sharon Springs, N.Y.—Sharon Sulphur Water
Teal Blue, Pint, smooth base, applied sloping double collar
mouth $300–400
American 1865–1870

John Graf—Milwaukee Wis
Aqua, 7½ in., iron pontil, applied mouth $40–80
American 1845–1855

Kissingen Water, Hanbury Smith
Deep Emerald Green, 7¼ in., smooth base, tooled mouth..........$20–35
American 1880–1890

L. Gahre, This Bottle Is Never Sold—Mineral Water, Bridgeton
Medium Emerald Green, 7¼ in., smooth base, applied blob type
mouth $250–350
American 1850–1860

Lithia Mineral Spring Co., Gloversville
Bluish Aqua, 7¾ in., smooth base, applied sloping collar
mouth $1200–1600
American 1865–1880 (rare)

Luke Beard, Howard St., Boston (Five-Pointed Star), This Bottle Is Never Sold
Cobalt Blue, 7⅜ in., iron pontil, applied sloping collar mouth........$125–150
American 1845–1860

McKinney Philada—Rice & Mineral Water
Medium Teal Blue, 7 in., iron pontil, applied mouth.................$80–120
American 1845–1855

Missisquoi, A, Springs
Medium Root Beer Amber, Quart, smooth base, applied sloping
double collar mouth...$100–150
American 1865–1880

Ponce De Leon Spring Water, St. Augustine, FL., 1870–1880, $4000–$6000; A.B. & D. Sands, New York, 1855–1865, $800–$1200; St. Louis Artesian Mineral Water by W.H. Stevens & Co., 1865–1875, $2500–$3500; Pavilion & United States Spring Co. Saratoga N.Y.—Pavilion Water Aperient, 1865–1875, $900–$1500.

N, Morristown, N.J.—Union Glass Works Philad., Superior Mineral Water
Teal Blue, 7⅜ in., iron pontil, applied blob type mouth.........$250–350
American 1845–1855

Oswego Deep Rock Mineral Water—This Bottle Must Be Returned
Deep Bluish Aqua, 9⅜ in., smooth base, applied blob type
mouth $100–200
American 1865–1875

Poland Water—Poland Mineral Spring Water (in Banner Around) Pmsw (Monogram) H Ricker & Sons Proprietors
Aqua, 11 in., smooth base, applied sloping collar mouth $125–175
American 1885–1895

Saint Leon Spring Water (Inside Diamond Around) Earl W. Johnson, 27, Congress St., Boston, Mass.
Medium Emerald Green, Pint, smooth base, applied sloping double collar
mouth $120–160
American 1870–1880

Saratoga, A, Spring Co, N.Y.
Medium Yellowish Olive Green, Pint, smooth base, applied sloping
double collar mouth..$175–250
American 1865–1875

Saratoga Red Spring
Medium Blue Green, Quart, smooth base, applied sloping double
collar mouth..$75–100
American 1865–1875

Saratoga Red Spring
Medium Blue Green, Pint, smooth base, applied sloping double
collar mouth..$50–75
American 1865–1875

Saratoga Seltzer Water
Deep Teal Blue, Pint, smooth base, applied mouth..................$100–150
American 1885–1895

Saratoga Vichy Spouting Spring
Aqua, Pint, smooth base, applied sloping double collar mouth......$70–100
American 1865–1875

Schanzenbacher Mineral Water, Louisville Ky
Aqua, 8 in., smooth base, applied mouth.....................................$40–80
American 1865–1875

Seitz & Bro—Easton Pa—Premium Mineral Waters
Cobalt Blue, 7⅝ in., iron pontil, applied blob type mouth $175–275
American 1845–1855

Spring (Star) Spring
Deep Olive Green, 9½ in., smooth base, applied sloping double
collar mouth..$80–120
American 1865–1875

St. Louis Artesian Mineral Water by W.H. Steven & Co.
Deep Blue Aqua, 9½ in., smooth base, applied mouth........$2500–3500
American 1865–1875

Star Spring Co (Star) Saratoga N.Y.
Deep Chocolate Amber (Black), 7¾ in., smooth base, applied sloping
double collar mouth..$100–150
American 1865–1875

Witter Springs Water,
San Francisco, 1880–1895,
$25–$45.

Strumatic Mineral Water, N, P.S.M. Co.
Deep Reddish Amber, 6⅞ in., smooth base, applied sloping double
collar mouth $1000–1500
American 1865–1880

Strumatic Mineral Water, N, P.S.M. Co.
Deep Reddish Amber, 7⅜, smooth base, applied sloping double
collar mouth $800–1200
American 1865–1880

Tarr & Smith (in Slug Plate) Boston Mineral Water
Emerald Green, 7⅜ in., iron pontil, applied blob type mouth $200–300
American 1845–1855

Teller's Mineral Water, Detroit, The Bottle Must Be Returned
Deep Cobalt Blue, 8⅜ in., smooth base, applied sloping blob type
mouth $300–400
American 1855–1865

The Ashton Mineral Water Co. LTD. Portland St, Ashton-u-Lyne
Yellow Amber, 7¼ in., smooth base, applied mouth $15–30
American 1845–1855

The Excelsior Water
Emerald Green, 7¼ in., iron pontil, applied blob type mouth $175–225
American 1845–1855

Tweddle's Celebrated Soda or Mineral Waters—Courtland Street, 38, New York
Cobalt Blue, 7⅜ in., iron pontil, applied sloping collar mouth........$125–150
American 1845–1860

W. Heiss Jr's, Superior Mineral Water, No 213N 2d St. Philada (Motif of Eagle, Shield, and Flags)
Medium Cobalt Blue, 7¼ in., iron pontil, applied mouth $125–150
American 1845–1855

W.W. Lappeus—Premium—Soda or Mineral Waters—Albany
Cobalt Blue 10-Sided, iron pontil, applied mouth.....................$80–120
American 1845–1860

Washington Lithia Well Mineral Water, Ballston Spa, N.Y.
Deep Bluish Aqua, 7¾ in., smooth base, applied sloping double
collar mouth $80–120
American 1865–1878

W.M.S. Co., San Francisco
Medium Amber, 9¼ in., smooth base, tooled mouth...................$30–60
American 1845–1855

Witter Springs Water
Amber, 9¼ in., smooth base, tooled mouth $30–60
American 1845–1860

V. Mager, 101 Elizabeth St, N.Y.—Union Glass Works Philad. Superior Mineral Water
Deep Cobalt Blue, 7⅜ in., iron pontil, applied blob type
mouth $275–325
American 1840–1855 (rare)

Geyser Natural Boiled Mineral Water, 1875–1885, $45–$75;
Jackson's Napa Soda Springs, 1870–1875, $300–$500;
Anaconda Bottling Co. P.S. & F. Prop, 1865–1875, $50–$100.

Vermont Spring, Saxe & Co/ Sheldon Vt.
Peach puce, Quart, smooth base, applied mouth.....................$250–350
American 1870–1880

Veronica Mineral Water
Medium Amber, 10¼ in., smooth base, tooled mouth.................$30–60
American 1845–1850

Vichy Water, Hanbury Smith
Teal Blue, Half-Pint, smooth base, applied sloping double collar
mouth $30–50
American 1865–1885

Victoria Springs, A, Frelichsburg, Canada
Deep Bluish Aqua, 9½ in., smooth base, applied sloping double
collar mouth..$1500–2200
American 1875–1885 (rare saratoga bottle)

Nursing Bottles

Nursing bottles, along with associated items such as sterilizers, bottle warmers, trading cards, advertisements, and other numerous items related to infant feeding have long been a favorite of many bottle collectors. In fact, in 1973, The American Collectors of Infant Feeders (ACIF) was founded by a group of devoted collectors to promote the hobby of collecting nursing bottles and related items. Today, that membership now extends throughout the United States and to Canada, Australia, Germany, and numerous other countries.

Nursing bottles have a colorful history dating back to the early 1600's. Then, nursing bottles were better known as "sucking bottles" and usually were made of leather or wood, the nipples fashioned from rags, skins, or sponges. Toward the end of the 1600's and into the 1700's, the pewter sucking bottle arrived on the scene. By the late 1790's and early 1800's, tubular shaped pottery nursing bottles were being used in England and eventually began to be manufactured in American Glass Houses. During the 1800's a competition arose between the American and English glass manufacturers. Dr. T.W. Dyott began advertising his free blown glass decanter and tubular nursing bottles in the 1820's, and Solomon Maw began to manufacture glass nursing bottles in England in 1832. And, by 1832, nursing bottles and nursing flasks were being advertised by numerous New York drug companies. In 1841, Charles Windship of Massachusetts registered the first nursing bottle with the United States Patent Office, and in 1845 the first rubber nipple was registered by Dr. Elijah Pratt of New York. This was a welcomed event for the babies of the world who up to that point had had to make do with hard nipples of pewter, silver, wood, or ivory.

The latter part of the 1800's brought about a virtual explosion of various designs and methods of nursing bottles and feeding devices. Here's a highlight of some of these important milestones:

1851—The first nursing bottle using a long sucking tube was introduced at the Great Exposition in England.

1854—Paneled glass nursing bottles fitted with an internal tube, stopper, and hard nipple were advertised by Bullock & Crenshaw.

1864—The turtle-shaped nursing bottle was patented in England and
brought over to the United States.

1869—The first nursing bottle with graduated markings was patented
by Drs.H. and A.M. Knapp of Providence, Rhode Island.

1872—The corset-shaped nursing bottle was patented by Milo S. Burr.

1873—The two-hole (vented) nursing bottle was patented by William Hobson.

1894—The wide mouthed Hygeia nursing bottle was patented by Dr.
William Decker.

1896—The Double ended Allenbury Nursing Bottle was patented in
England.

With the invention of the Owens Automatic Bottle Machine in 1903, blown in a mold bottles (BIM) were phased out, and the early 1900's saw a new tapered wide mouth nursing bottle in the 8ounce size manu-factured by companies such as Pyrex, Hygeia, Vita-Flo, Curity, and Arm-strong. One of the most popular brands was introduced in 1947, Evenflo. And circa 1905, the first style to be manufactured by the Automatic Bottle Machine, the flask shaped nursing bottle, was phased out of use. Even though today's nursing bottles have replaced their glass with plastic, we can still enjoy these rare and unique collectibles of the past.

Acme Nursing, WT&C (Fancy Monogram Embossed in 8-Pointed Star) Bottle
Clear, Turtle type, BIM, tooled lip with long neck.......................$25–30
American 1882–1910

Alexandra SFG Co. (Fancy Monogram) Feeder
Clear, Standing Turtle, BIM, tooled lip with long neck................$25–35
American 1880–1890

Selection of rib-pattern chestnut flasks, 1820–1830, $200–$1000 (each).

Umbrella ink, 1860–1870, $75–$100.

Selection of barber bottles, 1885–1925, $75–$700 (each);
Paper shaving vase, 1885–1925, $700–$1000.

Selection of milk quarts, 1940–1950, $35–$75 (each).

Figural fountain bottle, 1885–1910, $300–$400; Figural madam bottle, 1890–1915, $800–$1000; Statue of Liberty jar, 1886–1890, $40–$60; D.D. Alsace—Depose figural bottle, 1885–1910, $400–$600; Figural Indian maiden, 1885–1915, $150–$250; Figural nightstick, 1885–1910, $100–$125; Saltglaze pottery pig, 1880–1895, $500–$900.

Quaker Club,
Old Rye,
S.B. Rothenberg,
1898–1899,
$65–$100.

Davy Crockett
Pure Old Bourbon,
1880–1905,
$35–$50.

Selection of
scrolled flasks,
1845–1855,
$200–$700
(each).

Selection of umbrella inks, $100–$300 (each); Turtle inks, $200–$700 (each);
Sandwich type inkwell, $1000–$1500; all 1845–1890.

Lewiston Brewing Co., 1920, $8–$12; Rocky Mountain Special Export Beer, 1925, $7–$10; Bock Beer, 1920, $7–$10; Butte Lager Beer, 1920, $5–$10.

Country-Music; Stone Fort—Applied Painted Label Soda, 1940–1955, $15 (each).

MainBrace Rum, 1950, $35–$65; Liquid Sunshine, Finest Rum, 1950, $45–$65.

Selection of violin bottles, 1875–1890, $65–$125 (each).

Miners Cash Grocery,
1880–1900,
$900–$1200

Kessler Dairy, 1900, $25–$50; Miners Dairy,
1900, $35–$50; Quality Cantrell Milk, 1900,
$35–$50.

Septicide medicine bottle
with shipping crate,
1885–1900, $25–$40
(bottle), $100 (crate).

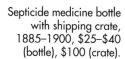

Selection of violin bottles,
1875–1890, $60–$125 (each).

Rocky Mountain Seltzer, 1900–1930,
$35–$55; Silver State Reno, 1900–1930,
$35–$55; Imperial Beverage Co.,
1900–1930, $35–$55.

Big Chief, 1955, $11; Big Chief, 1948, $35; Big Chief, 1967, $9;
Big Chief, 1970, $9; Big Chief, 1962, $21; Big Chief, 1962, $27;
Big Chief, 1960, $26; Big Chief, 1955, $22.

Mandalay Punch $5; Mount Zircon $5; Evervess $50; Pepsi-Cola
$8; Pepsi-Cola $19; Pepsi-Cola $45; Pepsi-Cola $15; 1947–1955.

Selection of colbalt blue
medicines, 1885–1900,
$25–$55 (each).

Miniature whiskey giveaways,
"Have a Camel" (complete set).

Ponce De Leon Spring Water, St. Augustine, FL, 1870–1880,
$2500–$3500; A.B. & D. Sands, New York, 1855–1865,
$1000–$1200; Bryant's Stomach Bitters, 1860–1870,
$5000–$6000; Pavilion & United States Spring Co.,
Saratoga, N.Y., Pavilion Water, Aperient, 1865–1875,
$1000–$1300; R.B. Cutter Pure Bourbon, 1855–1865,
$250–$275.

Teddy's Pet Peaceful
Nights—For Your Baby,
1904, $210;
Comfy, 1925, $170;
The Little Papoose—Patd,
1865–1885, $325;
Sweet Babee Nurser—
Patd May 3–10,
1910–1920, $85;
Medallion Nursing
Bottle—Trade-M.S. Burr &
Co., 1878–1895, $60.

Selection of fruit jars,
1850–1900;
$50–$500 (each).

Selection of various inks, whiskeys, fruit jars, bitters, mineral waters, colognes, black glass, 1820–1890.

Selection of various inks, ink wells, flasks, target balls, bitters, fruit jars, medicine bottles, figurals, demi-johns, 1820–1890.

Baby (Picture of Seated Bunny) Bunting
Clear, Oval, ABM, 4-ounce scales on reverse.................................$8–10
American 1930–1945

Baby, Lying on Its Tummy (Embossed Picture)
Clear, oval, ABM, 8-ounce scale on reverse, "K" within keystone on
base (Knox Glass Bottle Co., Knox, PA)...$15–20
America 1930–1940

Baby Nurser
Clear, Flask type, BIM, tooled lip, M.B.W./U S A on base (Millville
Bottle Works, Millville, NJ)..$20–30
American 1903–1915

**Babys Delight (Embossed Picture of Seated Baby Drinking from
Turtle Bottle)**
Clear, Turtle type, BIM, tooled lip with neck ring...................$100–130
American 1890–1900

Beck's Security Nursing Bottle (Embossed in Shield on Shoulder)
Clear, round, ABM, "Beck's" on base..$10–15
Canada 1927–1937

Betsy Brown Safety Nursing Bottle
Clear, Flask type, BIM, sheared lip with screw threads on
neck..$30–40
American 1897–1910

Betsy Brown Sterilizer
Clear, Round, BIM, sheared lip with screw threads on neck, Pat. July
6th 97 (embossed "M" within diamond) on base......................$75–100
American 1897–1910

Betsy Jane Nurser, It Tilts
Clear, ABM, "National Baby Products Co., Denver, Colo" (on
base) $20–30
American 1934–1944

Bostonia
Clear, Flask type, BIM, tooled lip, "M" on base $30–40
American 1900–1910

Betsy Brown Sterilizer, 1897–1910, $75–$100; The Superior—SB, 1890–1900, $75–$110; Baby's Delight, 1890–1900, $65–$130; Perfection Feeding Cup for Hospital and Home, 1895–1910, $50–$80; Betty Jane Nurser, 1934–1944, $20–$35.

Bostonia
Clear, round, ABM $15–25
American 1910–1925

Bulldog (Embossed Picture of a Standing Bulldog)
Clear, wide mouth cylinder, ABM, #2 on base $8–10
American 1930–1944

Burr's Patent Nursing Bottle (Embossed Picture of Fitted Bottle) Patd Nov. 26th 1872
Aqua, corset type, BIM, tooled lip, smooth base $100–140
American 1872–1880

Cat (Embossed Picture of Seated Cat)
Clear, wide mouth cylinder, ABM $15–30
American 1930–1944

Cleaneasy Sanitary Sterlilizer—Whitall Tatum Company
Clear, round, BIM , tooled lip, W.T.Co. and "B" embossed on base.
American 1895–1910 ....$15–20

Cleanfont Vented Nursing Bottle, Fox Fultz & Webster, New York & Boston, Patented Oct 25 1892
Clear, Turtle type, BIM, tooled lip $75–110
American 1892–1900

Clean-Well Sanitary Sterilizer Bottle, 12oz
Clear, round, BIM, tooled lip L W T CO/New York (on base)....$10–20
American 1900–1910

Comfy (Embossed Mickey Mouse Type Cartoon Character)
Clear, oval, ABM, "2" (on base)..$140–170
Canadian 1925

Davol (in Oval Seal), Anticolic Brand Nurser with 'Dual-purpose' Nipple
Clear, Screw-top wide mouth, ABM $8–10
American 1950–1970

Dimples/Hygienic Feeding Bottle
Clear, Double-ended, "Dimples" embossed between "Hygienic" and "Feeding Bottle", 7¾ in. length...$60–80
English 1920–1940

Dr. Doyle's Anti-colic Nurser Bottle Sanitary Pat. Oct.14th .08 Mfg by Physicians Specialties Mfg. Co. Inc. Pittsburgh Pa.
Clear, ABM, screw on cap, ground lip $250–325
American 1908–1915

Flask-Type Nurser
Clear, 7¼ in., BIM, tooled lip, "32" (on base) $15–30
American 1890–1910

Franklin
Clear, flask type, ABM $10–15
American 1905–1915

Handy, Wt Co. (Fancy Monogram) Nurser
Clear, Flask type, BIM, tooled lip, Pat. Feb 24 1891/W.T.& Co./E/ U.S.A. (on base) $30–40
American 1891–1910

Hygeia, Pat. Dec.5th 1916, Made in U.S.A.
Clear, Wide mouth cylinder, ABM, Hygeia (on base)..................$20–30
American 1916–1944

Infant Nursing Bottle
Bluish Aqua, 5⅝ in., smooth base, tooled mouth $40–60
American 1880–1910

Infants Nursing Bottle—Inb (2-in.-Tall Fancy Monogram)
Aqua, Standing turtle, BIM, straight neck with ring, WT & Co. (on
base) $15–20
American 1876–1910

Kingwood Jerseys—Sterilized Milk
Clear, 8½ in., round with round bottom, BIM, tooled lip, Blown in
three-piece mold..$35–40
American 1890–1910

Little Darling (Embossed Picture of a Baby Lying on a Pillow)
Clear, Oval, "S" (in circle on base—Swindell Bros., Baltimore,
Md) $85–110
American 1930–1940

Mammary Nurser
Clear, Breast-shaped, 4⅜ in. diameter, three-piece mold with
concave base, flared lip..$450–550
American 1845–1865 (believed to have been the first known nursing
bottle patented in the United States)

Marisco Infant Feeders—Approximate Capacity
Clear, 5 in., open at opposite end with small rolled lip $175–230
American 1950–1960 (unusual)

Medallion Nursing Bottle (Embossed Around Perimeter of a Double-Lined Oval Enclosing the Profile Bust of Man) Trade Mark—M.S.Burr & Co. Proprietors Boston Mass.
Aqua, Standing turtle, BIM, tooled lip, straight neck with
ring $50–60
American 1878–1895

Santro Pat—Registered-Baby's Delight, Help to Mothers, 1910–1920, $100–$150; Turtle type Nurser, 1880–1910, $300–$400; Burr's Patent Nursing Bottle, 1872–1880, $100–$150; Dr. Doyle's Anti-Colic Nurser Bottle, 1908–1915, $250–$325; The Graduated Nursing Bottle, 1900–1910, $20–$25.

Pennsylvania Tin Feeder
Tin, Round body, 4½ in. from base to top of domed lid........$300–400
American 1800–1840

Pyrex—Wide Mouth Nurser
Clear, Hexagon, ABM, Made in U.S.A. (on base)...........................$5–10
American 1930–1950

Royal Nursing Bottle, W.J. Gilmore & Co. Pittsburgh, Penn'a', W.T. & Co. (Monogram Inside Star)
Clear, 6¼ in., smooth base, tooled mouth $40–60
American 1880–1910

S. Mawson & Sons. London, C&S MWM (Fancy Monogram in Trefoil Design) Trade Mark
Clear, Torpedo type, BIM, tooled lip with inside screw threads.......$100–120
English 1900–1920

Santro Pat. Registered—Baby's Delight, Help to Mothers
Clear, Modified Flask type, BIM, tooled lip, MADE IN AUSTRIA (on base)...$100–140
Austria 1910–1920

Pennsylvania Tin Feeder, 1800–1840, $300–$400; The Best Pat
Sep.1.91 The Gotham Co. N.Y., 1891–1900, $65–$84; Lacteal or
Mammary Nurser, 1845–1865, $450–$550; Early Earthenware or
Water Carrying Vessel, 300 B.C.-Late 19ᵗʰ Century, $35–$50; Figural
Cologne Bottle "Baby and Cabbage Leaves" or "Moses in the
Bulrushes," 1880–1900, $45–$60.

Sweet Babee Nurser Pat'd May 3–10, Easily Cleaned and Hygienic
Clear, Wide mouth cylinder, ABM $65–85
American 1910–1920

The 'Allenburys' Feeder, Made in England
Clear, Double-ended, BIM, tooled lip..$20–40
English 1915–1925

The Best, Pat Sep.1. 91, The Gotham Co. N.Y.
Clear, Turtle type, BIM, tooled lip, 8 ounce scale embossed on
front...$65–85
American 1891–1900

The Eagle, M.S. Burr & Co. Boston (Eagle in Circle) Trade Mark, Nursing Bottle
Clear, Standing Turtle, BIM, tooled lip, neck ring.......................$45–65
American 1878–1885

The Empire (Large WT & Co Fancy Monogram) Nursing Bottle
Clear, Standing Turtle, BIM, tooled lip with neck ring................$10–15
American 1880–1909

The Graduated Nursing Bottle
Clear, Flask type, BIM, tooled lip...$20–25
American 1900–1910

The Hygienic (in Script) Feeder
Clear, 3½ in. Oval, Double-Ended, BIM......................................$10–15
English 1910–1925

The Little Papoose—Patd
Clear, Turtle type, BIM, tooled lip, neck ring.........................$275–325
English 1865–1885

The Monarch Nurser, Oval Flint Bottle
Clear, Turtle type, BIM, tooled lip $25–30
American 1890–1900

The National Feeding Bottle
Clear, Standing turtle, BIM, tooled lip with inside screw
threads...$30–35
English 1880–1910

The Peerless Nurser
Greenish-Aqua, Turtle type, BIM, tooled lip, neck ring...............$30–40
American 1878–1890

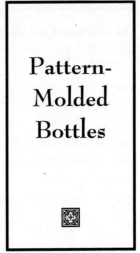

Pattern-Molded Bottles

A pattern-molded bottle is one that is blown into a ribbed or otherwise pattern mold. This group includes globular and chestnut flasks. One of these, the Stiegel bottle, manufactured during the late eighteenth century, is considered very rare and valuable. The two types of Stiegel bottles manufactured at the Stiegel Glass Factory are the Diamond daisy and Hexagon designs.

Since pattern-molded bottles are among the more valuable and rare pieces, collectors need to familiarize themselves with the types, sizes, colors, and the various manufacturers of these bottles.

Blown Three-Mold Decanter
Pure Olive Green, 7⅞ in., pontil base, flared lip.................$1000–1500
American 1815–1830

Blown Three-Mold Toilet Water Bottle
Deep Cobalt Blue, 5¾ in., pontil base, flared lip.....................$200–300
American 1815–1830

Eight-Pillar Molded Decanter
Milky Cobalt Blue, 6⅜ in., pontil applied foot, tooled
mouth $1200–1600
American 1850–1865 (rare)

Figural Flask
Deep Cobalt Blue, 4 in., pontil base, sheared lip $150–250
American 1850–1870 (resembles a clam)

Pitkin Flask, 1815–1825, $350–$450; Midwestern Rib-Pattern Chestnut Flask, 1820–1830, $200–$300; Midwestern Grandfather Flask, 1820–1835, $1500–$2000; Pitkin Flask, 1830–1850, $400–$600.

Flattened Chestnut Flask
Yellow Olive, 5⅜ in., pontil base, sheared lip..........................$150–250
American 1820–1835

Globular Shaped Bottle
Aqua, 8 in., pontil base, rolled mouth...$70–90
American 1820–1835

Midwestern Club Bottle
Bluish Aqua, 10½ in., 24 Rib Pattern, pontil base, applied sloping collar mouth..$175–225
American 1820–1835

Midwestern Globular Bottle
Deep Bluish Aqua, 8⅝ in., 24 Broken Rib Pattern, pontil base, applied mouth..$150–200
American 1825–1835

Midwestern Globular Bottle
Deep Reddish Amber, 8⅜ in., 24 Rib Pattern, pontil base, rolled lip...$350–450
American 1820–1835

Midwestern Globular Bottle
Medium Amber, 8⅜ in., 24 Rib Pattern, pontil base, rolled
lip $375–425
American 1820–1835

Midwestern Grandfather Flask
Medium Amber, 8⅝ in., 24 Vertical Rib Pattern, pontil base, tooled
lip $1500–2200
American 1820–1835

Pattern Molded Chestnut Flask
Deep Cobalt Blue, 4⅜ in., Diamond Pattern, pontil base, flared
lip $500–700
European 1870–1900

Pattern Molded Chestnut Flask
Medium Pinkish Amethyst, 6 in., 16 Vertical Rib Pattern, Pontil
base, sheared lip..$700–900
American 1820–1830

Pattern Molded Chestnut Flask
Cobalt Blue, 6⅞ in., 12 Vertical Rib Pattern, pontil base, applied
sloping collar mouth $50–75
European 1820–1870

Pattern Molded Chestnut Flask
Pinkish Amethyst, 6⅝ in., 18 Vertical Rib Pattern, pontil base,
sheared lip...$50–75
European 1820–1870

Pattern Molded Chestnut Flask
Medium Cobalt Blue, 4⅞ in., 17 Vertical Rib Pattern, pontil base,
flared lip..$500–700
American 1820–1840

Pattern Molded Chestnut Flask
Pale Green, 6¾ in., 18 Rib Pattern, pontil base, sheared
lip $140–160
American 1820–1835

Pattern Molded Chestnut Flask
Deep Cobalt Blue, 3½ in., 20 Rib Pattern broken by a 16 Vertical Rib
Pattern, pontil base, flared lip..$400–600
American 1820–1840

Pattern Molded Chestnut Flask
Reddish Amber, 4⅞ in., 24 Vertical Rib Pattern, pontil base, rolled
lip $225–325
American 1820–1835

Pattern Molded Chestnut Flask
Greenish Aqua, 6⅞ in., 24 Rib Pattern, pontil base, sheared
lip $140–180
American 1820–1835

Pattern Molded Chestnut Flask
Pale Greenish Aqua, 5½ in., 32 Broken Rib Pattern, pontil base,
sheared lip..$175–250
American 1820–1835

Pattern Molded Chestnut Flask
Deep Colbalt Blue, 3⅞ in., 42 Broken Rib Pattern, pontil base,
sheared lip..$175–350
American 1830–1860

Pattern Molded Club Bottle
Aqua, 7⅞ in., 24 Rib Pattern, pontil base, rolled lip...............$125–150
American 1820–1830

Pattern Molded Club Bottle
Aqua, 8⅛ in., 16 Vertical Rib Pattern, pontil base, applied
mouth $150–200
American 1820–1830

Pattern Molded Diamond-Daisy Stiegel Pocket Bottle
Brilliant Amethyst, 5⅛ in., pontil base, sheared mouth $2000–4000
American 1763–1774 (American Flint Glass Manufactory, Manheim,
Pennsylvania)

Pattern Molded Diamond Stiegel Type Pocket Flask
Brilliant Medium Amethyst, 5¾ in., pontil base, tooled
mouth $2000–4000
American 1763–1774 (American Flint Glass Manufactory, Manheim,
Pennsylvania)

Pattern Molded Flask
Red Amber, 4¾ in., 14 Rib Pattern, pontil base, sheared
lip $400–600
American 1820–1830

Pattern Molded Flask
Honey Amber, 5½ in., 13 row hobnail pattern, pontil base, sheared
lip $800–1200
American 1820–1835

Pattern Molded Flask
Medium to Deep Amber, 5¾ in. 24 Broken Rib pattern, pontil base,
sheared lip $4000–6000
American 1820–1835

Pattern Molded Flask
Clear glass, 5¼ in., pontil base, flared lip $60–90
European 1820–1880

Pattern Molded Flask
Light Copper Puce, 5¼ in., pontil base, flared lip $60–90
European 1820–1880

Pattern Molded Footed Chestnut Flask
Medium Pinkish Amethyst, 3½ in., 18 Vertical Rib Pattern, pontil
base, sheared lip $275–400
American 1820–1840

Pattern Molded Grandfather Flask
Golden Amber with Red tone, 8⅝ in., 24 Vertical Rib Pattern, pontil
base, sheared mouth..$1200–2400
American 1815–1840

Pattern Molded Pocket Flask
Medium Bluish Green, 5⅞ in., 24 Rib Pattern, pontil base, sheared
mouth $100–200
American 1800–1830

Pattern Molded Pocket Flask
Medium Bluish Green, 6⅜ in., 24 Vertical Rib Pattern, pontil base,
tooled mouth..$100–200
American 1800–1830

Pattern Molded Toilet Water Bottle

Cobalt Blue, 5⅛ in., 16 Vertical Rib Pattern, pontil base, rolled & flared lip..$175–250
American 1820–1840

Pinch Waist Spirits Bottle

Light Colbalt, 6¼ in., 20 Broken Rib Pattern, polished pontil, applied pewter neck ring...$400–600
European 1810–1860

Pitkin Flask

Medium Emerald Green, 5¼ in., 16 Vertical Rib Pattern, pontil base, sheared lip...$250–350
American 1780–1810

Pitkin Flask

Deep Emerald Green, 5⅞ in., 24 Broken Rib Pattern, pontil base, sheared lip..$325–400
American 1780–1810

Pitkin Flask

Medium Emerald Green, 7 in., 24 Broken Rib Pattern, pontil base, rolled lip...$200–300
American 1780–1820

Pitkin Flask

Aquamarine, 6½ in., 31 Rib Pattern, pontil base, sheared mouth...$150–300
American 1815–1840 (Rare color)

Pitkin Flask

Pale Aqua, 5 in., 32 Broken Rib Pattern, pontil base, sheared lip...$250–350
American 1790–1820

Pitkin Flask

Light Yellow Olive, 5 in., 36 Broken Rib Pattern, pontil base, sheared lip..$300–400
American 1790–1815

Pitkin Flask
Yellow Olive, 6 in., 36 Rib Pattern, pontil base, sheared
lip $125–250
American 1783–1830

Teardrop Flask
Deep Cobalt Blue, 8¾ in., 16 Rib Pattern, pontil base, sheared
lip $300–400
American 1840–1870

Teardrop Flask
Deep Cobalt Blue, 8½ in., 25 Rib Pattern, pontil base, sheared
lip $275–375
American 1850–1870

Ten-Pillar Molded Decanter
Milky Cobalt Blue, 6⅜ in., polished pontil, flared lip..........$1400–1800
American 1850–1870

Poison Bottles

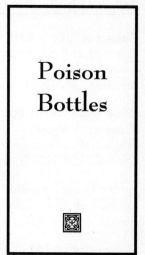

Poison bottles are a unique category for collecting by the very nature of their contents. While most people assume that poison bottles are plain, the fact is that most are very decorative in order to make them easily identifiable as containers of toxic substances. Around 1853, the American Pharmaceutical Association recommended laws for identification of all poison bottles. In 1872, the American Medical Association also recommended that poison bottles be identified with a rough surface on one side and the word *poison* on the other. As so often happened during that era, passing of these laws was very difficult and the manufacturers were left to do whatever they wanted. Because a standard wasn't established, a varied group of bottle shapes, sizes, and patterns were manufactured, including the skull and crossbones, or skulls, leg bones, and coffins.

These bottles were manufactured with quilted or ribbed surfaces and diamond/lattice-type patterns for identification by touch. Colorless bottles are very rare since most poison bottles were produced in dark shades of blue and brown, another identification aid. When collecting these bottles, caution must be exercised since it is not uncommon to find a poison bottle with its original contents. If the bottle has the original glass stopper the value will greatly increase.

Chester A. Baker, Boston
Cobalt Blue, 4⅛ in., smooth base (C.L.G. Co. Patent Applied For), tooled lip $350–450
American 1890–1910 (rare)

Chester A. Baker, Boston
Cobalt Blue, 5 in., smooth base (C.L.G. Co. Patent Applied For),
tooled lip $200–300
American 1890–1910 (scarce)

(Skull and Crossed Bones) De-Dro Gift Flasche Der Deutscher Drogisten Verbandes
Medium Moss Green, 4⅜ in., smooth base, ABM lip...............$400–500
German 1910–1920 (extremely rare)

Doctor Oreste, Sinadide's Medicinal Preparations, Orestorine
Deep Cobalt Blue Coffin, 4 in., smooth base, tooled mouth....$200–300
American 1885–1900

Dodge—Poison (64 oz Graduation) Dodger
Clear Glass, 11½ in., smooth base, tooled lip..............................$60–80
American 1890–1910

Durfee Embalming Fluid Co., Grand Rapids Mich—Poison
Clear Glass, 8⅝ in., smooth base, tooled lip............................$100–150
American 1890–1910

Embossed Skull Poison Bottle
Clear glass, 4⅛ in., smooth base (Patd June 8 1875), tooled
lip $1200–1400
American 1875–1885

Federation Francaise Droguistes Marchands De Couleurs
Pale Yellow Green, 10¾ in., smooth base (1 Litre Modele Depose),
ABM lip $250–350
French 1920–1930

(Skull and Crossed Bones) Poison—Jacobs—Tablets (Skull and Crossed Bones) Poison
Medium Amber, 2⅜ in., smooth base, tooled mouth.............$800–1200
American 1890–1910

J.W. McBeath Kimberely Poison
Cobalt Blue, 5⅜ in., smooth base (W.T. & CO. U.S.A. Pat. Dec 11,
1894), tooled lip $250–350
American 1885–1900

Poison—H.K. Mulford Company, Chemists Philadelphia, 1900–1910, $50–$75.

Lattice and Diamond Pattern (Label—Aqua Ammonia)
Cobalt Blue, 5½ in., smooth base, tooled mouth $80–120
American 1890–1910

Lattice and Diamond Pattern (Label—Hydrochloric Acid)
Medium Cobalt Blue, 4⅝ in., smooth base, tooled mouth $80–100
American 1890–1910

Lattice and Diamond Pattern (Label—Potassium Hydroxide)
Cobalt Blue, 3¾ in., smooth base, tooled mouth $80–100
American 1890–1910

Poison—(Label—Bi-Chloride of Mercury, Mays Drug Co. Pittsburgh)
Cobalt Blue Coffin, 3½ in., smooth base, tooled lip $100–150
American 1890–1910

Poison
Cobalt Blue submarine, 2 in. H, 3 in. L, smooth base (Registered No. 336907) tooled mouth $150–250
English 1890–1910

Poison Flask
Clear glass, 6⅛ in., pontil base, applied mouth $125–150
European 1830–1850

Poison Flask
Clear glass, 6 in., pontil base, rolled lip $70–90
European 1850–1870

Poison—Poison
Medium Amber, 8 in., smooth base, tooled mouth....................$80–120
American 1890–1910

Poison—Poison (Label—Mercuric Chloride, The Norwich Pharmacal Company, Norwich, New York)
Medium Cobalt Blue Coffin, 7½ in., smooth base (Norwich U.S.A.), tooled mouth...$1200–1600
American 1890–1910

Poison—Poison (Label—Mercury Bichloride, Rexall Drug Co.)
Clear glass, 5¼ in., smooth base, tooled lip..............................$200–300
American 1890–1910 (scarce in colorless glass)

Poison (Label—Poison 200 Toxitabellae Hydrargyrl Chloridi Corrasivi, E.R. Aquibb & Sons, New York)
Cobalt Blue, 5¼ in., smooth base, tooled mouth.....................$250–350
American 1890–1910

Poison (Five-Pointed Star) Above and Below Skull and Crossed Bones) Poison
Yellow Amber, 4¾ in., smooth base (S & D), tooled mouth $500–650
American 1890–1910

Poison—Bowman's Drug Store—Poison
Deep Cobalt Blue, 3⅜ in., smooth base (C.L.G. Co. Patent Appl'd For), tooled lip..$150–250
American 1890–1910

Poison—Davis & Geck, Inc. (Monogram in Diamond), Brooklyn, N.Y. U.S.A.
Cobalt Blue, 3¼ in., smooth base, tooled mouth..................$800–1400
American 1890–1910 (unique, only one with Davis & Geck embossing)

Poison (Motif of Skull and Crossed Bones) Demert Drug & Chemical Co. Spokane
Cobalt Blue, 5⅝ in., smooth base (W.T. CO. U.S.A.), tooled mouth $1500–2500
American 1890–1910 (rare)

Poison—F.A. Thompson & Co. Detroit Poison
Yellow Amber Coffin, 3⅛ in., smooth base, tooled lip $1000–1500
American 1890–1910

Poison—Jno Wyeth & Bro. Philadelphia—Poison
Cobalt Blue, 2⅝ in., smooth base, tooled lip $75–100
American 1890–1910

Poison—Jno Wyeth & Bro. Phildaelphia—Poison
Amber, 2¾ in., smooth base, ABM lip $75–100
American 1890–1910

Poison—Poison, Kilner Bros. Makers
Amber, 14 in., smooth base, tooled mouth..................................$70–90
American 1890–1910

Poison Bottle—Lin. Belladon. Poison
Deep Green, 8 in., polished pontil, tooled lip $125–150
English 1880–1900

Poison—Ser C Sol, Elliott—Poison—Not to Be Taken—Ser C Sol, Elliott Poison—Not to Be Taken
Medium Golden Amber, 5¼ in., smooth base (embossed crown),
tooled mouth..$200–300
European 1890–1910 (extremely rare, only three known pieces)

(Skull & Crossbones) Poison Tinct Iodine
Cobalt Blue, 2⅛ in., smooth base, tooled lip $75–100
American 1890–1910

Poison—The Owl Drug Co (Motif of Owl on Mortar and Pestle)
Cobalt Blue, 3½ in., smooth base, tooled lip $60–90
American 1890–1910

Poison—The Owl Drug Co (Motif of Owl on Mortar and Pestle)
Cobalt Blue, 4½ in., smooth base, tooled lip $70–90
American 1890–1910

Poison—The Owl Drug Co (Motif of Owl on Morar and Pestle)
Cobalt Blue, 6 in., smooth base, tooled lip................................$150–225
American 1890–1910

Poison—The Owl Drug Co (Motif of Owl on Mortar and Pestle)
Cobalt Blue, 6½ in., smooth base, tooled mouth......................$175–250
American 1890–1910

Poison—The Owl Drug Co (Motif of Owl on Mortar and Pestle)
Cobalt Blue, 9½ in., smooth base, tooled mouth....................$500–700
American 1890–1910

Poison—Pat. Appl'd for
Medium Cobalt Blue, 2⅞ in., smooth base (Pat June 26th 1894),
tooled lip $1400–1600
American 1890–1910

Poison and Poison (Star Above and Below Skull and Crossed Bones) Poison
Cobalt Blue, 2¾ in., smooth base, sheared lip.............................$25–40
American 1910–1912

Poison—Wyeth
Cobalt Blue, 2¼ in., smooth base, ABM lip $100–150
American 1910–1920

Poisonous Not Be Taken, Buffalo Ammonia, a Powerful Cleanser for General Cleaning Purposes Address American Bluing Co. Buffalo, N.Y.
Deep Olive Amber, 9⅜ in., smooth base, applied sloping double
collar mouth $70–90
American 1890–1910

Pottery—Poison Crock, Swift's Arsenate of Lead, Manufactured Only by the Merrimac Chemical Co., Boston, U.S.A.
Cream Color, 6½ in., smooth base $50–80
American 1890–1910

Vapo Cresolene Co.—Patd U.S. July 17 91 Eng July 1891
Deep Cobalt Blue, 4 in., smooth base, tooled mouth...............$175–225
American 1891–1900 (scarce in cobalt)

(Skull and Crossed Bones)—Vorsicht Gift (Skull and Crossed Bones)
Deep Yellowish Olive Green, 9⅝ in., smooth base (1000), ABM
lip $150–250
German 1910–1925

Sarsaparilla Bottles

Sarsaparilla was advertised as a "cure-all" elixir, which actually makes these bottles a subset of the "Cures" or "Bitters" category. In the seventeenth century, sarsaparilla was touted as a blood purifier and later as a cure for the dreaded venereal disease, syphilis. As time passed, sarsaparilla was recognized as nothing more than the "snake oil" sold at the medicine shows. As you can see from the image of "The Red Root of Jamaica" label (below), the bottle labels were unique and very ornate. One of the most popular brands among collectors is Doctor Townsend, which was advertised as "The Most Extraordinary Medicine in the World." Usually, these bottles are aqua or green. Blues and other dark colors are rarer.

Dr. B.W. Hair's Sarsaparilla
Bluish Aqua, 9⅝ in., open pontil, applied mouth....................$400–500
American 1845–1855 (rare)

Dr. De Andries Sarsparilla Bitter—E.M. Rusha New Orleans
Amber, 10 in., smooth base, applied sloping collar mouth......$500–700
American 1865–1875

Dr. Fox's Sarsaparilla for the Blood
Whimsy Flip Hat, Clear glass, 1½ in., smooth base, tooled
rim...$125–150
American 1890–1910 (scarce dose glass)

Dr. Moorehouse's—Sarsaparilla (Motif of Eagle)/ Trade Mark
Deep Olive Green, 9¼ in., smooth base, applied sloping collar
mouth..$175–225
Australian 1855–1870 (Extremely Rare)

Dr. Henry's Sarsaparilla,
1880–1890, $75–$125.

Hall's Sarsaparilla,
1855–1865, $50–$80.

Dr. S. Rose's—Sarsaparilla—Philadelphia
Deep Teal Blue, 9¼ in., iron pontil, applied mouth $2500–3500
American 1845–1855 (rare in this color)

Dr. Townsends Sarsaparilla Albany NY
Amber, 9½ in., open pontil, applied sloping collar mouth......$100–200
American 1845–1855

Dr. Townsends Sarsaparilla Albany Ny
Amber, 9⅞ in., graphite pontil, applied top..............................$90–180
American 1845–1855

Dr. Webster's Sarsaparilla Ithica
Bluish Aqua, 6½ in., open pontil, applied sloping collar
mouth $250–350
American 1840–1855 (rare)

Edward Wilder's Sarsaparilla & Potash (Motif of Five Story Building)
Edward Wilder & Co/Wholesale Druggists/Louisville, Ky
Clear glass, 8¼ in., smooth base, tooled mouth.........................$80–120
American 1865–1875

Ellis's Sarsaparilla Compound—Empire State Drug Company
Clear, 9⅛ in., smooth base, applied top.......................................$30–50
American 1880–1900

Genuine Phoenix Sarsaparilla Louisville Ky.
Yellowish Grass Green, 9 in., smooth base, applied sloping collar
mouth $1000–1500
American 1860–1870 (extremely rare)

Genuine—Sand's Sarsaparilla New York
Aqua, 10 in., pontil, applied double collar mouth $200–300
American 1845–1855

Gray's Sarsaparilla—Irwin M. Gray & Co. Montrose, Pa
Bluish Aqua, 8½ in., smooth base, tooled mouth $100–150
American 1890–1900 (extremely rare)

I. D. Bull's Extract/Sarsaparilla—Hartford, Con
Aqua, 8 in., pontil, applied mouth...$90–125
American 1845–1855

Dr. Guystott's Yellow Dock &
Sarsaparilla, 1845–1855,
$90–$150.

Kelley & Co—Sarsasparilla—J.L. Kelley & Co/Chemists/Portland, Me
Aqua, 6⅞ in., pontil, applied mouth $90–125
American 1845–1855

Log Cabin Sarsaparilla Rochester, N.Y.
Medium Amber, 9 in., smooth base (Pat Sept 6 87), applied
mouth $100–150
American 1880–1890

Masury's Sarsaparilla Cathartic
Aqua, 6⅝ in., pontil, applied mouth $250–350
American 1845–1855

Old Dr. Townsends Sarsaparilla New York
Amber, 9⅞ in., iron pontil, applied top $100–200
American 1845–1855

Sand's Sarsaparilla New York
Aqua, 6¼ in., pontil, applied sloping collar mouth $80–120
American 1845–1855

The C.D. Co's Sarsaparilla Resolvent
Amber, 9 in., smooth base, tooled mouth................................$125–150
American 1870–1890

Thos. A. Hurley—Compound Syrup of Sarsaparilla—Louisville Ky.
Bluish Aqua, 9½ in., smooth base, applied collar mouth $60–90
American 1855–1865

Turner's Sarsaparilla Buffalo N.Y.
Deep Aqua, 12¼ in., smooth base, applied sloping collar
mouth $300–400
American 1855–1865

Wilsons Tonic & Sarsaparillian Elixir J.W. Brayley Proprietor
Aqua, 8⅞ in., smooth base, tooled mouth $90–125
American 1860–1870

Worlds Columbian Sarsaparilla Worchester. Mass—Worlds Columbian Sarsaparilla Co
Clear glass, 8¾ in., smooth base, tooled mouth.........................$90–125
American 1860–1870

Wynkoop's Katharismic Sarsaparilla New York
Medium Cobalt Blue, 10 in., iron pontil, applied sloping collar
mouth $4500–6500
American 1845–1855 (rarest of Wynkoop grouping)

Snuff Bottles

Snuff was basically composed of tobacco mixed with ingredients of salt, different scents, and flavors such as cinnamon and nutmeg. It was usually mixed in a powder form, and inhaling snuff was much more fashionable than smoking or chewing tobacco. It was yet another substance touted as a cure-all, in this case for sinus problems, headaches, and numerous other problems.

Most of the snuff bottles from the eighteenth and early nineteenth centuries were embossed, dark brown or black, with straight sides. They were either square or rectangular in shape, with beveled edges and narrow bodies with wide mouths. In the latter part of the nineteenth century, the bottles were colorless or aqua and rectangular or cylindrical, with occasional embossing and possibly labels.

2nd Quality Manufactured and Sold by Levi Garrett & Son, No.1128 So Front Street, Philad (Label)
Golden Yellow, 4 in., pontil, tooled flared mouth....................$150–250
American 1840–1860

Barrel Snuff Jar
Deep Red Puce, 7¼ in., pontil base, sheared lip......................$400–700
European 1750–1800

Black Glass Tall Snuff Jar
Medium Olive Amber, 11¼ in., pontil base on deep kickup, applied string lip $400–600
European 1750–1800

Black Glass Tall Snuff Jar
Deep Olive Amber, 12⅞ in., pontil base on deep kickup, applied string lip $400–600
European 1750–1800

E. Roome Troy New York
Yellow Amber, 4¼ in., pontil base, tooled lip.........................$200–300
American 1845–1855

E. Roome Troy New York, French Rapee Snuff Manufactured by Edw'd Roome 2193 River St. Troy, 134 Water St., New York (Label)
Olive Amber, 4¼ in., pontil base, flared lip............................$275–375
American 1830–1855

MCCCOBOY Warranted Snuff Micklefield
Clear glass, 3⅞ in., pontil base, rolled lip...............................$140–180
English 1820–1835 (rare embossed snuff bottle)

Rectangular Snuff Bottle
Yellowish Olive Amber, 4 in., pontil base, tooled lip..................$70–90
American 1830–1845

Rectangular Snuff Bottle
Olive Green, 4⅞ in., pontil base, tooled and flared lip $120–140
American 1820–1835

E. Roome, Troy, New York, 1845, $50–$100.

Rectangular Snuff Bottle
Deep Yellowish Amber, 4⅜ in., pontil base, tooled lip.............$70–100
American 1835–1845

Rectangular Snuff Bottle
Medium Yellow Olive, 4⅜ in., pontil base, tooled lip $100–150
American 1820–1835 (scarce)

Rectangular Snuff Bottle
Light Blue Green, 5⅞ in., pontil base, tooled and flared
lip $100–150
American 1840–1850

Rectangular Snuff Bottle
Deep Olive Green, 6¾ in., pontil base, tooled and rolled
lip $150–200
American 1820–1835

Square Snuff Bottle
Yellow Amber, 4⅛ in., pontil base, tooled and flared lip $140–180
American 1835–1845

Square Snuff Bottle
Deep Red Amber, 4¼ in., pontil base, tooled and flared
lip $150–200
American 1830–1845

Square Snuff Bottle
Emerald Green, 4¼ in., pontil base, tooled lip $400–600
American 1830–1845 (rare)

Square Snuff Bottle
Olive Green, 4⅝ in., smooth base, tooled lip...........................$150–200
American 1850–1860

Square Snuff Bottle
Olive Amber, 6⅛ in., pontil base, tooled and flared lip $250–350
American 1820–1835

Tall Snuff Bottle
Olive Green, 9⅜ in., smooth base, sheared lip $250–325
American 1850–1860

Soda Bottles

After years of selling, buying, and trading, I think that the soda bottle supports one of the largest collector groups in the United States. Even collectors who don't normally seek out soda bottles always seem to have a few on their tables for sale (or under the table).

Soda bottles, as a rule, are not unique in design since the manufacturers had the task of producing bottles as cheaply as possible to keep up with demand. The only way to distinguish among bottles is by the lettering, logos, embossing, or labels (not very common).

Soda is basically artificially flavored or unflavored carbonated water. In 1772, an Englishman named Joseph Priestley succeeded in defining the process of carbonation. Small quantities of unflavored soda were sold by Professor Benjamin Silliman in 1806. By 1810, New York druggists were selling homemade seltzer as a cure-all for stomach problems. By 1881, flavoring was included in these seltzers.

The first commercially sold soda was Imperial Inca Cola, its name inspired by the Native American Indian, which promoted medical benefits. The first truly successful cola drink was developed in 1886 by Dr. John Styth Pemberton of Atlanta, Georgia. It's known today as Coca-Cola. Carbonated water was added to Coca-Cola in 1887. By 1894, bottled Coca-Cola was taking off. The familiar configuration of the Coke bottle as we now know it was designed in 1915 by Alex Samuelson. Numerous inventors attempted to ride on the coattails of Coke's success. The most successful of these inventors was Caleb Bradham, who started Brad's drink in 1890, and in 1896 changed its name to Pep-Kola. In

1898, it was changed to Pipi-Cola, and by 1906 to Pepsi-Cola. The taste war goes on today.

With the advent of the soda bottle and the use of carbonation, the age of closure inventions set in. Various entrepreneurs developed the Hutchinson-type wire stoppers, lighting stoppers, and cod stoppers.

A. Wagner & Co. Philada—W
Deep Emerald Green, 7¼ in., smooth base, applied mouth $60–90
American 1855–1865

B. Bick Cincinnati—This Bottle Is Never Sold
Deep Cobalt Blue, 7½ in., iron pontil, applied mouth $300–400
American 1845–1855

B.R. Lipencott & Co. Stockton
Cobalt Blue, 7¼ in., iron pontil, applied mouth....................$800–2000
American 1852–1858

Bridgeton Glass Works/ N.J.
Medium Green, 7 in., smooth base, applied sloping double collar mouth $70–80
American 1855–1870

Williams & Severance,
1852–1854, $300–$500.

California Natural Seltzer Water H&G (Bear on Back)
Light Green, 6⅞ in., smooth base, applied top $60–120
American 1875–1885

Ch. Gloeser Philada (In a Slug Plate)
Deep Blue Green, 7⅜ in., iron pontil, applied sloping double collar
mouth $70–90
American 1845–1855

C.H. Richardson, Trenton N.J. (Peened out Letter 'R' on Reverse)
Medium Teal Blue, 7⅛ in., smooth base, applied blob type
mouth $70–90
American 1860–1875

Chalybeate Water/ of The/ American Spa Spring Co.
Medium Blue Green, 9⅜ in., smooth base, applied mouth......$600–900
American 1865–1875

Clarke & Co./New York
Medium Teal Blue, 7⅚ in., iron pontil, applied sloping double
collar mouth $250–350
American 1850–1860

Congress & Empire Spring Co/E/Saratoga, N.Y.
Deep Olive Green, 9⅜ in., smooth base, applied sloping double
collar mouth $50–70
American 1865–1875

C. Whittmore New York
Medium Emerald Green, 8¼ in., iron pontil, applied
mouth $275–375
American 1845–1855 (scarce)

D. Strecker Phila (In a Slug Plate)
Medium Teal Blue Green, 7 in., iron pontil, applied sloping double
collar mouth $80–120
American 1845–1855

David Lord/Manayunk/Pa
Medium Green, 7 in., smooth base, applied sloping double collar
mouth $80–120
American 1855–1865

Crystal S.W.CO., SF, Cider,
1886, $75–$150.

Ditz & Ellerkemp San Francisco Soda Works
Light to Medium Bluish Aqua, 7 in., iron pontil, applied
mouth $500–1000
American 1868–1872

D.L. Ormsby, New York, Union Glass Works, Phila
Deep Cobalt Blue, 7⅜ in., iron pontil, applied blob type
mouth $175–250
American 1845–1855

Eastern Cider Co.
Medium Amber, 7¼ in., iron pontil, applied mouth $100–200
American 1877–1882

Friederich Rau Philada—R
Deep Emerald Green, 7½ in., iron pontil, applied sloping double
collar mouth $70–90
American 1845–1855

George Ch Gemuenden—Brown Stout
Blue Green, 6¾ in., iron pontil, applied double collar mouth.....$150–250
American 1845–1855

Empire Soda Works, D&M,
San Francisco, 1864–1865,
$50–$150.

Geo. Eagle
Medium Blue Green, 6⅞ in., iron pontil, applied sloping collar
mouth $600–800
American 1845–1855 (rare)

Geo. W. Flanagen/Brown Stout (In a Slug Plate)
Deep Emerald Green, 6⅞ in., iron pontil, applied mouth $40–60
American 1865–1875

H. Mau & Co. Eureka, Nev.
Light Green, 7 in., smooth base, applied mouth $40–100
American 1882–1886

H. Verhage, Cincinnati, Ohio—This Bottle Is Never Sold
Light Cobalt Blue, 7⅜ in., smooth base, applied mouth..........$175–275
American 1845–1855

Hagerty's Glass Works N.Y. (On Base)
Bluish Aqua, 6⅜ in., smooth base, applied blob type
mouth $100–150
American 1855–1865

Hoffman & Berry Phila (In a Slug Plate)
Deep Blue Green, 7 in., iron pontil, applied double collar
mouth $100–150
American 1845–1855

I. Houghland Leadville, Col. I.C. Co. (On Reverse)
Aqua Green, 7 in., iron pontil, applied mouth.........................$200–400
American 1879–1880

I. Sutton Cincinnati
Medium Cobalt Blue, 7½ in., iron pontil, applied mouth $500–700
American 1845–1855 (rare)

J. Aufrecht, Philada (In a Slug Plate)
Deep Blue Green, 7¼ in., smooth base, applied sloping double
collar mouth $80–120
American 1845–1855

J. Bodine & Sons
Deep Blue Green, 7¼ in., iron pontil, applied mouth.............$175–250
American 1845–1855

Cottle Post & Co, Portland, OGN,
1877–1887, $750–$1400.

J. Eves Soda Water Manr—This Bottle Is Never Sold 1862
Ice Blue Torpedo, 7⅞ in., smooth base, applied blob type
mouth $350–450
Canadian 1862–1870 (very rare)

J. McLaughlin Philada (In a Slug Plate)
Deep Emerald Green, 6½ in., iron pontil, applied sloping collar
mouth $50–70
American 1845–1855

J. Monier & Co. CL—FR—NA
Emerald Green, 7 in., iron pontil, applied top $300–600
American 1856–1858 (rare)

J. Monier & Co. CL—FR—NA
Cobalt Blue, 7 in., iron pontil, applied top............................$500–1200
American 1856–1858

J. Reynolds Bottlers, Philada (In a Slug Plate)
Deep Blue Green, 7⅛ in., iron pontil, applied sloping double collar
mouth $70–90
American 1845–1855

J. Sloan, Philada (In a Slug Plate)
Medium Blue Green, 7 in., iron pontil, applied sloping collar
mouth $70–90
American 1845–1855

J.T. Brown, Chemist, Boston—Double, Soda Water
Teal Blue Green Torpedo, 9⅛ in., smooth base, applied blob type
mouth $250–350
American 1850–1860

J.H. Pollard, Boston
Deep Emerald Green, 6⅞ in., iron pontil, applied sloping double
collar mouth $80–120
American 1855–1870

J.L. Smith/Phila
Teal, 7 in., iron pontil, applied mouth $35–50
American 1845–1855

B.R. Lippincott, Stockton Superior
Mineral Water, Union Glass Works,
1852–1858, $1000–$2000.

Thomas Leonard Sonora Soda Works,
Sonora, Cal., 1845–1855,
$50–$125.

J.P. Robinson, Salem N.J.—R
Medium Green, 6⅞ in., smooth base, applied mouth..............$100–150
American 1855–1870

Jacob Sherer, Philada
Aqua, 7 in., smooth base, applied mouth.....................................$20–30
American 1855–1865

John B. Welscher, Philada (In a Slug Plate)
Deep Teal Green, 7¼ in., smooth base, applied sloping double
collar mouth...$70–100
American 1855–1865

John Clark, FP, Balto—C
Deep Emerald Green, 6¾ in., iron pontil, applied sloping collar
mouth..$100–150
American 1845–1855

John Cooper, Philada—C
Medium Blue Green, 7 in., iron pontil, applied mouth...............$35–50
American 1845–1855

Johnston & Co. (Star) Phila
Blue Green, 7 in., smooth base, applied mouth...........................$20–30
American 1855–1865

Jos. Crowther
Blue Green, 7½ in., smooth base, applied mouth.......................$25–35
American 1850–1870

Kehoe & Purcell/Trenton/N.J.
Deep Blue Green, 7 in., smooth base, applied mouth..................$70–90
American 1855–1865

Kimball & Co.
Cobalt Blue, 7¼ in., iron pontil, applied mouth......................$300–600
American 1853–1856

L.Gahre/Bridgeton/N.J.—G
Light Blue Green, 7 in., smooth base, applied sloping double collar
mouth $70–80
American 1855–1870 (rare in this color)

L. Fisher, Philada—F
Deep Blue Green, 7¼ in., iron pontil, applied sloping double collar
mouth $70–90
American 1845–1855

Lewis & Scott, Phila—L&S
Aqua, 7 in., smooth base, applied mouth $20–30
American 1855–1865

Lynch & Clarke/New York
Deep Olive Amber, 7 in., pontil base, applied mouth............$800–1200
American 1855–1865 (rare)

Lynch & Clarke/New York
Deep Yellowish Olive Amber, 7⅜ in., pontil base, applied sloping
double collar mouth..$275–375
American 1855–1865

W.A. Boots, 1883, $45–$55; Deer Lodge Soda Factory,
1880–1885, $45–$55; Deer Lodge Soda Factory,
1880–1885, $45–$55.

M. Mooney Visalia
Deep Green, 7³⁄₈ in., smooth base, blob top..................................$40–80
American 1872–1881

M. & J. Duffy/Phila—Brow/Stout (In a Slug Plate)
Deep Emerald Green, 7 in., smooth base, applied sloping double
collar mouth..$40–60
American 1855–1865

M.M. Ketner and J. Aulenbach, Pottsville—Union Glass Works, Phila
Deep Bluish Aqua, 7¹⁄₄ in., iron pontil, applied blob type
mouth $150–200
American 1845–1855

Monteith & Co., Philada—M
Aqua, 7 in., smooth base, applied mouth....................................$30–40
American 1850–1860

O'Kane & Maginnis/C. May N.J.
Medium Teal Blue, 6⁷⁄₈ in., smooth base, applied sloping double
collar mouth..$100–150
American 1855–1870 (rare)

P. Divine Bottler, Pilada
Medium Blue Green, 7 in., iron pontil, applied mouth................$35–50
American 1845–1855

P. Duross/Phila (In a Slug Plate)
Deep Emerald Green, 7¼ in., iron pontil, applied double collar
mouth $80–120
American 1845–1855

R'D McLaughlin (Trade Mark—Inside Mortar and Pestle)—Toronto
Bluish Aqua Torpedo, 9¼ in., smooth base, tooled mouth......$300–400
Canadian 1880–1890

R & H Colombia, Cal
Light Green, 6⅝ in., graphite pontil, applied mouth $300–700
American 1852–1856

S & B/Ashland/Pa
Light Blue Green, 6⅝ in., smooth base, applied mouth...............$25–35
American 1860–1870

San Jose Soda Works
Deep Bluish Aqua, 7 in., smooth base, applied mouth $100–200
American 1870–1886

Schick & Fett/Reading/Pa—S&F
Olive Green, 7¼ in., smooth base, applied mouth........................$35–50
American 1860–1870

Southwick & Tupper—New York
Medium Cobalt Blue, 7½ in., iron pontil, applied sloping collar
mouth $100–150
American 1845–1855

Taylor & Co. Valparaiso Chili Soda Water
Medium Emerald Green, 7¼ in., iron pontil, applied
mouth $100–200
American 1845–1855

Tarr & Smith/Worcester St./Boston
Medium Emerald Green, 7 in., smooth base, applied gloppy
mouth $70–90
American 1855–1865

Mokelumne Hill Soda Works,
1845–1855, $50–$100.

Twitchell, T, Philada
Emerald Green, 7 in., smooth base, applied mouth $25–35
American 1850–1860

W & B Shasta Union Glass Works Philad Superior Mineral Water
Cobalt Blue, 7¼ in., iron pontil, applied mouth..................$3000–8000
American 1850–1857 (rare)

W. Coughlan Baltimore
Deep Blue Green, 6⅞ in., iron pontil, applied blob type
mouth $175–275
American 1845–1855 (scarce)

Wm. W. Lappeus—Premium—Soda or—Mineral Waters—Albany
Medium Sapphire Blue, 7¼ in., iron pontil, applied blob type
mouth $175–250
American 1845–1855

Target Balls

Target balls, which are small rounded bottles, were filled with confetti, ribbon, and other items. They were used for target practice from the 1850s to the early 1900s. They gained considerable popularity during the 1860s and 1870s with the Buffalo Bill Cody and Annie Oakley Wild West shows. Around 1900, clay pigeons started to be used in lieu of target balls. Because they were made to be broken, they are unfortunately extremely difficult to find, and are very rare, collectible, and valuable.

Bogardus Glass Ball Pat'd Apr 10, 1877
Yellow Amber, 2¾ in., rough sheared lip.............................$1500–2500
American 1877–1885 (rare)

C. Newman
Medium Yellowish Amber, 2⅝ in., rough sheared mouth......$700–1000
American 1880–1890 (rare)

Carnival Shooting Ball
Cobalt Blue, 1⅛ in., rough sheared mouth $70–90
English 1880–1900 (used in carnival shooting arcades)

Carnival Shooting Ball
Sapphire Blue, 1¼ in., rough sheared mouth..............................$70–90
English 1880–1900 (used in carnival shooting arcades)

For Hockeys Patent Trap
Light Smoky Green, 2⅜ in., rough sheared lip........................$400–700
English 1880–1890 (scarce)

For Hockeys Patent Trap
Medium Green, 2½ in., rough sheared lip $500–700
English 1880–1890 (scarce)

From /J.H. Johnson /Great Western Gun Works/169 Smithfield Street/Pittsbugh, PA—Rifles Shotguns/Revolvers Ammunition/Fishing Tackle/Choke Boring, Reparing/ &C/Write for Price List
Root Beer Amber, 2½ in., rough sheared lip........................$3500–5500
American 1880–1890 (rare)

Glashutteneotte Jun Charlottenburg L
Yellow Olive, 2⅝ in., rough sheared mouth............................$700–900
German 1880–1890 (rare)

Glashutten Dr. A. Frank Charlottenburg
Deep Yellow Olive, 2⅝ in., rough sheared lip $500–700
German 1880–1890

Gurd & Son 185 Dundas Street London Ont
Medium Amber, 2⅝ in., rough sheared mouth........................$400–700
Canadian 1880–1890 (scarce)

Ilmenau (Thur) Sophienhuttein
Bright Lime Green, 2¾ in., rough sheared lip......................$1000–1500
German 1880–1900 (rare)

Ira Paine's Filled Ball Pat. Oct 23 1877 (Large Letter Embossing)
Yellow Amber, 2⅝ in., rough sheared lip................................$250–350
American 1877–1890

Ira Paine's Filled Ball Pat. Oct 23 1877 (Small Letter Embossing)
Yellow Amber, 2⅝ in., rough sheared lip................................$250–350
American 1877–1890

Ira Paine's Filled—Ball Pat Apl'd For
Golden Yellow Amber, 2¾ in., rough sheared lip....................$500–700
American 1877

Liddle & Keading Agents
Deep Bluish Aqua, 2¾ in., sheared lip $4000–6000
American 1880–1890

London—B.M.P. (Range Ball)
Deep Cobalt Blue, 2 in., rough sheared lip on long neck........$250–350
English 1880–1890

N.B. Glass Works Perth
Bluish Aqua, 2⅝ in., flat smooth base, rough sheared lip.......$100–150
English 1880–1890

N.B. Glass Works Perth
Light Sapphire Blue, 2⅝ in., rough sheared lip.......................$100–150
English 1880–1890

Sure Break Patent Apl'd For
Medium Amber, 2½ in., rough sheared mouth...................$6000–8000
American 1880–1900

Target Ball (Man Shooting in Circle)
Medium Amethyst, 2¾ in., sheared lip....................................$300–400
American 1880–1895

Target Ball (Man Shooting in Circle)
Light Pink Amethyst, 2¾ in., sheared lip $300–400
American 1880–1895

Target Ball (Motif of Man Shooting)
Cobalt Blue, 2⅝ in., rough sheared mouth $375–475
English 1880–1890

N.B. Glass Works Perth, 1880–1890, $100–$150; Ilmenau (Thur) Sophienhuttein, 1880–1900, $1000–$1500; Sure Break—Patent, Apl'd For, 1880–1900, $6000–$8000; Van Cutsem—A St. Quentin, 1880–1890, $70–$100; Bogardus Glass Ball Patd apr. 10 1877, 1877–1890, $400–$600.

Target Ball (Motif of Man Shooting)
Medium Amethyst, 2⅝ in., rough sheared lip..........................$275–375
American 1880–1890

Target Ball (Motif of Man Shooting)
Dark Amethyst, 2⅝ in., rough sheared mouth.........................$275–375
English 1880–1890

Target Ball (Motif of Man Shooting)
Deep Moss Green, 2⅝ in., rough sheared mouth.....................$275–375
English 1870–1890 (scarce color)

Target Ball
Medium Cobalt Blue, 2⅛ in., rough sheared mouth..................$80–120
English 1880–1900

Target Ball
Cobalt Blue, 2⅝ in., sheared and flared mouth.......................$100–150
French 1880–1890

Target Ball
Medium Sapphire Blue, 2¾ in., rough sheared mouth $175–225
English 1880–1890 (scarce)

W.W. Greener St. Marys Works Birmm & 68 Haymarket London
Cobalt Blue, 2¾ in., rough sheared lip.....................................$120–160
English 1880–1890

Van Cutsem—a St. Quentin (on Center Band)
Deep Cobalt Blue, 2¾ in., rough sheared mouth.....................$100–150
French 1880–1890

Warner Bottles

The Warner bottle was named for H. H. Warner, who sold a number of remedies developed by a Dr. Craig. Warner developed his bottle for those and other cures and began producing great volumes and varieties (over twenty) in 1879 in Rochester, New York.

Warner bottles can frequently be found with their original labels and boxes, giving additional value to these already expensive and rare bottles.

H.H. Warner & Co. Ltd. Melbourne
Amber, 9⅝ in., smooth base, tooled mouth $15–25
Australian 1880–1890

H.H. Warner & Co. Ltd. Melbourne
Yellow Amber, 5½ in., smooth base, tooled mouth $40–70
Australian 1890–1920

Log Cabin Sarsaparilla Rochester N.Y.
Medium Amber, 9 in., smooth base (Pat Sept 6 87) applied
mouth $100–175
American 1880–1890

Log Cabin Sarsaparilla Rochester N.Y.
Chocolate Amber, 8⅞ in., smooth base (Pat Sept 6 87) $125–175
American 1887–1895

Tippecanoe—H.H. Warner (Figural Fish Bottle)
Amber, 9⅝ in., smooth base, applied mouth $20–30
American 1880–1890

Tippecanoe—H.H. Warner & Co. (Figural Log)
Amber, 9 in., smooth base (Pat Nov. 20 83/Rochester/N.Y.), applied
disc type mouth $70–90
American 1880–1890

Tippecanoe—H.H. Warner & Co. (Figural Log)
Amber, 9⅛ in., smooth base (Pat Nov 20 83 Rochester NY) applied
mouth $60–80
American 1875–1885

Warner's Safe Cure (Motif of Safe) Frankfurt A/M
Deep Olive Green, 9 in., smooth base, applied mouth $350–450
German 1890–1900

Warner's Safe Cure (Motif of Safe) Pressburg
Blood Red, 9½ in., smooth base, applied mouth $400–600
German 1880–1895 (Rare)

Warner's Safe Cure (Motif of Safe) Melbourne Aus/London Eng/ Toronto Can/Rochester NY USA
Root Beer Amber, 9½ in., smooth base, applied double collar
mouth $100–150
American 1880–1890

Warner's Safe Cure (Motif of Safe) Melbourne Aus/London, Eng/ Toronto, Can/Rochester, N.Y. USA
Reddish Amber, 9⅝ in., smooth base, applied double collar
mouth $100–150
American 1880–1890

Warner's Safe Cure (Motif of Safe) Trade Mark Frankfurt A/M
Medium Amber, 9¼ in., smooth base, ABM mouth.................$275–475
German 1900–1910

Warner's Safe Cure (Motif of Safe) Trade Mark Frankfurt A/M
Deep Olive Green, 9⅛ in., smooth base, applied mouth $500–700
German 1885–1895

Warner's Safe Cure (Motif of Safe) Trade Mark London
Medium Olive Green, 9⅜ in., smooth base, applied blob type
mouth $150–200
English 1880–1900

Warner's Safe Nervine,
1875–1885, $300–$400.

Warner's Safe Diabetes Cure (Motif of Safe) Melbourne Aus./London Eng/Toronto Can/Rochester N.Y. U.S.A.
Medium Amber, 9½ in., smooth base, applied double collar
mouth $250–350
Australian 1890–1900 (rare)

Warner's Safe Kidney & Liver Cure
Amber, 9⅝ in., smooth base, applied mouth $20–30
American 1880–1890

Warner's Safe Kidney & Live Cure (Motif of Safe) Trade Mark Rochester, N.Y.
Golden Yellow with Amber tone, 9⅝ in., smooth base, applied
double collar mouth...$150–250
American 1880–1890

Warner's Safe Nervine (Motif of Safe) Rochester, N.Y. (In a Slug Plate)
Medium Amber, 5⅛ in., smooth base, tooled mouth.................$75–100
American 1880–1895

Warner's Safe Tonic, Rochester
N.Y., 1875–1885, $250–$350.

Warner's Safe Nervine (Motif of Safe) Rochester, N.Y.
Golden amber, 7⅜ in., smooth base, tooled mouth...................$80–140
American 1880–1895

Warner's Safe Nervine (Motif of Safe) Trade Mark London
Copper color, 7⅜ in., smooth base, applied mouth...................$80–120
English 1885–1895

Warner's Safe Remedy (Motif of Safe) Rochester, N.Y.
Amber, 5½ in., smooth base, tooled mouth $15–25
American 1880–1900

Warner's Safe Rheumatic Cure (Motif of Safe) London
Yellow Topaz, 9¼ in., smooth base, applied mouth $175–225
American 1885–1900

Warner's Safe Rheumatic Cure (Motif of Safe)
Amber, 9½ in., smooth base, applied blob type mouth...........$125–175
American 1875–1895

Whiskey Bottles

Whiskeys, sometimes referred to as spirits, come in an array of sizes, designs, shapes, and colors. The whiskey bottle dates back to the nineteenth century and the avid collector can acquire rare and valuable pieces.

In 1860, E. G. Booz manufactured a whiskey bottle in the design of a cabin embossed with the year 1840 and the words "Old Cabin Whiskey." One theory has it that the word *booze* was derived from his name to describe hard liquor. The Booz bottle is given the credit of being the first to emboss a name on whiskey bottles.

After the repeal of Prohibition in 1933, the only inscription that could be found on any liquor bottle was "Federal Law Forbids Sale or Re-use of This Bottle," which was continued through 1964.

A. Frohmann & Co, Philadelphia
Yellow Olive, 11 in., smooth base, tooled mouth.......................$75–100
American 1880–1895

A.C. Nolet (In a Slug Plate)—Aromatic—Schiedam—Schnapps
Medium Olive Green, 7¼ in., smooth base, applied sloping collar mouth $100–150
American 1880–1895

Alfred Moog, Pensacola, Fla
Amber, smooth base, 4½ in., tooled mouth $20–35
American 1890–1910

Tea Kettle Old Bourbon,
1871–1887, $300–$500.

Thos. Taylor & Co., Sole Agents for
P. Vollmers, Louisville, K.Y.
1880–1886, $400–$600.

American Vintage Co
Orange Amber, 11½ in., smooth base, applied sloping double collar
mouth $150–200
American 1880–1890

Back Bar Bottle—American Eagle
Clear, 8¾ in., smooth base, tooled lip..$30–60
American 1890–1910

**Back Bar Bottle—Established 1793 Coates & Co.'s Original Plymouth
Gin Black Friars Distillery, Plymouth, England (White Enamel
Lettering)**
Clear, 8½ in., polished pontil, tooled mouth $200–300
English 1890–1910

Back Bar Bottle—Jackson Rye
Clear, 9¼ in., smooth base, tooled lip..$30–60
American 1890–1910

Back Bar Bottle—Suspects His Master (Bull Dog Listing to a Jug of Whiskey with the Words 'Brown Forman Co. Distillers Louisville, Ky')
Clear, 8¾ in., smooth base, tooled lip..$30–60
American 1890–1910

Barry & Patten 116 & 118 Montgomery St. San Francisco
Medium Dark Amber, 9 in., graphite pontil, applied top.....$1000–2000
American 1850–1856 (rare—only one of three known examples)

Bininger's Travelers Guide, A.M. Bininger & Co., No 19 Broad St NY
Amber, Teardrop Flask, 6¾ in., smooth base, applied double collar
mouth $200–300
American 1860–1870

Blanchard & Co Inc. Importers, Boston, Mass
Amber, 6 in., smooth base, tooled lip..$15–25
American 1890–1915

Booth 7 Co Sacramento (Picture of Anchor and Rope)
Light Amethyst, 10½ in., smooth base, tooled top $200–300
American 1890–1894

Boulevard O.K. Bourbon H. Buneman Sole Agent S.F. Cal (Picture of Belt Buckle)
Medium to Deep Amber, 12½ in., smooth base, tooled top....$300–500
American 1896–1904

Brandes Brothers, New York
Amber, 9 in., smooth base, tooled lip..$20–25
American 1890–1915

Brent, Warder & Co.—Louisville, Ky
Medium Copper Puce, Barrel, 6⅞ in., smooth base, applied
mouth $1500–2000
American 1865–1875

B.T. & P. Oak Run Whiskey (Sample Size)
Yellowish Amber, 4¼ in., smooth base, tooled lip...................$400–600
American 1890–1910

Buffalo Old Bourbon (Motif of Buffalo), Geo. E. Dierssen & Co, Sacramento, Cal
Clear, 11⅞ in., smooth base, tooled mouth $700–1000
American 1890–1910 (scarce)

C.A. Richards & Co, 99 Washington St, Boston (Label—Plantation Bourbon, This Brand of Pure Bourbon Is Only Genuine When It Bears the Signature
Red Amber, 9½ in., smooth base, applied sloping collar
mouth $125–175
American 1855–1875

Cartan, McCarthy & Co (Monogram) San Francisco
Medium Amber, 12 in., smooth base, applied mouth $400–600
American 1880–1894

Chapin & Gore
Amber, 11¼ in., smooth base, applied mouth $50–80
American 1880–1890

Chestnut Grove Whiskey, C.W.
Medium Amber, 8⅞ in., open pontil, applied mouth and
handle..$140–180
American 1860–1870

Chevalir's Ginger Brandy, Trademark (Monogram)
Medium Amber, 11¼ in., smooth base, tooled top...................$200–400
American 1884–1888

C.R. Gibson, Salamanca N.Y.
Amber, 7 in., smooth base, tooled lip...$25–35
American 1890–1915

Dr. Warren's Pure Ginger Brandy, Homer Williams & Co, Proprietors, San Francisco, Cal
Amber, 11 in., smooth base, tooled lip...$15–20
American 1895–1901

Duffy's Malt Whiskey Company, D.M.W.Co. (Monogram), Rochester, N.Y. U.S.A.
Amber, 10⅛ in., smooth base (PATD. AUG. 24 1886), ABM lip.....$20–35
American 1880–1910

Durham Whiskey (Picture of Bull)
Medium Orange Red, 11 in., smooth base, applied top..........$300–750
American 1876–1882

Dyottville Glass Works Phila
Amber, 11⅜ in., smooth base, applied sloping double collar
mouth...$20–30
American 1860–1870

Eagle Glen Whiskey 59 Market Street S.F. Werle & Wiloh (Picture of Eagle and Shield)
Medium Amber, 12¼ in., smooth base, tooled top.................$400–600
American 1907–1916

E.G. Booz's Old Cabin Whiskey—1840—120 Walnut St, Philadelphia
E.G. Booz's Old Cabin Whiskey
Medium Amber, 7¾ in., smooth base, applied sloping collar
mouth...$175–250
American 1855–1865

Wolters Bros & Co, 115 & 117
Front St., S.F., 1886–1895,
$500–$1000.

United We Stand, Whisky,
Charles Kohn & Co., 1884–1888,
$1000–$1500.

El Pinal Vineyard, Bown & Schram, San Francisco Distributors
Medium Olive Yellow, 5 in., smooth base, tooled lip $150–225
American 1890–1910 (rare)

E & J. Burke's—Schiedam—Schnapps
Deep Olive Amber, 8 in., smooth base, applied sloping collar
mouth $80–120
American 1880–1890

Fleckenstein & Mayer, Portland, Oregon (Monogram)
Medium Deep Amber, 11⅛ in., smooth base, tooled top $1500–2500
American 1871–1909

Forest Lawn, J.V.H.
Deep Olive Green, 7½ in., iron pontil, applied mouth............$375–475
American 1855–1865 (From the San Francisco Dig of 1998)

From the Montego Bay Aerated Water Factory
Deep Olive Green, 9 in., round bottom, applied mouth..............$20–30
American 1880–1895

Full Weight Pure Rye Whiskey, This Bottle Is the Property of Wm. Edwards & Col, Cleveland, Ohio, U.S.A.
Grass Green, 6¾ in., smooth base, tooled mouth $75–125
American 1880–1895

Garfield Whiskey Bottle (with Label Underglass Recessed Shield and Picture of James Garfield)
Amber, 12½ in., smooth base, applied top $2500–3000
American 1880

Greeting, Theodore Netter, 1232 Market St., Philadelphia Pa
Cobalt Blue, Barrel, 5⅞ in., smooth base, tooled mouth $200–400
American 1890–1910

G.W. Middleton, What, 1825 Whiskey, Philada (on Applied Seal)
Dark Red Amber, 9¼ in., smooth base, tooled mouth $75–100
American 1880–1895

H. Brickwedel & Co. Wholesale Liquor Dealers 208 & 210 Front Street S.F.
Medium Amber, Half-pint, smooth base, applied top...............$300–500
American 1880–1883

H. Rickett's Glass Works Bristol
Amber, 8¾ in., pontil base, applied sloping double collar
mouth $25–35
American 1860–1870

**H.B. Kirk & Co., Wine Merchant, New York, Estabd 1853 (Label—
Old Hermitage Pure Rye Sour Mash Whisky W.A. Gaines & Co.,
Frankfort, Kentucky)**
Bluish Aqua, 7⅞ in., smooth base, tooled mouth $200–300
American 1885–1890

Hencken & Schroder, Our Choice, OK, Sole Agents, S.F.
Clear, 11¼ in., smooth base, tooled top.....................................$50–75
American 1895–1896

Hilderbrandt, Posner & Co. S.F. (Monogram)
Light Amber, 10½ in., smooth base, tooled top......................$100–200
American 1884–1890

Hopatkong Whiskey, J.C. Hess & Co. Phila
Deep Cobalt Blue, 10⅜ in., smooth base, applied mouth........$500–700
American 1875–1885 (rare in this color, only three known to exist)

Hudson G. Wolfe's (Large Embossed Bell)—Bell Schnapps
Medium Amber, 9⅞ in., smooth base, applied mouth.............$140–180
American 1870–1880 (rare)

**I. Goldberg—Distiller—171 E. Broadway—Houston Cor. Clinton
St—5th Ave Cor. 115th St. New York City**
Deep Amber, 12¼ in., smooth base, tooled mouth......................$60–90
American 1880–1890

I. Nelson's, Old Bourbon, Maysville, Ky.
Golden Amber, Barrel, 7⅜ in., smooth base, applied disc type
mouth $2000–3000
American 1860–1870 (extremely rare—less than five known examples)

J. Hayes & Co., Wholesale Dealers, Manchester. NH
Amber, 10 in., smooth base, tooled lip.......................................$15–25
American 1890–1915

Pottery Whiskey Jug "Glenco Brand—Scotch Whiskey", 1890–1910, $120–$160; Pottery Whiskey Jug "Pennsylvania Club Pure Rye Whiskey", 1890–1910, $300–$400; Pottery Whiskey Jug "Cruiskeen Lawn Mitchell's Old Irish Whisky" Belfast, 1885–1910, $60–$80; Pottery Whiskey Jug, Established 1902 Dufftown Glenlivet District Dawson's Perfection Old Scotch Whisky, 1890–1910, $200–$300; Pottery Whiskey Jug, Spring Lake, Hand Made Sour Mash Bourbon, Klein Bros. & Hyman, Cincinnati, Proprietors, 1890–1925, $400–$600.

J.J. Melchers W7—Schiedam—Aromatic Schnapps
Medium Olive Green, 7¼ in., smooth base, applied mouth........$40–70
American 1860–1870

J.T. Gayen—Schiedam—Schnapps
Medium Yellow Olive-Green, 7⅝ in., smooth base, applied mouth $80–140
American 1880–1890

Jas. A. Jackson & Co's—Cocktail
Medium Amber, Handled jug, 8¾ in., smooth base, applied mouth $375–475
American 1860–1870

Joseph N Galway, New York (Label—Old Continental Whiskey, from Joseph N. Galway, 42nd St. Opp. Grand Central Depot New York, 1860 Bourbon)
Deep Amber, 8¾ in., smooth base, applied sloping collar mouth $100–150
American 1860–1870

Kane, O'Leary & Co. 221 7 223 Bush St. S.F.
Medium Amber, 9½ in., smooth base, tooled type $1000–2000
American 1879–1881

Keller, Srass Distilling, Registered Distillers, Kansas City, Mo U.S.A.
Clear, 11⅛ in., smooth base, tooled mouth $25–40
American 1890–1910

K.B. Daly, 118 Wall St. New York
Deep Amber, 8⅞ in., smooth base, applied double collar
mouth $100–150
American 1865–1875

Label under Glass Back Bar Bottle—Established 1855, Robert Johnston Distiller of Copper Double Distilled Rye Wheat and Malt Whiskies, Warranted Without the Use of Steam, the Only Whiskey Fit for Medicinal Use & Co. Greencastle, Franklin Co. Pa
Clear, 11⅜ in., smooth base, tooled mouth $700–900
American 1880–1900 (extremely rare)

McKennas Nelson County Extra Kentucky Bourbon Whiskey, W&K Sole Agents
Medium Amber, 10½ in., smooth base, applied top............$1000–2000
American 1874–1878

Meyerfeld, Mitchell & Co, Days of 49 (in Two Diamonds) Trade, Mark, Cincinnati & SNA Francisco
Clear, 10¾ in., smooth base, ring lip...$20–25
American 1895–1905

Millers Extra Trade Mark, E. Martin Co., Old Bourbon
Yellow Olive, 7½ in., smooth base, applied mouth..............$1500–2500
American 1875–1880

Mohawk Whiskey, Pure, Rye, Patented, Feb 11 1868
Golden Amber, 12⅝ in., smooth base, rolled lip.................$1400–1800
American 1868–1875

N.M. Uri & Co., Inc., Louisville. Ky
Amber, 4½ in., smooth base, tooled mouth.................................$25–40
American 1890–1910

California Brandy, The Rosenblatt Co., San Francisco, California, 1890–1910, $25–$40.

N. Van Beil, 88, Chamber St. New York
Medium Yellow Olive, 11½ in., smooth base, applied seal, sloping double collar mouth...$300–400
American 1855–1870 (rare)

Old Joe Gideon, Whiskey, St. Louis 190, Portland, Ore
Amber, 6 in., smooth base, tooled lip...$20–25
American 1890–1915

Old Slaters Premium Bourbon Henry Rosenbrock, Carson, Nev
Medium Golden Amber, 11½ in., smooth base (S.F.P.G.W.), tooled top $200–300
American 1865–1887

M. Gruenberg & Co, Old Judge Ky Bourbon San Francisco (Original Label)
Amber, 10½ in., smooth base, applied top $300–500
American 1879–1881

Peerless Whiskey Wolf Wreden Co Sole Agents S.F.
Medium Amber, 12 in., smooth base, tooled lip $600–1000
American 1891–1898 (rare)

Kentucky Reserve (pinch bar bottle), 1890–1910, $75–$100.

Perrine's—Apple—Ginger—Phila (on Roof Panels)—Perrine's (Motif of Apple) Ginger—Depot No 37, Nth Front St, Philada
Golden Yellow, 10⅛ in., smooth base, tooled mouth $125–150
American 1865–1875

P.J. Desmond Pure Liquor, Park St, Lawrence, Mass
Amber, 9½ in., smooth base, applied mouth $50–60
American 1880–1890

P.J. Mullane, 35th St & 10th Ave, 50th St and 10th Ave, N.Y. (Label—Boyer's Bengal Liquid Blue Manufactured by Boyer & Co Philadelphia)
Golden Olive, 10⅛ in., smooth base, tooled mouth $70–90
American 1890–1910

Preoria Rye Is Betterk L& A Scharff Bottlers, St. Louis, Mo
Golden Amber, 9½ in., smooth base, applied mouth $150–250
American 1880–1895

R.B. Cutter—Louisvile, Ky
Medium Amber, 8¾ in., smooth base, applied mouth and
handle $70–90
American 1860–1870

R.B. Cutter Pure Bourbon
Strawberry Puce, 8¾ in., iron pontil base, applied mouth and
handle $175–275
American 1855–1865

Roanoke Rye Shea Bocqueraz &Co.
Medium Amber, 11½ in., smooth base, tooled lip...................$175–250
American 1898–1905

Royal Club—Schnapps—Schiedam
Yellowish Olive Green, 7¾ in., smooth base, applied sloping collar
mouth $80–120
American 1880–1900

R & S (Monogram) Roehling & Schutz, Inc., Chicago
Amber, 9¾ in., smooth base, tooled mouth $200–300
American 1880–1890

S.A. Casse—1695—Madison Ave. N.Y.—1301 Wilkins Ave. N.Y.
Medium Amber, 13⅜ in., smooth base, tooled mouth...............$80–100
American 1890–1910

Old Barbee Whiskey, Butte, Mont; Peach Blossom Bourbon
Whiskey, Butte, Mont; Beartooth Bourbon Whiskey, Red Lodge,
Mont. All circa 1900–1930; All $10–$15 (each).

Schiedam—Aromatic, Schnapps
Olive Green, 7⅞ in., smooth base, applied mouth........................$40–70
American 1860–1870

Security Distilling Co, Chicago, U.S.A.
Amber, 4½ in., smooth base, tooled mouth.................................$25–35
American 1890–1910

Silver Stream Schnapps—W & A Gilbey
Olive Green with Amber tone, 8⅜ in., smooth base, applied sloping
collar mouth...$80–140
American 1880–1890

Smokine, Imported and Bottled, by Alfred Andersen & Co, The Western Importers, Minneapolis, Minn and Winnipeg, Man (Figural Log Cabin)
Amber, 6⅝ in., smooth base, tooled mouth..............................$80–100
American 1890–1910

Sontaw's Old Cabinet Whiskey (On Applied Seal)
Medium Amber, 8⅜ in., smooth base, applied sloping collar
mouth..$275–375
American 1860–1870

The Duffy Malt Whiskey Company, D.M.W. Co (Monogram), Rochester N.Y. U.S.A.
Medium Amber, 10 in., smooth base, ABM lip $20–30
American 1875–1890

This Bottle Is the Property of John De Kuyper & Son, Rotterdam
Medium Olive Green, Coffin Flask, 5⅞ in., smooth base, applied
mouth...$80–120
American 1880–1895

Trade Mark Registered, Full Measure, Pint, A. William & Son, Estab 1870 Family Wine Store, 410 Hanover St., Boston
Aqua, smooth base, 8 in., smooth base, tooled lip.......................$15–25
American 1890–1915

Vollmar Schnapps
Bluish Aqua, 8 in., smooth base, tooled mouth...........................$70–90
American 1890–1900

Hill and Hill, Dillon, Mont, 1900–1930, $15.

Vonthofen's—Aromatic Schiedam, Schnapps
Deep Green, 9½ in., smooth base, applied sloping collar
mouth $300–400
American 1855–1870 (rare)

WM. McCully & Co Pittsburgh—Patent (on Shoulder)
Yellowish Amber, 11½ in., smooth base, applied double collar
mouth $40–60
American 1860–1870

Wormer's Bro's S.F. Fine Old Cognac
Olive Amber, 6⅛ in., smooth base, applied double collar
mouth $7000–10,000
American 1865–1867 (rare)

Young & Holmes—Cincinnati, O
Amber, 9½ in., smooth base, applied sloping collar mouth $175–275
American 1865–1875

New Bottles
(Post–1900)

New Bottles: Post– 1900

The bottles listed in this section have been broken down solely by characteristics of the bottles themselves. The contents of these groups hold little interest for the collector. New bottles covered in this section are valuable precisely for their decorative, appealing, and sometimes unique designs.

The goal of most new-bottle collectors is to collect a complete set of items designed and produced by a favorite manufacturer. As it is with the reproductions of old bottles such as Coca-Cola, or new items such as the Avon items, the right time to purchase is when the first issue comes out on the retail market, or prior to retail release if possible. As with the old bottles, I have provided a good cross section of new bottles in various price ranges and categories rather than listing only the rarest or most collectible pieces.

The pricing shown reflects the value of the particular item listed. Newer bottles are usually manufactured in limited quantities without any reissues. Since retail prices are affected by factors such as source, type of bottle, desirability, condition, and the possibility that the bottle was produced exclusively as a collectors' item, the pricing can fluctuate radically at any given time.

Avon
Bottles

The cosmetic empire known today as Avon began as the California Perfume Company, was the creation of D. H. McConnell, a door-to-door book salesman who gave away perfume samples to stop the doors from slamming in his face. As time went on, McConnell gave up on books and concentrated on selling perfumes. Although based in New York, the name Avon was used in 1929 along with the name California Perfume Company or C.P.C. After 1939, the company operated exclusively under the name Avon. Bottles embossed with C.P.C. are very rare and collectible owing to the small quantities issued and the even smaller quantity that have been well preserved.

Today Avon offers the collector a wide range of products in bottles shaped like cars, people, chess pieces, trains, animals, sporting items (footballs, baseballs, etc.), and numerous other objects. The most scarce pieces and sought-after are the pre–World War II figurals. They're very hard to find, but almost all are well preserved.

To those who collect Avon items, anything Avon related is considered collectible. That includes boxes, brochures, magazine ads, or anything else labeled with the Avon name. Since many people who sell Avon items are unaware of the individual piece value, a collector can find great prices at swap meets, flea markets, and garage sales. While this book offers an excellent detailed cross section of Avon collectibles, I recommend that serious collectors obtain Bud Hastings's new *14th Edition of Avon Products & California Perfume Co. (CPC) Collector's Encyclopedia,* which offers pricing and pictures on thousands of Avon & California Perfume Co. (CPC) products from 1886 to present.

Remember When Gas Pump, 4 oz,
Red Painted Over Clear Glass, Red
and White Plastic Cap—Came in
Deep Woods or Wild Country,
1976–1977, $10–$15.

A Man's World, Globe on Stand 1969 ....$7–10

A Winner, Boxing Gloves 1960 ....$20–25

Abraham Lincoln, Wild Country After Shave 1970–1972 ....$3–5

After Shave on Tap, Wild Country $3–5

Aladdin's Lamp 1971 ....$7–10

Alaskan Moose 1974 ....$5–8

Alpine Flask 1966–1967 ....$35–45

American Belle, Sonnet Cologne 1976–1978................................$5–7

American Buffalo 1975...$6–8

American Eagle Pipe 1974–1975 ....$6–8

American Eagle, Windjammer After Shave 1971–1972................$3–4

American Ideal Perfume, California Perfume Comp.
1911 ....$125–140

American Schooner, Oland After Shave 1972–1973 ....$4–5

Andy Capp Figural (England) 1970 ....$95–105

Angler, Windjammer After Shave 1970 ....$5–7

Apple Blossom Toilet Water 1941–1942 ....$50–60

Apothecary, Lemon Velvet Moist Lotion 1973–1976....................$4–6

Apothecary, Spicy After Shave 1973–1974................................$4–5

Aristocrat Kittens Soap (Walt Disney)................................$5–7

Armoire Decanter, Charisma Bath Oil 1973–1974 ....$4–5

Armoire Decanter, Elusive Bath Oil 1972–1975 ....$4–5

Auto Lantern 1973 ....$6–8

Auto, Big Mack Truck, Windjammer After Shave 1973–1975 ....$5–6

Auto, Cord, 1937 Model, Wild Country After Shave
1974–1978..$7–8

Auto, Country Vendor, Wild Country After Shave 1973.............$7–8

Auto, Dusenberg, Silver, Wild Country After Shave
1970–1972..$8–9

Auto, Dune Buggy, Sports Rally Bracing Lotion 1971–1973 ......$4–5

Auto, Electric Charger, Avon Leather Cologne 1970–1972 ....$6–7

Auto, Hayes Apperson, 1902 Model, Avon Blend 7 After Shave
1973–1974..$5–7

Auto, Maxwell 23, Deep Woods After Shave 1972–1974 ....$5–6

Auto, MG, 1936, Wild Country After Shave 1974–1975.............$4–5

Auto, Model A, Wild Country After Shave 1972–1974 ....$4–5

Auto, Red Depot Wagon, Oland After Shave 1972–1973 ....$6–7

Auto, Rolls Royce, Deep Woods After Shave 1972–1975...........$6–8

Auto, Stanley Steamer, Windjammer After Shave 1971–1972 ....$6–7

Auto, Station Wagon, Tai Winds After Shave 1971–1973...........$7–8

Auto, Sterling 6, Spicy After Shave 1968–1970............................$6–7

Auto, Sterling Six II, Wild Country After Shave 1973–1974......$4–5

Auto, Stutz Bearcat, 1914 Model, Avon Blend 7 After Shave
1974–1977...$5–6

Auto, Touring T, Tribute After Shave, 1969–1970......................$6–7

Auto, Volkswagen, Red, Oland After Shave 1972.........................$5–6

Avon Calling, Phone, Wild Country After Shave
1969–1970..$15–20

Avon Dueling Pistol II, Black Glass 1972 ....$10–15

Avonshire Blue Cologne 1971–1974..$4–5

Baby Grand Piano, Perfume Glace 1971–1972............................$8–10

Baby Hippo 1977–1980..$4–5

Ballad Perfume, 3 Drams, ⅜ Ounce 1939..............................$100–125

Bath Urn, Lemon Velvet Bath Oil 1971–1973 ....$4–5

Beauty Bound Black Purse 1964...$45–55

Bell Jar Cologne 1973...$5–10

Benjamin Franklin, Wild Country After Shave 1974–1976.........$4–5

Big Game Rhino, Tai Winds After Shave 1972–1973 .... $ 7–8

Big Whistle 1972..$4–5

Bird House Power Bubble Bath 1969..$7–8

Bird of Paradise Cologne Decanter 1972–1974............................$4–5

Blacksmith's Anvil, Deep Woods After Shave 1972–1973...........$4–5

Bloodhound Pipe, Deep Woods After Shave 1976 ....$5–6

Blue Blazer After Shave Lotion 1964...$25–30

Chevy '55 1974–1975...$6–8

Christmas Ornament, Green or Red 1970–1971..........................$1–2

Christmas Ornament, Orange, Bubble Bath 1970–1971...............$2–3

Christmas Tree Bubble Bath 1968...$5–7

Classic Lion, Deep Wood After Shave 1973–1975......................$4–5

Club Bottle, 1906 Avon Lady 1977...$25–30

Club Bottle, 1st Annual 1972..$150–200

Club Bottle, 2nd Annual 1973...$45–60

Club Bottle, 5th Annual 1976..$25–30

Club Bottle, Bud Hastin 1974...$70–95

Club Bottle, CPC Factory 1974...$30–40

Collector's Pipe, Windjammer After Shave 1973–1974...............$3–4

Colt Revolver 1851 1975–1976..$10–12

Corncob Pipe After Shave 1974–1975.......................................$4–6

Corvette Stingray '65 1975...$5–7

Covered Wagon, Wild Country After Shave 1970–1971.............$4–5

Daylight Shaving Time 1968–1970...$5–7

Defender Cannon 1966...$20–24

Dollar's 'N' Scents 1966–1967...$20–24

Dutch Girl Figurine, Somewhere 1973–1974.............................$8–10

Duck After Shave 1971..$4–6

Dueling Pistol 1760 1973–1974...$9–12

Dueling Pistol II 1975..$9–12

Eight Ball Decanter, Spicy After Shave 1973............................$3–4

Electric Guitar, Wild Country After Shave 1974–1975...............$4–5

Enchanted Frog Cream Sachet, Sonnet 1973–1976....................$3–4

Jaguar Car 1973–1976 ....$6–8

Jolly Santa 1978 ....$6–7

Joyous Bell 1978..$5–6

King Pin 1969–1970 ....$4–6

Kodiak Bear 1977 ....$5–10

Koffee Klatch, Honeysuckle Foam Bath Oil 1971–1974...............$5–6

Liberty Bell, Tribute After Shave 1971–1972................................$4–6

Liberty Dollar, After Shave 1970–1972 ....$4–6

Lincoln Bottle 1971–1972...$3–5

Lip Pop Colas, Cherry 1973–1974 ....$1–2

Lip Pop Colas, Cola 1973–1974 ....$1–2

Lip Pop Colas, Strawberry 1973–1974 ....$1–2

Longhorn Steer 1975–1976 ....$7–9

Looking Glass, Regence Cologne 1970–1972 ....$7–8

Mallard Duck 1967–1968 ....$8–10

Mickey Mouse, Bubble Bath 1969 ....$10–12

Mighty Mitt Soap on a Rope 1969–1972.......................................$7–8

Ming Cat, Bird of Paradise Cologne 1971 ....$5–7

Mini Bike, Sure Winner Bracing Lotion 1972–1973.....................$3–5

Nile Blue Bath Urn, Skin So Soft 1972–1974 ....$3–4

Nile Blue Bath Urn, Skin So Soft 1972–1974 ....$4–6

No Parking 1975–1976 ....$5–7

Old Faithful, Wild Country After Shave 1972–1973.....................$4–6

One Good Turn, Screwdriver 1976 ....$5–6

Opening Play, Dull Golden, Spicy After Shave 1968–1969.......$8–10

Opening Play, Shiny Golden, Spicy After Shave
1968–1969...$14–17

Owl Fancy, Roses, Roses 1974–1976...$3–4

Owl Soap Dish and Soaps 1970–1971...$8–10

Packard Roadster 1970–1972..$4–7

Pass Play Decanter 1973–1975..$6–8

Peanuts Gang Soaps 1970–1972..$8–9

Pepperbox Pistol 1976..$5–10

Perfect Drive Decanter 1975–1976..$7–9

Pheasant 1972–1974..$7–9

Piano Decanter, Tai Winds After Shave 1972....................................$3–4

Pipe, Full, Decanter, Brown, Spicy After Shave 1971–1972........$3–4

Pony Express, Avon Leather After Shave 1971–1972.................$3–4

Pony Post "Tall" 1966–1967..$7–9

Pot Belly Stove 1970–1971..$5–7

President Lincoln, Tai Winds After Shave 1973...........................$6–8

President Washington, Deep Woods After Shave 1974–1976.....$4–5

Quail 1973–1974..$7–9

Rainbow Trout, Deep Woods After Shave 1973–1974.................$3–4

Road Runner, Motorcycle...$4–5

Rook, Spicy After Shave 1973–1974..$4–5

Royal Coach, Bird of Paradise Bath Oil 1972–1973....................$4–6

Scent with Love, Elusive Perfume 1971–1972.............................$9–10

Scent with Love, Field Flowers Perfume 1971–1972.................$9–10

Scent with Love, Moonwind Perfume 1971–1972.......................$9–10

Side-wheeler, Tribute After Shave 1970–1971.............................$4–5

Side-wheeler, Wild Country After Shave 1971–1972 ....$3–4

Small World Perfume Glace, Small World 1971–1972 ....$3–4

Snoopy Soap Dish Refills 1968–1976 ....$3–4

Snoopy's Bubble Tub 1971–1972 ....$3–4

Spark Plug Decanter 1975–1976...$2–5

Spirit of St. Louis, Excalibur After Shave 1970–1972 ....$3–5

Stage Coach, Wild Country After Shave 1970–1977....................$5–6

Tee Off, Electric Pre-shave, 1973–1975 ....$2–3

Ten Point Buck, Wild Country After Shave 1969–1974.............$5–7

Twenty-Dollar Gold Piece, Windjammer After Shave
1971–1972 ....$4–6

Uncle Sam Pipe, Deep Woods After Shave 1975–1976 ....$4–5

Viking Horn 1966...$12–16

Western Boot, Wild Country After Shave 1973–1975 ....$2–3

Western Saddle 1971–1972 ....$7–9

Wild Turkey 1974–1976..$6–8

World's Greatest Dad Decanter 1971...$4–6

Ballantine Bottles

Ballantine bottles, which are brightly colored and ceramic, contain imported Scotch whiskey and usually read "Blended Scotch Whisky, 14 Years Old." The majority of these bottles' designs are based on sporting or outdoor themes, such as ducks or fishermen with their heads represented by the bottle cap. The more collectible items, however, are the older bottles (1930), which are nonfigural and very decorative.

Charioteer...$5–10

Discus Thrower...$5–10

Duck...$8–10

Fisherman...$10–12

Gladiator...$5–10

Golf Bag..$8–10

Mallard Duck...$6–8

Mercury...$5–10

Old Crow Chessman..$9–10

Scottish Knight..$10–12

Seated Fisherman..$10–12

Ballantine's Liqueur Blended Scotch Whisky, Product of Scotland, 1950–1955, $50–$75.

Silver Knight $12–15

Zebra $12–15

Barsottini Bottles

The Barsottini bottle, which is manufactured in Italy, does not use any American or nongeographic themes for the U.S. marketplace. These bottles are ceramic and come in gray and white to represent the brickwork of buildings, and usually represent European subjects such as the Eiffel Tower or the Florentine Steeple.

Alpine Pipe, 10 inches $8–12

Antique Automobile, Ceramic, Coupe $6–9

Antique Automobile, Open Car $6–9

Clock, with Cherub $30–40

Clowns, Ceramic, 12 in. each $9–12

Eiffel Tower, Gray and White, 15 inches $8–12

Florentine Cannon "L," 15 in. $14–20

Florentine Steeple, Gray and White $9–12

Monastery Cask, Ceramic, 12 in. $14–20

Paris Arc de Triomphe, 7½ in. $10–12

Pisa's Leaning Tower, Gray and White $10–12

Roman Coliseum, Ceramic $7–10

Trivoli Clock, Ceramic, 15 in. $12–15

Jim Beam Bottles

The James B. Beam distilling company was founded in 1778 by Jacob Beam in Kentucky and now bears the name of Colonel James B. Beam, Jacob Beam's grandson. Beam whiskey was very popular in the South during the nineteenth and early twentieth centuries but not produced on a large scale. Because of low production, the early Beam bottles are very rare, collectible, and valuable.

In 1953, the Beam company packaged bourbon in a special Christmas/ New Year ceramic decanter, which was a rarity for any distiller. When the decanters sold well, Beam decided to redevelop its method of packaging, which led to production of a wide variety of different series in the 1950s. The first of these were the ceramics of 1953. In 1955 the executive series was issued to commemorate the 160th anniversary of the corporation. In 1955, Beam introduced the Regal China series to honor significant people, places, and events with a concentration on America and contemporary situations. In 1956, political figures were introduced with the elephant and the donkey as well as special productions for customer specialties, which were made on commission. In 1957, the trophy series came along to signify various achievements within the liquor industry. And, in 1958, the state series was introduced to commemorate the admission of Alaska and Hawaii into the Union. The practice has continued with Beam still producing decanters commemorating all fifty states.

In total, over 500 types of Beam bottles have been issued since 1953.

AC Spark Plug 1977
Replica of a spark plug in white, green, and gold........................$22–26

AHEPA 50th Anniversary 1972
Regal China bottle designed in honor of AHEPA's (American
Hellenic Education Progressive Association) 50th anniversary $4–6

Aida 1978
Figurine of character from the opera *Aida* $140–160

Akron Rubber Capital 1973
Regal China bottle honoring Akron, Ohio....................................$15–20

Alaska 1958
Regal China, 9½ in., star-shaped bottle $55–60

Alaska 1964–1965
Re-issue of the 1958 bottle...$40–50

Alaska Purchase 1966
Regal China, 10 in., blue and gold bottle $4–6

American Samoa 1973
Regal China, reflects the seal of Samoa...$5–7

American Veterans...$4–7

Antique Clock $35–45

Antioch 1967
Regal China, 10 in., commemorates Diamond Jubilee of Regal........$5–7

Antique Coffee Grinder 1979
Replica of a box coffee mill used in mid-19th century $10–12

Antique Globe 1980
Represents the Martin Behaim globe of 1492...................................$7–11

Antique Telephone (1897) 1978
Replica of an 1897 desk phone, second in a series.......................$50–60

Antique Trader 1968
Regal China, 10½ in., represents *Antique Trader* newspaper............$4–6

Appaloosa 1974
Regal China, 10 in., represents favorite horse of the Old
West...$12–15

Arizona 1968
Regal China, 12 in., represents the State of Arizona......................$4–6

Armadillo..$8–12

Armanetti Award Winner 1969
Honor's Armanetti, Inc., of Chicago as "Liquor Retailer of the
Year"...$6–8

Armanetti Shopper 1971
Reflects the slogan "It's fun to Shop Armanetti-Self Service Liquor
Store," 11¾ in. $6–8

Armanetti Vase 1968
Yellow-toned decanter embossed with flowers..................................$5–7

Bacchus 1970
Issued by Armanetti Liquor Stores of Chicago, Illinois, 11¾ in. $6–9

Barney's Slot Machine 1978
Replica of the world's largest slot machine.................................$14–16

Barry Berish 1985
Executive series $110–140

Barry Berish 1986
Executive series, bowl...$110–140

Bartender's Guild 1973
Commemorative honoring the International Bartenders Assn...........$4–7

Baseball 1969
Issued to commemorate the 100th anniversary of baseball. $18–20

Beam Pot 1980
Shaped like a New England bean pot, Club bottle for the New England
Beam Bottle and Specialties Club..$12–15

Beaver Valley Club 1977
A club bottle to honor the Beaver Valley Jim Beam Club of
Rochester $8–12

Bell Scotch 1970
Regal China, 10 ½ in., in honor of Arthur Bell & Sons.................$4–7

Beverage Association, NLBA...$4–7

The Big Apple 1979
Apple-shaped bottle with "The Big Apple" over the top.................$8–12

Bing's 31st Clam Bake Bottle 1972
Commemorates 31st Bing Crosby National Pro-Am Golf Tournament
in January 1972..$25–30

Bing Crosby National Pro-Am 1970 ....$4–7

Bing Crosby National Pro-Am 1971 ....$4–7

Bing Crosby National Pro-Am 1972 ....$15–25

Bing Crosby National Pro-Am 1973 ....$18–23

Bing Crosby National Pro-Am 1974 ....$15–25

Bing Crosby National Pro-Am 1975 ....$45–65

Bing Crosby 36th 1976...$15–25

Bing Crosby National Pro-Am 1977 ....$12–18

Bing Crosby National Pro-Am 1978 ....$12–18

Black Katz 1968
Regal China, 14½ in. $7–12

Blue Cherub Executive 1960
Regal China, 12½ in. $70–90

Blue Daisy 1967
Also know as Zimmerman Blue Daisy.......................................$10–12

Blue Gill, Fish..$12–16

Blue Goose Order..$4–7

Blue Jay 1969...$4–7

Blue Goose 1979
Replica of blue goose, authenticated by Dr. Lester Fisher, dir. of
Lincoln Park Zoological Gardens in Chicago.............................$7–9

Blue Hen Club $12–15

Blue Slot Machine 1967..$10–12

Bobby Unser Olsonite Eagle 1975
Replica of the racing car used by Bobby Unser...........................$40–50

Bob DeVaney...$8–12

Bob Hope Desert Classic 1973
First genuine Regal China bottle created in honor of the Bob Hope Desert
Classic..$8–9

Bob Hope Desert Classic 1974 ....$8–12

Bohemian Girl 1974
Issued for the Bohemian Cafe in Omaha, Nebraska to honor the Czech
and Slovak immigrants in the United States, 14¼ in. $10–15

Bonded Gold $4–7

Bonded Mystic 1979
Urn-shaped bottle, burgundy-colored...$4–7

Bonded Silver..$4–7

Boris Godinov, with Base 1978
2nd in opera series...$350–450

Bourbon Barrel...$18–24

Bowling Proprietors..$4–7

Boys Town of Italy 1973
Created in honor of the Boys Town of Italy....................................$7–10

Bowl 1986
Executive series $20–30

Broadmoor Hotel 1968
To celebrate the 50th anniversary of this famous hotel in Colorado
Springs, Colorado—1918–The Broadmoor–1968 ....$4–7

Buffalo Bill 1971
Regal China, 10½ in., commemorates Buffalo Bill............................$4–7

Bull Dog 1979
Honors the 204th anniversary of the United States Marine
Corps $15–18

Cable Car 1968
Regal China, 4½ in. $4–6

Caboose 1980...$50–60

California Mission 1970
This bottle was issued for the Jim Beam Bottle Club of Southern
California in honor of the 20th anniversary of the California
Missions, 14 in. $10–15

California Retail Liquor Dealers Association 1973
Designed to commemorate the 20th anniversary of the California
Retail Liquor Dealers Association..$6–9

Cal-Neva 1969
Regal China, 9½ in. $5–7

Camellia City Club 1979
Replica of the cupola of the State Capitol building in
Sacramento $18–23

Cameo Blue 1965
Also known as the Shepherd Bottle...$4–6

Cannon 1970
Bottle issued to commemorate the 175th anniversary of the Jim Beam
Co. Some of these bottles have a small chain shown on the cannon and
some do not. Those without the chain are harder to find and more
valuable, 8 in.
Chain $2–4
No Chain..$9–13

Canteen 1979
Replica of the exact canteen used by the Armed Forces $8–12

Captain and Mate 1980 ....$10–12

Cardinal (Kentucky Cardinal) 1968 ....$40–50

Carmen 1978
Third in the opera series..$140–180

Carolier Bull 1984
Executive series $18–23

Catfish...$16–24

Cathedral Radio 1979
Replica of one of the earlier dome-shaped radios.........................$12–15

Cats 1967
Trio of cats: Siamese, Burmese, and Tabby.....................................$6–9

Cedars of Lebanon 1971
This bottle was issued in honor of the Jerry Lewis Muscular
Dystrophy Telethon in 1971...$5–7

Charisma 1970
Executive series $4–7

Charlie McCarthy 1976
Replica of Edgar Bergen's puppet from the 1930s........................$20–30

Cherry Hills Country Club 1973
Commemorating 50th anniversary of Cherry Hills Country Club....$4–7

Cheyenne, Wyoming 1977...$4–6

Chicago Cubs, Sports Series $30–40

Chicago Show Bottle 1977
Commemorates 6th Annual Chicago Jim Beam Bottle Show........$10–14

Christmas Tree $150–200

Churchill Downs—Pink Roses 1969
Regal China, 10¼ in. $5–7

Churchill Downs—Red Roses 1969
Regal China, 10¼ in. $9–12

Circus Wagon 1979
Replica of a circus wagon from the late 19th century...................$24–26

Civil War North 1961
Regal China, 10¼ in. $10–15

Civil War South 1961
Regal China, 10¼ in. $25–35

Clear Crystal Bourbon 1967
Clear glass, 11½ in. $5–7

Clear Crystal Scotch 1966..$9–12

Clear Crystal Vodka 1967..$5–8

Cleopatra Rust 1962
Glass, 13¼ in. $3–5

Cleopatra Yellow 1962
Glass, 13¼ in., rarer than Cleopatra Rust......................................$8–12

Clint Eastwood 1973
Commemorating Clint Eastwood Invitational Celebrity Tennis
Tournament in Pebble Beach $14–17

Cocktail Shaker 1953
Glass, Fancy Disp. Bottle, 9¼ in. $2–5

Coffee Grinder..$8–12

Coffee Warmers 1954
Four types are known: Red, Black, Gold, and White....................$7–12

Coffee Warmers 1956
Two types with metal necks and handles $2–5

Coho Salmon 1976
Official seal of the National Fresh Water Fishing Hall of Fame is on
the back...$10–13

Colin Mead..$180–210

Cobalt 1981
Executive Series...$18–23

Collector's Edition 1966
Set of six glass famous paintings: *The Blue Boy*, *On the Terrace*, *Mardi Gras*, *Austide Bruant*, *The Artist Before His Easel*, and *Laughing Cavalier* (each) $2–5

Collectors Edition Volume II 1967
A set of six flask-type bottles with famous pictures: *George Gisze*, *Soldier and Girl*, *Night Watch*, *The Jester*, *Nurse and Child*, and *Man on Horse* (each)...$2–5

Collectors Edition Volume III 1968

A set of eight bottles with famous paintings: *On the Trail, Indian Maiden, Buffalo, Whistler's Mother, American Gothic, The Kentuckian, The Scout,* and *Hauling in the Gill Net* (each)..$2–5

Collectors Edition Volume IV 1969

A set of eight bottles with famous paintings: *Balcony, The Judge, Fruit Basket, Boy with Cherries, Emile Zola, The Guitarist Zouave,* and *Sunflowers* (each)..$2–5

Collectors Edition Volume V 1970

A set of six bottles with famous paintings: *Au Cafe, Old Peasant, Boaring Party, Gare Saint Lazare, The Jewish Bride,* and *Titus at Writing Desk* (each)..$2–5

Collectors Edition Volume VI 1971

A set of three bottles with famous art pieces; *Charles I, The Merry Lute Player,* and *Boy Holding Flute* (each)...$2–5

Collectors Edition Volume VII 1972

A set of three bottles with famous paintings: *The Bag Piper, Prince Baltasar,* and *Maidservant Pouring Milk* (each) $2–5

Collectors Edition Volume VIII 1973

A set of three bottles with famous portraits: *Ludwig van Beethoven, Wolfgang Mozart,* and *Frédéric François Chopin* (each).......................$2–5

Collectors Edition Volume IX 1974

A set of three bottles with famous paintings: *Cardinal, Ring-Neck Pheasant,* and the *Woodcock* (each) $3–6

Collectors Edition Volume X 1975

A set of three bottles with famous pictures: *Sailfish, Rainbow Trout,* and *Largemouth Bass* (each) $3–6

Collectors Edition Volume XI 1976

A set of three bottles with famous paintings: *Chipmunk, Bighorn Sheep,* and *Pronghorn Antelope* (each)..$3–6

Collectors Edition Volume XII 1977

A set of four bottles with a different reproduction of James Lockhart on the front (each)..$3–6

Collectors Edition Volume XIV 1978
A set of four bottles with James Lockhart paintings: *Raccoon, Mule Deer, Red Fox,* and *Cottontail Rabbit* (each) $3–6

Collectors Edition Volume XV 1979
A set of three flasks with Frederic Remington's painting: *The Cowboy 1902, The Indian Trapper 1902,* and *Lieutenant S.C. Robertson 1890* (each) $2–5

Collectors Edition Volume XVI 1980
A set of three flasks depicting duck scenes: *The Mallard, The Redhead,* and *The Canvasback* (each) $3–6

Collectors Edition Volume XVII 1981
A set of three flasks bottles with James Lockhart paintings: *Great Elk, Pintail Duck,* and the *Horned Owl* (each) $3–6

Colorado 1959
Regal China, 10¾ in. $20–25

Colorado Centennial 1976
Replica of Pikes Peak $8–12

Colorado Springs $4–7

Computer, Democrat 1984 .... $12–18

Computer, Republican 1984 .... $12–18

Convention Bottle 1971
Commemorate the first national convention of the National Association of Jim Beam Bottle and Specialty Clubs hosted by the Rocky Mountain Club, Denver, Colorado $5–7

Convention Number 2 1972
Honors the second annual convention of the National Association of Jim Beam Bottle and Specialty Clubs in Anaheim, CA $20–30

Convention Number 3—Detroit 1973
Commemorates the third annual convention of Beam Bottle Collectors in Detroit $10–12

Convention Number 4—Pennsylvania 1974
Commemorates the annual convention of the Jim Beam Bottle Club in Lancaster, PA $80–100

Convention Number 5—Sacramento 1975
Commemorates the annual convention of the Camellia City Jim Beam
Bottle Club in Sacramento, CA...$5–7

Convention Number 6—Hartford 1976
Commemorates the annual convention of the Jim Beam Bottle Club
in Hartford, CN..$5–7

Convention Number 7—Louisville 1978
Commemorates the annual convention of the Jim Beam Bottle Club
in Louisville, KY..$5–7

Convention Number 8—Chicago 1978
Commemorates the annual convention of the Jim Beam Bottle Club
in Chicago, IL...$8–12

Convention Number 9—Houston 1979
Commemorates the annual convention of the Jim Beam Bottle Club
in Houston, TX..$20–30
Cowboy, beige..$35–45
Cowboy, in color...$35–45

Convention Number 10—Norfolk 1980
Commemorates the annual convention of the Jim Beam Bottle Club at
the Norfolk Naval Base...$18–22
Waterman, pewter...$35–45
Waterman, yellow..$35–45

Convention Number 11—Las Vegas 1981
Commemorates the annual convention of the Jim Beam Bottle Club
in Las Vegas, NV...$20–22
Showgirl, blonde $45–55
Showgirl, brunette $45–55

Convention Number 12—New Orleans 1982
Commemorates the annual convention of the Jim Beam Bottle Club
in New Orleans, LA $30–35
Buccaneer, gold $35–45
Buccaneer, in color..$35–45

Convention Number 13—St. Louis 1983 (Stein)
Commemorates the annual convention of the Jim Beam Bottle Club
in St. Louis, MO $55–70
Gibson girl, blue $65–80
Gibson girl, yellow $65–80

Convention Number 14—Florida, King Neptune 1984
Commemorates the annual convention of the Jim Beam Bottle Club
in Florida...$15–20
Mermaid, blonde $35–45
Mermaid, brunette...$35–45

Convention Number 15—Las Vegas 1985
Commemorates the annual convention of the Jim Beam Bottle Club
in Las Vegas, NV..$40–50

Convention Number 16—Pilgrim Woman, Boston 1986
Commemorates the annual convention of the Jim Beam Bottle Club
in Boston $35–45
Minuteman, color $85–105
Minuteman, pewter $85–105

Convention Number 17—Louisville 1987
Commemorates the annual convention of the Jim Beam Bottle Club
in Louisville, KY..$55–75
Kentucky Colonel, blue..$85–105
Kentucky Colonel, gray..$85–105

Convention Number 18—Bucky Beaver 1988 ....$30–40
Portland rose, red..$30–40
Portland rose, yellow...$30–40

Convention Number 19—Kansas City 1989
Commemorates the annual convention of the Jim Beam Bottle Club
in Kansas City, MO..$40–50

Cowboy 1979
Awarded to collectors who attended the 1979 convention for
the International Association of Beam Clubs................................$35–50

CPO Open $4–7

Crappie 1979
Commemorates the National Fresh Water Fishing Hall of Fame $10–14

Dark Eyes Brown Jug 1978 ....$4–6

D-Day $12–18

Delaware Blue Hen Bottle 1972
Commemorates the State of Delaware $4–7

Delco Freedom Battery 1978
Replica of a Delco battery..$18–22

Delft Blue 1963..$3–5

Delft Rose 1963 ....$4–6

Del Webb Mint 1970
Metal stopper...$10–12
China stopper...$50–60

Devil Dog..$15–25

Dial Telephone 1980
Fourth in a series of Beam telephone designs................................$40–50

Dodge City 1972
Issued to honor the centennial of Dodge City $5–6

Doe 1963
Regal China, 13½ in. $10–12

Doe—Reissued 1967 ....$10–12

Dog 1959
Regal China, 15¼ in. $20–25

Don Giovanni 1980
The fifth in the opera series $140–180

Donkey and Elephant Ashtrays 1956
Regal China, 12 in. (pair)..$12–16

Donkey and Elephant Boxers 1964 (pair) $14–18

Donkey and Elephant Clowns 1968
Regal China, 12 in. (pair)...$4–7

Donkey and Elephant Football Election Bottles 1972
Regal China, 9½ in. (pair)..$6–9

Donkey New York City 1976
Commemorates the National Democratic Convention in New York
City..$10–12

Duck 1957
Regal China, 14¼ in. $15–20

Ducks and Geese 1955 ....$5–8

Ducks Unlimited Mallard 1974..$40–50

Ducks Unlimited Wood Duck 1975 ....$45–50

Ducks Unlimited 40th Mallard Hen 1977 ....$40–50

Ducks Unlimited Canvasback Drake 1979 ....$30–40

Ducks Unlimited Blue-winged Teal 1980
The sixth in a series, 9½ in. $40–45

Ducks Unlimited Green-winged Teal 1981.................................$35–45

Ducks Unlimited Wood Ducks 1982...$35–45

Ducks Unlimited American Wigeon PR 1983 ....$35–45

Ducks Unlimited Mallard 1984...$55–75

Ducks Unlimited Pintail Pr 1985...$30–40

Ducks Unlimited Redhead 1986 ....$15–25

Ducks Unlimited Blue Bill 1987 ....$40–60

Ducks Unlimited Black Duck 1989 ....$50–60

Eagle 1966
Regal China, 12½ in. $10–13

Eldorado 1978...$7–9

Election, Democrat 1988...$30–40

Election, Republican 1988 ....$30–40

Elephant and Donkey Supermen 1980 (set of two) $10–14

Elephant Kansas City 1976
Commemorates the National Republican Convention in New York
City $8–10

Elks $4–7

Elks National Foundation $8–12

Emerald Crystal Bourbon 1968
Green glass, 11½ in. $3–5

Emmett Kelly 1973
Likeness of Emmett Kelly as sad-faced Willie the Clown $18–22

Emmett Kelly, Native Son $50–60

Ernie's Flower Cart 1976
In honor of Ernie's Wines and Liquors of Northern Calif............$24–28

Evergreen, Club Bottle $7–10

Expo 1974
Issued in honor of the World's Fair held in Spokane, Wash...........$5–7

Falstaff 1979
Second in Australian Opera series, limited edition of 1,000
bottles $150–160

Fantasia Bottle 1971 ....$5–6

Fathers Day Card $15–25

Female Cardinal 1973 ....$8–12

Fiesta Bowl, Glass $8–12

Fiesta Bowl 1973
The second bottle created for the Fiesta Bowl $9–11

Figaro 1977
Character Figaro from the opera *Barber of Seville* $140–170

Fighting Bull $12–18

Fiji Islands $4–6

First National Bank of Chicago 1964
Commemorates the 100th anniversary of the First National Bank of Chicago. Approximately 130 were issued, with 117 being given as mementos to the bank directors with none for public distribution. This is the most valuable Beam Bottle known. Also, beware of reproductions...$1900–2400

Fish 1957
Regal China, 14 in. $15–18

Fish Hall of Fame..$25–35

Five Seasons 1980
Club bottle for the Five Seasons Club of Cedar Rapids honors the State of Iowa $10–12

Fleet Reserve Association 1974
Issued by the Fleet Reserve Association to honor the Career Sea Service on their 50th anniversary...$5–7

Florida Shell 1968
Regal China, 9 in. $4–6

Floro de Oro 1976 ....$10–12

Flower Basket 1962
Regal China, 12¼ in. $30–35

Football Hall of Fame 1972
Reproduction of the New Professional Football Hall of Fame Building $14–18

Foremost—Black and Gold 1956
First Beam bottle issued for a liquor retailer, Foremost Liquor Store of Chicago $225–250

Foremost—Speckled Beauty 1956
The most valuable of the Foremost bottles $500–600

Fox 1967, Blue Coat $65–80

Fox 1971, Gold Coat $35–50

Fox, Green Coat $12–18

Fox, White Coat $20–30

Fox, on a Dolphin $12–15

Fox, Uncle Sam..$5–6

Fox, Kansas City, Blue, Miniature................................$20–30

Fox, Red Distillery $1100–1300

Franklin Mint..$4–7

French Cradle Telephone 1979
Third in the Telephone Pioneers of America series......................$20–22

Galah Bird 1979 ....$14–16

Gem City, Club Bottle $35–45

George Washington Commemorative Plate 1976
Commemorates the U.S. Bicentennial, 9½ in. $12–15

German Bottle—Weisbaden 1973 ....$4–6

German Stein $20–30

Germany 1970
Issued to honor the American Armed Forces in Germany $4–6

Glen Campbell 51st 1976
Honors the 51st Los Angeles Open at the Riviera Country Club in
February 1976...$7–10

Golden Chalice 1961..$40–50

Golden Jubilee 1977
Executive Series $8–12

Golden Nugget 1969
Regal China, 12½ in. $35–45

Golden Rose 1978 ....$15–20

Grand Canyon 1969
Honors the Grand Canyon National Park 50th anniversary $7–9

Grant Locomotive 1979 ....$55–65

Gray Cherub 1958
Regal China, 12 in. $240–260

Great Chicago Fire Bottle 1971
Commemorates the great Chicago fire of 1871 and to salute Mercy
Hospital, which helped the fire victims..$18–22

Great Dane 1976 ....$7–9

Green China Jug 1965
Regal Glass, 12½ in. $4–6

Hank Williams, Jr....$40–50

Hannah Dustin 1973
Regal China, 14½ in. $10–12

Hansel and Gretel Bottle 1971...$44–50

Harley Davidson 85th Anniversary Decanter $175–200

Harley Davidson 85th Anniversary Stein..............................$180–220

Harolds Club—Man-in-a-Barrel 1957
First in a series made for Harolds Club in Reno, Nevada........$380–410

Harolds Club—Silver Opal 1957
Commemorates the 25th anniversary of Harolds Club $20–22

Harolds Club—Man-in-a-Barrel 1958.....................................$140–160

Harolds Club—Nevada (Gray) 1963
Created for the "Nevada Centennial—1864–1964 as a state" bottle.
This is a rare and valuable bottle $90–110

Harolds Club—Nevada (Silver) 1964 ....$90–110

Harolds Club—Pinwheel 1965...$40–45

Harolds Club—Blue Slot Machine 1967 ....$10–14

Harolds Club—VIP Executive 1967
Limited quantity issued...$50–60

Harolds Club—VIP Executive 1968...$55–65

Harolds Club—Gray Slot Machine 1968....................................$4–6

Harolds Club—VIP Executive 1969
This bottle was used as a Christmas gift to the casino's
executives...$260–285

Harolds Club—Covered Wagon 1969–1970 ....$4–6

Harolds Club 1970 ....$40–60

Harolds Club 1971 ....$40–60

Harolds Club 1972 ....$18–25

Harolds Club 1973 ....$18–24

Harolds Club 1974 ....$12–16

Harolds Club 1975 ....$12–18

Harolds Club VIP 1976 ....$18–22

Harolds Club 1977 ....$20–30

Harolds Club 1978 ....$20–30

Harolds Club 1979 ....$20–30

Harolds Club 1980 ....$25–35

Harolds Club 1982 ....$110–145

Harp Seal $12–18

Harrahs Club Nevada—Gray 1963
This is the same bottle used for the Nevada Centennial and Harolds
Club...$500–550

Harry Hoffman $4–7

Harveys Resort Hotel at Lake Tahoe..$6–10

Hatfield 1973
The character of Hatfield from the story of the Hatfield and McCoy
feud...$15–20

Hawaii 1959
Tribute to the 50th state..$35–40

Hawaii—Reissued 1967...$40–45

Hawaii 1971 ....$6–8

Hawaii Aloha 1971 ....$6–10

Hawaiian Open Bottle 1972
Honors the 1972 Hawaiian Open Golf Tournament.........................$6–8

Hawaiian Open 1973
Second bottle created in honor of the United Hawaiian Open Golf
Classic...$7–9

Hawaiian Open 1974
Commemorates the 1974 Hawaiian Open Golf Classic....................$5–8

Hawaiian Open Outrigger 1975 ....$9–11

Hawaiian Paradise 1978
Commemorates the 200th anniversary of the landing of Captain
Cook...$15–17

Hemisfair 1968
Commemorates the "Hemisfair 68–San Antonio" $8–10

Herre Brothers $22–35

Hobo, Australia..$10–14

Hoffman 1969 ....$4–7

Holiday-Carolers $40–50

Holiday-Nutcracker $40–50

Home Builders 1978
Commemorates the 1979 convention of the Home Builders $25–30

Hone Heke...$200–250

Honga Hika 1980
First in a series of Maori warrior bottles. Honga Hika was a war-chief
of the Ngapuke tribe...$220–240

Horse (Appaloosa) $8–12

Horse (Black) $18–22

Horse (Black) reissued 1967 ....$10–12

Horse (Brown)...$18–22

Horse (Brown) reissued 1967 ....$10–12

Horse (Mare and Foal)..$35–45

Horse (Oh Kentucky)...$70–85

Horse (Pewter)..$12–17

Horse (White)...$18–20

Horse (White) reissued 1967...$12–17

Horseshoe Club 1969..$4–6

Hula Bowl 1975...$8–10

Hyatt House—Chicago..$7–10

Hyatt House—New Orleans..$8–11

Idaho 1963...$30–40

Illinois 1968
Honors the Sesquicentennial 1818–1968 of Illinois.........................$4–6

Indianapolis Sesquicentennial...$4–6

Indianapolis 500...$9–12

Indian Chief 1979...$9–12

International Chili Society 1976...$9–12

Italian Marble Urn 1985
Executive series...$12–17

Ivory Ashtray 1955...$8–10

Jackalope 1971
Honors the Wyoming Jackalope...$5–8

Jaguar..$18–23

Jewel T Man—50th Anniversary..$35–45

John Henry 1972
Commemorates the legendary Steel Drivin' Man.............................$18–22

Joliet Legion Band 1978
Commemorates the 26th national championships.............................$15–20

Kaiser International Open Bottle 1971
Commemorates the 5th Annual Kaiser International Open Golf
Tournament $5–6

Kangaroo 1977 ....$10–14

Kansas 1960
Commemorates the "Kansas 1861–1961 Centennial"...................$35–45

Kentucky Black Head—Brown Head 1967
    Black Head..$12–18
    Brown Head...$20–28
    White Head $18–23

Kentucky Derby 95th, Pink, Red Roses 1969 ....$4–7

Kentucky Derby 96th, Double Rose 1970 ....$15–25

Kentucky Derby 97th 1971 ....$4–7

Kentucky Derby 98th 1972 ....$4–6

Kentucky Derby 100th 1974 ....$7–10

Key West 1972
Honors the 150th anniversary of Key West, Florida........................$5–7

King Kamehameha 1972
Commemorates the 100th anniversary of King Kamehameha
Day $8–11

King Kong 1976
Commemorates Paramount's movie release in December 1976 ......$8–10

Kiwi 1974...$5–8

Koala Bear 1973 ....$12–14

Laramie 1968
Commemorates the "Centennial Jubilee Laramie Wyo.
1868–1968"...$4–6

Largemouth Bass Trophy Bottle 1973
Honors the National Fresh Water Fishing Hall of Fame $10–14

Las Vegas 1969
Bottle used for Customer Specials, casino series.........................$4–6

Light Bulb 1979
Honors Thomas Edison..$14–16

Lombard 1969
Commemorates "Village of Lombard, Illinois—1869 Centennial
1969"..$4–6

London Bridge...$4–7

Louisville Downs Racing Derby 1978..$4–6

Louisiana Superdome..$8–11

LVNH Owl...$20–30

Madame Butterfly 1977
Figurine of Madame Butterfly, music box plays "One Fine Day"
from the opera $340–370

The Magpies 1977
Honors an Australian football team $18–20

Maine 1970 ....$4–6

Majestic 1966..$20–24

Male Cardinal...$18–24

Marbled Fantasy 1965...$38–42

Marina City 1962
Commemorates modern apartment complex in Chicago...............$10–15

Marine Corps $25–35

Mark Antony 1962 ....$18–20

Martha Washington 1976 ....$5–6

McCoy 1973
Character of McCoy from the story of the Hatfield and McCoy
feud..$14–17

McShane—Mother-of-Pearl 1979
Executive series $85–105

McShane—Titans 1980 ....$85–105

McShane—Cobalt 1981
Executive series $115–135

McShane—Green Pitcher 1982
Executive series $80–105

McShane—Green Bell 1983
Executive series $80–110

Mephistopheles 1979
Figurine depicts Mephistopheles from the opera *Faust*, music box
plays soldiers' chorus $160–190

Michigan Bottle 1972 ....$7–9

Milwaukee Stein $30–40

Minnesota Viking 1973 ....$9–12

Mint 400 1970 ....$80–105

Mint 400 1970
Commemorates the annual Del Webb Mint 400 ....$5–6

Mint 400 1971 ....$5–6

Mint 400 1972
Commemorates the 5th annual Del Webb Mint 400 ....$5–7

Mint 400 1973
Commemorates the 6th annual Del Webb Mint 400 ....$6–8

Mint 400 1974 ....$4–7

Mint 400 7th Annual 1976 ....$9–12

Mississippi Fire Engine 1978 ....$120–130

Model A Ford 1903 (1978) $38–42

Model A Ford 1928 (1980) $65–75

Montana 1963
Tribute to "Montana, 1864 Golden Years Centennial 1964" $50–60

Monterey Bay Club 1977
Honors the Monterey Bay Beam Bottle and Specialty Club $9–12

Mortimer Snerd 1976...$24–28

Mother-of-Pearl 1979..$10–12

Mount St. Helens 1980
Depicts the eruption of Mount St. Helens...................................$20–22

Mr. Goodwrench 1978..$24–28

Musicians on a Wine Cask 1964...$4–6

Muskie 1971
Honors the National Fresh Water Fishing Hall of Fame...............$14–18

National Tobacco Festival 1973
Commemorates the 25th anniversary of the National Tobacco
Festival...$7–8

Nebraska 1967..$7–9

Nebraska Football 1972
Commemorates the University of Nebraska's national championship
football team of 1970–1971...$5–8

Nevada 1963...$34–38

New Hampshire 1967...$4–8

New Hampshire Eagle Bottle 1971..$18–23

New Jersey 1963..$40–50

New Jersey Yellow 1963..$40–50

New Mexico Bicentennial 1976..$8–12

New Mexico Statehood 1972
Commemorates New Mexico's 60 years of statehood...................$7–9

New York World's Fair 1964...$5–6

North Dakota—1965..$45–55

Northern Pike 1977
The sixth in a series designed for the National Fresh Water Fishing
Hall of Fame...$14–18

Nutcracker Toy Soldier 1978..$90–120

Ohio 1966 ....$5–6

Ohio State Fair 1973
In honor of the 120th Ohio State Fair..............................$5–6

Olympian 1960 ....$2–4

One Hundred First Airborne Division 1977
Honors the division known as the Screaming Eagles......................$8–10

Opaline Crystal 1969 ....$4–6

Oregon 1959
Honors the centennial of the state....................................$20–25

Oregon Liquor Commission $25–35

Osco Drugs...$12–17

Panda 1980..$20–22

Paul Bunyan $4–7

Pearl Harbor Memorial 1972
Honoring the Pearl Harbor Survivors Association......................$14–18

Pearl Harbor Survivors Association 1976 ....$5–7

Pennsylvania 1967..$4–6

Pennsylvania Dutch, Club Bottle $8–12

Permian Basin Oil Show 1972
Commemorates the Permian Basin Oil Show in Odessa, Texas........$4–6

Petroleum Man...$4–7

Pheasant 1960...$14–18

Pheasant 1961 reissued; also '63, '66, '67, '68............................$8–11

Phi Sigma Kappa (Centennial Series) 1973
Commemorates the 100th anniversary of this fraternity..................$3–4

Phoenician 1973 ....$6–9

Pied Piper of Hamlin 1974...$3–6

Ponderosa 1969
A replica of the Cartwrights of "Bonanza" TV fame..........................$4–6

Ponderosa Ranch Tourist 1972
Commemorates the one millionth tourist to the Ponderosa
Ranch...$14–16

Pony Express 1968...$9–12

Poodle—Gray and White 1970...$5–6

Portland Rose Festival 1972
Commemorates the 64th Portland, Oregon Rose Festival.................$5–8

Portola Trek 1969
Bottle was issued to celebrate the 200th anniversary of San
Diego..$3–6

Poulan Chain Saw 1979..$24–28

Powell Expedition 1969
Depicts John Wesley Powell's survey of the Colorado River.............$3–5

Preakness 1970
Issued to honor the 100th anniversary of the running of the
Preakness...$5–6

Preakness Pimlico 1975...$4–7

Presidential 1968
Executive series...$4–7

Prestige 1967
Executive series...$4–7

Pretty Perch 1980
8th in a series, this fish is used as the official seal of the National
Fresh Water Fishing Hall of Fame..$13–16

Prima Donna 1969...$4–6

Professional Golf Association...$4–7

Queensland 1978..$20–22

Rabbit...$4–7

Rainbow Trout 1975
Produced for the National Fresh Water Fishing Hall of Fame $12–15

Ralph Centennial 1973
Commemorates the 100th anniversary of the Ralph Grocery
Company $10–14

Ralphs Market...$8–12

Ram 1958 ....$40–55

Ramada Inn 1976 ....$10–12

Red Mile Racetrack..$8–12

Redwood 1967 ....$6–8

Reflections 1975
Executive series $8–12

Regency 1972...$7–9

Reidsville 1973
Issued to honor Reidsville, North Carolina on its centennial $5–6

Renee the Fox 1974
Represents the companion for the International Association of Jim
Beam Bottle and Specialties Club's mascot..$7–9

Rennie the Runner 1974...$9–12

Rennie the Surfer 1975...$9–12

Reno 1968
Commemorates "100 Years—Reno" $4–6

Republic of Texas 1980 ....$12–20

Republican Convention 1972 ....$500–700

Republican Football 1972..$350–450

Richard Hadlee..$110–135

Richards—New Mexico 1967
Created for Richards Distributing Co. of Albuquerque, New
Mexico $8–10

Robin 1969...$5–6

Rocky Marciano 1973..$14–16

Rocky Mountain, Club Bottle..$10–15

Royal Crystal 1959...$3–6

Royal Di Monte 1957...$45–55

Royal Emperor 1958 ....$3–6

Royal Gold Diamond 1964..$30–35

Royal Gold Round 1956 ....$80–90

Royal Opal 1957...$5–7

Royal Porcelain 1955 ....$380–420

Royal Rose 1963..$30–35

Ruby Crystal 1967..$6–9

Ruidoso Downs 1968
Pointed ears..$24–26
Flat ears..$4–6

Sahara Invitational Bottle 1971
Introduced in honor of the Del Webb 1971 Sahara Invitational Pro-
Am Golf Tournament...$6–8

San Bear—Donkey 1973
Political series...$1500–2000

Samoa..$4–7

San Diego 1968
Issued by the Beam Co. for the 200th anniversary of its founding in
1769 ....$4–6

San Diego—Elephant 1972...$15–25

Santa Fe 1960..$120–140

SCCA, Etched $15–25

SCCA, Smoothed $12–18

Screech Owl 1979..$18–22

Seafair Trophy Race 1972
Commemorates the Seattle Seafair Trophy Race..............................$5–6

Seattle World's Fair 1962...$10–12

Seoul—Korea 1988..$60–75

Sheraton Inn...$4–6

Short Dancing Scot 1963...$50–65

Short-timer 1975...$15–20

Shriners 1975...$10–12

Shriners—Indiana...$4–7

Shriners Pyramid 1975
Issued by the El Kahir Temple of Cedar Rapids, Iowa.................$10–12

Shriners Rajah 1977...$24–28

Shriners Temple 1972..$20–25

Shriners Western Association...$15–25

Sierra Eagle...$15–22

Sigma Nu Fraternity 1977..$9–12

Sigma Nu Fraternity—Kentucky...$8–12

Sigma Nu Fraternity—Michigan..$18–23

Smiths North Shore Club 1972
Commemorating Smith's North Shore Club, at Crystal Bay, Lake
Tahoe...$10–12

Smoked Crystal 1964..$6–9

Snow Goose 1979...$8–10

Snowman...$125–175

South Carolina 1970
In honor of celebrating its tricentennial 1670–1970.........................$4–6

South Dakota—Mount Rushmore 1969.....................................$4–6

South Florida—Fox on Dolphin 1980
Bottled sponsored by the South Florida Beam Bottle and Specialties
Club...$14–16

Sovereign 1969
Executive series $4–7

Spengers Fish Grotto 1977...$18–22

Sports Car Club of America...$5–7

Statue of Liberty 1975 ....$8–12

Statue of Liberty 1985 ....$18–20

St. Bernard 1979..$30–35

St. Louis, Club Bottle $10–15

St. Louis Arch 1964 ....$10–12

St. Louis Arch—Reissue 1967.......................................$16–18

St. Louis Statue 1972..$8–10

Sturgeon 1980
Exclusive issue for a group that advocates the preservation of
sturgeons...$14–17

Stutz Bearcat 1914, 1977...$45–55

Submarine—Diamond Jubilee.......................................$35–45

Submarine Redfin 1970
Issued for Manitowoc Submarine Memorial Association $5–7

Superdome 1975
Replica of the Louisiana Superdome...$5–8

Swagman 1979
Replica of an Australian hobo called a swagman who roamed that
country looking for work during the depression $10–12

Sydney Opera House 1977 ....$9–12

Tall Dancing Scot 1964 ....$9–12

Tavern Scene 1959...$45–55

Telephone No. 1 1975
Replica of a 1907 phone of the Magneto wall type......................$25–30

Telephone No. 2 1976
Replica of an 1897 desk set...$30–40

Telephone No. 3 1977
Replica of a 1920 cradle phone...$15–20

Telephone No. 4 1978
Replica of a 1919 dial phone $40–50

Telephone No. 5 1979
Replica of a pay phone $25–35

Telephone No. 6 1980
Replica of a battery phone...$20–30

Telephone No. 7 1981
Replica of a digital dial phone..$35–45

Ten-pin 1980...$8–11

Texas Hemisfair $7–11

Texas Rose 1978
Executive series $14–18

Thailand 1969..$4–6

Thomas Flyer 1907, 1976B $60–70

Tiffany Poodle 1973
Created in honor of Tiffany, the poodle mascot of the National
Association of the Jim Beam Bottle and Specialties Clubs $20–22

Tiger—Australian..$14–18

The Tigers 1977
Issued in honor of an Australian football team.............................$20–24

Titian 1980..$9–12

Tobacco Festival $8–12

Tombstone $4–7

Travelodge Bear $4–7

Treasure Chest 1979..$8–12

Trout Unlimited 1977
To honor the Trout Unlimited Conservation Organization...........$14–18

Truth or Consequences Fiesta 1974
Issued in honor of Ralph Edwards radio and television show $14–18

Turquoise China Jug 1966 ....$4–6

Twin Bridges Bottle 1971
Commemorates the largest twin bridge between Delaware and New
Jersey $40–42

Twin Cherubs 1974
Executive series $8–12

Twin Doves 1987
Executive series $18–23

US Open 1972
Honors the US Open Golf Tourney at Pebble Beach, Calif............$9–12

Vendome Drummers Wagon 1975
Honored the Vendomes of Beverly Hills, Calif..............................$60–70

VFW Bottle 1971
Commemorates the 50th anniversary of the Department of Indiana
VFW $5–6

Viking 1973...$9–12

Volkswagen Commemorative Bottle—Two Colors 1977
Commemorates the Volkswagen Beetle..$40–50

Vons Market...$28–35

Walleye Pike 1977
Designed for the National Fresh Water Fishing Hall of Fame......$12–15

Walleye Pike 1987..$17–23

Washington 1975
A state series bottle to commemorate the Evergreen State...............$5–6

Washington—the Evergreen State 1974
The club bottle for the Evergreen State Beam Bottle and Specialties
Club..$10–12

Washington State Bicentennial 1976...$10–12

Waterman 1980 ....$100–130

Western Shrine Association 1980
Commemorates the Shriners convention in Phoenix, Arizona $20–22

West Virginia 1963 ....$130–140

White Fox 1969
Issued for the 2nd anniversary of the Jim Beam Bottle and
Specialties Club in Berkeley, Calif.................................$25–35

Wisconsin Muskie Bottle 1971 ....$15–17

Woodpecker 1969..$6–8

Wyoming 1965..$40–50

Yellow Katz 1967
Commemorates the 50th anniversay of the Katz Department
Stores...$15–17

Yellow Rose 1978
Executive series $7–10

Yellowstone Park Centennial.....................................$4–7

Yosemite 1967..$4–6

Yuma Rifle Club $18–23

Zimmerman—Art Institute $5–8

Zimmerman Bell 1976
Designed for Zimmerman Liquor Store of Chicago.........$6–7

Zimmerman Bell 1976..$6–7

Zimmerman—Blue Beauty 1969.................................$9–12

Zimmerman—Blue Daisy $4–6

Zimmerman Cherubs 1968..$4–6

Zimmerman—Chicago $4–6

Zimmerman—Elforado $4–7

Zimmerman—Glass 1969...$7–9

Zimmerman Oatmeal Jug $40–50

Zimmerman—The Peddler Bottle 1971 ....$4–6

Zimmerman Two-Handled Jug 1965 ....$45–60

Zimmerman Vase, Brown...$6–9

Zimmerman Vase, Green $6–9

Zimmerman—50th Anniversary $35–45

Automobile and Transportation Series

Chevrolet
1957 Convertible, Black, New..$85–95

1957 Convertible, Red, New $75–85

1957, Black...$70–80

1957, Dark Blue, PA $70–80

1957, Red $80–90

1957, Sierra Gold $140–160

1957, Turquoise..$50–70

1957, Yellow Hot Rod..$65–75

Camaro 1969, Blue...$55–65

Camaro 1969, Burgundy $120–140

Camaro 1969, Green $100–120

Camaro 1969, Orange $55–65

Camaro 1969, Pace Car $60–70

Camaro 1969, Silver...$120–140

Camaro 1969, Yellow, PA...$55–65

Corvette 1986, Pace Car, Yellow, New $60–85

Corvette 1984, Black...$70–80

Corvette 1984, Bronze $100–200

Corvette 1984, Gold..$100–120

Corvette 1984, Red $55–65

Corvette 1984, White..$55–65

Corvette 1978, Black...$140–170

Corvette 1978, Pace Car...$135–160

Corvette 1978, Red $50–60

Corvette 1978, White...$40–50

Corvette 1978, Yellow..$40–50

Corvette 1963, Black, PA...$75–85

Corvette 1963, Blue, NY..$90–100

Corvette 1963, Red $60–70

Corvette 1963, Silver $50–60

Corvette 1955, Black, New..$110–140

Corvette 1955, Copper, New $90–100

Corvette 1955, Red, New $110–140

Corvette 1954, Blue, New $90–100

Corvette 1953, White, New..$100–120

Dusenburg
Convertible, Cream $130–140

Convertible, Dark Blue $120–130

Convertible, Light Blue..$80–100

Convertible Coupe, Gray $160–180

Ford
International Delivery Wagon, Black...$80–90

International Delivery Wagon, Green..$80–90

Fire Chief 1928 ....$120–130

Fire Chief 1934 ....$60–70

Fire Pumper Truck 1935 ....$45–60

Model A, Angelos Liquor...$180–200

Model A, Parkwood Supply..$140–170

Model A 1903, Black..$35–45

Model A 1903, Red $35–45

Model A 1928 ....$60–80

Model A Fire Truck 1930..$130–170

Model T 1913, Black..$30–40

Model T 1913, Green...$30–40

Mustang 1964, Black...$100–125

Mustang 1964, Red...$35–45

Mustang 1964, White..$25–35

Paddy Wagon 1930 ....$100–120

Phaeton 1929 ....$40–50

Pickup Truck 1935..$20–30

Police Car 1929, Blue $75–85

Police Car 1929, Yellow $350–450

Police Patrol Car 1934...$60–70

Police Tow Truck 1935..$20–30

Roadster 1934, Cream, PA, New $80–90

Thunderbird 1956, Black..$60–70

Thunderbird 1956, Blue, PA $70–80

Thunderbird 1956, Gray $50–60

Thunderbird 1956, Green $60–70

Thunderbird 1956, Yellow $50–60

Woodie Wagon 1929 ....$50–60

Mercedes
1974, Blue $30–40

1974, Gold $60–80

1974, Green $30–40

1974, Mocha $30–40

1974, Red $30–40

1974, Sand Beige, PA $30–40

1974, Silver, Australia $140–160

1974, White $35–45

Trains
Baggage Car $40–60

Box Car, Brown $50–60

Box Car, Yellow $40–50

Bumper $5–8

Caboose, Gray $45–55

Caboose, Red $50–60

Casey Jones with Tender $65–80

Casey Jones Caboose $40–55

Casey Jones Accessory Set $50–60

Coal Tender, No Bottle $20–30

Combination Car $55–65

Dining Car...$75–90

Flat Car $20–30

General Locomotive...$60–70

Grant Locomotive $50–65

Log Car..$40–55

Lumber Car...$12–18

Observation Car..$15–23

Passenger Car...$45–53

Tank Car $15–20

Track...$4–6

Turner Locomotive $80–100

Watertower...$20–30

Wood Tender $40–45

Wood Tender, No Bottle $20–25

Other

Ambulance..$18–22

Army Jeep...$18–20

Bass Boat $12–18

Cable Car $25–35

Circus Wagon $20–30

Ernie's Flower Cart $20–30

Golf Cart $20–30

HC Covered Wagon 1929..$10–20

Jewel Tea...$70–80

Mack Fire Truck 1917 ....$120–135

Mississippi Pumper Firetruck 1867..$115–140

Bischoff Bottles

Bischoffs, which was founded in Trieste, Italy, in 1777, issued decorative figurals in the eighteenth century, long before any other company. The early bottles are rare because of the limited production and the attrition of extent bottles over the years. Modern-day Bischoffs were imported into the United States beginning in 1949. Collectors haven't shown intense interest in modern imports and since sales have not been made often enough to have establish values, prices are not included in this book. Three other types of Bischoffs will be covered: Kord Bohemian decanters, Venetian glass figurals, and ceramic decanters and figurals.

Kord Bohemian Decanters

These decanters were hand-blown and hand-painted glass bottles created in Czechoslovakia by the Kord Company, with a tradition of Bohemian cut, engraved, etched, and flashed glass. Stoppers and labels with the bottles are considered very rare and valuable today. The cut-glass and ruby-etched decanters were imported to the United States in the early 1950s. The ruby-etched is considered rare only if complete with the stopper.

In addition, most of these decanters have a matching set of glasses, which increases the value if the entire set is intact.

Amber Flowers 1952
A two-toned glass decanter, 15½ in., Dark Amber stopper $30–40

Amber Leaves 1952
Multi-toned bottle with long neck, 13½ in. $30–40

Anisette 1948–1951
Clear glass bottle with ground glass stopper, 11 in. $20–30

Bohemian Ruby-Etched 1949–1951
Round decanter, tapered neck, etched stopper, 15½ in. $30–40

Coronet Crystal 1952
A round tall bottle, multi-toned with a broad band of flowers, leaves, and scrolls circle, 14 in. $30–40

Cut Glass Decanter (Blackberry) 1951
A geometric design, handcut overall, ground stopper, 10½ in.
....$32–42

Czech Hunter 1958
Round thick clear glass, heavy round glass base, 8½ in. $18–26

Czech Hunter's Lady 1958
"Mae West" shaped decanter of cracked clear glass, 10 in. $18–26

Dancing—Country Scene 1950
Clear glass handblown decanter with peasant boy and girl doing a country dance beside a tree, 12¼ in. $25–35

Dancing—Peasant Scene 1950
Decanter is of pale and amber glass, peasants in costume dancing to music of bagpipes, 12 in. $25–35

Double-Dolphin 1949–1969
Fish-shaped twin bottles joined at the bellies, handblown clear glass $20–30

Flying Geese Pitcher 1952
Green glass handle and stopper, glass base, 9½ in. $15–25

Flying Geese Pitcher 1957
Clear-crystal-handled pitcher, gold stopper, 9½ in. $15–25

Horse Head 1947–1969
Pale amber-colored bottle in the shape of a horse's head, round pouring spout on top, 8 in. $15–25

Jungle Parrot—Amber Glass 1952
Hand-etched jungle scenes with a yellow amber color, 15½ in. $25–35

Jungle Parrot—Ruby Glass 1952
Hand-etched jungle scenes with a ruby-colored body, 15½ in. $20–30

Old Coach Bottle 1948
Pale amber color, round glass stopper, 10 in. $25–35

Old Sleigh Bottle 1949
Glass decanter, handpainted, signed, 10 in. $22–32

Wild Geese—Amber Glass 1952
Tall round decanter with tapering etched neck, flashed with a yellow
amber color, 15½ in. $25–35

Wild Geese—Ruby Glass 1952
Tall round decanter with tapering etched neck, flashed with Ruby
Red Color, 15½ in. $25–35

Venetian Glass Figurals

These figurals are produced in limited editions by the Serguso Glass
Company in Morano, Italy, and are unique in design and color with
birds, fish, cats, and dogs.

Black Cat 1969
Glass black cat with curled tail, 12 in. long..................................$18–25

Dog—Alabaster 1966
Seated alabaster glass dog, 13 in. long...$33–45

Dog—Dachschund 1966
Alabaster long dog with brown tones, 19 in. long $40–50

Duck 1964
Alabaster glass tinted pink and green, long neck, upraised wings, 11
in. long..$42–52

Fish—Multicolor 1964
Round fat fish, alabaster glass. Green, rose, yellow $18–25

Fish—Ruby 1969
Long, flat, ruby glass fish, 12 in. long $25–35

Ceramic Decanters and Figurals

These are some of the most interesting, attractive, and valuable of the Bischoff collection and are made of ceramic, stoneware, and pottery. Decanters complete with handles, spouts, and stoppers command the highest value.

African Head 1962...$15–18

Alpine Pitcher 1969 ....$25–30

Amber Flower 1952...$30–35

Amber Leaf 1952 ....$30–35

Amphora, 2 Handles 1950...$20–25

Ashtray, Green Striped 1958..$10–15

Bell House 1960 ....$30–40

Bell Tower 1960 ....$15–30

Boy (Chinese) Figural 1962 ....$30–40

Boy (Spanish) Figural 1961..$25–35

Candlestick 1958..$20–25

Candlestick, Clown 1963..$8–10

Cat, Black 1969 ....$20–25

Clown with Black Hair 1963...$30–40

Clown with Red Hair 1963 ....$15–25

Chariot Urn 1966 (2 Sections) $20–25

Christmas Tree 1957...$50–55

Deer Figural 1969 ....$20–25

Egyptian Dancing Figural 1961..$12–17

Egyptian Pitcher—2 Musicians 1969...$15–24

Borghini Bottles

Borghini bottles, ceramics of modernistic style with historical themes, are manufactured in Pisa, Italy. These bottles vary greatly in price depending on distribution points. The lowest values are in areas closest to the point of distribution or near heavy retail sales. Recent bottles are stamped "Borghini Collection Made in Italy."

Cats
Black with red ties, 6 in. $11–15

Cats
Black with red ties, 12 in. $10–15

Female head
Ceramic, 9½ in. $11–15

Penguin
Black and white, 6 in. $8–11

Penguin 1969
Black and white, 12 in. $12–16

Ezra Brooks Bottles

The Ezra Brooks Distilling Company did not start to issue figurals until 1964, ten years after the Jim Beam company, and quickly became a strong rival owing to effective distribution, promotion techniques, original designs, and choice of subjects.

While many of the Brooks bottles depict the same themes as the Jim Beam series (sports and transportation), they also produced bottles based on original subjects. The Maine lobster looks good enough to put on anyone's dinner table. The most popular series depict antiques such as an Edison phonograph and a Spanish cannon. Yearly new editions highlight American historical events and anniversaries. One of my favorites is the Bucket of Blood (1970)—from the Virginia City, Nevada, saloon by the same name—in a bucket-shaped bottle.

While these bottles are still filled with Kentucky bourbon, most purchases of these figural bottles are made by collectors.

Alabama Bicentennial 1976 ....$12–14

American Legion 1971
Distinguished embossed star emblem from World War I $20–30

American Legion 1972
Salutes Illinois American Legion 54th National Convention $45–55

American Legion 1973
Salutes Hawaii, which hosted the American Legion's 54th National
Convention $10–12

American Legion—Denver 1977 ....$19–22

American Legion—Miami Beach 1973..$8–12

Amvets—Dolphin 1974..$8–10

Amvets—Polish Legion 1973..$14–18

Antique Cannon 1969..$6–9

Antique Phonograph 1970..$8–12

Arizona 1969
Man with burro in search of Lost Dutchman Mine........................$4–8

Auburn 1932 Classic Car 1978..$18–20

Badger No. 1 Boxer 1973..$9–11

Badger No. 2 Football 1974..$10–14

Badger No. 3 Hockey 1974..$9–12

Baltimore Oriole Wildlife 1979..$20–30

Bare Knucklefighter 1971..$5–7

Baseball Hall of Fame 1973..$20–22

Baseball Player 1974..$14–16

Bear 1968..$5–9

Beaver 1973..$10–15

Bengal Tiger Wildlife 1979..$20–30

Betsy Ross 1975..$8–12

Bicycle, Penny-Farthington 1973..$10–15

Big Bertha
Nugget Casino's very own elephant with a raised trunk..............$10–13

Big Daddy Lounge 1969
Salute to South Florida's state liquor chain and Big Daddy
Lounges..$4–6

Bighorn Ram 1973..$14–18

Bird Dog 1971..$12–14

Bordertown
Salutes Borderline Club on border of California and Nevada.........$5–10

Bowler 1973 ....$4–6

Bowling Tenpins 1973 ....$9–12

Brahma Bull 1972...$10–12

Bucket of Blood 1970
Salutes the famous Virginia City, Nevada saloon. Bucket-shaped
bottle...$5–7

Bucking Bronco, Rough Rider 1973 ....$7–9

Bucky Badger, Football $20–25

Bucky Badger, Hockey 1975..$18–24

Bucky Badger, No. 1 Boxer 1973 ....$9–12

Buffalo Hunt 1971 ....$5–7

Bulldog 1972
Mighty canine mascot and football symbol $10–14

Bull Moose 1973..$12–15

Busy Beaver..$4–7

Cabin Still $20–35

Cable Car 1968..$5–6

California Quail 1970 ....$8–10

Canadian Honker 1975 ....$9–12

Canadian Loon Wildlife 1979 ....$25–35

Cardinal 1972 ....$20–25

Casey at Bat 1973 ....$6–10

Ceremonial Indian 1970 ....$15–18

CB Convoy Radio 1976 ....$5–9

Charolais Beef 1973 ....$10–14

Cheyenne Shoot-out 1970
Honoring the Wild West and its Cheyenne Frontier Days.............$6–10

Chicago Fire 1974...$20–30

Chicago Water Tower 1969..$8–12

Christmas Decanter 1966..$5–8

Christmas Tree 1979...$13–17

Churchill 1970
Commemorating "Iron Curtain" speech at Westminster College by
Churchill..$5–9

Cigar Store Indian 1968..$4–6

Classic Firearms 1969
Embossed gun set consisting of Derringer, Colt .45, Peacemaker, Over
and Under Flintlock, and Pepper Box....................................$15–19

Clowns, Imperial Shrine 1978.......................................$9–11

Clown Bust No. 1 Smiley 1979.....................................$22–28

Clown Bust No. 2 Cowboy 1979..................................$20–25

Clown Bust No. 3 Pagliacci 1979.................................$15–22

Clown Bust No. 4 Keystone Cop..................................$30–40

Clown Bust No. 5 Cuddles...$20–30

Clown Bust No. 6 Tramp..$20–30

Clown with Accordion 1971...$15–18

Clown with Balloon 1973...$20–32

Club Bottle, Birthday Cake...$9–12

Club Bottle, Distillery..$9–12

Club Bottle 1973
The third commemorative Ezra Brooks Collectors Club in the shape
of America...$14–18

Clydesdale Horse 1973...$8–12

Colt Peacemaker Flask 1969 ....$4–8

Conquistadors
Tribute to the great Drum and Bugle Corps $6–9

Conquistadors Drum and Bugle 1972 ....$12–15

Corvette Indy Pace Car 1978 ....$45–55

Corvette 1957 Classic 1976 ....$110–140

Court Jester $5–7

Dakota Cowboy 1975 ....$34–44

Dakota Cowgirl 1976 ....$20–26

Dakota Grain Elevator 1978 ....$20–30

Dakota Shotgun Express 1977 ....$18–22

Dead Wagon 1970
Made to carry gunfight loser to Boot Hill $5–7

Delta Belle 1969 ....$6–7

Democratic Convention 1976 ....$10–16

Derringer Flask 1969 ....$5–8

Dirt Bike, Riverboat 1869 ....$10–16

Distillery 1970
Reproduction of the Ezra Brooks Distillery in Kentucky $9–11

Duesenberg $24–33

Elephant 1973 ....$7–9

Elk
Salutes those organizations who practiced benevolence and
charity $20–28

English Setter—Bird Dog 1971 ....$14–17

Equestrienne 1974 ....$7–10

Esquire, Ceremonial Dancer $10–16

Farthington Bike 1972 ....$6–8

Golden Horseshoe 1970
Salute to Reno's Horseshoe Club $7–9

Golden Rooster No. 1
Replica of solid gold rooster on display at Nugget Casino in Reno,
Nevada $35–50

Gold Prospector 1969 ....$5–9

Gold Seal 1972 ....$12–14

Gold Turkey $35–45

Go Tiger Go 1973 ....$10–14

Grandfather Clock 1970 ....$5–7

Grandfather Clock 1970 ....$12–20

Greater Greensboro Open 1972 ....$16–19

Greater Greensboro Open 1972 ....$15–20

Greater Greensboro Open Golfer 1973 ....$17–24

Greater Greensboro Open Map 1974 ....$29–36

Greater Greensboro Open Cup 1975 ....$25–30

Greater Greensboro Open Club and Ball 1977 ....$20–25

Great Stone Face—Old Man of the Mountain 1970 ....$10–14

Great White Shark 1977 ....$8–14

Hambletonian 1971 ....$13–16

Happy Goose 1975 ....$12–15

Harolds Club Dice 1968 ....$8–12

Hereford 1971 ....$12–15

Hereford 1972 ....$12–15

Historical Flask Eagle 1970 ....$3–5

Historical Flask Flagship 1970 ....$3–5

Historical Flask Liberty 1970 ....$3–5

Katz Cats 1969
Siamese cats are symbolic of Katz Drug Co. of Kansas City,
Kansas $8–12

Katz Cats Philharmonic 1970
Commemorating its 27th annual Star Night....................................$6–10

Keystone Cop 1980 ....$32–40

Keystone Cops 1971 ....$25–35

Killer Whale 1972 ....$15–20

King of Clubs 1969..$4–6

King Salmon 1971 ....$18–24

Liberty Bell 1970..$5–6

Lincoln Continental Mark I 1941 ....$20–25

Lion on the Rock 1971 ....$5–7

Liquor Square 1972..$5–7

Little Giant 1971
Replica of the first horse-drawn steam engine to arrive at the Chicago
fire in 1871 ....$11–16

Maine Lighthouse 1971...$18–24

Maine Lobster 1970 ....$15–18

Man-o-War 1969 ....$10–16

M & M Brown Jug 1975b $15–20

Map, USA Club Bottle 1972..$7–9

Masonic Fez 1976..$12–15

Max, the Hat, Zimmerman 1976..$20–25

Military Tank 1971 ....$15–22

Minnesota Hockey Player 1975..$18–22

Minuteman 1975..$10–15

Missouri Mule, Brown 1972 .... $7–9

Moose 1973 .... $20–28

Motorcycle $10–14

Mountaineer 1971
One of the most valuable Ezra Brooks figural bottles $40–55

Mr. Foremost 1969 .... $7–10

Mr. Maine Potato 1973 .... $6–10

Mr. Merchant 1970 .... $6–10

Mule $8–12

Mustang Indy Pace Car 1979 .... $20–30

Nebraska—Go Big Red! $12–15

New Hampshire State House 1970 .... $9–13

North Carolina Bicentennial 1975 .... $8–12

Nugget Classic
Replica of golf pin presented to golf tournament participants $7–12

Oil Gusher $6–8

Old Captial 1971 .... $30–40

Old Ez No. 1 Barn Owl 1977 .... $25–35

Old Ez No. 2 Eagle Owl 1978 .... $40–55

Old Ez No. 3 Show Owl 1979 .... $20–35

Old Man of the Mountain 1970 .... $10–14

Old Water Tower 1969
Famous landmark, survived the Chicago fire of 1871 .... $12–16

Oliver Hardy Bust $12–18

Ontario 500 1970 .... $18–22

Overland Express 1969 .... $17–20

Over-Under Flintlock Flask 1969 .... $6–9

Panda—Giant 1972...$12–17

Penguin 1972 ....$8–10

Penny Farthington High-wheeler 1973.............................$9–12

Pepperbox Flask 1969..$4–6

Phoenix Bird 1971...$20–26

Phoenix Jaycees 1973..$10–14

Phonograph...$15–20

Piano 1970 ....$12–13

Pirate 1971 ....$6–10

Polish Legion American Vets 1978..................................$18–26

Portland Head Lighthouse 1971
Honors the lighthouse that has guided ships safely into Maine
Harbor since 1791..$18–24

Pot-bellied Stove 1968 ....$5–6

Queen of Hearts 1969
Playing card symbol with royal flush in hearts on front of the
bottle..$4–6

Raccoon Wildlife 1978...$30–40

Ram 1973 ....$13–18

Razorback Hog 1969 ....$12–18

Razorback Hog 1979 ....$20–30

Red Fox 1979...$30–40

Reno Arch 1968
Honoring the Biggest Little City in the World, Reno, Nevada $4–8

Sailfish 1971 ....$7–11

Salmon, Washington King 1971.......................................$20–26

San Francisco Cable Car 1968..$4–8

Sea Captain 1971 ....$10–14

Sea Lion—Gold 1972 ....$11–14

Senators of the US 1972
Honors the senators of the United States of America $10–13

Setter 1974 ....$10–15

Shrine King Tut Guard 1979 ....$16–24

1804 Silver Dollar 1970 ....$5–8

Silver Saddle 1973 ....$22–25

Silver Spur Boot 1971
Cowboy-boot-shaped bottle with silver spur buckled on; "Silver
Spur–Carson City Nevada" embossed on side of boot...................$7–11

Simba 1971 ....$9–12

Ski Boot 1972 ....$5–7

Slot Machine 1971
A replica of the original nickel Liberty Bell slot machine invented
by Charles Fey in 1895 ....$18–24

Snowmobiles 1972 ....$8–11

South Dakota Air National Guard 1976 ....$18–22

Spirit of '76 1974 ....$5–7

Spirit of St. Louis 1977, 50th Anniversary $6–11

Sprint Car Racer $30–40

Stagecoach 1969 ....$10–12

Stan Laurel Bust 1976 ....$10–16

Stock Market Ticker 1970
A unique replica of a ticker-tape machine $8–11

Stonewall Jackson 1974 ....$22–28

Strongman 1974 ....$8–12

Sturgeon 1975 ....$20–28

John L. Sullivan 1970 ....$15–20

Syracuse—New York 1973 ....$11–16

Tank Patton 1972
Reproduction of a U.S. Army tank $16–20

Tecumseh 1969
Figurehead of the U.S.S. *Delaware*, this decanter is an embossed replica
of the statue at the United States Naval Academy $5–6

Telephone 1971
Replica of the old-time upright handset telephone $16–19

Tennis Player 1972..$8–12

Terrapin, Maryland 1974...$14–16

Texas Longhorn 1971 ....$18–22

Ticker Tape 1970 ....$8–12

Tiger on Stadium 1973
Commemorates college teams who have chosen the tiger as their
mascot...$12–17

Tom Turkey $18–24

Tonopah 1972...$12–15

Totem Pole 1972 ....$10–14

Tractor 1971
A mode of the 1917 Fordson made by Henry Ford.......................$9–11

Trail Bike Rider 1972 ....$10–12

Trojan Horse 1974 ....$15–18

Trojans—USC Football 1973 ....$10–14

Trout & Fly 1970..$7–11

Truckin' & Vannin' 1977 ....$7–12

Vermont Skier 1972...$10–12

VFW—Veterans of Foreign Wars 1973......................................$6–10

Virginia—Red Cardinal 1973 ....$15–20

Walgreen Drugs 1974 ....$16–24

Weirton Steel 1973 ....$15–18

Western Rodeos 1973 ....$17–23

West Virginia—Mountaineer 1971 ....$65–75

West Virginia—Mountain Lady 1972 ....$14–20

Whale 1972 ....$14–20

Wheat Shocker 1971
The mascot of the Kansas football team in a fighting pose $5–7

Whiskey Flasks 1970
Reproduction of collectible American patriotic whiskey flask of the
1800s: Old Ironsides, Miss Liberty, American Eagle, Civil War
Commemorative...$12–14

Whitetail Deer 1947 ....$18–24

White Turkey 1971 ....$20–25

Wichita $4–8

Wichita Centennial 1970 ....$4–6

Winston Churchill 1969 ....$6–10

Zimmerman's Hat 1968
A salute to "Zimmerman's—World's Largest Liquor Store"................$5–6

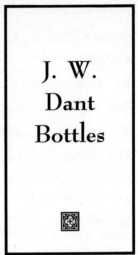

J. W. Dant Bottles

J.W. Dant Distilling Company also produces bottles similar to the Brooks and Beam bottles, and they likewise have strong collector appeal. These bottles usually depict American themes such as patriotic events and folklore in addition to various animals.

Because Dant has such a liking for American history and traditions, most of these bottles are decorated with historical scenes in full color. Some bottles carry an embossed American eagle and shield with stars. These bottles are all limited editions and the molds are not reused.

Alamo $4–6

American Legion $3–7

Atlantic City $4–6

Bobwhite $6–8

Boeing 747 ....$5–8

Boston Tea Party, Eagle to Left $4–6

Boston Tea Party, Eagle to Right $9–12

Bourbon $3–5

Paul Bunyan $5–7

California Quail $7–9

Chukar Partridge $7–9

Clear Tip Pinch $7–9

Constitution and Guerriere $5–7

Duel Between Burr and Hamilton.......................................$8–10

Eagle...$6–9

Fort Sill Centennial 1969 ....$7–11

Patrick Henry $4–7

Indianapolis 500 ....$7–11

Mountain Quail..$7–9

Mount Rushmore $5–9

Prairie Chicken $5–7

Reverse Eagle $5–8

Ring-necked Pheasant..$7–9

Ruffed Grouse $4–7

San Diego $4–6

Speedway 500 ....$6–9

Stove—Potbelly $9–11

Washington Crossing Delaware $5–7

Woodcock...$6–9

Wrong-Way Charlie..$15–20

Garnier
Bottles

Garnet Et Cie, a French firm founded in 1858, has long been given credit for being the pioneer of the modern collectible liquor bottle because they introduced the Garnier figural bottles in 1899. During Prohibition and World War II, there was a temporary halt in production but they quickly resumed manufacturing in the 1950s.

Those bottles manufactured prior to World War II are the most rare and valuable but are not listed in this book owing to the difficulty of establishing valid price levels. Among them are the Cat (1930), Clown (1910), Country Jug (1937), Greyhound (1930), Penguin (1930), and Marquise (1931).

Aladdin's Lamp 1963 ....$40–50

Alfa Romeo 1913, 1970 ....$20–30

Alfa Romeo 1929, 1969 ....$20–30

Alfa Romeo Racer 1969 ....$20–30

Antique Coach 1970..$25–30

Apollo 1969
Apollo spaceship, 13½ in. $17–22

Aztec Vase 1965 ....$15–20

Baby Foot—Soccer Shoe 1963
Black with white trim 3¾ in. × 8½ in. $10–20
1962 soccer shoe, large...$7–11

Baby Trio 1963...$7–10

Bacchus Figural 1967...$20–25

Bahamas
Black policeman, white jacket and hat, black pants, red stripe, gold
details...$15–24

Baltimore Oriole 1970..$10–16

Bandit Figural 1958...$10–14

Bedroom Candlestick 1967..$20–25

Bellows 1969..$14–21

Bird Ashtray 1958...$3–4

Bluebird 1970...$12–18

Bouquet 1966...$15–25

Bull (and matador) Animal Figural 1963.............................$17–23

Burmese Man Vase 1965..$15–25

Canada..$11–14

Candlestick 1955...$25–35

Candlestick Glass 1965..$15–25

Cannon 1964...$50–60

Cardinal State Bird—Illinois 1969......................................$12–15

Cat—Black 1962..$15–25

Cat—Gray 1962...$15–25

Chalet 1955..$40–50

Chimney 1956...$55–65

Chinese Dog 1965..$15–25

Chinese Statuette—Man 1970..$15–25

Chinese Statuette—Woman 1970..$15–25

Christmas Tree 1956..$60–70

Citroën 1922, 1970 ....$20–30

Clasic Ashtray 1958 ....$20–30

Clock 1958..$20–30

Clown's Head 1931 ....$65–75

Clown Holding Tuba 1955...$15–25

Coffee Mill 1966...$20–30

Coffee Pot 1962 ....$30–35

Columbine Figural 1968
Female partner..$20–30
Harlequin...$30–40

Diamond Bottle 1969 ....$10–15

Drunkard—Drunk on Lamppost $15–20

Duckling Figural 1956 ....$18–26

Duo 1954
Two clear glass bottles stacked, two pouring spouts $12–18

Egg Figural 1956 ....$70–80

Eiffel Tower 1951
13½ in. $15–25
12½ in. $14–20

Elephant Figural 1961..$20–30

Empire Vase 1962 ....$10–18

Fiat 500 1913, 1970
Yellow Body..$20–30

Fiat Nuevo 1913, 1970
Blue Body $20–30

Flask Garnier 1958...$9–12

Flying Horse Pegasus 1958 ....$50–60

Football Player 1970 ....$13–17

Ford 1913, 1970...$20–30

Fountain 1964...$25–35

Giraffe 1961..$20–35

Goldfinch 1970...$12–16

Goose 1955...$14–24

Grenadier 1949...$55–65

Harlequin Standing 1968...$13–19

Harlequin with Mandolin 1958..$30–40

Hockey Player 1970...$15–20

Horse Pistol 1964..$15–25

Hula Hoop 1959..$25–30

Hunting Vase 1964..$25–35

Hussar 1949
French cavalry soldier of 1800s...$25–35

India...$10–15

Indian 1958..$15–20

Indy 500, no. 1 1970...$35–40

Jockey 1961...$25–35

Lancer 1949..$15–22

Locomotive 1969...$15–25

Log—Round 1958...$20–30

London—Bobby...$12–18

Loon 1970..$10–18

Maharajah 1958..$70–80

M.G. 1933, 1970...$15–25

Mockingbird 1970...$8–14

Montmartre Jug 1960...$12–18

Monuments 1966
A cluster of Parisian monuments..............................$15–25

Napoleon on Horseback 1969................................$20–30

Nature Girl 1959 ....$10–15

New York Policeman...$9–13

Packard 1930, 1970...$20–30

Painting 1961...$25–35

Paris, French Policeman..$10–15

Paris Taxis 1960...$20–30

Partridge 1961 ....$25–35

Pheasant 1969..$25–35

Pigeon—Clear Glass 1958 ....$10–15

Pony 1961 ....$25–35

Poodle 1954 ....$12–15

Renault 1911 1969..$20–30

Road Runner 1969..$10–15

Robin 1970...$10–15

Rocket 1958 ....$10–15

Rolls-Royce 1908, 1970 ....$20–30

Rooster 1952..$15–25

Saint Tropez Jug 1961B..$20–30

Scarecrow 1960..$25–35

Sheriff 1958..$15–25

Snail 1950 ....$58–68

Soccer Shoe 1962 ....$30–40

S.S. *France*—Large 1962...$80–130

S.S. *France*—Small 1962...$50–60

S.S. *Queen Mary* 1970 ....$25–35

Stanley Steamer 1907, 1970...$20–30

Teapot 1961 ....$15–25

Teapot 1935 ....$20–30

Trout 1967 ....$17–22

Valley Quail 1969...$8–12

Violin 1966 ....$30–36

Watch—Antique 1966..$20–30

Water Pitcher 1965 ....$12–18

Young Deer Vase 1964...$25–35

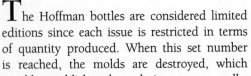

Hoffman
Bottles

The Hoffman bottles are considered limited editions since each issue is restricted in terms of quantity produced. When this set number is reached, the molds are destroyed, which quickly establishes these designs as very collectible, rare, and valuable.

While these bottles often reflect European figures in various occupations, they have also focused on American subjects. These include the 1976 Bicentennial bottle and the 1976 Hippie bottle.

Occupation Series
Mr. Bartender with Music Box
"He's a Jolly Good Fellow" $25–30

Mr. Charmer with Music Box
"Glow Little Glow Worm"..$10–15

Mr. Dancer with Music Box
"The Irish Washerwoman" $18–22

Mr. Doctor with Music Box
"As Long as He Needs Me"..$20–25

Mr. Fiddler with Music Box
"Hearts and Flowers"...$20–22

Mr. Guitarist with Music Box
"Johnny Guitar"...$20–22

Mr. Harpist with Music Box
"Do-Re-Mi" $10–15

Mr. Lucky with Music Box
"When Irish Eyes Are Smiling"..$15–20

Mrs. Lucky with Music Box
"The Kerry Dancer"..$12–15

Mr. Policeman with Music Box
"Don't Blame Me'"..$30–35

Mr. Sandman with Music Box
"Mr. Sandman"...$10–20

Mr. Saxophonist with Music Box
"Tiger Rag" $15–20

Mr. Shoe Cobbler
"Danny Boy"..$15–20

Bicentennial Series 4/5 Qt. Size
Betsy Ross with Music Box
"Star-Spangled Banner"...$30–40

Generation Gap
Depicts "100 Years of Progress," 2-oz. size $30–38

Majestic Eagle with Music Box
"America the Beautiful" $60–80

C.M. Russell Series 4/5 Qt. Size
Buffalo Man 1976...$20–25

Cowboy 1978..$30–35

Flathead Squaw 1976..$15–20

Half-Breed Trader 1978 ....$40–45

I Rode Him 1978..$35–40

Indian Buffalo Hunter 1978 ....$40–45

Last of Five Thousand 1975 ....$14–18

Northern Cree 1978..$35–40

Prospector 1976..$25–30

Japanese Bottles

While bottle making in Japan is an ancient art, the collectible bottles now produced are mainly for export purposes. Greater numbers of these bottles, now available in the American marketplace, have kept prices reasonable.

Daughter $12–18

Faithful Retainer $25–35

Golden Pagoda $12–18

"Kiku" Geisha, Blue 13¼ in. $20–30

Maiden $12–18

Noh Mask $12–18

Okame Mask $50–70

Playboy $14–24

Princess $14–24

Red Lion Man $40–60

Sake God, Colorful Robe, Porcelain 10 in. $20–30

Sake God, White, Bone China 10 in. $12–15

White Lion Man $35–50

White Pagoda $15–20

"Yuri" Geisha, Pink, Red Sash 13¼ in. $35–45

House of Koshu
Angel, with Book 7 oz. $5–10

Angel, Sitting on a Barrel 17 oz. $5–10

Beethoven Bust 7 oz. $5–10

Centurian Bust 7 oz. $5–10

Children 7 oz. $7–10

Declaration of Independence $4–6

Geisha, Blue..$40–45

Geisha, Cherry Blossom...$30–35

Geisha, Lily..$25–35

Geisha, Violet..$30–40

Geisha, Wisteria $30–40

Geisha, Lavender with Fan..$45–50

Geisha, Reclining...$60–70

Geisha, Sitting...$45–50

Lionman, Red...$40–45

Lionman, White $80–95

Pagoda, Green $25–30

Pagoda, White $20–25

Pagoda, Gold $15–20

Sailor with a Pipe..$6–10

Kamotsuru Bottles
Daokoru, God of Wealth $9–13

Ebisu, God of Fishermen...$10–15

Goddess of Art...$10–12

Hotei, God of Wealth...$7–10

Kentucky Gentlemen Bottles

These bottles are similar in design to the Beam and Brooks bottles but are released less frequently. As a rule, these bottles reflect clothing of various periods of American history, most notably around the Civil War time frame.

Confederate Infantry
In gray uniform with sword, 13½ in. $10–15

Frontiersman (1969)
Coonskin cap, fringed buckskin, power horn, long rifle, 14 in. $12–15

Kentucky Gentlemen (1969)
Figural bottle, frock coat, top hat and cane; "Old Colonel," gray ceramic, 14 in. $12–15

Pink Lady (1969)
Long bustle skirt, feathered hat, pink parasol, 13¼ in. $20–32

Revolutionary War Officer
In dress uniform and boots, holding sword, 14 in. $12–16

Union Army Sergeant
In dress uniform with sword, 14 in. $9–13

Lionstone
Bottles

Lionstone bottles, manufactured by Lionstone Distillery, reflect a great deal of realism in their designs in terms of components and details. Their "Shootout at OK Corral" work, for example, consists of three bottles with nine figures and two horses.

The Lionstone bottles are issued in series form and include a sport, circus, and bicentennial series. The most popular among collectors is the Western series. Since prices of these bottles have continued to be firm in the market, the collector should always be on the lookout for old, uncirculated stock.

Bar Scene No. 1	$125–140
Bartender	$18–22
Belly Robber	$12–16
Blacksmith	$20–30
Molly Brown	$18–25
Buffalo Hunter	$25–35
Calamity Jane	$18–23
Camp Cook	$13–17
Camp Follower	$9–12
Canadian Goose	$45–55
Casual Indian	$8–12

Cavalry Scout..$8–12

Cherry Valley Club $50–60

Chinese Laundryman..$12–15

Annie Christmas $10–15

Circuit Judge..$8–12

Corvette, 1.75 Liters $60–75

Country Doctor...$12–18

Cowboy...$8–10

Frontiersman $14–16

Gambel's Quail...$8–12

Gentleman Gambler..$25–35

God of Love $17–22

God of War $17–22

Gold Panner $25–35

Highway Robber...$15–20

Jesse James $18–23

Johnny Lightning $50–65

Judge Roy Bean...$20–30

Lonely Luke $45–60

Lucky Buck...$18–24

Mallard Duck $35–45

Miniatures—Western (Six) $85–110

Mint Bar with Frame..$700–900

Mint Bar with Nude and Frame...............................$1000–1250

Mountain Man...$15–20

Annie Oakley...$14–16

Pintail Duck $40–55

Proud Indian $10–14

Railroad Engineer $15–18

Renegade Trader $15–18

Riverboat Captain $10–15

Roadrunner..$28–36

Saturday Night Bath..$60–70

Sheepherder...$25–35

Sheriff $10–12

Sod Buster $13–16

Squawman $20–30

Stagecoach Driver $45–60

STP Turbocar $40–50

STP Turbocar with Gold and Platinum (Pair) $150–185

Telegrapher..$15–20

Tinker $25–35

Tribal Chief...$25–35

Al Unser No. 1 ....$15–20

Wells Fargo Man $8–12

Woodhawk..$15–17

Bicentennial Series
Firefighters No. 1 ....$110–120

Mail Carrier..$23–29

Molly Pitcher...$10–12

Paul Revere..$10–12

Betsy Ross $15–25

Sons of Freedom..$25–34

George Washington $15–25

Winter at Valley Forge $16–20

Bicentennial Westerns
Barber..$30–40

Firefighter No. 3 ....$60–70

Indian Weaver..$20–24

Photographer $34–40

Rainmaker...$22–28

Saturday Night Bath..$50–65

Trapper $30–36

Bird Series (1972–1974)
Bluebird—Eastern..$18–24

Bluebird—Wisconsin $20–30

Bluejay $20–25

Peregrine Falcon $15–18

Meadowlark $15–20

Mourning Doves...$50–70

Swallow...$15–18

Circus Series (Miniatures)
The Baker $10–15

Burmese Lady...$10–15

Fat Lady..$10–15

Fire-eater..$10–15

Giant with Midget $10–15

Giraffe-necked Lady...$10–14

Snake Charmer $10–15

Strong Man...$10–15

Sword Swallower $10–15

Tattooed Lady $10–15

Dog Series (Miniatures)
Boxer...$10–15

Cocker Spaniel..$9–12

Collie..$10–15

Pointer $10–15

Poodle $10–15

European Worker Series
The Cobbler $20–35

The Horseshoer...$20–35

The Potter...$20–35

The Silversmith...$25–35

The Watchmaker..$20–35

The Woodworker...$20–35

Oriental Worker Series
Basket Weaver..$25–35

Egg Merchant $25–35

Gardener..$25–35

Sculptor $25–35

Tea Vendor..$25–35

Timekeeper..$25–35

Sports Series
Baseball...$22–30

Basketball $22–30

Boxing...$22–30

Football...$22–30

Hockey $22–30

Tropical Bird Series (Miniatures)
Blue-Crowned Chlorophonia $12–16

Emerald Toucanet..$12–16

Northern Royal Flycatcher...$12–16

Painted Bunting $12–16

Scarlet Macaw $12–16

Yellow-Headed Amazon..$12–16

Miscellaneous Lionstone Bottles
Buccaneer...$25–35

Cowgirl $45–55

Dancehall Girl...$50–55

Falcon $15–25

Firefighter No. 2 ....$80–100

Firefighter No. 3 ....$25–35

Firefighter No. 5, 60th Anniversary $22–27

Firefighter No. 6, Fire Hydrant....................................$40–45

Firefighter No. 6, in Gold or Silver $250–350

Firefighter No. 7, Helmet...$60–90

Firefighter No. 8, Fire Alarm Box $45–60

Firefighter No. 8, in Gold or Silver $90–120

Firefighter No. 9, Extinguisher $55–60

Firefighter No. 10, Trumpet...$55–60

Firefighter No. 10, Gold $200–260

Firefighter No. 10, Silver..$125–175

Indian Mother and Papoose...$50–65

The Perfesser..$40–45

Roses on Parade...$60–80

Screech Owls...$50–65

Unser-Olsonite Eagle $35–45

Miscellaneous Miniatures
Bartender $12–15

Cliff Swallow Miniature...$9–12

Dancehall Girl Miniature...$15–22

Firefighter Emblem..$24–31

Firefighter Engine No. 8 ....$24–31

Firefighter Engine No. 10 ....$24–31

Horseshoe Miniature $14–20

Kentucky Derby Race Horse, Cannonade $35–45

Lucky Buck...$10–12

Rainmaker...$10–15

Sahara Invitational No. 1...$35–45

Sahara Invitational No. 2...$35–45

Sheepherder..$12–15

Shootout at OK Corral, Set of Three $250–300

Woodpecker $10–15

Luxardo
Bottles

The Girolamo Luxardo bottle is made in Torreglia, Italy, and was first imported into the United States in 1930. The Luxardo bottle usually contained wine or liquors, as Luxardo also produces wine.

Luxardo bottles are well designed and meticulously colored, adding to the desirability of this line. Most of these bottles are figural and consist of historical subjects and classical themes. The most popular bottle, the Cellini, was introduced in the early 1950s and is still used. The names and dates of many of the earlier bottles are not known owing to lack of owners' records. Bottles in mint condition with the original label, and with or without contents, are very rare, collectible, and valuable. One of the rarer and more valuable of these bottles is the Zara, which was made prior to World War II.

Alabaster Fish Figural (1960–1968)..$30–40

Alabaster Goose Figural (1960–1968)
Green and white, wings..$25–35

Ampulla Flask (1958–1959)..$20–30

Apothecary Jar (1960)
Handpainted multicolor, green and black $20–30

Assyrian Ashtray Decanter (1961)
Gray, tan, and black..$15–25

Autumn Leaves Decanter (1952)
Handpainted, two handles $35–45

Autumn Wine Pitcher (1958)
Handpainted country scene, handled pitcher $30–40

Babylon Decanter (1960)
Dark green and gold $16–23

Bizantina (1959)
Gold embossed design, wide body $28–38

Blue and Gold Amphora (1968)
Blue and gold with pastoral scene in white oval $20–30

Blue Fimmetta or Vermillian (1957)
Decanter...$20–27

Brocca Pitcher (1958)
White background pitcher with handle, multicolor flowers, green
leaves $28–37

Buddha Goddess Figural (1961)
Goddess head in green-gray stone...$14–19
Miniature $11–16

Burma Ashtray Specialty (1960)
Embossed white dancing figure, dark green background..............$20–25

Burma Pitcher Specialty (1960)
Green and gold, white embossed dancing figure $14–19

Callypso Girl Figural (1962)
Black West Indian girl, flower headdress in bright color. $20–25

Candlestick Alabaster (1961)..$30–35

Cellini Vase (1958–1968)
Glass and silver decanter, fancy..$14–19

Cellini Vase (1957)
Glass-and-silver-handled decanter with serpent handle................$14–19

Ceramic Barrel (1968)
Barrel shaped with painted flowers...$14–19

Cherry Basket Figural (1960)
White basket, red cherries $14–19

Classical Fragment Specialty (1961)
Roman female figure and vase $25–33

Cocktail Shaker (1957)
Glass and silver decanter, silver painted top $14–19

Coffee Carafe Specialty (1962)
Old-time coffeepot, white with blue flowers $14–19

Curva Vaso Vase (1961)
Green, green and white, ruby red $22–29

Deruta Amphora (1956)
Colorful floral design on white $11–16

Deruta Cameo Amphora (1959)
Colorful floral scrolls and cameo head on eggshell white $25–35

Deruta Pitcher (1953)
Multicolor flowers on base perugia $11–16

Diana Decanter (1956)
White figure of Diana with deer on black $11–16

Dogal Silver and Green Decanter (1952–1956)
Handpainted gondola $14–19

Dogal Silver Ruby (1952–1956)
Handpainted gondola $14–18

Dogal Silver Ruby Decanter (1956)
Handpainted Venetian scene and flowers $17–22

Dogal Silver Smoke Decanter (1952–1955)
Handpainted gondola $14–19

Dogal Silver Smoke Decanter (1953–1954)
Handpainted gondola $11–16

Dogal Silver Smoke Decanter (1956)
Handpainted silver clouds and gondola $11–16

Dogal Silver Smoke Decanter (1956)
Handpainted gondola, buildings, flowers......................................$14–18

Dolphin Figural (1959)
Yellow, green, blue...$42–57

"Doughnut" Bottle (1960)...$15–20

Dragon Amphora (1953)
Two-handled white decanter with colorful dragon and flowers....$10–15

Dragon Amphora (1958)
One handle, white pitcher, color dragon................................$14–18

Duck—Green Glass Figural (1960)
Green and amber duck, clear glass base $35–45

Eagle (1970)..$45–55

Egyptian Specialty (1960)
Two-handled amphora, Egyptian design on tan and gold...........$14–19

Etruscan Decanter (1959)
Single-handled black Greek design on tan background...............$14–19

Euganean Bronze (1952–1955)..$14–19

Euganean Coppered (1952–1955)...................................$13–18

Faenza Decanter (1952–1956)
Colorful country scene on white single-handled decanter. $21–28

Fighting Cocks (1962)
Combination decanter and ashtray $14–19

Fish—Green and Gold Glass Figural (1960)
Green, silver, and gold, clear glass base................................$30–40

Fish—Ruby Murano Glass Figural (1961)
Ruby-red tone of glass $30–40

Florentine Majolica (1956)
Round-handled decanter, painted pitcher................................$20–30

Gambia (1961)
Black princess, kneeling holding tray $8–12

Golden Fakir, Seated Snake Charmer with Flute and Snakes
1961 Gold $26–37
1960 Black and Gray $26–37

Gondola (1959)
Highly glazed abstract gondola and gondolier in black $21–27

Gondola (1960)...$14–19

Grapes, Pear Figural...$25–40

Mayan (1960)
Mayan temple god head mask $15–25

Mosaic Ashtray (1959), Combination Decanter Ashtray
Black, yellow, green 11½ in. $15–25
Black, green; miniature 6 in. $10–14

Nubian
Kneeling black figure..$14–19

Opal Majolica (1957)
Two gold handles, translucent top $14–19

Penguin Murano Glass Figural (1968)
Black and white penguin $25–30

Pheasant Murano Glass Figural (1960)
Red and clear glass on a crystal base $35–45

Pheasant Red and Gold Figural (1960)
Red and gold glass bird..$40–60

Primavera Amphora (1958)
Two-handled vase shape $14–19

Puppy Cucciolo Glass Figural (1961)
Amber and green glass..$26–37

Puppy Murano Glass Figural (1960)
Amber glass $26–37

Silver Blue Decanter (1952–1955)
Handpainted silver flowers and leaves............................$22–28

Silver Brown Decanter (1952–1955)
Handpainted silver flowers and leaves..$26–37

Sir Lancelot (1962)
Figure of English knight in full armor $14–19

Springbok Amphora (1952)
Leaping African deer $14–19

Squirrel Glass Figural (1968)
Amethyst-colored squirrel on crystal base $40–50

Sudan (1960)
African motif in browns, blue, yellow and gray............................$14–19

Torre Rosa (1962)
Rose-tinted tower of fruit...$16–24

Torre Tinta (1962)
Multicolored tower of fruit...$18–22

Tower of Fruit (1968)
Various fruit in natural colors..$16–24

Tower of Fruit Majolicas Torre Bianca (1962)
White and gray tower of fruit...$16–24

McCormic Bottles

These pieces, like Kentucky Gentlemen and others, are similar in design to the Beam and Brooks bottles but are released in limited numbers.

The McCormic bottles, which originally or still contain McCormick Irish Whiskey, are manufactured in different series, including cars, famous Americans, frontiersmen decanters, and gunfighters. The famous Americans series has been produced most often and represents celebrities from Colonial times to the twentieth century.

Barrel Series
Barrel, with Stand and Shot Glasses 1958 ....$25–30

Barrel, with Stand and Plain Hoops 1968 ....$15–20

Barrel, with Stand and Gold Hoops 1968 ....$20–25

Bird Series
Blue Jay 1971 ....$20–25

Canadian Goose, Miniature $18–25

Gambel's Quail 1982 ....$45–55

Ring-Neck Pheasant 1982 ....$45–55

Wood Duck 1980 ....$30–35

Car Series
Packard 1937 ....$25–35

The Pony Express...$20–25

The Sand Buggy Commemorative Decanter...........................$35–50

Confederate Series
Jeb Stuart...$25–35

Jefferson Davis $25–30

Robert E. Lee $25–35

Stonewall Jackson...$25–35

Country and Western Series
Hank Williams Sr. 1980 ....$50–55

Hank Williams Jr. 1980 ....$70–80

Tom T. Hall 1980...$32–42

Elvis Presley Series
Elvis '55 1979 ....$40–50

Elvis '55 Mini..$25–35

Elvis '55 Mini 1980..$20–30

Elvis '68 1980 ....$40–50

Elvis '68 Mini 1980..$25–35

Elvis '77 1978 ....$65–80

Elvis '77 Mini 1979..$32–40

Elvis Bust 1978..$24–35

Elvis Designer I
Music Box Plays "Are You Lonesome Tonight?"..................$85–100

Elvis Designer II
Music Box Plays "It's Now or Never" $140–160

Elvis Gold 1979..$180–220

Elvis Karate $100–130

Elvis Sergeant..$190–210

Elvis Silver 1980..$120–135

Famous American Portrait Series

Abe Lincoln with Law Book in Hand....................................$35–45

Alexander Graham Bell with Apron.................................$10–15

Captain John Smith...$12–20

Charles Lindbergh...$24–28

Eleanor Roosevelt...$12–20

George Washington Carver...$28–40

Henry Ford..$20–25

Meriwether Lewis...$16–20

Pocahontas..$30–42

Robert E. Perry...$25–35

Thomas Edison...$35–45

Ulysses S. Grant with Coffeepot and Cup.......................$15–25

William Clark...$15–20

Football Mascots

Alabama Bamas...$26–34

Arizona Sun Devils...$39–48

Arizona Wildcats...$21–27

Arkansas Hogs 1972...$42–48

Auburn War Eagles..$16–24

Baylor Bears 1972..$24–30

California Bears...$20–25

Drake Bulldogs, Blue Helmet and Jersey 1974.................$15–20

Georgia Bulldogs, Black Helmet and Red Jersey...............$12–19

Georgia Tech Yellowjackets..$15–25

Houston Cougars 1972..$20–30

Indiana Hoosiers 1974 ....$15–25

Iowa Cyclones 1974 ....$45–55

Iowa Hawkeyes 1974 ....$60–70

Iowa Purple Panthers $32–42

Louisiana State Tigers 1974 ....$15–20

Michigan State Spartans...$15–20

Michigan Wolverines 1974..$15–25

Minnesota Gophers 1974..$8–12

Mississippi Rebels 1974..$8–12

Mississippi State Bulldogs, Red Helmet and Jersey 1974........$12–18

Nebraska Cornhuskers 1974 ....$12–18

Nebraska Football Player $35–45

Nebraska, Johnny Rogers, No. 1 ....$230–260

New Mexico Lobo...$32–40

Oklahoma Sooners Wagon 1974..$20–28

Oklahoma Southern Cowboy 1974..$14–18

Oregon Beavers 1974 ....$10–18

Oregon Ducks 1974..$12–18

Purdue Boilermaker 1974 ....$15–25

Rice Owls 1972...$20–30

SMU Mustangs 1972 ....$17–24

TCU Horned Frogs 1972 ....$25–30

Tennessee Volunteers 1974...$8–12

Texas A&M Aggies 1972...$22–30

Texas Tech Raiders 1972 ....$20–26

Texas Horns 1972 ....$23–33

Washington Cougars 1974 ....$20–25

Washington Huskies 1974 ....$15–25

Wisconsin Badgers 1974 ....$15–25

Frontiersmen Commemorative Decanters 1972
Daniel Boone $15–22

Davy Crockett $17–25

Jim Bowie $12–15

Kit Carson $14–18

General
A & P Wagon $50–55

Airplane, *Spirit of St. Louis* 1969 ....$60–80

American Bald Eagle 1982 ....$30–40

American Legion Cincinnati 1986 ....$25–35

Buffalo Bill 1979 ....$70–80

Cable Car $25–30

Car, Packard 1980 ....$30–40

Chair, Queen Anne $20–30

Ciao Baby 1978 ....$20–25

Clock, Cuckoo 1971 ....$25–35

De Witt Clinton Engine 1970 ....$40–50

French Telephone 1969 ....$20–28

Globe, Angelica 1971 ....$25–32

Henry Ford 1977 ....$20–24

Hutchinson Kansas Centennial 1972 ....$15–25

Jester 1972 ....$20–28

Jimmy Durante 1981
With music box, plays "Inka Dinka Do" $31–40

Joplin Miner 1972 .... $15–25

JR Ewing 1980
With music box, plays theme song from "Dallas" $22–27

JR Ewing, Gold-colored $50–55

Julia Bulette 1974 .... $140–160

Lamp, Hurricane $13–18

Largemouth Bass 1982 .... $20–28

Lobsterman 1979 .... $20–30

Louis Armstrong $60–70

Mark Twain 1977 .... $18–22

Mark Twain, Mini $13–18

McCormick Centennial 1956 .... $80–120

Mikado 1980 .... $60–80

Missouri Sesquicentennial China 1970 .... $5–7

Missouri Sesquicentennial Glass 1971 .... $3–7

Ozark Ike 1979 .... $22–27

Paul Bunyan 1979 .... $25–30

Pioneer Theatre 1972 .... $8–12

Pony Express 1972 .... $20–25

Renault Racer 1969 .... $40–50

Sam Houston 1977 .... $22–28

Stephen F. Austin 1977 .... $14–18

Telephone Operator $45–55

Thelma Lu 1982 .... $25–35

US Marshal 1979 .... $25–35

Will Rogers 1977..$18–22

Yacht Americana 1971 ....$30–38

Gunfighter Series
Bat Masterson $20–30

Billy the Kid...$25–30

Black Bart $26–35

Calamity Jane...$25–30

Doc Holiday $25–35

Jesse James...$20–30

Wild Bill Hickok...$21–30

Wyatt Earp $21–30

Jug Series
Bourbon Jug $62–70

Gin Jug $6–10

Old Holiday Bourbon 1956 ....$6–18

Platte Valley 1953 ....$3–6

Platte Valley, ½ Pt. $3–4

Vodka Jug...$6–10

King Arthur Series
King Arthur on Throne..$30–40

Merlin the Wise Old Wizard with His Magical Robe 1979.....$25–35

Queen Guinevere, the Gem of the Royal Court.................$12–18

Sir Lancelot of the Lake in Armor, a Knight of
Roundtable $12–18

The Literary Series
Huck Finn 1980...$20–25

Tom Sawyer 1980...$22–26

Miniatures

Charles Lindbergh Miniature 1978..$10–14

Confederates Miniature Set (Four) 1978 ....$40–50

Henry Ford Miniature 1978 ....$10–14

Mark Twain Miniature 1978 ....$12–18

Miniature Gunfighters (Eight) 1977 ....$110–140

Miniature Noble 1978..$14–20

Miniature Spirit of '76 1977 ....$15–25

Patriot Miniature Set (Eight) 1976.......................................$250–350

Pony Express Miniature 1980..$15–18

Will Rogers Miniature 1978...$12–16

The Patriots

Benjamin Franklin 1975 ....$13–17

Betsy Ross 1975 ....$20–25

George Washington 1975 ....$20–27

John Paul Jones 1975...$15–20

Patrick Henry 1975 ....$14–18

Patrick Henry, Miniature $12–15

Paul Revere 1975..$20–25

Spirit of '76 1976 ....$50–60

Thomas Jefferson 1975 ....$14–18

Pirate Series

Pirate No. 1 1972..$10–12

Pirate No. 2 1972..$10–12

Pirate No. 3 1972..$8–12

Pirate No. 4 1972..$8–12

Pirate No. 5 1972...$8–12

Pirate No. 6 1972...$8–12

Pirate No. 7 1972...$8–12

Pirate No. 8 1972...$8–12

Pirate No. 9 1972...$8–12

Pirate No. 10 1972...$20–28

Pirate No. 11 1972...$20–28

Pirate No. 12 1972...$20–28

Rural Americana Series
Woman Feeding Chickens 1980 ....$25–35

Woman Washing Clothes 1980 ....$30–40

Shrine Series
Circus..$20–35

Dune Buggy 1976 ....$25–35

Imperial Council...$20–25

Jester (Mirth King) 1972 ....$30–40

The Noble 1976...$25–32

Sports Series
Air Race Propeller 1971..$15–20

Air Race Pylon 1970 ....$10–15

Johnny Rodgers No. 1 1972...$160–195

Johnny Rodgers No. 2 1973...$70–85

KC Chiefs 1969 ....$18–25

KC Royals 1971..$10–15

Muhammad Ali 1980..$20–30

Nebraska Football Player 1972 ....$33–45

Skibob 1971 ....$10–11

Train Series
Jupiter Engine 1969 ....$20–25

Mail Car 1970...$25–28

Passenger Car 1970..$35–45

Wood Tender 1969 ....$14–18

Miniature Bottles

When a discussion on bottle collecting begins, it's clear that most collectors focus their attention on the physically large bottles such as beer, whiskey, or maybe bitters. But there is a very distinct group of collectors who eschew big finds and set their sights on the small. Their quest for that special find leads them into the world of miniatures. Until I started bottle collecting, the only miniature bottles that I knew of were the ones other passengers bought on airline trips. Today, there is tremendous enthusiasm for miniature bottle collecting. Not only are there specialty clubs and dealers across the United States but throughout the world in the Middle East, Japan, England, Scotland, Australia, and Italy, to name just a few. The new collector will soon discover that all miniatures are unique and extremely fascinating in their own way. Because of their low average cost, $1 to $5 per bottle, and the relatively small amount of space required to store them, starting a collection is easy. As is the case with the large bottles, there are some rare and expensive miniatures.

A number of miniatures were manufactured in the 1800s, although the majority date from the late 1920s and the 1950s, with peak production in the 1930s. While miniatures are still produced today, some of the most interesting and sought after are those produced prior to 1950. The state of Nevada legalized the sale of miniatures in 1935, Florida in 1935, and Louisiana in 1934.

If you're looking for a nineteenth-century miniature you might seek out miniature beer bottles. They are a good example of a kind of bottle that was produced for uses other than containing beer. Most of the major breweries produced them as advertisements, novelties, and promotional items. In fact, most of the bottles did not contain beer. A number of these bottles came with perforated caps so that they could be used as salt and pepper shakers. The Pabst Blue Ribbon Beer Company was the first brewery to manufacture a beer bottle miniature commemorating the Milwaukee Convention of Spanish-American War Veterans in 1889. Pabst's last miniature was manufactured around 1942. Most of the miniature beers you'll find today date from before World War II. In 1899 there were as many as 1,507 breweries, of which all produced miniatures.

Beyond the whiskey, beer, and soda pop bottles identified in this chapter, don't overlook earlier chapters that focus on other miniatures, including Luxardo's, Garnier, Lionstone, Drioli, and Barsottini.

Collecting miniature liquor bottles has become a special interest for some. A number of the state liquor stamps from the early 1930s and 1940s have specific series numbers that have a value to stamp collectors.

Beer Bottles

A-1 Pilsner Beer, Arizona Brewing Co. (AZ-3)
Foil paper label, 4 in., Phoenix, AZ, 1958......................................$5–10

Acme Lager Beer, California Brewing Co. (CA-5)
Decal label, 4¼ in., San Francisco, CA, 1936..............................$30–50

Apache Beer, Arizona Brewing Co. (AZ-1)
Decal label, 4¼ in., Phoenix, AZ, 1936.......................................$75–150

Astra Exclusiv (GER-1)
Paper label, 4 in., Germany, 1960..$5–10

Balboa Lager, Panama Brewing & Refining Co. (PAN-3)
Decal paper label, 4¼ in., Panama, 1936......................................$30–50

Bohemian Beer, Philip Best Brewing Co. (WI-3)
Paper label, 5 in., Milwaukee, WI, 1889...................................$100–150

Bohemian Export, Bartholomay Brewery Co. (NY-1)
Paper label, 6 in., Rochester, NY, 1900 ....$100–150

Carlsberg Pilsner, Carlsberg, Leverandor, Til (DEN-3)
Paper label, 4 in., Til, Denmark, 1955...$10–20

Canadian Ace Beer, Canadian Ace Brewing Co. (IL-14)
Paper label, 4¼ in., Chicago, IL, 1948...$5–10

Collection of Springbank
Campbeltown Single Malt
Whiskys, 1950–1955, $50–$75
(each).

Conrad Seipp Br'g Co. (IL-5)
Embossed/embossed, 5 in., Chicago, IL, 1890 ....$100–150

Coors Export Lager Beer, Adolph Coors Co. (CO-5)
Ceramic, 3⅝ in., Golden, CO, 1937...$20–30

Coors Export Lager Beer, Adolph Coors Co. (CO-6)
Ceramic, 4¼ in., Golden, CO, 1933...$20–30

Dos Equis (MEX-4)
Paper label, 4¼ in., Mexico, 1958 ....$10–20

Drewerys Ale, Drewerys Ltd., U.S.A. Inc. (IN-5)
Paper label, 3 in., South Bend, IN, 1948......................................$10–20

Eastside Beer, Pabst Brewing Co. (CA-13)
Foil paper label, 4¼ in., Los Angeles, CA 1954............................$10–20

Edelweiss Maltine, P. Schoenhofen Brewing Co. (IL-1)
Paper label/embossed, 4 in., Chicago, IL, 1900 ....$100–150

Export Beer, L. Hoster Brewing Co. (OH-1)
Paper label, 5 in., Columbus, OH, 1900..................................$100–150

Export Beer, Sheridan Brewing Co. (WY-1)
Decal paper label, 3 in., Sheridan, WY, 1940..............................$50–75

Falstaff Beer, Falstaff Brewing Co. (CA-15)
Foil paper label, 4¼ in., San Jose, CA, 1953 ....$5–10

George Brehn, Baltimore County, Md. (MD-1)
Paper label/embossed, 5 in., Baltimore, MD, 1895 ....$100–150

Goebels Export Beer, Goebel Brewing Co. (MI-1)
Paper label, 5 in., Detroit, MI..$100–150

Guinness Extra Stout, Arthur Guinness (IRL-30)
Foil paper label, 4¼ in., Dublin, Ireland, 1960 ....$10–20

Indianapolis Brewing Co. (IN-1)
Paper label/embossed, 5 in., Indianapolis, IN $100–150

Jackson Koehler's Lager Beer, Erie Brewing Co. (PA-1)
Paper label, 5 in., Erie, PA, 1900..$100–150

John Weiland Lager Beer, San Francisco Breweries, Ltd. (CA-2)
Paper label/embossed, 5 in., San Francisco, CA , 1900............$100–150

Koenig Brau, Bismark Brewing Co. (IL-12)
Decal paper label, 3 in., Chicago, IL, 1940 ....$20–30

Lone Star Beer, Harry Mitchell Brewing Co. (TX-1)
Decal paper label, 4¼ in., San Antonio, TX, 1950 ....$10–20

O & E Scotch Whisky,
James B. Rintoul (Edinburgh) Ltd.,
1940–1950, $50–$75.

Mather's Black Beer, J.E. Mather & Sons, Ltd. (ENG-2)
Paper label, 4¼ in., England, 1960..$10–20

Meister Brau, Peter Hand Brewery Co. (IL-18)
Paper label, 3 in., Chicago, IL, 1948 ....$10–20

New Brew, Theo. Hamm Brewing Co. (MN-1)
Paper label, 5 in., St, Paul, MN, 1900 ....$100–150

Primo Lager Beer, Hawaii Brewing Corp., Ltd. (HA-1)
Decal paper label, 3 in., Honolulu, HI, 1940 ....$100–150

Rainier Beer, Seattle Brewing & Malting Co. (WA-1)
Paper label, embossed, 6 in., Seattle, WA, 1900 ....$100–150

Red Lion Lager Beer, Red Lion Ale & Porter Co. (CA-1)
Paper label/embossed, 5 in., San Francisco, CA, 1911 ....$100–150

Superior (MEX-1)
Enamel label, 4¼ in., Mexico, 1965 ....$10–20

Trivoli Lager Beer, Fredericksburg Brewery (CA-3)
Paper label/embossed, 5 in., San Jose, CA, 1905......................$100–150

Trophy Beer, Birk Bros. Brewing Co. (IL-22)
Paper label, 4¼ in., Chicago, IL, 1950...$5–10

Walter's Beer, The Walter Brewing Co. (CO-1)
Foil paper label, 4 in., Pueblo, CO, 1956......................................$20–30

Walter's Gold Label Beer, The Walter Brewing Co. (CO-2)
Decal paper label, 3¼ in., Pueblo, CO, 1936.............................$75–100

Whiskey (Circa 1928–1935)
Bardstown.. $150

Baltimore Club.. $100

Bridge Club $75

Captain John Smith.. $125

Claycross $60

Copley Club $200

Dower House.. $125

Frisco Times Spirit... $125

G & G Special $100

Hawthorne $150

Highgate .... $ 100

Kentucky Hill .... $ 125

Little Frisco $175

Lucky Strike $125

Montecito .... $ 125

Old Colonel Dan $175

Old Joe $50

Old Miner $125

Old Rose $100

Our Cask $150

Prince Of York $75

Rock Ridge $200

Sportsman $200

Square Rigger $125

Three Rivers $150

University Club $60

War Admiral $100

Scotch Whiskey
Alison's Braes O'Angus $90

The Argosy $130

Auld Gaffer $90

B. Grant's $250

Ben Brae $85

Black Bear $95

Black Watch $40

The Cabinet Whisky $275

Campbeltown (1919) $350

Red Cameron's Rum, 1950–1955, $35–$55.

Carter's Black & Gold $125

Dalmore Highland Malt $250

Deep Red Label $135

Glen Dawn $175

Glendronach—Most Suitable for Medicinal Purposes $350

Gleneagles $325

Grants Stand Fast $85

Hedges & Butler Vat $90

Hunting Squire $110

Kinloch's $50

Lovell's Nip O' Scotch $350

Old Black Bottle $250

Purple Heather $175

Royal Marshall $365

Scotch Plaid $170

Thomson Gold Seal $130

Washington House $45

Soda Bottles
A-Treat
Green, 3 in., Paper label $18

Andersons
Clear, 5 in., ACL (painted) $25

Black Rock
Clear, 4 in., Decal label $15

Bryants
Clear, 4 in., Embossed $20

Canada Dry
Clear, 3 in., ACL (painted) $3

Canada Dry
Light Green, 4 in., Decal label $15

Clawson Bros
Light Green, 4 in., Embossed $22

Coca-Cola
Red, plastic, 1 in., Embossed $4

Coca-Cola
Green, plastic, 1 in., Embossed $5

Coca-Cola
Clear, 2 in., Embossed $7

Coca-Cola
Amber, 3 in., Embossed $8

Coca-Cola—1984 Olympics (Japan)
Clear, 3 in., ACL (painted), White name $6

College Inn
Clear, 6 in., Embossed $15

Crush
Clear, 3 in., Decal label $12

Stewart's Genuine W-D Ex-Services
Rum, 1939–1945, $50–$75.

Crush
Orange, plastic, 5 in., ACL (painted) $20

Double Cola
Clear, 4 in., ACL (painted) $15

Dr Pepper
Clear, 3 in., Embossed $22

Eagle
Clear, 4 in., Embossed $7

Fanta
Amber, 3 in., ACL (painted) $8

Frostie
Clear, 2 in., Paper label $3

Hippo
White Glass, 3 in., ACL (painted) $25

Hires
Light Green, 4 in., Embossed $18

Knapp's
Clear, 4 in., Embossed.. $15

Lime Cola
Clear, 5 in., ACL (painted)... $25

Millers A
Clear, 5 in., ACL (painted)... $9

Mission
Clear, 3 in., Decal label.. $14

Moxie
Colored plastic, 1 in., Paper label (key chain)................................. $6

Nesbitts
Clear, 3 in., Decal label.. $17

Pep-Up
Clear, 5 in., ACL (painted)... $25

Pepsi-Cola
Clear, 4 in., Decal label.. $25

Pepsi-Cola
Colored plastic, 2 in., Paper label... $9

Pluto Water
Green, 4 in., Paper label... $17

Royal Crown
Clear, 4 in., Decal label.. $22

7 UP
Clear, 3 in., Paper label.. $20

Solon Springs
Green, 5 in., ACL (painted)... $25

Sprite
Green, 3 in., ACL (painted)... $7

Squirt
Clear, 3 in., Decal label.. $12

Welch's
Clear, 5 in., Embossed.. $8

Old Blue Ribbon Bottles

These bottles, like other figurals, are manufactured to contain Old Blue Ribbon liquor.

The Blue Ribbon bottles are noted for distinct realism of historical themes and depictions of railroad cars from the nineteenth century. In addition, Blue Ribbon is the only manufacturer to produce a hockey series, with each bottle commemorating a different hockey team.

Air Race Decanter $18–26

Blue Bird $14–19

Caboose Mkt $20–30

Eastern Kentucky University $15–21

Jupiter '60 Mail Car $13–17

Jupiter '60 Passenger Car $16–23

Jupiter '60 Wood Tender $13–17

Jupiter '60 Locomotive $15–22

KC Royals $19–26

Pierce Arrow $13–15

Santa Maria Columbus Ship $15–20

Titanic Ocean Liner $35–45

Transportation Series
Balloon $9–12

Fifth Avenue Bus $14–21

Prairie Schooner $10–11

River Queen $10–15

River Queen, Gold $20–25

Hockey Series
Boston Bruins $14–18

Chicago Black Hawks $14–18

Detroit Red Wings $14–18

Minnesota North Start $14–18

New York Rangers $14–18

St. Louis Blues $14–18

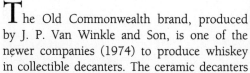

Old Commonwealth Bottles

The Old Commonwealth brand, produced by J. P. Van Winkle and Son, is one of the newer companies (1974) to produce whiskey in collectible decanters. The ceramic decanters themselves are manufactured in the Orient, while the whiskey is made and the bottling is done at the Hoffman Distilling Company in Lawrenceburg, Kentucky.

Today, the majority of the decanters are produced in regular and miniature sizes. The titles of most pieces appear on the bottle's front plaque.

Alabama Crimson Tide 1981
University of Alabama symbol $23–30

Bulldogs 1982
The mascot of the Georgia Bulldogs..$20–30

Chief Illini No. 1 1979
The mascot for the University of Illinois......................................$70–85

Chief Illini No. 2 1981
The mascot for the University of Illinois......................................$55–65

Chief Illini No. 3 1979
The mascot for the University of Illinois......................................$65–75

Coal Miner No. 1 1975
Standard size $80–100
Mini 1980..$20–30

Coal Miner No. 2 1976
Standard size $20–30
Mini 1982..$19–23

Coal Miner No. 3 1977
Standard size $28–36
Mini 1981..$20–25

Coal Miner—Lunch Time No. 4 1980
Standard size $33–43
Mini $15–20

Cottontail 1981 ....$25–35

Elusive Leprechaun 1980..$24–30

Fisherman, "A Keeper" 1980..$20–30

Golden Retriever 1979 ....$30–40

Kentucky Thoroughbreds 1976 ....$30–40

Kentucky Wildcat $32–42

LSU Tiger 1979 ....$45–55

Lumberjack...$15–25

Missouri Tiger..$35–45

Old Rip Van Winkle No. 1 1974......................................$40–50

Old Rip Van Winkle No. 2 1975......................................$35–45

Old Rip Van Winkle No. 3 1977......................................$30–40

Pointing Setter Decanter 1965 ....$16–23

Quail on the Wing Decanter 1968 ....$7–12

Rebel Yell Rider 1970...$23–32

Rip Van Winkle Figurine 1970..$32–40

Songs of Ireland 1972..$15–20

Sons of Erin 1969 ....$6–9

South Carolina Tricentennial 1970................................$12–19

Tennessee Walking Horse 1977...$24–35

USC Trojan 1980
Standard size $45–55
Mini $11–16

Weller Masterpiece 1963 ....$26–35

Western Boot Decanter 1982
Standard size $20–25
Mini $8–12

Western Logger 1980 ....$25–34

Wildcats 1982 ....$40–46

Wings Across the Continent 1972......................................$16–23

Yankee Doodle $25–32

Modern Firefighters Series
Modern Hero No. 1 1982
Standard size $25–35
Mini $8–12

The Nozzleman No. 2 1982
Standard size $30–40
Mini $17–24

On Call No. 3 1982
Standard size $45–55
Mini $15–24

Fallen Comrade No. 4 1982
Standard size $30–40
Mini $17–25

Waterfowler Series
Waterfowler No. 1 1979 ....$40–50

Here They Come No. 2 1980..$32–42

Good Boy No. 3 1981..$32–42

Old Fitzgerald Bottles

These bottles are manufactured by the Old Fitzgerald Distilling Company to package its whiskey and bourbon. These bottles are often called Old Cabin Still bottles, for one of the brand names under which they were distributed and sold.

These bottles are issued in both decanter and figural designs in various types and colors portraying different Irish and American subjects. Runs are produced in very limited quantities.

Americas Cup Commemorative 1970 .... $15–22

Blarney Castle 1970 .... $12–19

Browsing Deer Decanter 1967 .... $15–22

California Bicentennial 1970 .... $15–22

Cabin Still, Hillbilly 1854 .... $75–80

Cabin Still, Hillbilly 1954 .... $15–20

Candelite Decanter 1955 .... $9–12

Colonial Decanter 1969 .... $4–7

Crown Decanter $5–9

Eagle 1973 .... $5–10

Gold Coast Decanter 1954 .... $10–15

"Golden Bough" Decanter 1971 .... $4–9

Gold Web Decanter 1953 ....$10–16

Hillbilly Pt. 1969 ....$13–18

Hillbilly Bottle 1954 Pt. $13–18

Hillbilly Bottle 1954 Qt. $13–18

Hillbilly Bottle 1954 Gal. (Very Rare) $60–85

Irish Charm 1977 ....$15–20

Irish Patriots 1971 ....$10–15

Jewel Decanter 1951–1952 ....$9–15

Leaping Trout Decanter 1969 ....$11–16

Leprechaun Bottle 1968 ....$25–32

LSU Alumni Decanter 1970 ....$25–32

Man O'War Decanter 1969 ....$5–9

Memphis Commemorative 1969 ....$8–12

Nebraska 1971 ....$27–32

Nebraska 1972 ....$18–25

Ohio State Centennial 1970 ....$12–18

Old Cabin Still Decanter 1958 ....$16–23

Pilgrim Landing Commemorative 1970 ....$14–24

Ski-Country Bottles

Those bottles are produced in limited editions and offer a variety of subjects such as Indians, owls, game birds, Christmas themes, and customer specialties. Because of the limited editions and high quality of detailing, these bottles are rated high on the wish lists of most collectors.

Animals
Badger Family
Standard size $35–45
Mini $16–24

Bobcat Family
Standard size $45–60
Mini $16–25

Coyote Family
Standard size $37–48
Mini $17–23

Kangaroo
Standard size $22–32
Mini $18–28

Koala $20–28

Raccoon
Standard size $36–45
Mini $25–30

Skunk Family
Standard size $40–50
Mini $22–26

Snow Leopard
Standard size $36–43
Mini $30–35

Birds
Blackbird
Standard size $34–40
Mini $29–30

Black Swan
Standard size $30–35
Mini $18–24

Blue Jay
Standard size $50–60
Mini $42–49

Cardinal
Standard size $55–70
Mini $35–45

Condor
Standard size $45–55
Mini $25–30

Gamecocks
Standard size $120–130
Mini $40–46

Gila Woodpecker
Standard size $55–65
Mini $26–32

Peace Dove
Standard size $50–60
Mini $20–26

Peacock
Standard size $80–100
Mini $45–60

Penguin Family
Standard size $45–55
Mini $21–27

Wood Duck
Standard size $175–200
Mini $125–150

Christmas
Bob Cratchit
Standard size $40–50
Mini $25–30

Mrs. Cratchit
Standard size $40–50
Mini $25–30

Scrooge
Standard size $40–50
Mini $15–20

Circus
Clown
Standard size $44–52
Mini $27–33

Elephant on Drum
Standard size $35–45
Mini $35–45

Jenny Lind, Blue Dress
Standard size $55–75
Mini $48–60

Lion on Drum
Standard size $31–36
Mini $23–28

Palomino Horse
Standard size $40–48
Mini $30–40

P.T. Barnum
Standard size $32–40
Mini $20–25

Ringmaster
Standard size $20–25
Mini $15–18

Tiger on Ball
Standard size $35–44
Mini $31–37

Tom Thumb
Standard size $20–25
Mini $16–21

Customer Specialties
Ahrens-Fox Engine $140–180

Bonnie and Clyde (Pair)
Standard size $60–70
Mini $55–62

Caveman
Standard size $16–23
Mini $18–22

Mill River Country Club..$38–47

Olympic Skier, Gold..$85–110

Olympic Skier, Red
Standard size $22–30
Mini $30–35

Olympic Skier, Blue
Standard size $25–32
Mini $35–40

Political Donkey and Elephant......................................$50–60

Domestic Animals
Basset Hound
Standard size $45–55
Mini $26–32

Holstein Cow $45–60

Eagles, Falcons, and Hawks
Birth of Freedom
Standard size $85–95
Mini $65–75

Eagle on the Water
Standard size $90–110
Mini $38–45

Easter Seals Eagle
Standard size $48–60
Mini $22–29

Falcon Gallon...$350–425

Gyrfalcon
Standard size $54–60
Mini $27–34

Happy Eagle
Standard size $85–105
Mini $80–95

Mountain Eagle
Standard size $130–150
Mini $100–120

Osprey Hawk
Standard size $140–160
Mini $100–120

Peregrine Falcon
Standard size $75–85
Mini $18–25

Prairie Falcon
Standard size $65–80
Mini $35–48

Red Shoulder Hawk
Standard size $60–70
Mini $34–40

Redtail Hawk
Standard size $75–95
Mini $33–40

White Falcon
Standard size $68–75
Mini $30–40

Fish
Muskellunge
Standard size $30–37
Mini $17–21

Rainbow Trout
Standard size $40–50
Mini $24–30

Salmon
Standard size $30–35
Mini $18–22

Trout $27–32

Game Birds
Banded Mallard $50–60

Chukar Partridge
Standard size $33–40
Mini $16–21

King Eider Duck $50–60

Mallard 1973 ....$50–60

Pheasant, Mini $52–62

Pheasant, Golden
Standard size $40–45
Mini $24–30

Pheasant in the Corn
Standard size $50–60
Mini $30–39

Pheasants Fighting
Standard size $70–80
Mini $35–45

Pheasants Fighting, ½ Gal $145–165

Pintail..$76–85

Prairie Chicken $55–65

Ruffed Grouse
Standard size $40–50
Mini $22–28

Turkey
Standard size $80–100
Mini $100–120

Grand Slam
Desert Sheep
Standard size $75–90
Mini $25–30

Mountain Sheep
Standard size $50–60
Mini $24–30

Stone Sheep
Standard size $50–65
Mini $27–34

Horned and Antlered Animals
Antelope...$45–60

Big-horn Ram
Standard size $65–75
Mini $25–31

Mountain Goat
Standard size $30–45
Mini $38–48

Mountain Goat, Gal..$525–600

White Tail Deer
Standard size $30–95
Mini $34–40

Indians
Ceremonial Antelope Dancer
Standard size $52–62
Mini $36–45

Ceremonial Buffalo Dancer
Standard size $150–185
Mini $32–38

Ceremonial Deer Dancer
Standard size $85–100
Mini $40–48

Ceremonial Eagle Dancer
Standard size $185–205
Mini $24–34

Ceremonial Falcon Dancer
Standard size $85–100
Mini $34–45

Ceremonial Wolf Dancer
Standard size $50–60
Mini $32–40

Chief No. 1
Standard size $105–125
Mini $14–20

Chief No. 2
Standard size $105–125
Mini $14–20

Cigar Store Indian $32–40

Dancers of the Southwest, Set
Standard size $250–300
Mini $140–175

Owls
Barn Owl
Standard size $48–55
Mini $20–24

Great Gray Owl
Standard size $48–55
Mini $20–25

Horned Owl
Standard size $60–70
Mini $70–80

Horned Owl, Gal. $700–800

Saw Whet Owl
Standard size $40–45
Mini $20–25

Screech Owl Family
Standard size $80–90
Mini $68–75

Spectacled Owl
Standard size $70–85
Mini $58–68

Rodeo
Barrel Racer
Standard Size $58–68
Mini $20–26

Bull Rider
Standard size $42–49
Mini $22–28

Wyoming Bronco
Standard size $48–66
Mini $25–35

Soda Bottles— Applied Color Label (ACL)

Anyone who has ever had a cold soda on a hot summer day from a bottle with a painted label probably didn't realize that the bottle would become rare and collectible. Today, collecting Applied Color Label (ACL) Soda Bottles has become one of the fastest-growing and most affordable areas of bottle collecting. In fact, this rapid growth has resulted in the Painted Soda Bottle Collectors Association, which is the nationwide collectors group dedicated to the promotion and preservation of ACL Soda Bottles.

So, what is an Applied Color Label soda bottle? The best description is this excerpt from an article written by Dr. J. H. Toulouse, a noted expert on bottle collecting and glass manufacturing in the late 1930s:

> One of the developments of the last few years has been that of permanent fused-on labels on glass bottles. The glass in a glass furnace is homogenous in character, all of one color and composition. When the bottles are ready for decoration, the color design is printed on them in the process that superficially resembles many printing or engraving processes. The color is applied in the form of a paste-like material, through a screen of silk, in which the design has been formed. The bottle which contains the impression of that design must be dried and then fired by conducting it thorough a lehr, which is a long, tunnel-like enclosure through which the bottles pass at a carefully controlled rate of speed and in which definite zones of temperature are maintained. The maximum temperature chosen is such that the glass body will not melt, but the softer glass involved in the color will melt and rigidly fuse on the glass beneath it.

The ACL Soda Bottle was conceived in the 1930s when Prohibition forced numerous brewing companies to experiment with soda. What started out as a temporary venture saved many brewing companies from bankruptcy; some companies never looked back. From the mid-1930s to the early 1960s, with the peak production falling in the 1940s and 1950s, many small, local bottlers throughout the United States created bottle labels that will forever preserve unique moments in American history. The labels featured western scenes, cowboys, Native Americans, biplanes to jets, clowns, famous figures, birds, bears, boats, Donald Duck, and even Las Vegas (Vegas Vic). Since Native Americans and cowboys were popular American figures, bottles depicting them are among the most popular and most collectible. In fact, the Big Chief ACL sodas are the most popular bottles, even more than the embossed types. These small bottlers actually produced the majority of the better-looking labels in contrast to the largely uniform bottles by major bottlers like Coca-Cola and Pepsi-Cola. Because these bottles were produced in smaller quantities, they are more rare and hence more valuable. While rarity will affect the dollar value, a bottle with a larger label is even more desirable for collectors. The most sought after bottles are those with a two-color label, each color adding more value to the bottle.

Unless otherwise noted, all of the soda bottles listed have a smooth base and a crown top:

Applied Color Label Bottles
A Kick (2 Old-Time Football Players)—Everett, WA
Clear, 8 oz., American 1941.. $190

Alpine Springs (Mountain & Birds)—Springfield, OH
Green, 12 oz., American 1954.. $15

Apollo (Bust of Apollo)—Apollo, PA
Clear, 12 oz., American 1955.. $60

Beehive (Beehive & 6 Bees)—Brigham City, UT
Clear, 10 oz., American 1951.. $25

Big Chief (Chief with Headdress)—Iola, Kansas
Clear, 10 oz., American 1955.. $11

Jumbo 60 oz., $25; Mammy 60 oz., $40; St. Louis Crystal Water Soda Co., $25; All circa 1935–1945.

Big Chief (Chief with Headdress)—Denver, CO
Clear, 12 oz., American 1948.. $35

Big Chief (Chief with Headdress)—McAllen, TX
Clear, 9 oz., American 1967.. $13

Bingo (Bingo Card)—St. Louis, MO
Clear, 12 oz., American 1948.. $100

Blackhawk (Indian on Arrowhead)—Rock Is., IL
Green, 6½ oz., American 1938 .... $245

Brook (Babbling Brook with Bridge)—Brookville, PA
Clear, 12 oz., American 1953.. $12

Calistoga (Calistoga Springs & Awards)—Calistoga, CA
Clear, 7 oz., American 1945 .... $25

Chief Washakie (Native American Chief with Headdress)—Worland, NY
Clear, 10 oz., American 1949.. $133

Chisca (Native American Profile)—Memphis, TN
Clear, 12 oz., American 1939.. $85

Cleo Cola (Egyptian Queen)—Topeka, KS
Dark Green, 12 oz., American 1938 .... $84

Cub (Bear Cub)—Shreveport, LA
Clear, 12 oz., American 1957... $10

Dad's Root Beer—Pittsburg, KS
Amber, 7 oz., American 1948... $7

Diamond Head (Diamond Head)—Honolulu, HI
Clear, 7 oz., American 1960.. $20

Drinkmor (Small Boy Holding Glass)—Richmond, MO
Clear, 12 oz., American 1959... $17

Dr. Sweet's Root Beer—Albuquerque
Clear, 10 oz., American 1946... $5

Duffy's—Denver, CO
Clear, 12 oz., American 1952... $8

Durhan's Hi-tide (Sailing Ship)
Clear, 8 oz., American 1954... $10

Eight Ball (8 Ball)—Altoona, PA
Amber, 7 oz., American 1946... $65

Collection of Pepsi-Cola Bottles; Prices L to R: $36, $11, $30, $44, $10, $10, $15, $11; Circa 1930–1976.

Frostie Root Beer—Breese, IL
Clear, 7 oz., American 1960... $6

Golden Bridge (Picture of Golden Gate Bridge)—S.F.—Oakland, CA
Clear, 7 oz., American 1949... $27

Good Guy (Stern-Looking Sheriff)—Tucson, AZ
Clear, 8 oz., American 1961... $41

Goody Root Beer—Maquoketa, IA
Clear, 10 oz., American 1976... $5

Grapeteen (Dancing Teenagers and Band)—Houston, TX
Clear, 6 oz., American 1946... $12

Grapette—St. Joseph, MO
Clear, 7 oz., American 1947... $6

High-n-Dry (Mountain Scene)—Calgary, CAN
Green, 7 oz., Canadian 1944... $43

Hires Root Beer—Philadelphia, PA
Clear, 8 oz., American 1949... $5

Honey's (Cheerleader)—Meadville, PA
Clear, 7 oz., American 1950... $65

Jet (Jet Airplane)—Waco, TX
Clear, 8 oz., American 1948... $31

Keep Kool (Baby Seal on Iceberg)—St. John's, Newfoundland
Clear, 7 oz., Canadian 1948... $58

Lakeside (Sailboats on Lake)—Erie, PA
Clear, 12 oz., American 1954... $25

La Victoria (Man Blowing Horn)—Tijuana, Mexico
Clear, 10 oz., Mexico 1949 .... $22

Lemonette—Richmond, MO
Clear, 6 oz., American 1948... $6

Lindy (Airplane)—Boone, IA
Clear, 10 oz., American 1950... $42

Pioneer Beverages, 10 oz., 1964, $25.

Long Branch Saloon (Saloon Scene)—Dodge City, KS
Green, 10 oz., American 1959.. $40

Mason's Root Beer—Chicago, IL
Amber, 10 oz., American 1960.. $5

Mok Hill (Miner Panning for Gold)—Mokelumne, CA
Clear, 32 oz., American 1943.. $35

Nugrape—Atlanta, GA
Clear, 10 oz., American 1969.. $3

Old Faithful (Old Faithful Scene)—Idaho Falls, ID
Clear, 12 oz., American 1945.. $70

Oregon Trail (Covered Wagon Scene)—Alliance & Sidney, NE
Clear, 11 oz., American 1940.. $26

Pahoa Soda Works (Palm Trees)—Pahoa, HI
Clear, 6½ oz., American 1949 .... $62

Pepsi-Cola—Malden, MO
Clear, 10 oz., American 1956.. $14

Peter Pan (Figure of Peter Pan)—Santa Barbara, CA
Clear, 9 oz., American 1948.. $52

Pick-up (Old-Fashioned Golfer)—Los Angeles, CA
Green, 7 oz., American 1942.. $37

Quality—Dr Pepper—Kansas City, MO
Clear, 7 oz., American 1944.. $14

Quality (Pheasant)—Norfolk, NE
Clear, 7 oz., American 1953.. $31

Rocket (Three–Stage Rocket Circling Earth)—Columbus, OH
Clear, 12 oz., American 1962.. $40

Royal Crown—Danville, KY
Light Green, 12 oz., American 1951.. $5

Roundup (Cowboy on Bucking Bronco)—Roundup, MT
Clear, 10 oz., American 1950.. $95

Santa Fe Trail (Covered Wagon Scene)—Denver, CO
Clear, 10 oz., American 1949.. $130

Silver State (Gold Miner and Mule)—Reno, NV
Clear, 7 oz., American 1940.. $70

Hermann, 1955, $15–$25.

Ski (Skier)—Canadian
Clear, 12 oz., French Canadian 1940.. $55

Skie's-Hie—Lawrence, KS
Clear, 10½ oz., American 1940 .... $10

Sky High (Airplane in Cloud)—Milwaukee, WI
Clear, 12 oz., American 1939.. $50

Smile (Two Orangehead Kewpie Dolls)—Honolulu, HI
Clear, 6½ oz., American 1953 .... $29

Sour Schnapps—Wauconda, IL
Dark Green, 7 oz., American 1958 .... $7

TNT (Explosive Clouds)—Cleveland, OH
Amber, 7 oz., American 1946.. $130

Tropic Cola (Palm Tree and Waves)—Canada
Clear, 10 oz., American 1950.. $12

Twenty-Four Special (Passenger Train)—Los Angeles, CA
Clear, 12 oz., American 1940.. $80

Uncle Sam's (Uncle Sam)—Houston, TX
Clear, 7 oz., American 1947... $75

Barrelhead Root Beer, 16 oz., 1979, $20; Black Jack, 7 oz., 1964,
$5; Cleo Cola, 12 oz., 1939, $70; Cleo Cola, 12 oz., 1939, $175;
Cleo Cola, 12 oz., 1939, $35; Clicquot Club, 15½ oz., 1940, $7;
Clicquot Club, 1940, 15½ oz., $7.

V D Korker—Brooklyn, NY
Dark Green, 7 oz., American 1948 .... $3

Vegas Vic (Vegas Vic's Face)—Las Vegas, NV
Clear, 10 oz., American 1957.. $100

Victory Root Beer ("Victory" Banner)—Pacoima, CA
Clear, 10 oz., American 1946... $34

Virginia Dare KRKR—Ex Springs, MO
Dark Green, 7 oz., American 1948 .... $3

White Rock—New York, NY
Dark Green, 7 oz., American 1965 .... $3

Winx (Winking Sun Face Character)—Philadelphia, PA
Green, 7 oz., American 1946... $100

Wishing Well (Soldier Figures)—London, Canada
Green, 10 oz., Canadian 1940... $22

Yosemite (Yosemite Park Scene)—Merced, CA
Clear, 9 oz., American 1938... $65

Embossed
Big Chief—Clinton, MO
Clear, 9 oz., American 1955... $10

Carnation—Mt. Vernon, MO
Clear, 8 oz., American 1956.. $5

CCBC—Big Chief (Picture of Indian Chief)—Sedalia, MO
Clear, 6½ oz., American 1928 .... $24

Coca-Cola—Kansas City, MO
Light Green, 6½ oz., American 1950... $7

Coca-Cola Bottling Co. Inc—Binghamton, NY
Medium Olive Yellow, 7¾ in., 12 oz., American 1900–1910........... $90

Full Flavor Beverages;
Delicious 5-HI Beverages;
Old Colony Beverages;
Circle Beverages. All
1950–1955, $5–$7
(each).

Crete (Star of Neck)—Crete, NE
Clear, 9 oz., American 1947 .... $3

Elk's (Picture of Elk)—Leavenworth, KS
Clear, 6½ oz., American 1925 .... $14

Jacob Ries—Shakopee, MN
Clear, 7 oz., American 1958 .... $4

Jumbo (Elephant Picture)
Clear, 60 oz., American 1930s $25

Lane's—Sioux City, IA
Clear, 7 oz., American 1962 .... $5

Mammy (Mammy with White Apron)
Clear, 60 oz., American 1930s $40

Mit-che—Eagle Lake, TX
Light Green, 6½ oz., American 1928 .... $3

O! Skinnay—Lexington, MO
Light Green, 6½ oz., American 1927 .... $8

Shaef's—Oakland, MD
Dark Green, 7 oz., American 1964 .... $3

St. Louis Crystal Water
Clear, 64 oz., American 1930s $5

Sun Fresh (Picture of Sun)—Birmingham, AL
Clear, 8 oz., American 1956... $16

Wright's—Greenwood, MS
Light Green, 6½ oz., American 1918... $10

Paper Labeled
Black Jack (Picture of King in Black Spade)—Shakopee, MN
Dark Green, 7 oz., American 1964 .... $4

Blatz—Milwaukee, WI
Amber, 24 oz., American 1931.. $20

Cleo-Cleo—St. Louis, MO
Dark Green, 12 oz., American 1939 .... $175

Manitou Ute Cola (Standing Ute Chief)—Manitou Springs, CO
Clear, 24 oz., American 1946... $12

Pop's Root Beer—Philadelphia, PA
Amber, 12 oz., American 1948.. $21

7 UP—Leavenworth, KS
Dark Green, 24 oz., American 1960 .... $5

Smile—St. Louis, MO
Clear, 6 oz., American 1947... $15

Tom Moore—Minneapolis, MN
Light Green, 12 oz., American 1925 .... $10

Uncle Dan's Root Beer (Uncle Dan with Mug)—Detroit, MI
Amber, 12 oz., American 1940.. $17

1894	1899–1902	1900——1916		1915	1923	1937	1957	1961	1975
				Nov. 16	Dec. 25	Aug. 3 (D-105529)	Applied Color Label (ACL)	One-Way Bottle (OWB)	One-Way Bottle (Plastic)

Chronology of the Glass Package for Coca-Cola, 1894–1975.

NARRATIVE FOR BOTTLES IN

CHRONOLOGY OF THE GLASS PACKAGE FOR COCA-COLA

1894—1975

(Left to Right)

1. Hutchinson-Style Bottle: Type unit in which Coca-Cola was first bottled in 1894 by Joseph A. Biedenharn, Vicksburg, Mississippi—the first Bottler of Coca-Cola.

2. Hutchinson-Style Bottle used 1899-1902: This style bottle was used briefly by Bottlers of Coca-Cola after November 1899 and before 1903.

3 and 4. Straight-sided bottle with the trade-mark Coca-Cola embossed in glass: Type unit designed for crown closures and distributed with the diamond-shaped label between 1900-1916, inclusive. Both flint and amber bottles were used by the Bottlers of Coca-Cola during this period.

5. The first glass package for Coca-Cola using classic contour design and introduced into the market in 1916.

6 and 7. Two successive designs with patent revisions used between 1923 (patent date: December 25, 1923) and 1951 when the 1937 patent (number D-105529) expired. In 1960, the contour design for the bottle was registered as a trademark.

8. Applied Color Label, for trade-mark Coca-Cola on panels, introduced on all sizes of classic contour bottles for Coca-Cola in 1957 and continued thereafter.

9. The no-return, or one-way glass bottle, first introduced in 1961; later modified for twist-top.

10. Experimental plastic 10-oz. package for Coca-Cola in classic contour design with twist-top cap; tested, 1970-1975. This package not in general circulation, Spring, 1975.

Trademarks

Identification by trademarks is an often overlooked method for determining the history, age, and value of a bottle. In addition, researching trademarks gives the bottle collector a deeper knowledge of the many glass manufacturers that produced these bottles and the bottling companies that provided the contents.

What is a trademark? By definition, a trademark is a word, name, letter, number, symbol, design, phrase, or a combination of all of these items that identifies and distinguishes a product from its competitors. For bottles, that mark usually appears on the bottom of the bottle and possibly on the label if a label still exists. Also, with a trademark, the protection for the manufacturer is in the symbol that distinguishes the product and not in the actual product itself.

Trademarks have been around for a long time. The first person to use an identification mark on glassware was a glassmaker called Ennion of Sidon who lived in the first century along with two of his students, Jason and Aristeas. They were actually the first glassmakers to letter their identification into the sides of the mold. Identifying marks have been found on antique Chinese porcelain, on pottery from ancient Greece and Rome, and on items from India dating back to 1300 B.C. In addition, stonecutters' marks have been found on many Egyptian structures dating back to 4000 B.C. In medieval times, while marks identified the source of the goods, the craft and merchant owners also relied upon the marks to single out their products from inferior goods and gain buyers' loyalties with particular products. Trademarks were then applied to just about everything: watermarks on paper, bread, leather goods, weapons. Gold and silversmiths also began to rely on trademarks. In the late 1600s, bottle manufacturers began to mark their products with a glass seal that was applied to the bottle while still hot. A die with the manufacturer's initials, date, or design was then pressed into the seal. For the glass manufacturer, the seal was important since it required no mold cutting and the mark could easily be seen by the buyer.

For collecting purposes, if you are able to determine the owner of the mark, as well as when it might have been used, you will likely be able to determine the date of the piece. If the mark was used over a long period of time, you will have to rely on other references to date the bottle. If the mark was not in use for long, it is much easier to pinpoint the age of the bottle. Unfortunately, most numbers appearing with trademarks are not a part of the trademark and therefore do not provide any useful information for dating your bottles. There are also very few instances of companies using identical marks, which is amazing considering how many companies have manufactured bottles.

For many manufacturers of antique bottles, protection for the trademark owner was virtually nonexistent. While the United States Constitution provided rights of ownership in copyrights and patents, there was no trademark protection until the United States Congress enacted the country's first federal trademark law in 1870. There are approximately 1,200 trademarks for bottles and fruit jars, which are comprised of 900 older marks (1830s–1940s) and 300 more modern marks (1940s to 1970). This chapter covers a large portion of both U.S. trademarks and foreign trademarks for bottles.

The words and letters in bold are the company's description and the trademarks as they appeared on the bottle. Each is followed by the complete name and location of the company and the approximate period of time during which the trademark was used.

United States Trademarks

A—Adams & Co., Pittsburgh, PA, 1861–1891

A—John Agnew & Son, Pittsburgh, PA, 1854–1866

A IN A CIRCLE—American Glass Works, Richmond, VA, and Paden City, WV, 1908–1935.

A & B TOGETHER (AB)—Adolphus Busch Glass Manufacturing Co, Belleville, IL, and St. Louis, MO, 1904–1907

ABC—Atlantic Bottle Co., New York City and Brackenridge, PA, 1918–1930

ABCo.—American Bottle Co., Chicago, IL, 1905–1916; Toledo, OH, 1916–1929

ABCO IN SCRIPT—Ahrens Bottling Company, Oakland, CA, 1903–1908

A B G M Co.—Adolphus Busch Glass Manufacturing Co., Belleville, IL, 1886–1907; St. Louis, MO, 1886–1928

A & Co.—John Agnew and Co., Pittsburgh, PA, 1854–1892

A C M E—Acme Glass Co., Olean, NY, 1920–1930

A & D H C—A. & D.H. Chambers, Pittsburgh, PA, Union Flasks, 1843–1886

AGCo—Arsenal Glass Co. (or Works), Pittsburgh, PA, 1865–1868

AGEE AND AGEE IN SCRIPT—Hazel Atlas Glass Co., Wheeling, WV, 1919–1925

AGNEW & CO.—Agnew & Co., Pittsburgh, PA, 1876–1886

AGWL,PITTS PA—American Glass Works, Pittsburgh, PA, 1865–1880, American Glass Works Limited, 1880–1905

AGW—American Glass Works, Richmond, VA, and Paden City, WV, 1908–1935

AMF & Co.—Adelbert M. Foster & Co., Chicago, IL, Millgrove, Upland, and Marion, IN 1895–1911

ANCHOR FIGURE WITH H IN CENTER—Anchor Hocking Glass Corp., Lancaster, OH, 1955

A. R. S.—A. R. Samuels Glass Co., Philadelphia, PA, 1855–1872

A S F W W VA.—A. S. Frank Glass Co., Wellsburg, WV, 1859

ATLAS—Atlas Glass Co., Washington, PA, and later Hazel Atlas Glass Co., 1896–1965

BALL AND BALL IN SCRIPT—Ball Bros. Glass Manufacturing Co., Muncie, IN, and later Ball Corp., 1887–1973

BAKER BROS. BALTO.MD.—Baker Brothers, Baltimore, MD, 1853–1905

BAKEWELL—Benjamin P. Bakewell Jr. Glass Co., 1876–1880

BANNER—Fisher-Bruce Co., Philadelphia, PA, 1910–1930

BB Co—Berney-Bond Glass Co., Bradford, Clarion, Hazelhurst, and Smithport, PA, 1900

BB & Co—Berney-Bond Glass Co., Bradford, Clarion, Hazelhurst, and Smithport, PA, 1900

BB48—Berney-Bond Glass Co., Bradford, Clarion, Hazelhurst, and Smithport, PA, 1920–1930

BERNARDIN IN SCRIPT—W. J. Latchford Glass Co., Los Angeles, CA, 1932–1938

THE BEST—Gillender & Sons, Philadelphia, PA, 1867–1870

B F B Co.— Bell Fruit Bottle Co., Fairmount, IN, 1910

B. G. Co.—Belleville Glass Co., IL, 1882

BISHOP'S—Bishop & Co., San Diego and Los Angeles, CA, 1890–1920

BK—Benedict Kimber, Bridgeport and Brownsville, PA, 1825–1840

BOYDS IN SCRIPT—Illinois Glass Co., Alton, IL, 1900–1930

BP & B—Bakewell, Page & Bakewell, Pittsburgh, PA, 1824–1836

BRELLE (IN SCRIPT) JAR—Brelle Fruit Jar Manufacturing Co., San Jose, CA, 1912–1916

BRILLIANTE—Jefferis Glass Co., Fairton, NJ, and Rochester, PA, 1900–1905

C IN A CIRCLE—Chattanooga Bottle & Glass Co. and later Chattanooga Glass Co., 1927–Present

C IN A SQUARE—Crystal Glass Co., Los Angeles, CA, 1921–1929

C IN A STAR—Star City Glass Co., Star City, WV, 1949–Present

CANTON DOMESTIC FRUIT JAR—Canton Glass Co., Canton, OH, 1890–1904

C & Co. OR C Co—Cunninghams & Co., Pittsburgh, PA, 1880–1907

CCCo—Carl Conrad & Co., St. Louis, Mo. (Beer), 1860–1883

C.V.Co. No. 1 & No 2—Milwaukee, WI, 1880–1881

C C Co.—Carl Conrad & Co., St. Louis, MO, 1876–1883

C C G Co.—Cream City Glass Co., Milwaukee, WI, 1888–1894

C.F.C.A.—California Fruit Canners Association, Sacramento, CA, 1899–1916

CFJCo—Consolidated Fruit Jar Co., New Brunswick, NJ, 1867–1882

C G I—California Glass Insulator Co., Long Beach, CA, 1912–1919

C G M Co—Campbell Glass Manufacturing Co., West Berkeley, CA, 1885

C G W—Campbell Glass Works, West Berkeley, CA, 1884–1885

C & H—Coffin & Hay, Hammonton, NJ, 1836–1838, or Winslow, NJ, 1838–1842

C L G Co.—Carr-Lowrey Glass Co., Baltimore, MD, 1889–1920

CLYDE, N. Y.—Clyde Glass Works, Clyde, NY, 1870–1882

THE CLYDE IN SCRIPT—Clyde Glass Works, Clyde, NY, 1895

C MILW—Chase Valley Glass Co., Milwaukee, WI, 1880–1881

COHANSEY—Cohansey Glass Manufacturing Co., Philadelphia, PA, 1870–1900

C R—Curling, Robertson & Co., Pittsburgh, PA, 1834–1857, or Curling, Ringwalt & Co., Pittsburgh, PA, 1857–1863

DB—Du Bois Brewing Co., Pittsburgh, PA, 1918

DEXTER—Franklin Flint Glass Works, Philadelphia, PA, 1861–1880

DIAMOND—(Plain) Diamond Glass Co., 1924–Present

THE DICTATOR—William McCully & Co., Pittsburgh, PA, 1855–1869

DICTATOR—William McCully & Co., Pittsburgh, PA, 1869–1885

D & O—Cumberland Glass Mfg. Co., Bridgeton, NJ, 1890–1900

D O C—D. O. Cunningham Glass Co., Pittsburgh, PA, 1883–1937

DOME—Standard Glass Co., Wellsburg, WV, 1891–1893

D S G Co.—De Steiger Glass Co., LaSalle, IL, 1879–1896

DUFFIELD—Dr. Samuel Duffield, Detroit, MI, 1862–1866 and Duffield, Parke & Co,. Detroit, MI, 1866–1875

DYOTTSVILLE—Dyottsville Glass Works, Philadelphia, PA, 1833–1923

E4—Essex Glass Co., Mt. Vernon, OH, 1906–1920

ECONOMY (IN SCRIPT) TRADE MARK—Kerr Glass Manufacturing Co., Portland, OR, 1903–1912

ELECTRIC TRADE MARK IN SCRIPT—Gayner Glass Works, Salem, NJ, 1910

ELECTRIC TRADE MARK—Gayner Glass Works, Salem, NJ, 1900–1910

ERD & CO., E R DURKEE—E. R. Durkee & Co., New York, NY, Post-1874

E R DURKEE & CO—E. R. Durkee & Co., New York, NY, 1850–1860

EUREKA 17—Eurkee Jar Co., Dunbar, WV, 1864

EUREKA IN SCRIPT—Eurkee Jar Co., Dunbar, WV, 1900–1910

EVERETT AND EHE—Edward H. Everett Glass Co. (Star Glass Works), Newark, OH, 1893–1904

EVERLASTING (IN SCRIPT) JAR—Illinois Pacific Glass Co., San Francisco, CA, 1904

F INSIDE A JAR OUTLINE—C. L. Flaccus Glass Co., Pittsburgh, PA, 1900–1928

F WM. FRANK & SONS—WM. Frank & Co., Pittsburgh, PA, 1846–1966, WM. Frank & Sons, Pittsburgh, PA, 1866–1876

F & A—Fahnstock & Albree, Pittsburgh, PA 1860–1862

FERG CO—F.E. Reed Glass Co., Rochester, NY, 1898–1947

FF & CO—Fahnstock, Fortune & Co., Pittsburgh, PA, 1866–1873

F G—Florida Glass Manufacturing Co., Jacksonville, FL, 1926–1947

FL OR FL & CO.—Frederick Lorenz & Co., Pittsburgh, PA, 1819–1841

FOLGER, JAF&Co., PIONEER, GOLDEN GATE—J. A. Folger & Co., San Francisco, CA, 1850–Present

G E M—Hero Glass Works, Philadelphia, PA, 1884–1909

G & H—Gray & Hemingray, Cincinnati, OH, 1848–1851; Covington, KY, 1851–1864

G & S—Gillinder & Sons, Philadelphia, PA, 1867–1871 and 1912–1930

GILLINDER—Gillinder Bros., Philadelphia, PA, 1871–1930

GILBERDS—Gilberds Butter Tub Co., Jamestown, NY, 1883–1890

GREENFIELD—Greenfield Fruit Jar & Bottle Co., Greenfield, IN, 1888–1912

G W K & Co.—George W. Kearns & Co., Zanesville, OH, 1848–1911

H (WITH VARYING NUMERALS)—Holt Glass Works, West Berkeley, CA, 1893–1906

H IN A DIAMOND—A.H. Heisey Glass Co., Oakwood Ave., Newark, OH, 1893–1958

HAZEL—Hazel Glass Co., Wellsburg, WV, 1886–1902

H.B.Co— Hagerty Bros. & Co., Brooklyn, NY, 1880–1900

HELME—Geo. W. Helme Co., Jersey City, NJ, 1870–1895

HEMINGRAY—Hemingray Brothers & Co. and later Hemingray Glass Co., Covington, KY, 1864–1933

H. J. HEINZ—H.J. Heinz Co., Pittsburgh, PA, 1860–1869

HEINZ & NOBLE—H.J. Heinz Co., Pittsburgh, PA, 1869–1872

F. J. HEINZ—H.J. Heinz Co., Pittsburgh, PA, 1876–1888

H. J. HEINZ Co.—H.J. Heinz Co., Pittsburgh, PA, 1888–Present

HELME—Geo. W. Helme Co., NJ, 1870–1890

HS IN A CIRCLE—Twitchell & Schoolcraft, Keene, NH, 1815–1816

I G Co.—Ihmsen Glass Co., Pittsburgh, PA, 1855–1896

I. G. Co—Ihmsen Glass Co., Pittsburgh, PA, 1895

I. G. Co.—Monogram, Illinois Glass Co. on fruit jar, 1914

IPGCO—Illinois Pacific Glass Company, San Francisco, CA, 1902–1926

IPGCO—(In Diamond), Illinois Pacific Glass Company, San Francisco, CA, 1902–1926

IG—Illinois Glass, F inside of a jar outline, C. L. Flaccus ½ glass ½ co., Pittsburgh, PA, 1900–1928

Ill. Glass Co.—1916–1929

I G—Illinois Glass Co., Alton, IL, before 1890

I G Co. in a diamond—Illinois Glass Co., Alton, IL, 1900–1916

Improved G E M—Hero Glass Works, Philadelphia, PA, 1868

I P G—Illinois Pacific Glass Co., San Francisco, CA, 1902–1932

I X L—I X L Glass Bottle Co., Inglewood, CA, 1921–1923

J in Square—Jeannette Glass Co., Jeannette, PA, 1901–1922

JAF & Co., Pioneer and Folger—J. A. Folger & Co., San Francisco, CA, 1850–Present

J D 26 S—Jon Ducan & Sons, New York, NY, 1880–1900

J. P. F.—Pitkin Glass Works, Manchester, CN, 1783–1830

J R—Stourbridge Flint Glass Works, Pittsburgh, PA, 1823–1828

JBS monogram—Joseph Schlitz Brewing Co., Milwaukee, WI, 1900

JT—Mantua Glass Works and later Mantua Glass Co., Mantua, OH, 1824

JT & Co—Brownsville Glass Works, Brownsville, PA, 1824–1828

Kensington Glass Works—Kensington Glass Works, Philadelphia, PA, 1822–1932

Kerr in script—Kerr Glass Manufacturing Co. and later Alexander H. Kerr Glass Co., Portland, OR; Sand Spring, OK; Chicago, IL; Los Angeles, CA, 1912–Present.

K H & G—Kearns, Herdman & Gorsuch, Zanesville, OH, 1876–1884

K & M—Knox & McKee, Wheeling, WV, 1824–1829

K & O—Kivlan & Onthank, Boston, MA, 1919–1925

K Y G W AND KYGW Co—Kentucky Glass Works Co., Louisville, KY, 1849–1855

L—W. J. Latchford Glass Co., Los Angeles, CA, 1925–1938

LAMB—Lamb Glass Co., Mt. Vernon, OH, 1855–1964

L & W—Lorenz & Wightman, PA, 1862–1871

LGW—Laurens Glass Works, Laurens, SC, 1911–1970

L G Co—Louisville Glass Works, Louisville, KY, 1880

LIGHTNING—Henry W. Putnam, Bennington, VT, 1875–1890

L K Y G W—Louisville Kentucky Glass Works, Louisville, KY, 1873–1890

"MASCOT, "MASON" AND M F G Co.—Mason Fruit Jar Co., Philadelphia, PA, 1885–1890

MASTADON—Thomas A. Evans Mastadon Works, and later Wm. McCully & Co. Pittsburgh, PA, 1855–1887

MB Co—Muncie Glass Co., Muncie, IN, 1895–1910

M B & G Co—Massillon Bottle & Glass Co., Massillon, OH, 1900–1904

M B W—Millville Bottle Works, Millville, NJ, 1903–1930

MG—Slant letters, Maywood Glass, Maywood, CA, 1930–1950

M.G. CO.—Modes Glass Co., Cicero, IN, 1895–1904

M. G. W.—Middletown Glass Co. NY, 1889

MOORE BROS.—Moore Bros., Clayton, NJ, 1864–1880

N—H. Northwood Glass Co., Wheeling, WV, 1902–1925

N B B G Co—North Baltimore Bottle Glass Co., North Baltimore, OH, 1885–1930

N G Co—Northern Glass Co., Milwaukee, WI, 1894–1896

N—W—Nivison-Weiskopf Glass Co., Reading, OH, 1900–1931

O IN A SQUARE—Owen Bottle Co., 1911–1929

O B C—Ohio Bottle Co., Newark, OH, 1904–1905

O-D-1-O & DIAMOND & I—Owens Ill. Pacific Coast Co., CA, 1932–1943. Mark of Owen-Ill. Glass Co. merger in 1930

PCGW—Pacific Coast Glass Works, San Francisco, CA, 1902–1924

PEERLESS—Peerless Glass Co., Long Island City, NY, 1920–1935 (was Bottler's & Manufacturer's Supply Co., 1900-1920)

P G W—Pacific Glass Works, San Francisco, CA, 1862–1876

PREMIUM—Premium Glass Co., Coffeyville, KS, 1908–1914

P in Square or Pine in Box— Pine Glass Corp., Okmulgee, OK, 1927–1929

P S—Puget Sound Glass Co., Anacortes, WA, 1924–1929

PUTNAM GLASS WORKS IN A CIRCLE—Putnam Flint Glass Works, Putnam, OH, 1852–1871

P & W—Perry & Wood and later Perry & Wheeler, Keene, NH, 1822–1830

QUEEN (IN SCRIPT) TRADE MARK ALL IN A SHIELD—Smalley, Kivian & Onthank, Boston, MA, 1906–1919

RAU'S—Fairmount Glass Works, Fairmount, IN, 1898–1908

R & C Co—Roth & Co., San Francisco, CA, 1879–1888

RED WITH A KEY THROUGH IT—Safe Glass Co., Upland, IN, 1892–1898

R G Co.—Renton Glass Co., Renton, WA, 1911

ROOT—Root Glass Co., Terre Haute, IN, 1901–1932

S—(inside of start)—Southern Glass Co., Los Angeles, CA, 1920–1929

SB & GCo—Streator Bottle & Glass Co., Streator, IL, 1881–1905

SF & PGW—San Francisco & Pacific Glass Works, 1876–1900

S & C—Stebbins & Chamberlain or Coventry Glass Works, Coventry, CT, 1825–1830

S F G W—San Francisco Glass Works, San Francisco, CA, 1869–1876

SQUIBB—E.R. Squibb, M.D., Brooklyn, NY, 1858–1895

STANDARD (IN SCRIPT, MASON)—Standard Coop. Glass Co. and later Standard Glass Co., Marion, IN, 1894–1932

STAR GLASS CO—Star Glass Co., New Albany, IN, 1867–1900

SWAYZEE—Swayzee Glass Co., Swayzee, IN, 1894–1906

T C W—T.C. Wheaton Co., Millville, NJ, 1888–Present

T W & Co.—Thomas Wightman & Co., Pittsburgh, PA, 1871–1895

T S—Coventry Glass Works, Coventry, CT, 1820–1824

U—Upland Flint Bottle Co., Upland, IN, 1890–1909

W & CO—Thomas Wightman & Co., Pottsburg, PA, 1880–1889

W C G Co—West Coast Glass Co., Los Angeles, CA, 1908–1930

WF & S MILW—William Franzen & Son, Milwaukee, WI, 1900–1929

W G W—Woodbury Glass Works, Woodbury, NJ, 1882–1900

WYETH—A drug manufacturer, 1880–1910

W T & Co—Whitall-Tatum & Co., Millville, NJ, 1857–1935

W T R Co.—W. T. Rawleigh Manufacturing Co., Freeport, IL, 1925–1936

Foreign Trademarks

A IN A CIRCLE—Alembic Glass, Industries Bangalore, India

BIG A IN CENTER OF IT GM—Australian Glass Mfg. Co., Kilkenny, So. Australia.

A.B.C.—Albion Bottle Co. Ltd., Oldbury, Nr. Birmingham, England.

A.G.W.—Alloa Glass Limited, Alloa, Scotland.

A G B Co.—Albion Glass Bottle Co., England, trademark is found under Lea & Perrins, 1880–1900

B & C Co. L—Bagley & Co. Ltd. Est. 1832 still operating (England)

AVH.A.—Van Hoboken & Co., Rotterdam, the Netherlands, 1800–1898

BEAVER—Beaver Flint Glass Co., Toronto, Ontario, Canada, 1897–1920

BOTTLE IN FRAME—Veb Glasvoerk Drebkau Drebkau, N. L. Germany

CROWN WITH 3 DOTS—Crown Glass, Waterloo, N.S. Wales

CS & Co.—Cannington, Shaw & Co., St. Helens, England, 1872–1916

CROWN WITH FIGURE OF A CROWN—Excelsior Glass Co., St. Johns, Quebec, and later Diamond Glass Co., Montreal, Quebec, Canada, 1879–1913

D IN CENTER OF A DIAMOND—Cominion Glass Co., Montreal, Quebec

D.B.—In a book frame, Dale Brown & Co., Ltd., Mesborough, York, England.

FISH—Veb Glasvoerk Stralau, Berlin

EXCELSIOR—Excelsior Glass Co., St. John, Quebec, Canada, 1878–1883

HH—Werk Hermannshutte, Czechoslovakia.

HAMILTON—Hamilton Glass Works, Hamilton, Ontario, Canada, 1865–1872

HAT—Brougba, Bulgaria

HUNYADI JANOS—Andreas Saxlehner, Budapest, Austria-Hungary, 1863–1900

IYGE—All in a circle, The Irish Glass Bottle, Ltd., Dublin.

KH—Kastrupog Holmeqaads, Copenhagen.

L—On a bell, Lanbert S.A. Belgium

LIP—Lea & Perrins, London, England, 1880–1900

LS—In a circle, Lax & Shaw Ltd., Leeds, York, England.

M—In a circle, Cristales Mexicanos, Monterey, Mexico.

N—In a diamond, Tippon Glass Co., Ltd., Tokyo, Japan.

NAGC—North American Glass Co., Montreal, Quebec, Canada, 1883–1890

P & J A—P. & J. Arnold, Ltd., London, England, 1890–1914

PG—Verreries De Puy De Dome, S. A. Paris

R—Louis Freres & Co., France, 1870–1890

S—In a circle, Vetreria Savonese. A. Voglienzone, S.A. Milano, Italy

S.A.V.A.—All in a circle, Asmara, Ethiopia.

S & M—Sykes & Macvey, Castleford, England, 1860–1888.

T—In a circle, Tokyo Seibin, Ltd., Tokyo, Japan

vFo—Vidreria Ind. Figuerras Oliveiras, Brazil

VT—Ve.Tri S.p.a., Vetrerie Trivemta, Vicenza, Italy

VX—Usine de Vauxrot, France

WECK—In a frame, Weck Glaswerk G. mb.H, ofigen, in Bonn, Germany

Y—In a circle, Etaria Lipasmaton, Athens, Greece

Bottle Clubs

Bottle Clubs are one of the best sources for beginners. They offer a great opportunity to meet veteran bottle collectors, learn from them, gather information, and in general have a good time. The bottle clubs listed here reflect the latest information available at the time of publication and are subject to change. The list represents an excellent cross section of the United States, Europe, and Asia-Pacific. Any active bottle club or organization that requires a change of information or wishes to be included in the next edition of *Bottles: Identification & Price Guide* should send the required information to Michael F. Polak, P.O. Box 30328, Long Beach, CA 90853.

Listed alphabetically by state, country, and club name

United States

ALABAMA

Alabama Bottle Collectors Society
2768 Hanover Circle
Birmingham, AL 35205
(205) 933-7902

Azalea City Beamers Bottle & Spec. Club
100 Bienville Avenue
Mobile, AL 36606
(205) 473-4251

Choctaw Jim Beam Bottle & Spec. Club
218 S. Hamburg Street
Butler, AL 36904
(205) 459-3140

Heart of Dixie Beam Bottle & Spec. Club
2136 Rexford Road
Montgomery, AL 36116

Mobile Bottle Collectors Club
8844 Lee Circle
Irvington, AL 36544
(205) 957-6725

Montgomery, Alabama, Bottle Club
1940A Norman Bridge Court
Montgomery, AL 36104

Montgomery Bottle & Insulator Club
2021 Merrily Drive
Montgomery, AL 36111
(205) 288-7937

North Alabama Bottle & Glass Club
P.O. Box 109
Decatur, AL 35602-0109

Tuscaloosa Antique Bottle Club
1617 11th Street
Tuscaloosa, AL 35401

Southern Beamers Bottle & Spec. Club
1400 Greenbrier Road, Apt. G-3
Anniston, AL 36201
(205) 831-5151

Vulcan Beamers Bottle & Spec. Club
5817 Avenue Q
Birmingham, AL 35228
(205) 831-5151

ALASKA
Alaska Bottle Club
8510 E. 10th
Anchorage, AK 99504

Arizona
Avon Collectors Club
P.O. Box 1406
Mesa, AZ 86201

Fort Smith Area Bottle Collectors Association
4618 S. "Q"
Fort Smith, AZ 72901

Kachina Ezra Brooks Bottle Club
3818 W. Cactus Wren Drive
Phoenix, AZ 85021

Phoenix A.B.C. Club
326 E. Huber St.
Mesa, AZ 85201

Pick & Shovel A.B.C. of Arizona, Inc.
P.O. Box 7020
Phoenix, AZ 85011

Southern AZ Historical Collector's Association, Ltd.
6211 Piedra Seca
Tucson, AZ 85718

Tri-City Jim Beam Bottle Club
2701 E. Utopia Road, Sp.#91
Phoenix, AZ 85024
(602) 867-1375

Valley of the Sun Bottle & Specialty Club
212 E. Minton
Tempe, AZ 85281

White Mountain Antique Bottle Collectors Association
P.O.Box 503
Eager, AZ 85925

Wildcat Country Beam Bottle & Spec. Club
2601 S. Blackmoon Drive
Tucson, AZ 85730
(602) 298-5943

ARKANSAS
Fort Smith Area Bottle Collectors Assn.
2201 S. 73rd Street
Ft. Smith, AR 72903

Hempsted County Bottle Club
710 S. Hervey
Hope, AR 71801

Indian Country A.B. & Relic Soc.
3818 Hilltop Dr.
Jonesboro, AR 72401

Little Rock Antique Bottle Collectors Club
16201 Highway 300
Roland, AR 72135

Madison County Bottle Collectors Club
Rt. 2, Box 304
Huntsville, AR 72740

Razorback Jim Beam Bottle & Spec. Club
2609 S. Taylor
Little Rock, AR 72204
(501) 664-1335

<u>CALIFORNIA</u>

American Cut Glass Assoc.
P.O. Box 482
Ramona, CA 92065-0482

Amethyst Bottle Club
3245 Military Avenue
Los Angeles, CA 90034

Antique Bottle Club Association of Fresno
P.O. Box 1932
Fresno, CA 93718

Antique Bottle Collectors of Orange County
223 E. Pomona
Santa Ana, CA 92707

Argonaut Jim Beam Bottle Club
8253 Citadel Way
Sacramento, CA 95826
(916) 383-0206

Avon Bottle & Specialties Collectors
Southern California Division
9233 Mills Avenue
Montclair, CA 91763

Bakersfield Bottle & Insulator Collectors
1023 Baldwin Road
Bakersfield, CA 93304

Bay Area Vagabonds Jim Beam Club
224 Castleton Way
San Bruno, CA 94066
(415) 355-4356

Bidwell Bottle Club
Box 546
Chico, CA 95926

Bishop Belles & Beaux Bottle Club
P.O. Box 1475
Bishop, CA 93514

Blossom Valley Jim Beam Bottle & Spec. Club
431 Grey Ghost Avenue
San Jose, CA 95111
(408) 227-2759

California Milk Bottle Collectors
2592 Mayfair Court
Hanford, CA 93230

California Miniature Bottle Club
1911 Willow Street
Alameda, CA 94501

California Ski Country Bottle Club
212 South El Molino Street
Alhambra, CA 91801

Camellia City Jim Beam Bottle Club
3734 Lynhurst Way
North Highlands, CA 95660

Cherry Valley Beam Bottle & Specialty Club
6851 Hood Drive
Westminster, CA 92683

Fiesta City Beamers
329 Mountain Drive
Santa Barbara, CA 93103

First Double Springs Collectors Club
13311 Illinois Street
Westminster, CA 92683

Five Cities Beamers
756 Mesa View Drive, Sp. 57
Arroyo Grande, CA 93420

Fresno Antique Bottle & Collectors Club
281 West Magill Avenue
Clovis, CA 93612

Glass Belles of San Gabriel
518 W. Neuby Avenue
San Gabriel, CA 91776

Glasshopper Figural Bottle Association
P.O. Box 6642
Torrance, CA 90504

Golden Gate Beam Club
35113 Clover Street
Union City, CA 94587
(415) 487-4479

Golden Gate Historical Bottle Society
P.O. Box 5331
Richmond, CA 94805

Greater Calif. Antique Bottle Collectors
P.O. Box 55
Sacramento, CA 95801

*Highland Toasters Beam Bottle & Spec.
Club*
1570 E. Marshall
San Bernardino, CA 92404
(714) 883-2000

Hoffman's Mr. Lucky Bottle Club
2104 Rhoda Street
Simi Valley, CA 93065

International Perfume Bottle Association
3519 Wycliffe Drive
Modesto, CA 95355

Jewels of Avon
2297 Maple Avenue
Oroville, CA 95965

Jim Beam Bottle Club
139 Arlington
Berkeley, CA 94707

Jim Beam Bottle Club of So. Calif
1114 Coronado Terrace
Los Angeles, CA 90066

Lilliputian Bottle Club
5626 Corning Avenue
Los Angeles, CA 90056
213-294-3231

Lionstone Bottle Collectors of America
P.O. Box 75924
Los Angeles, CA 90075

Livermore Avon Club
6385 Claremont Avenue
Richmond, CA 94805

Lodi Jim Beam Bottle Club
429 E. Lodi Avenue
Lodi, CA 95240

Los Angeles Historical Bottle Club
2842 El Sol Drive
Lancaster, CA 93535

*Miniature Bottle Club of Southern
California*
836 Carob
Brea, CA 92621

Mission Bells (Beams)
1114 Coronada Terrace
Los Angeles, CA 90026

Mission Trail Historical Bottle Club
1475 Teton Avenue
Salinas, CA 93906

Modesto Beamers
1429 Glenwood Drive
Modesto, CA 95350
(209) 523-3440

Modesto Old Bottle Club (MOBC)
P.O. Box 1791
Modesto, CA 95354

*Monterey Bay Beam Bottle & Specialty
Club*
P.O. Box 258
Freedom, CA 95019

Motherlode Antique Bottle Club
P.O. Box 165
Downieville, CA 95936

Mt.Bottle Club
422 Orpheus
Encinitas, CA 92024

Mt.Diablo Bottle Club
4166 Sandra Circle
Pittsburg, CA 94565

Mt.Diablo Bottle Society
1699 Laguna #110
Concord, CA 94520

Napa-Solano Bottle Club
1409 Delwood
Vallejo, CA 94590

National Insulator Assoc.
28390 Saffron Ave.
Highland, CA 92346
(909) 862-4312

Northern California Jim Beam Bottle &
Specialty Club
P.O.Box 186
Montgomery Creek, CA 96065

Northwestern Bottle Collectors
Association
P.O. Box 1312
Healdsburg, CA 95448

Northwestern Bottle Collectors
Association
1 Keeler Street
Petaluma, CA 94952

Ocean Breeze Beamers
4841 Tacayme Drive
Oceanside, CA 92054
(714) 757-9081

Orange County Jim Beam Bottle &
Specialties Club
546 W. Ash Ave.
Fullerton, CA 92632-2702
(714) 875-8241

Original Sippin Cousins Ezra Brooks
Specialties Club
12206 Malone Street
Los Angeles, CA 90066

Pepsi-Cola Collectors Club
P.O. Box 817
Claremont, CA 91711

Pepsi-Cola Collectors Club
P.O. Box 1275
Covina, CA 91722

Painted Soda Bottle Collectors Assn
9418 Hilmer Dr.
LaMesa, CA 91942
(619) 461-4354

Peninsula Bottle Club
P.O. Box 886
Belmont, CA 94002

Quail Country Jim Beam Bottle & Spec.
Club
625 Pleasant
Coalinga, CA 93210

Queen Mary Beam & Specialty Club
P.O. Box 2054
Anaheim, CA 92804

Relic Accumulators
P.O. Box 3513
Eureka, CA 95501

Santa Barbara Beam Bottle Club
5307 University Drive
Santa Barbara, CA 93111

Santa Barbara Bottle Club
P.O. Box 30171
Santa Barbara, CA 93105

San Bernardino County Historical Bottle
and Collectible Club
P.O. Box 6759
San Bernardino, CA 92412
(619) 244-5863

San Diego Antique Bottle Club
P.O. Box 5137
San Diego, CA 92165
(619) 274-5519

San Diego Jim Beam Bottle Club
2620 Mission Village Drive
San Diego, CA 92112

San Joaquin Valley Jim Beam Bottle &
Specialties Club
4085 N. Wilson Avenue
Fresno, CA 93704

San Jose Historical Bottle Club Assn
P.O. Box 5432
San Jose, CA 95150
(408) 259-7564

San Luis Obispo Bottle Society
124-21 Street
Paso Robles, CA 93446
(805) 238-1848

Santa Maria Beam & Spec. Club
528 E. Harding
Santa Maria, CA 93454
(805) 922-1238

Sequoia Antique Bottle Society
1900 4th Avenue
Kingsburg, CA 93631

Sequoia Antique Bottle and Collectors
Society
P.O. Box 3695
Visalia, CA 93278
(209) 686-1873

Shasta Antique Bottle Collectors Assn
Rt. 1, Box 3147-A
Anderson, CA 96007

Sierra Gold Ski Country Bottle Club
5081 Rio Vista Avenue
San Jose, CA 95129

Ski-Country Bottle Club of Southern
California
3148 N. Walnut Grove
Rosemead, CA 91770

Solar Country Beamers
940 Kelly Drive
Barstow, CA 92311
(714) 256-1485

South Bay Antique Bottle Club
2589½ Valley Drive
Manhattan Beach, CA 90266

Southern Wyoming Avon Bottle Club
301 Canyon Highlands Drive
Oroville, CA 95965

Stockton Historical Bottle Society, Inc.
P.O. Box 8584
Stockton, CA 95204

Sunnyvale Antique Bottle Collectors Assn
613 Torrington
Sunnyvale, CA 94087

Superior California Bottle Club
3220 Stratford Avenue
Redding, CA 96001

Taft Antique Bottle Club
P.O. Box 334
Taft, CA 93268

Tehama County Antique Bottle Club
Rt. 1, Box 775
Red Bluff, CA 96080
(916) 527-1680

The California Miniature Club
1911 Willow St.
Alameda, CA 94501

Tinseltown Beam Club
4117 E. Gage Avenue
Bell, CA 90201
(213) 699-8787

Wildwind Jim Beam Bottle & Spec. Club
905 Eaton Way
Sunnyvale, CA 94087
(408) 739-1558

'49er Historical Bottle Assn
P.O. Box 561
Penryn, CA 95663
(916) 663-3681

COLORADO
American Breweriana Association, Inc.
P.O. Box 11157
Pueblo, CO 81001

Antique Bottle Collectors of Colorado
17238 E. Greenwood
CO 80013

Avon Club of Colorado Springs, CO
707 N. Farragut
Colorado Springs, CO 80909

Colorado Mile-High Ezra Brooks Bottle Club
7401 Decatur Street
Westminster, CO 80030

Lionstone Western Figural Club
P.O. Box 2275
Colorado Springs, CO 80901

Mile-Hi Jim Beam Bottle & Spec. Club
13196 W. Green Mountain Drive
Lakewood, CO 80228
(303) 986-6828

National Ski Country Bottle Club
1224 Washington Avenue
Golden, CO 80401
(303) 279-3373

Northern Colorado Antique Bottle Club
227 W. Beaver Avenue
Ft. Morgan, CO 80701

Northern Colorado Beam Bottle & Spec. Club
3272 Gunnison Drive
Ft. Collins, CO 80526
(303) 226-2301

Ole Foxie Jim Beam Club
7530 Wilson Court
Westminster, CO 80030
(303) 429-1823
Attn: Shirley Engel, President

Pikes Peak Antique Bottle & Collectors Club
308 Maplewood Drive
Colorado Springs, CO
80907-4326

Southern Colorado Antique Bottle Club
843 Ussie Ave
Canon City, CO 81212
(719) 275-3719

Telluride Antique Bottle Collectors
P.O. Box 344
Telluride, CO 81435

Western Slope Bottle Club
P.O. Box 354
Palisade, CO 81526
(303) 464-7727

CONNECTICUT
Connecticut Specialty Bottle Club, Inc.
P.O. Box 624
Stratford, CT 06497

The National Assn. of Milk Bottle
Collectors
4 Ox Bow Road
Westport, CT 06880-2602
(203) 227-5244

Sommers Antique Bottle Club
27 Park Lane
Glastonbury, CT 06033

Southern Connecticut Antique Bottle
Collectors Assn.
11 Paquonnock Road
Trumbull, CT 06033

DELAWARE

Blue Hen Jim Beam Bottle & Spec. Club
303 Potomac Drive
Wilmington, DE 19803
(302) 652-6378

Delmarva Antique Bottle Collectors
57 Lakewood Drive
Lewes, DE 19958

Mason-Dixon Bottle Collectors Assn
P.O. Box 505
Lewes, DE 19958

Tri-State Bottle Collectors and Diggers
Club
2510 Cratchett Road
Wilmington, DE 19808

FLORIDA

Antique Bottle Collectors of Florida, Inc.
2512 Davie Boulevard
Ft. Lauderdale, FL 33312

Assn. of Florida Antique Bottle
Collectors
P.O. Box 3105
Sarasota, FL 34230
(813) 923-6550

Bay Area Historical Bottle Collector
P.O. Box 3454
Apollo Beach, FL 32210

Central Florida Insulator Collectors Club
707 N.E. 113th St.
Miami, FL 33161-7239

Central Florida Jim Beam Bottle Club
1060 W. French Avenue
Orange City, FL 32763
(904) 775-7392

Crossarms Collectors Club
1756 N.W. 58th Avenue
Lauderhill, FL 33313

Emerald Coast Bottle Collectors
714 St. Croix Cove
Niceville, FL 32578

Everglades Antique Bottle Club
6981 S.W. 19th Street
Pompano, FL 33068

Everglades Antique Bottle & Collectors
Club
400 S. 57 Terrace
Hollywood, FL 33023
(305) 962-3434

International Perfume Bottle Assn.
3314 Shamrock Rd.
Tampa, FL 33629
(813) 837-5845

Longwood Bottle Club
P.O. Box 437
Longwood, FL 32750

Mid-State Antique Bottle Collectors
3400 East Grant Street
Orlando, FL 32806

M.T. Bottle Collectors Assn., Inc.
P.O. Box 1581
Deland, FL 32721

Original Florida Keys Collectors Club
P.O. Box 212
Islamorada, FL 33036

Pensacola Bottle & Relic Collectors Assn
1004 Freemont Avenue
Pensacola, FL 32505

Ridge Area Antique Bottle Collectors
1219 Carlton
Lake Wales, FL 33853

Sanford Antique Bottle Collectors
2656 Grandview Avenue
Sanford, FL 33853
(305) 322-7181

*Sarasota-Mantee Tailgators Antique
Bottle Club*
P.O. Box 3105
Sarasota, FL 34230

*South Florida Jim Beam Bottle & Spec.
Club*
7741 N.W. 35th Street
West Hollywood, FL 33024

Suncoast Antique Bottle Club
6720 Park St.
South Pasadena, FL 33707

*The Antique Bottle and Glass Collectors
of North FL*
P.O. Box 380022
Jacksonville, FL 32205-9266

Treasure Coast Bottle Collectors
6301 Lilyan Parkway
Ft. Pierce, FL 34591

*West Coast Florida Ezra Brooks Bottle
Club*
1360 Harbor Drive
Sarasota, FL 33579

GEORGIA
*Bulldog Double Springs Bottle Collector
Club of Augusta, Georgia*
1916 Melrose Drive
Augusta, GA 30906

Cavanagh's Coca-Cola Collectors Society
1000 Holcomb Woods Parkway
Roswell, GA 30076

Coastal Empire Bottle Club
P.O. Box 3714, Station B
Savannah, GA 31404

Coca-Cola Collectors Club International
P.O. Box 49166
Atlanta, GA 30359-1166

The Desoto Trail Bottle Collectors Club
406 Randolph Street
Cuthbert, GA 31740

The Dixie Jewels Insulator Club
6220 Carriage Court
Cummings, GA 30130
(707) 781-5021

Flint Antique Bottle & Coin Club
C/O Cordele-Crisp Co., Recreation
Dept
204 2nd Street North
Cordele, GA 31015

Georgia Bottle Club
2996 Pangborn Road
Decatur, GA 30033

Macon Antique Bottle Club
P.O. Box 5395
Macon, GA 31208

The Middle Georgia Antique Bottle Club
2746 Alden Street
Macon, GA 31206

Peachstate Bottle & Specialty Club
5040 Vallo Vista Court
Atlanta, GA 30342

*Peanut State Jim Beam Bottle & Spec.
Club*
767 Timberland Street
Smyrna GA 30080
(404) 432-8482

Southeastern Antique Bottle Club
P.O. Box 657
Decatur, GA 30033

Southeastern Antique Bottle Club
143 Scatterfoot Drive
Peachtree City, GA 30269

HAWAII
Hauoli Beam Bottle Collectors Club of
Hawaii
45-027 Ka-Hanahou Place
Kaneohe, HI 96744

Hawaii Historic Bottle Collectors Club
P.O. Box 90456
Honolulu, HI 96835

Hilo Bottle Club
287 Kanoelani Street
Hilo, HI 96720

IDAHO
Buhl Antique Bottle Club
500 12th
N. Buhl, ID 83316

Eagle Rock Beam & Spec. Club
3665 Upland Avenue
Idaho Falls, ID 83401
(208) 522-7819

Em Tee Bottle Club
P.O. Box 62
Jerome, ID 83338

Fabulous Valley Antique Bottle Club
P.O. Box 8051
Boise, ID 83707

Idaho Beam & Spec. Club
2312 Burrell Avenue
Lewiston, ID 83501
(208) 743-5997

Inland Empire Jim Beam Bottle &
Collectors' Club
1117 10th Street
Lewiston, ID 83501

ILLINOIS
Antique Bottle Club of Northern Illinois
P.O. Box 553
Richmond, IL 60071

Alton Area Bottle Club
2448 Alby Street
Alton, IL 62002
(618) 462-4285

Blackhawk Jim Beam Bottle & Spec.
Club
2003 Kishwaukee Street
Rockford, IL 61101

Central Illinois Jim Beam Bottle & Spec.
Club
3725 S. Sand Creek Road
Decatur, IL 62521

Central & Midwestern States Beam &
Spec. Club
44 S. Westmore
Lombard, IL 60148

Chicago Ezra Brooks Bottle & Spec.
Club
3635 W. 82nd Street
Chicago, IL 60652

Chicago Jim Beam Bottle & Spec. Club
1305 W. Marion Street
Joliet, IL 60436

Dreamers Beamers
5721 Vial Parkway
LaGrange, IL 60525
(312) 246-4838

Eagle Jim Beam Bottle & Spec. Club
1015 Hollycrest, P.O. Box 2084 CFS
Champaign, IL 61820
(217) 352-4035

1st Chicago Antique Bottle Club
P.O. Box A3382
Chicago, IL 60690

Greater Chicago Insulator Club
11728 Leonardo Dr.
St. John, IN 46373

Heart of Illinois Antique Bottle Club
2010 Bloomington Road
East Peoria, IL 61611

International Assn. of Jim Beam Bottle
and Specialties Clubs
2015 Burlington Ave.
Kewanee, IL 61443
www.2.tee.com.net/~eagle.beam-wade
collectables.htm

Land of Lincoln Bottle Club
2515 Illinois Circle
Decatur, IL 62526

Lewis & Clark Jim Beam Bottle & Spec.
Club
P.O. Box 451
Wood River, IL 62095

Louis Joliet Bottle Club
12 Kenmore
Joilet, IL 60433

Metro East Bottle & Jar Assn
309 Bellevue Drive
Delleville, IL 62223

North Shore Jim Beam Bottle Spec. Club
542 Glendale Road
Glenview, IL 60025

Pekin Bottle Collectors Assn.
409 E. Forrest Hill Ave.
Peoria, IL 61603

Rock River Valley Jim Beam Bottle &
Spec. Club
1107 Avenue A.
Rock Falls, IL 61071
(815) 625-7075

Starved Rock Jim Beam Bottle & Spec.
Club
P.O. Box 177
Ottawa, IL 61350
(815) 433-3269

Sweet Corn Capital Bottle Club
1015 W. Orange
Hoopeston, IL 60942

The Greater Chicago Insulator Club
34273 Homestead Rd.
Gurnee, IL 60031
(708) 855-9136

Tri-County Jim Beam Bottle Club
3702 W. Lancer Road
Peoria, IL 61615
(309) 691-8784

INDIANA
American Collectors of Infant Feeders
5161 W. 59th St.
Indianapolis, IN 46254
(317) 291-5850

City of Bridges Jim Beam Bottle & Spec.
Club
1017 N. 6th Street
Logansport, IN 46947
(219) 722-3197

Crossroads of America Jim Beam Bottle
Club
114 S. Green Street
Brownsburg, IN 46112
(317) 852-5168

Fort Wayne Historical Bottle Club
P.O. Box 475
Huntertown, IN 46748

Hoosier Jim Beam Bottle & Spec. Club
P.O. Box 24234
Indianapolis, IN 46224

Jelly Jammers
6086 West Boggstown Road
Boggstown, IN 46110

Lafayette Antique Bottle Club
3664 Redondo Drive
Lafayette, IN 47905

Mid-West Antique Fruit Jar & Bottle
Club
1201 W. Cowing Dr.
Flat Rock, IN 47234

The Ohio Valley Antique Bottle and Jar
Club
214 John Street
Aurora, IN 47001

Steel City Ezra Brooks Bottle Club
Rt. 2, Box 32A
Valparaiso, IN 46383

We Found 'Em Bottle & Insulator Club
P.O. Box 578
Bunker Hill, IN 46914

Iowa

Five Seasons Beam & Spec. Club of
Iowa
609 32nd Street, NE
Cedar Rapids, IA 52402
(319) 365-6089

Gold Dome Jim Beam Bottle & Spec.
Club
2616 Hull
Des Moines, IA 50317
(515) 262-8728

Hawkeye Jim Beam Bottle Club
658 Kern Street
Waterloo, IA 60703
(319) 233-9168

Iowa Antique Bottlers
Route 1, Box 145
Milton, IA 52570

Iowa Great Lakes Jim Beam Bottle &
Spec. Club
Green Acres Mobile Park, Lot 88
Estherville, IA 51334
(712) 362-2759

Larkin Bottle Club
107 W. Grimes
Red Oak, IA 51566

Midlands Jim Beam Bottle & Spec. Club
Rt. 4
Harlan, IA 51537
(712) 744-3686

Quad Cities Jim Beam Bottle & Spec.
Club
2425 W. 46th Street
Davenport, IA 52806

Shot Tower Beam Club
284 N. Booth Street
Dubuque, IA 52001
(319) 583-6343

Kansas

Air Capital City Jim Beam Bottle &
Spec. Club
3256 Euclid
Wichita, KS 67217
(316) 942-3162

Bud Hastin's National Avon Collector's
Club
P.O. Box 11530
Ft. Lauderdale, FL 33339

Cherokee Strip Ezra Brooks Bottle &
Spec. Club
P.O. Box 631
Arkansas City, KS 67005

Jayhawk Bottle Club
7919 Grant
Overland Park, KS 66212

Kansas City Bottle Collectors
1050 West Blue Ridge Blvd
Kansas City, MO 64145

National Depression Glass Assoc.
P.O. 8264
Wichita, KS 67208

No. Central Kansas Antique Bottle &
Collectors Club
5425 186th Blvd
Russell, KS 67665

Southeast Kansas Bottle & Relic Club
Route 2, Box 107
Humboldt, KS 66748

Walnut Valley Jim Beam Bottle & Spec.
Club
P.O. Box 631
Arkansas City, KS 67005
(316) 442-0509

KENTUCKY

Derby City Jim Beam Bottle Club
4105 Spring Hill Road
Louisville, KY 40207

Gold City Jim Beam Bottle Club
286 Metts Court, Apt. 4
Elizabethtown, KY 42701
(502) 737-9297

Kentuckiana Antique Bottle & Outhouse
Society
4017 Shady Villa Drive
Louisville, KY 40219

Kentucky Bluegrass Ezra Brooks Bottle
Club
6202 Tabor Drive
Louisville, KY 40218

Kentucky Cardinal Beam Bottle Club
428 Templin
Bardstown, KY 41104

Louisville Bottle Collectors
11819 Garrs Avenue
Anchorage, KY 40223

LOUISIANA

Ark-La-Tex Jim Beam Bottle & Spec.
Club
1902 Carol Street
Bossier City, LA 71112
(318) 742-3550

Bayou Bottle Bugs
216 Dahlia
New Iberia, LA 70560

"Cajun Country Cousins" Ezra Brooks
Bottle & Spec. Club
1000 Chevis Street
Abbeville, LA 70510

Crescent City Jim Beam Bottle & Spec.
Club
733 Wright Avenue
Gretna, LA 70053
(504) 367-2182

Dixie Diggers Bottle Club
P.O. Box 626
Empire, LA 70050

Historical Bottle Assn. of Baton Rouge
1843 Tudor Drive
Baton Rouge, LA 70815

New Orleans Antique Bottle Club
2605 Winifred Sreet
Metairie, LA 70003

North East Louisiana Antique Bottle
Club
P.O. Box 4192
Monroe, LA 71291
(318) 322-8359

Sanford's Night Owl Beamers
Rt. 2, Box 102
Greenwell Springs, LA 70739
(504) 261-3658

Shreveport Antique Bottle Club
1157 Arncliffe Drive
Shreveport, LA 71107
(504) 221-0089

MAINE
Dirigo Bottle Collectors Club
R.F.D. 3
Dexter, ME 04930
(207) 924-3443

Jim Beam Collectors Club
10 Lunt Road
Falmouth, ME 04105

New England Antique Bottle Club
RFD 1, Box 408
North Berwick, ME 03906

New England Bottle Club
45 Bolt Hill Road
Eliot, ME 03903

Pine Tree State Beamers
15 Woodside Avenue
Saco, ME 04072
(207) 284-8756

Tri-County Bottle Collectors Assn.
R.F.D. 3
Dexter, ME 04930

MARYLAND
Baltimore Antique Bottle Club
P.O. Box 36061
Towson, MD 21286-6061

International Chinese Snuff Bottle
Society
2601 North Charles Street
Baltimore, MD 21218

Mid-Atlantic Miniature Whiskey Bottle
Club
208 Gloucester Drive
Glen Burnie, MD 21061
(301) 766-8421

MASSACHUSETTS
Berkshire Antique Bottle Assn.
Box 971
Lenox, MA 01240

Little Rhody Bottle Club
2739 Elm Street
Dighton, MA 02715

Merrimack Valley Antique Bottle Club
3 Forrest St.
Chelmsford, MA 01824-2861
(978) 256-9561

National American Glass Club
P.O. Box 8489
Silver Spring, MD 20907

Scituate Bottle Club
54 Cedarwood Road
Scituate, MA 02066

Violin Bottle Collectors Association of
America
24 Sylvan St.
Danvers, MA 01923

Yankee Pole Cat Insulator Club
c/o Jill Meier
103 Cantebury Court
Carlisle, MA 01741-1860
(508) 369-0208

MICHIGAN
Central Michigan Krazy Korkers Bottle
Club
Mid-Michigan Community College
Clare Avenue
Harrison, MI 48625

Chief Pontiac Antique Bottle Club
13880 Neal Road
Davisburg, MI 48019
c/o Larry Blascyk
(313) 634-8469

Dickinson County Bottle Club
717 Henford Avenue
Iron Mountain, MI 49801

Flint Antique Bottle Collectors Assn.
450 Leta Avenue
Flint, MI 48507

Flint Antique Bottle & Collectors Club
6349 W. Silver Lake Road
Linden, MI 48451

Flint Eagles Ezra Brooks Club
1117 W. Remington Avenue
Flint, MI 48507

Grand Rapids Antique Bottle Club
1368 Kinney N.W.
Walker, MI 49504

Grand Valley Bottle Club
31 Dickinson S.W.
Grand Rapids, MI 49507

Great Lakes Miniature Bottle Club
P.O. Box 230460
Fairhaven, MI 48023

Huron Valley Bottle Club
12475 Saline-Milan Road
Milan, MI 48160

Huron Valley Bottle & Insulator Club
2475 West Walton
Waterford, MI 48329-4435

Kalamazoo Antique Bottle Club
1121 Maywood
Kalamazoo, MI 49001

Lionstone Collectors Bottle & Spec. Club of Michigan
3089 Grand Blanc Road
Swartz Creek, MI 48473

Manistee Coin & Bottle Club
207 E. Piney Road
Manistee, MI 49660

Metro Detroit Antique Bottle Club
410 Lothrop Road
Grosse Point Farms, MI 48236

Michigan Bottle Collectors Assn.
144 W. Clark Street
Jackson, MI 49203

Michigan's Vehicle City Beam Bottles & Spec. Club
907 Root Street
Flint, MI 48503

Mid-Michee Pine Beam Club
609 Webb Drive
Bay City, MI 48706

Northern Michigan Bottle Club
P.O. Box 421
Petoskey, MI 49770

Red Run Jim Beam Bottle & Spec. Club
172 Jones Street
Mt. Clemens, MI 48043
(313) 465-4883

West Michigan Avon Collectors
331 Bellevue S.W.
Wyoming, MI 49508

W.M.R.A.C.C.
331 Bellevue S.W.
Grand Rapids, MI 49508

Wolverine Beam Bottle & Spec. Club of Michigan
36009 Larchwood
Mt. Clemens, MI 48043

World Wide Avon Bottle Collectors Club
22708 Wick Road
Taylor, MI 48180

Ye Old Corkers
c/o Janet Gallup
Box 7
Gastor, MI 49927

MINNESOTA
Hey! Rube Jim Beam Bottle Club
1506 6th Avenue N.E.
Austin, MN 55912
(507) 433-6939

Lake Superior Antique Bottle Club
P.O. Box 67
Knife River, MN 55609

Minnnesota 1st Antique Bottle Club
5001 Queen Ave N.
Minneapolis, MN 55430

North-Star Historical Bottle Assn. Inc.
3308-32 Ave. So.
Minneapolis, MN 55406

Paul Bunyan Jim Beam Bottle & Spec.
Club
Rt. 8, Box 656
Bemidji, MN 56601
(218) 751-6635

Society of Inkwell Collectors
5136 Thomas Ave. S.
Minneapolis, MN 55410

Truman, Minnesota Jim Beam Bottle &
Spec. Club
Truman, MN 56088
(507) 776-3487

Viking Jim Beam Bottle & Spec. Club
8224 Oxborough Avenue S.
Bloomington, MN 55437
(612) 831-2303

MISSISSIPPI
Chimneyville Beam Bottle & Spec. Club
2918 Larchmont
Jackson, MS 39209-6129
(601) 352-6069

Gum Tree Beam Bottle Club
104 Ford Circle
Tupelo, MS 38801

Magnolia Beam Bottle & Spec. Club
1079 Maria Drive
Jackson, MS 39204-5518
(601) 372-4464

Middle Mississippi Antique Bottle Club
P.O. Box 233
Jackson, MS 39205

Oxford Antique Bottlers
128 Vivian Street
Oxford, MS 38633

South Mississippi Antique Bottle Club
203 S. 4th Avenue
Laurel, MS 39440

MISSOURI
Antique Bottle Club of Central Missouri
726 W. Monroe
Mexico, MO 65265
(314) 581-1391

Arnold, Missouri Jim Beam Bottle &
Spec. Club
1861 Jean Drive
Arnold, MO 63010
(314) 296-0813

Barnhart, Missouri Jim Beam Bottle &
Spec. Club
2150 Cathlin Court
Barnhart, MO 63012

Chesterfield Jim Beam Bottle & Spec.
Club
2066 Honey Ridge
Chesterfield, MO 63017

"Down in the Valley" Jim Beam Bottle
Club
528 St. Louis Avenue
Valley Park, MO 63088

The Federation of Historical Bottle Clubs
10118 Schuessler
St. Louis, MO 63128
(314) 843-7573

Florissant Valley Jim Beam Bottles &
Spec. Club
25 Cortez
Florissant, MO 63031

Greater Kansas City Jim Beam Bottle &
Spec. Club
P.O. Box 6703
Kansas City, MO 64123

Kansas City Antique Bottle Collectors
Assn.
1131 E. 77 Street
Kansas City, MO 64131

Maryland Heights Jim Beam Bottle &
Spec. Club
2365 Wesford
Maryland Heights, MO 63043

Midwest Miniature Bottle Collectors
12455 Parkwood Lane
Blackjack, MO 63033

Missouri Arch Jim Beam Bottle & Spec.
Club
2900 N. Lindbergh
St. Ann, MO 63074
(314) 739-0803

Mound City Jim Beam Decanter
Collectors
42 Webster Acres
Webster Groves, MO 63119

North-East County Jim Beam Bottle &
Spec. Club
10150 Baron Drive
St. Louis, MO 63136

Rock Hill Jim Beam Bottle & Spec. Club
9731 Graystone Terrace
St. Louis, MO 63119
(314) 962-8125

Show Me Jim Beam Bottle & Spec. Club
Rt. 7, Box 314-D
Springfield, MO 65802
(417) 831-8093

St. Charles, Missouri Jim Beam Bottle &
Spec. Club
122 S. Cardinal
St. Charles, MO 63301

St. Louis Antique Bottle Collectors Assn.
2236 Highway N
Pacific, MO 63039

St. Louis Jim Beam Bottle & Spec. Club
2900 Lindbergh
St. Ann, MO 63074
(314) 291-3256

Troy, Missouri Jim Beam Bottle & Spec.
Club
121 E. Pershing
Troy, MO 63379

Vera Young, Avon Times
P.O. Box 9868
Kansas City, MO 64134
816-537-8223

West County Jim Beam Bottle & Spec.
Club
11707 Momarte Lane
St. Louis, MO 63141

NEBRASKA

Cornhusker Jim Beam Bottle & Spec.
Club
5204 S. 81st Street
Ralston, NE 68127
(402) 331-4646

Nebraska Antique Bottle & Collectible
Club
7913 Edgewood Blvd
La Vista, NE 68128

Nebraska Big Red Bottle & Spec. Club
N Street Drive-in, 200 S. 18th Street
Lincoln, NE 68508

NEVADA

Las Vegas Antique Bottle & Collectibles
Club
3901 E. Stewart #16
Las Vegas, NV 89110
(702) 452-1263

Las Vegas Bottle Club
2632 E. Harman
Las Vegas, NV 89121
(702) 731-5004

Lincoln County Antique Bottle Club
P.O. Box 191
Calente, NV 89008
(702) 726-3655

Reno/Sparks Antique Bottle Club
P.O. Box 1061
Verdi, NV 89439

Virginia & Truckee Jim Beam Bottle &
Spec. Club
P.O. Box 1596
Carson City, NV 89701

NEW HAMPSHIRE

Central New Hampshire Antique Bottle
Club
FRD 2, Box 1A, Winter Street
Tilton, NH 03276

Merrimack Valley Antique Bottle Club
776 Harvey Rd.
Manchester, NH 03103
(503) 623-4101

New England Antique Bottle Club
4 Francove Drive
Somersworth, NH 03878-2339

Yankee Bottle Club
382 Court Street
Keene, NH 03431-2534

NEW JERSEY

Antique Bottle Collectors Club of
Burlington County
18 Willow Road
Bordentown, NJ 08505

Artifact Hunters Assn. Inc
c/o 29 Lake Road
Wayne, NJ 07470

Central Jersey Bottle & Collectible Club
92 North Main Street
New Egypt, NJ 98553

Glass Research Society of New Jersey
Wheaton Village
Millville, NJ 08332

The Jersey Devil Bottle Diggers Club
14 Church Street
Mt. Holly, NJ 08060

*Jersey Jackpot Jim Beam Bottle & Spec.
Club*
197 Farley Avenue
Fanwood, NJ 07023
(201) 322-7287

Jersey Shore Bottle Club
P.O. Box 995
Toms River, NJ 08753

New Jersey Ezra Brooks Bottle Club
S. Main Street
Cedarville, NJ 08311

North Jersey Antique Bottle Club Assn.
88 Jackson St.
South River, NJ 07035

*South Jersey Heritage Bottle & Glass
Club, Inc.*
65 N. Main St.
Woodstown, NJ 08098

Sussex County Antique Bottle Collectors
Division of Sussex County Historical
Society
82 Main Street
Newton, NJ 07860

Trenton Jim Beam Bottle Club, Inc.
17 Easy Street
Freehold, NJ 07728

West Essex Bottle Club
76 Beaufort Avenue
Livingston, NJ 07039

New Mexico
Cave City Antique Bottle Club
Rt. 1, Box 155
Carlsbad, NM 88220

New Mexico Historical Bottle Society
140 W. Coronado Road
Santa Fe, NM 87501

Roadrunner Bottle Club of New Mexico
2341 Gay Road S.W.
Albuquerque, NM 87105

New York
Auburn Bottle Club
297 S. Street Road
Auburn, NY 13021

Ball Metal Container Group
One Adams Road
Saratoga Springs, NY 12866-9036

Capital District Insulator Club
41 Crestwood Drive
Schenectady, NY 12306

*Catskill Mountains Jim Beam Bottle
Club*
Six Gardner Avenue
Middletown, NY 10940

*Chautauqua County Bottle Collectors
Club*
Morse Motel, Main Street
Sherman, NY 14781

Eastern Monroe County Bottle Club
c/o Bethelem Lutheran Church
1767 Plank Road
Webster, NY 14580

Empire State Bottle Collectors Assn.
P.O. Box 3421
Syracuse, NY 13220
(315) 689-6460

Empire State Jim Beam Bottle Club
P.O. Box 561, Main Street
Farmingdale, NY 11735

Finger Lakes Bottle Collectors Assn.
5 Tanbark Circle
Freeville, NY 13068

Genessee Valley Bottle Collectors Assn.
166 Haley Road
Ontario, NY 14519

Greater Catskill Antique Bottle Club
P.O. Box 411
Liberty, NY 14850

Hudson River Jim Beam Bottle & Spec.
Club
48 College Road
Monsey, NY 10952

Hudson Valley Bottle Club
201 Filors Lane
Stony Point, NY 10980

Lions Club of Ballston Spa
37 Grove Street
Ballston Spa, NY 12020

Long Island Antique Bottle Assn.
10 Holmes Court
Sayville, NY 11782

Mohawk Valley Antique Bottle Club
8646 Aitken Avenue
Whitesboro, NY 13492

National Bottle Museum
76 Milton Avenue
Ballston Spa, NY 12020
(518) 885-7589

National Insulator Association
41 Crestwood Drive
Schenectady, NY 12306

North County Bottle Collectors Assn.
Rt. 1
Canton, NY 13617

Saratoga Type Bottle Collectors Society
531 Rt. 42
Sparrow Bush, NY 12780

Southern Tier Bottle & Insulator
Collectors Assn.
47 Dickinson Avenue
Port Dickinson, NY 13901

The Corning Museum of Glass
One Museum Way
Corning, NY 14830-2253

The Whimsey Club
20 William Street
Dansville, NY 14437

Tryon Bottle Badgers
P.O. Box 146
Tribes Hill, NY 12177

Warwick Valley Bottle Club
P.O. Box 393
Warwick, NY 10990

Western New York Bottle Club Assn.
62 Adams Street
Jamestown, NY 14701
(716) 487-9645
Attn: Tom Karapantso

Western New York Bottle Collectors
87 S. Bristol Avenue
Lockport, NY 14094

Western New York Miniature Liquor
Club
P.O. Box 182
Cheektowaga, NY 14225

West Valley Bottleique Club
P.O. Box 204
Killbuck, NY 14748
(716) 945-5769

Whimsey Glass Club
20 William Street
Danville, NY 14437

NORTH CAROLINA

Blue Ridge Bottle and Jar Club
Dogwood Lane
Black Mountain, NC 28711

Carolina Jim Beam Bottle Club
1014 N. Main Street
Burlington, NC 27215

Catawba Valley Jim Beam Bottle &
Spec. Club
265 5th Avenue, N.E.
Hickory, NC 28601
(704) 322-5268

Goldsboro Bottle Club
2406 E. Ash Street
Goldsboro, NC 27530

Kinston Collectors Club, Inc.
1905 Greenbriar Rd
Kinston, NC 28501-2129
(919) 523-3049

Pelican Sand Dunners Jim Beam
Bottle & Spec. Club
Lot 17-J, Paradise Bay Mobile Home
Park, P.O. Box 344
Salter Path, NC 28575
(919) 247-3290

Tar Heel Jim Beam Bottle & Spec. Club
6615 Wake Forest Road
Fayetteville, NC 20301
(919) 488-4849

The Johnnyhouse Inspector's Bottle Club
1972 East US 74 Highway
Hamlet, NC 28345

The Robeson Antique Bottle Club
1830 Riverside Blvd
Lumberton, NC 28358

Western North Carolina Antique Bottle
Club
P.O. Box 1391
Candler, NC 28715

Wilmington Bottle & Artifact Club
183 Arlington Drive
Wilmington, NC 28401
(919) 763-3701

Wilson Antique Bottle & Artifact Club
Rt. 5, P.O. Box 414
Wilson, NC 27893

Yadkin Valley Bottle Club
General Delivery
Gold Hill, NC 28071

OHIO

Beam on the Lake Bottle & Spec. Club
9151 Mentor Avenue, F 15
Mentor, OH 44060
(215) 255-0320

Buckeye Bottle Club
229 Oakwood Street
Elyria, OH 44035

Buckeye Jim Beam Bottle Club
1211 Ashland Avenue
Columbus, OH 43212

Carnation City Jim Beam Bottle Club,
Vernon E. Brunt
135 W. Virginia
Sebring, OH 44672
(216) 938-6817

Central Ohio Bottle Club
931 Minerva Avenue
Columbus, OH 43229

Collectors of Findlay Glass
P.O. Box 256
Findlay, OH 45939-0256

Diamond Pin Winners Avon Club
5281 Fredonia Avenue
Dayton, OH 45431

The Federation of Historical Bottle Clubs
c/o Gary Beatty, Treasurer
9326 Court Road 3C
Galion, OH 44833

Findlay Antique Bottle Club
407 Cimarron Ct.
Findlay, OH 45840
(419) 422-3183

Gem City Beam Bottle Club
1463 E. Stroop Road
Dayton, OH 45429

Glass Collectors Club of Toledo
6122 Cross Trails Rd.
Sylvania, OH 43560-1714

Greater Cleveland Jim Beam Club
5398 W. 147th Street
Brook Park, OH 44142
(216) 267-7665

Heart of Ohio Bottle Club
P.O. Box 353
New Washington, OH 44854
(419) 492-2829

Jeep City Beamers
531A Durango
Toledo, OH 43609
(419) 382-2515

Maple Leaf Beamers
8200 Yorkshire Road
Mentor, OH 44060
(216) 255-9118

Midwest Miniature Bottle Club
5537 Cleander Dr.
Cincinnati, OH 45238

National Fenton Glass Society
P.O. Box 4008
Marietta, OH 45750

Northern Ohio Jim Beam Bottle Club
43152 Hastings Road
Oberlin, OH 44074
(216) 775-2177

North Eastern Ohio Bottle Club
P.O. Box 57
Madison, OH 44057
(614) 282-8918

Northwest Ohio Bottle Club
104 W. Main
Norwalk, OH 44857

Ohio Bottle Club
P.O. Box 585
Barberton, OH 44203
(216) 753-2115

Ohio Ezra Brooks Bottle Club
8741 Kirtland Chardon Road
Kirtland Hills, OH 44094

Pioneer Beamers
38912 Butternut Ridge
Elyria, OH 44035
(216) 458-6621

Rubber Capitol Jim Beam Club
151 Stephens Road
Akron, OH 44312

Southwestern Ohio Antique Bottle & Jar Club
273 Hilltop Drive
Dayton, OH 45415
(513) 836-3353

St. Bernard Swigin Beamers
4327 Greenlee Avenue
Cincinnati, OH 45217
513-641-3362

Superior Bottle Club
22000 Shaker Boulevard
Shaker Heights, OH 44122

OKLAHOMA

Bar-Dew Antique Bottle Club
817 E. 7th Street
Dewey, OK 74029

Frontier Jim Beam Bottle & Spec. Club
P.O. Box 52, Meadowbrook Trailer
Village, Lot 101
Ponca City, OK 74601
(405) 765-2174

Green County Jim Beam Bottle & Spec.
Club
Rt. 2, P.O. Box 233
Chouteau, OK 74337
(918) 266-3512

Midwest Miniature Bottle Collector
3108 Meadowood Drive
Midwest City, OK 73110-1407

Oklahoma Territory Bottle & Relic Club
1300 S. Blue Haven Dr.
Mustang, OK 73064
(405) 376-1045

Sooner Jim Beam Bottle & Spec. Club
5913 S.E. 10th
Midwest City, OK 73110
(405) 737-5786

Tri-State Historical Bottle Club
817 E. 7th Street
Dewey, OK 74029

Tulsa Antique & Bottle Club
P.O. Box 4278
Tulsa, OK 74159-0278
(918) 446-6774

OREGON

Central Oregon Bottle & Relic Club
671 N.E. Seward
Bend, OR 97701

Empire City Old Bottle Society
1991 Sherman Avenue, Suite #206
North Bend, OR 97459

Frontier Collectors
504 N.W. Bailey
Pendleton, OR 97801

Gold Diggers Antique Bottle Club
1958 S. Stage Road
Medford, OR 97501

Lewis & Clark Historical Bottle &
Collectors Soc.
8018 S.E. Hawthorne Boulevard
Portland, OR 97501

Lewis & Clark Historical Bottle Society
4828 N.E. 33rd
Portland, OR 97501

Northwest Mini Bottle Club
P.O. Box 6551
Portland, OR 97228

Oregon Beamers Beam Bottle & Spec.
P.O. Box 7
Sheridan, OR 97378

Oregon Bottle Collectors Assn.
3565 Dee Highway
Hood River, OR 97031

Pioneer Fruit Collectors Assn.
P.O. Box 175
Grand Ronde, OR 97347

Siskiyou Antique Bottle Collectors Assn.
2668 Montana Drive
Medford, OR 97504

PENNSYLVANIA

American Collectors of Infant Feeders
1849 Ebony Drive
York, PA 17402-4706

Beaver Valley Jim Beam Club
1335 Indiana Avenue
Monaca, PA 15061

Bedford County Bottle Club
P.O. Box 116
Loysburg, PA 16659

Camoset Bottle Club
P.O. Box 252
Johnstown, PA 15901

Christmas Valley Beamers
150 Second Street
Richlandtown, PA 18955
(215) 536-4636

Classic Glass Bottle Collectors
2 Cogan Station, PA 17728

Coal Crackers Bottle Club
Rod Walck, 168 Sunrise Terrace Ln.
Lehighton, PA 18235
(610) 377-1484

Delaware Valley Bottle Club
12 Belmar Road
Halboro, PA 19040

Del Val Miniature Bottle Club
57-104 Delaire Landing Road
Philadelphia, PA 19114

Eastern Coast Breweriana Assoc.
P.O. Box 349
West Point, PA 19846

East Coast Double Springs Spec. Bottle
Club
P.O. Box 419
Carisle, PA 17013

East Coast Ezra Brooks Bottle Club
2815 Fiddler Green
Lancaster, PA 17601

Endless Mountain Antique Bottle Club
P.O. Box 75
Granville Summit, PA 16926

Eric Bottle Club
P.O. Box 373
Erie, PA 16512

Flood City Jim Beam Bottle Club
231 Market Street
Johnstown, PA 15901

Forks of the Delaware Bottle Club Assn.
3105 Hecktown Road
Nazareth, PA 18045

Indiana Bottle Club
240 Oak Street
Indiana, PA 15701

Jefferson County Antique Bottle Club
6 Valley View Drive
Washington, PA 15301

Keystone Flyers Jim Beam Bottle Club
288 Hogan Boulevard, Box 42
Lock Haven, PA 17745
(717) 748-6741

Kiski Mini Beam and Spec. Club
c/o John D. Ferchak Jr.
816 Cranberry Drive
Monroeville, PA 15146
(412) 372-0387

Laurel Valley Bottle Club
P.O. Box 201
Hostetter, PA 15638
(412) 238-9046

Ligonier Historic Bottle Club
P.O. Box 188
Ligonier, PA 15658

Middletown Area Bottle Collectors Assn.
P.O. Box 1
Middletown, PA 17057
(717) 939-0288

National Milk Glass Collectors Society
500 Union Cemetery Rd.
Greensburg, PA 15601

Pagoda City Beamers
735 Florida Avenue, Riverview Park
Reading, PA 19605
(215) 929-8924

Penn Beamers' 14th
15 Gregory Place
Richboro, PA 18954

Pennsylvania Bottle Collectors
251 Eastland Ave
York, PA 17402

Pennsylvania Dutch Jim Beam Bottle
Club
812 Pointview Avenue
Ephrate, PA 17522

Philadelphia Bottle Club
8203 Elberon Avenue
Philadelphia, PA 19111

Pittsburgh Antique Bottle Club
3226 Latonia Avenue
Pittsburgh, PA 15216

Pittsburgh Bottle Club
1528 Railroad Street
Sewickley, PA 15143

Susquehanna Valley Jim Beam Bottle &
Spec. Club
64 E. Park Street
Elizabethtown, PA 17022
(717) 367-4256

The American Collectors of Infant
Feeders
1849 Ebony Drive
York, PA 17402-4706

Valley Forge Jim Beam Bottle Club
1219 Ridgeview Drive
Phoenixville, PA 19460

Washington County Antique Bottle Club
RD 2—Box 342
Carmichaela, PA 15320

RHODE ISLAND

Seaview Jim Beam Bottle & Spec. Club
362 Lakepoint Drive
Harrisburg, PA 17111
(717) 561-2517

SOUTH CAROLINA

Anderson Collectors Club
2318 Hwy. 29
N. Anderson, SC 29621

Palmetto State Beamers
908 Alton Circle
Florence, SC 29501
(803) 669-6515

South Carolina Bottle Club
238 Farmdale Drive
Lexington, SC 29073

TENNESSEE

Cotton Carnival Beam Club
P.O. Box 17951
Memphis, TN 38117

East Tennessee Bottle Society
220 Carter School Road
Strawberry Plains, TN 37871

Memphis Bottle Collectors Club
3706 Deerfield Cove
Bartlett, TN 38135

Middle Tennessee Bottle Collectors Club
1221 Nichol Lane
Nashville, TN 37205

Music City Beam Bottle Club
2008 June Drive
Nashville, TN 37214
(615) 883-1893

Alamo City Jim Beam Bottle & Spec.
Club
5785 FM 1346, P.O. Box 20442
San Antonio, TX 78220

Cowtown Jim Beam Bottle Club
2608 Roseland
Ft. Worth, TX 76103
(817) 536-4335

Dr. Pepper Collectors Club
P.O. Box 153221
Irving, TX 75015

El Paso Insulator Club
Martha Stevens, Chairman
4556 Bobolink
El Paso, TX 79922

The Exploration Society
603 9th Street NAS
Corpus Christi, TX 78419
(361) 922-2902

Foursome (Jim Beam)
1208 Azalea Drive
Longview, TX 75601

Gulf Coast Bottle & Jar Club
P.O. Box 1754
Pasadena, TX 77501
(713) 592-3078

Houston Glass Club
5338 Creekbend Drive
Houston, TX 77096

North Texas Longhorn Bottle Club
4205 Donnington Drive
Plano, TX 75072

Republic of Texas Jim Beam Bottle &
Spec. Club
616 Donley Drive
Euless, TX 76039

Sidewinders Jim Beam Club
522 Reinosa Drive
Garland, TX 75043

Utah Antique Bottle & Relic Club
517 South Hayes
Midvale, UT 84047

Utah Antique Bottle Club
P.O. Box 15
Ogden, UT 84402

Apple Valley Bottle Collectors Club
P.O. Box 2201
Winchester, VA 22604

Buffalo Beam Bottle Club
P.O. Box 434
Buffalo Junction, VA 24529
(804) 374-2041

Chesapeake Bay Beam Bottle & Spec.
Club
515 Briar Hill Road
Norfolk, VA 23502
(804) 461-3763

Country Cousins Beam Bottle & Spec.
Club
Rt. 2, Box 18C
Dinwiddle, VA 23841
(804) 469-7414

Historical Bottle Diggers of Virginia
242 East Grattan Street
Harrisonburg, VA 22801

Merrimac Beam Bottle & Spec. Club
433 Tory Road
Virginia Beach, VA 23462
(804) 497-0969

Metropolitan Antique Bottle Club
109 Howard Street
Domfries, VA 22026
(804) 221-8055

National Privy Diggers Assn.
614 Park Dr.
Mechanicsville, VA 23111
(804) 746-9854

Potomac Bottle Collectors
8411 Porter Ln.
Alexandria, VA 22308
(703) 360-8181

Richmond Area Bottle Collectors Assn.
3511 Clydewood Ave.
Richmond, VA 23234

Shenandoah Valley Beam Bottle & Spec. Club
11 Bradford Drive
Front Royal, VA 22630
(703) 743-6316

Tidewater Beam Bottle & Spec. Club
P.O. Box 14012
Norfolk, VA 23518

Ye Old Bottle Club
General Delivery
Clarksville, VA 23927

WASHINGTON

Apple Capital Beam Bottle & Spec. Club
300 Rock Island Road
E. Wenatchee, WA 98801
(509) 884-6895

Blue Mountain Jim Beam Bottle & Spec. Club
P.O. Box 147, Russet Road
Walla Walla, WA 99362
(509) 525-1208

Cascade Treasure Club
254 N.E. 45th
Seattle, WA 98105

Chinook Ezra Brooks Bottle Club
233 Kelso Drive
Kelso, WA 98626

Inland Empire Bottle & Collectors Club
7703 E. Trent Avenue
Spokane, WA 99206

Mt. Rainer Ezra Brooks Bottle Club
P.O. Box 1201
Lynwood, WA 98178

Northwest Treasure Hunters Club
E. 107 Astor Drive
Spokane, WA 99208

Pacific Northwest Avon Bottle Club
25425 68th S.
Kent, WA 98031

Skagit Bottle & Glass Collectors
1314 Virginia
Mt. Vernon, WA 98273

Violin Bottle Collectors Association of America
21815 106th Street East
Buckley, WA 98321

Washington Bottle Collectors Assn.
5492 Hannegan Road
Bellingham, WA 98226

WEST VIRGINIA

Blennerhassett Jim Beam Club
Rt. 1, 26 Popular Street
Davisville, WV 26142
(304) 428-3184

Fenton Art Glass Collectors
P.O. Box 384
Williamstown, WV 26187

Wild Wonderful W. Virginia Jim Beam
Bottle & Spec. Club
3922 Hanlin Way
Weirton, WV 26062
(304) 748-2675

WISCONSIN
Antique Bottle Club of Northern Illinois
P.O. Box 571
Geneva, WI 53147

Badger Jim Beam Club of Madison
P.O. Box 5612
Madison, WI 53705

Belle City Jim Beam Bottle Club
8008 104th Avenue
Kenosha, WI 53140
(414) 694-3341

Bucken Beamers Bottle Club of
Milwaukee, WI
16548 Richmond Drive
Menomonee Falls, WI 53051
(414) 251-1772

Central Wisconsin Bottle Collectors
1608 Main Street
Stevens Point, WI 54481

Cream Separator Collectors Association
W20772 State Road 95
Arcadia, WI 54612

Heart of the North Beam Bottle and
Bottle Club
1323 Eagle Street
Rhinelander, WI 54501
(715) 362-6045

Lumberjack Beamers
414 N. 5th Avenue
Wausau, WI 54401
(715) 842-3793

Milwaukee Antique Bottle & Advertising
Club, Inc.
4090 Lake Drive
West Bend, WI 53095

Milwaukee Jim Beam Bottle and Spec.
Club, Ltd.
N. 95th Street W.
16548 Richmond Drive
Menomonee Falls, WI 53051

Packerland Beam Bottle & Spec. Club
1366 Avondale Drive
Green Bay, WI 54303
(414) 494-4631

South Central Wisconsin Bottle Club
c/o Dr. T.M. Schwartz, Rt. 1
Arlington, WI 53911

Sportsman's Jim Beam Bottle Club
6821 Sunset Strip
Wisconsin Rapids, WI 54494
(715) 325-5285

WYOMING
Cheyenne Antique Bottle Club
4417 E. 8th Street
Cheyenne, WY 82001

Insubott Bottle Club
P.O. Box 34
Lander, WY 82520

International Perfume Bottle Assoc.
Box 529
Vienna, VA 22183

Foreign Clubs

AUSTRALIA
Miniature Bottle Collectors of Australia
P.O. Box 59
Ashburton, Victoria 3147 Australia

CANADA
Bytown Bottle Seekers' Club
564 Courtenay Ave.
Ottawa, Ontario, Canada K2A 3B3

Four Seasons Bottle Collectors Club
8 Stillbrook Court
West Hill, Ontario, Canada M1E3N7

Sleeping Giant Bottle Club
P.O. Box 1351
Thunder Bay, Ontario, Canada P7C
5W2

CHINA
Hong Kong Miniature Liquor Club LTD
180 Nathan Road
Bowa House
Tsim Sha Tsui
Kowloon, Hong Kong
(852) 721-3200

ENGLAND
The Mini Bottle Club
47 Burradon Rd.
Burradon, Cramlington
Northumberland, NE 237NF England

GERMANY
*Miniatur Flaschensammler Deutschlands
E.V:*
Keltenstrasse 1a
5477 Nickenich, Germany

ITALY
Club Delle Mignonnettes
Via Asiago 16
60124 Ancona, AN, Italy

JAPAN
Osaka Miniature Bottle Club
11-2 Hakucho 1-Chome
Habikinoshi, Osaka 583, Japan

Miniature Bottle Club of Kobe
3-5-41, Morigocho
Nada-ku, Kobe, 657 Japan

NEW ZEALAND
Port Nicholson Miniature Bottle Club
86 Rawhiti Rd.
Pukerua Bay
Wellington, New Zealand

Bottle Dealers

Listed alphabetically by state and city

Domestic Dealers

ALABAMA

Bert & Margaret Simard
Rt. 1 Box 49D
Ariton, AL 36311
(334) 762-2663
Ink Bottles & Ink Wells

Steve Holland
1740 Serene Dr.
Birmingham, AL 35215
(205) 853-7929

Walkers Antique Bottles
2768 Hanover Circle
Birmingham, AL 35205
(205) 933-7902
Medicines & Crown Sodas

Terry & Katie Gillis
115 Mountain Dr.
Fort Payne, AL 35967
(205) 845-4541

C.B. & Barbara Meares
Rt. 3, Box 161
Fort Payne, AL 35967
(205) 638-6225

Frank & Nancy Harrison
815 Troy Street
Gadsden, AL 35901
(205) 546-9112
Glassware & Stoneware

Ken Roberts
218 Cumberland Dr.
Huntsville, AL 35803
(205) 880-1460
Glass Insulators

Loretta & Mack Wimmer
3012 Cedar Crescent Dr.
Mobile, AL 36605

Old Time Bottle House & Museum
306 Parker Hills Dr.
Ozark, AL 36360
Stone Jugs & Fruit Jars

Elroy Webb
203 Spanish Main
Spanish Fort, AL 36527
(334) 626-1067
Bottles, Appraisals

Ed's Lapidary Shop
7927 Historic Mobile Parkway
Hwy. 90
Theodore, AL 36582
(205) 653-0713

ARIZONA

Antiques ETC.
5753 W. Glendale Ave.
Glendale, AZ
(602) 939-2732

Now, Then, & Always Inc.
7021 N. 57th Drive
Glendale, AZ 85301
(602) 931-1116

Bruce Young
Lake Havasu City, AZ 86403
(602) 855-3396—Insulators

Michael & Karen Miller
9214 W. Gary Rd.
Peoria, AZ 85345
(602) 486-3123
Arizona Bottles

Antiques, Interiors & Memories
3026 N. 16th St.
Phoenix, AZ
(602) 277-0433

The Antique Center
3601 E. Indian School Rd.
Phoenix, AZ 85018
(602) 957-3600

The Brewery
1605 N. 7th Ave.
Phoenix, AZ 85007
(602) 252-1415
Brewery Items

Bryan Grapentine
1939 W. Waltann Lane
Phoenix, AZ 85023
(602) 993-9757
Bottles & Advertising

Ray & Dyla Lawton
Box 374
Pinetop, AZ 85935
(602) 366-4449

Russ & Pat Peterson
814 N. 86th Way
Scottsdale, AZ 85252
(602) 970-3380
Dr Pepper Bottles

The Antique Center
1290 N. Scottsdale Rd.
Tempe, AZ 85281
(602) 966-3350

Keith Curtis
6871 E. Lurlene Dr.
Tucson, AZ 85703
(602) 790-4336

ARKANSAS

Buddy's Bottles
30 N. Taylor
Ashdown, AR 71822
(501) 898-3790
Hutchinson Sodas & Medicines

Charles & Mary Garner
620 Carpenter Dr.
Jacksonville, AR 72076
(501) 982-8381

Don & Jackie Leonard
1118 Green Mt. Dr.
Little Rock, AR 72211
(501) 224-5432
Bottles

Terry Fields
Route 1, Box 167-7
McCrory, AR 72101
(501) 697-3132
Bottles & Indian Artifacts

Rufus Buie
P.O. Box 226
Rison, AR 71665
(501) 325-6816

Edwin R. Tardy
16201 Hwy 300
Roland, AR 72135
(501) 868-9548
Coca-Cola Bottles

CALIFORNIA
Al Halpern
P.O. Box 2081
Anaheim, CA 92804
(714) 776-1371
Miniature Bottles

D & E Collectables & Antiques
14925 Apple Valley Road
Apple Valley, CA 92307
(619) 946-1767
Bottles

Diane Pingree
345 Commercial St.
Auburn, CA 95603
(916) 885-5537

Tom Chapman
2433 Apache Drive
Bishop, CA 93514
(619) 872-2427
California & Nevada Bottles

Leigh R. Giarde
P.O. Box 366
Bryn Mawr, CA 92318
(909) 792-8681
Dairy Nostalgia

Walter Yeargain
6222 San Lorenzo Dr.
Buena Park, CA 90620
(714) 826-5264
Bottles

Fred Hawley
1311 Montero Ave.
Burlingame, CA 94010
(415) 342-7085
Miniature Bottles

Wayne Hortman
P.O. Box 183
Butler, CA 31006
(912) 862-3699

John L. Thomas
4805 Grace St. Apt C
Capitola, CA 95010
(408) 475-3223
Western Whiskey Bottles

Bruce D. Kendall
Erma's Country Store
P.O. Box 1761
Carmel, CA 93921
(408) 394-3257

Eloise Haltman
P.O. Box 399
Cathedral City, CA 92234
(619) 328-5321
Glass Insulators

Don Ayers
P.O. Box 1515
Chico, CA 95927
(916) 895-0813
Coca-Cola Bottles

Barbara Edmundson
701 E. Lassen #308
Chico, CA 95973
(916) 343-8460
Shot Glasses

Randy Taylor
P.O. Box 1065
Chico, CA 95927
(530) 345-0519
Fruit Jars

Tom Bloomenrader
6200 Desimore Ln. #38A
Citrus Heights, CA 95621
(916) 729-5744

Duke Jones
P.O. Box 642
Citrus Heights, CA 95610
(916) 725-1989
California Embossed Beers

John Walker
281 W. Magill Ave.
Clovis, CA 93612
(209) 297-4613 Bottles

Stoney & Myrt Stone
1925 Natoma Dr.
Concord, CA 94519
(415) 685-6326

Russell Brown
P.O. Box 441
Corona, CA 91720
(714) 737-7164

Gary & Harriet Miller
5034 Oxford Dr.
Cypress, CA 90630
(714) 828-4778

Jim & Monica Baird
P.O. Box 106
Descanso, CA 91916
(619) 445-4771
Western Americana

Jay Turner
5513 Riggs Rd.
El Cajon, CA 92019
(619) 445-3039
Bottles

Tim Blair
418 W. Palm Ave.
El Segundo, CA 90245
(310) 640-2089
Los Angeles Bottles

Ken Salter
P.O. Box 1549
El Cerrito, CA 94530
(510) 527-5779
French & U.S. Mustards

Floyd Brown
532 South "E" Street
Exeter, CA 93221
(209) 592-2525
Marbles, Games, and Related Items

Mike & Joyce Amey
625 Clay St.
Fillmore, CA 93015
(805) 524-3364

James Musser
P.O. Box T
Forest Knolls, CA 94933
(415) 488-9491
Bottles (Heroin, Cocaine, Opium)

Gary Egorov
346 E. Cornell
Fresno, CA 93704
(209) 228-1772
Gems

Dan Andrews
19032 S. Vermont Ave, Ste 244
Gardena, CA 90248
Brewery Items

Vincent Madruga
P.O. Box 1261
Gilroy, CA 95021
(408) 847-0639
Bitters, Whiskeys, Historicals

Gary & Sheran Johnston
22853 De Berry
Grand Terrace, CA 92313
(909) 783-4101
Fruit Jars

Scott Grandstaff
Box 154
Happy Camp, CA 96039
(916) 493-2032
Mason's SGCO (Monogram) Pat.
1858's

Kitty Roach
Box 409
Happy Camp, CA 96039
(916) 493-2032
Whittemore Bottles

Mike & Deanna Delaplain
P.O. Box 787
Hemet, CA 92343
(714) 766-9725

Gene & Phyllis Kemble
14733 Poplar St.
Hesperia, CA 92345
(714) 244-5863

Larry Caddell
15881 Malm Circle
Huntington Beach, CA 92647
(714) 897-8133

Jim & Sandy Lindholm
2001 Sierra
Kingsburg, CA 93631
(209) 897-4083
Western Bottles, Machine & Hand-
Made Marbles, Free Appraisals

Joss Grandeau
P.O. Box 1508
Laguna Beach, CA 92652
(714) 588-6091
Milk Bottles

Fred Padgett
P.O. Box 1122
Livermore, CA 94551-1122
(510) 443-8841
Glass Insulators & Bottles

Ted Haigh
1852 Miceltorena
Los Angeles, CA 90026
(213) 666-4408
Miniature Bottles

Chiisasi Bin Imports
P.O. Box 90245
Los Angeles, CA 90009
(310) 370-8993
Miniature Bottles

Louis & Cindy Pellegrini
1231 Thurston
Los Altos, CA 94022
(415) 965-9060

John & Estelle Hewitt
366 Church St.
Marietta, CA 30060
(404) 422-5525

Steve Viola
827 Wake Forest Rd.
Mountain View, CA 94043
(415) 968-0849
Glass Insulators

John Hiscox
10475 Newtown Rd.
P.O. Box 704
Nevada City, CA 95959
Bottles

Chuck Erickson
155 N. Singingwood #58
Orange, CA 92669
(714) 771-2286
Los Angeles Bottles, Whiskeys

Les Whitman
1328 Huntoon
Oroville, CA 95965
(916) 532-6377
Bottles & Beer Cans

Gary Frederick
1030 Mission St.
Pasadena, CA 91030
(818) 799-1917
Soda Pop Bottles, Owls, Medicines

Henry & Cecilia Guillen
5595 Smoketree Ave.
29 Palms, CA 92277
(619) 367-6009
Bottles

Pat & Shirley Patocka
P.O. Box 326
Penryn, CA 95663
(916) 663-3681
Insulators

Bob's Bottle Shop
Robert Glover
2500 Hwy 128
Philco, CA 95466
(707) 895-3259
Bottles & Fruit Jars

Mel & Barbara De Mello
P.O. Box 186
Pollock Pines, CA 95726
(916) 644-6133
Antique Advertising

Robert Jones
1866 N. Orange Grove #202
Pomona, CA 91767
(909) 920-0840
Rexall Drug Bottles & Items

Stan Wilker
P.O. Box 2081
Rancho Palos Verdes, CA 90274
(310) 377-7780
Gaming & Western Americana

Charlie's Ore House
POB 293, 153 Butte
Randsburg, CA 93554
(760) 374-2238

J. Bart Parker
P.O. Box 356
Randsburg, CA 93554
(760) 374-2382
Louis Taussig Whiskey Items, Tokens

Emma's Trunk, Bill & Sue Morse
1701 Orange Tree Lane
Redlands, CA 92374
(909) 798-7865

Byrl & Grace Rittenhouse
3055 Birch Way
Redding, CA 96002
(916) 243-0320

Ralph Hollibaugh
8266 Cascade Blvd.
Redding, CA 96008
(916) 243-4672

Doug Hansen
865 Commerce
Redding, CA 96002
(916) 547-3152

Tom Aldama
15245 Fawndale Rd. #2
Redding, CA 96003
(916) 275-1048
Painted Label Sodas

Shawn McAlister
333 Calle Miramar #C
Redondo Beach, CA 90277
(310) 791-0440
Whiskeys, Bitters, Colored Sodas

Jeff Hargrove
2002 Midway Road
Ridgecrest, CA 93555
(619) 446-8986
Glass Insulators

Harold & Virginia Lyle
11259 Gramercy Pl.
Riverside, CA 92505
(714) 689-3662
Bottles

James Fennelly
520 54th St.
Sacramento, CA 95819
(916) 457-3695
Bottles—Ezra Brooks, Jim Beams, Ski
Country

Bill Grolz
22 Mad River Ct.
Sacramento, CA 95831
(916) 424-7283
Violin Bottles

Frank Feher
1624 Maryland Avenue
West Sacramento, CA 95691
(916) 371-7731
Glass Insulators

George & Rose Reidenbach
2816 "P" St.
Sacramento, CA 95816
(916) 451-0063

Grant Salzman
427 Safflower Place
West Sacramento, CA 95691
(916) 372-7272
Glass Insulators

Peck & Audie Markota
4627 Oakhallow Dr.
Sacto, CA 95842
(916) 334-3260

Dwayne & Ofelia Anthony
1066 Scenic Dr.
San Bernardino, CA 92408
(909) 888-6417
Insulators, Fruit Jars, Poison Bottles

Clarice Gordon
3269 N. Mtn. View Dr.
San Diego, CA 92116
(619) 282-5101
Glass Insulators

Norm & Doris James
San Diego, CA 92115
(619) 466-0652
Insulators

Al Sparacino
743 La Huerta Way
San Diego, CA 92154
(619) 690-3632
Miniature Bottles

Thierry Stanich
946 Terra Bella Ave.
San Jose, CA 95125
(408) 267-7703
Miniature Bottles (Cognacs)

Jim Gibson
8573 Atlas View Dr.
Santee, CA 92071
Bottles

Bill Groves
2620 Sutter St.
San Francisco, CA 94115
(415) 922-6248

Randolph M. Haumann
415 Amherst St.
San Francisco, CA 94134
(415) 239-5807
Colored Figural Bitters

Terry & Peggy Wright
6249 Lean Ave.
San Jose, CA 95123
(408) 578-5580

Ed & Diane Kuskie
1030 W. MacArthur #154
Santa Ana, CA 92707
(714) 435-1054
Bottles

Valvern & Mary Kille Mcluff
214 S. Ranch Rd.
Santa Maria, CA 93454
(805) 925-7014

Derek Abrams
129 E. El Camino
Santa Maria, CA 93454
(805) 922-4208
Whiskeys, Western Bottles

Fireside Cellars
1421 Montana Ave.
Santa Monica, CA 90403
(310) 393-2888
Miniature Bottles

Lewis Lambert
Santa Rosa, CA
(707) 823-8845
Early Western Bottles

James Doty
2026 Finch Ct.
Simi Valley, CA 93063
Insulators

T.R. Schweighart
1123 Santa Luisa Dr.
Solana Beach, CA 92075

Flask Liquor, Inc.
12194 Ventura Blvd.
Studio City, CA 91604
(818) 761-5373
Miniature Bottles

Frank & Judy Brockman
104 W. Park
Stockton, CA 95202
(209) 948-0746

The Glass Bottle
22 Main St. Hwy. 49
Sutter Creek, CA 95685
(209) 267-0122
Figurals, Perfumes, Whiskey, Milks

John R. Swearingen
3227 N. Wildhorse Ct.
Thousand Oaks, CA 91360
(805) 492-5036
Fruit Jars

Rich Burnham
P.O. Box 4056
Torrance, CA 90503
(310) 320-2552
Civil War Relics

David Spaid
2916 Briarwood Dr.
Torrance, CA 90505
(310) 534-4943
Miniature Bottles

Steve & Cris Curtiss
34641 S. Bernard Dr.
Tracy, CA 95376
(209) 836-0903
Northern & Central Calif. Hutch &
Sodas

Nancy Clayton
P.O. Box 3566
Tustin, CA 92681-3566
(909) 395-2727
Miniature Bottles

Dennis Rogers
2459 Euclid Crescent East
Upland, CA 91784
(909) 982-3416
Cathedral Pickle Bottles

Tom Quinn
P.O. Box 5503
Vallejo, CA 94591
(707) 864-0564
Western Whiskeys

Don & Linda Yount
P.O. Box 4459
Ventura, CA 93004
(805) 656-2707
Bottles

Tom Eccles
747 Magnolia
West Covina, CA 91791
(818) 339-9107
Sarsaparilla Bottles

Les & Pat Whitman
219 Fir St., P.O. Drawer KK
Westwood, CA 96137
(916) 256-3437
Sodas

David Hall
1217 McDonald Ave.
Wilmington, CA 90744
(310) 834-6368
Glass Insulators

Betty & Ernest Zumwalt
5519 Kay Dr.
Windsor, CA 95492
(707) 545-8670

Mitri Manneh
11415 Whittier Blvd
Whittier, CA 90601
(310) 692-2928
Miniature Bottles

Sleep's Siskiyou Specialties
217 W. Mine P.O. Box 689
Yreka, CA 96097

Mike & Lilarae Smith
P.O. Box 2347
Yucca Valley, CA 92286
(760) 228-9640
Indian Bottles

COLORADO
Ken Schneider
7156 Jay St.
Arvada, CO 80003
Colorado Bottles

Michael Bliss
Ft. Collins, CO 80525
(970) 225-0800
Insulator & Bottles

Mike & Jodee Holzwarth
2224 Laporte Ave.
Ft. Collins, CO 80521
(970) 224-4464
Colorado Bottles

Fort Collins Bottles
Bill Thomas
2000 Rangeview Dr.
Ft. Collins, CO 80524
(303) 493-8177
Miniature Bottles

Remember When-
Ron Jones
2204 W. Colorado Ave.
Colorado Springs, CO 80904
Collectibles

Jim Keilman
3101 F Road
Grand Junction, CO 81501
(303) 434-3275
Bottles, Bimal Miniatures

Marc Sagrillo
555 Aspen Ridge Drive
Lafayette, CO 80026
(303) 661-9800
Colorado Bottles

Marietta LeBlanc
5592 W. Geddes Place
Littleton, CO 80123
(303) 979-4943
Miniature Bottles

Jim Bishop
Box 5554
Snowmass Village, CO 81615
(303) 923-2348
Miniature Liquor

CONNECTICUT
Woodland Antiques
P.O. Box 277
Mansfield Center
Ashford, CT 06250
(203) 429-2983
Flasks, Bitters, Inks

Todd James Maynard
P.O. Box 326
Centerbrook, CT 06409
(860) 767-9037
Saratoga Type Mineral Water Bottles

Stephen Link
953 Post Rd.
Fairfield, CT 06430

B'Thea's Cellar
31 Kensington St.
Hartford, CT 06112
(203) 249-4686

Mary's Old Bottles
White Hollow Rd.
Lakeville, CT 06039
(203) 435-2961

Doug MacGillvary
79 New Bolton Road
Manchester, CT 06040
(203) 649-0477
Northeast Insulators

Bob's Old Bottles
656 Noank Rd., Rt. 215
Mystic, CT 06355
(203) 536-8542

Gerald "J" Jaffee & Lori Waldeck
P.O. Box 1741
New Haven, CT 06507
(203) 787-4232
Poisons & Insulators

Time in a Bottle
Gail Quick
Rt. 25
Hawleyville, CT 06440
(203) 426-0031

Albert Corey
153 W. Main St.
Niantic, CT 06357
(203) 739-7493

Bill Stankard
61 Old Post Rd.
Saybrook, CT 06475
(203) 388-2435

George E. Johnson
2339 Litchfield Rd.
Watertown, CT 06795
(203) 274-1785

Norman & Elizabeth Heckler
Woodstock, CT 06282
(203) 974-1634

Al & Ginny Way
68 Cooper Drive
Waterbury, CT 06704
(203) 575-9964
Insulators

DELAWARE
Rowland L. Hearn
10 Wordsworth Drive
Wilmington, Delaware 19808
(302) 994-2036
Delaware Books & Bottles

<u>FLORIDA</u>

E.S. & Romie Mackenzie
Box 57
Brooksville, FL 33510
(904) 796-3400

Larry Craft
403 Woodville Hwy
Crawfordville, FL 32327
(904) 421-6907
Insulators

Bill Derrick
P.O. Box 140088
Gainesville, FL 32614
(352) 332-0315
Soda Pop Bottles

Bud Hastings
P.O. Box 11530
Ft. Lauderdale, Fl 33339
(305) 566-0691

M & S Bottles and Antiques
421 Wilson St.
Fort Meade FL 33841
(941) 285-9421

Gore's Shoe Repair
410 Orange Ave.
Ft. Pierce, FL 33450
Florida Bottles & Black Glass

Pat Besinger
5719 Casino Drive
Holiday, FL 34690
(813) 934-3986
Nursing Bottles

This-N-That Shop
Albert B. Coleman
P.O. Box 185
Hollister, FL 32047
(904) 328-3658

Hickory Stick Antiques
400 So. 57 Terr.
Hollywood, FL 33023
(904) 962-3434
Canning Jars, Black Glass, Household
Bottles

The Browns
6512 Mitford Rd.
Jacksonville, FL 32210
(904) 771-2091
Sodas, Mineral Waters, Milk, Black
Glass

Pacer Henry
5858 Theed Street
Jacksonville, FL 32211
(904) 744-8458
Florida Pottery Jugs & Crocks

Dwight Pettit
33 Sea Side Dr.
Key Largo, FL 33037
(305) 852-8338

Carl Sturm
88 Sweetbriar Branch
Longwood, FL 32750
(407) 332-7689
Cure Bottles

Gerae & Lynn McLarty
6705 Dogwood Ct.
New Port Richey, FL 33552
(813) 849-7166

Mike Kollar
50 Sylvania Pl.
Ormond, FL 32074

Jon Vander Schouw
P.O. Box 1151
Palmetto, FL 33561
(813) 722-1375

Alan McCarthy
2415 W. 15th St.
Panama City, FL 32401
(904) 784-3903
Black Glass, Early Medicines

Tom & Alice Moulton
2903 Aston Avenue
Plant City, FL 33567
(813) 754-1396
Insulators & Fruit Jars

Hidden Bottle Shop
2656 Grandview
Sanford, FL 32771
(813) 322-7181

Juanne & Ed Herrold
P.O. Box 3105
Sarasota, FL
(941) 923-6550
Bitters, Cathedral Pickles

Harry O. Thomas
2721 Parson's Rest
Tallahassee, FL 32308
(904) 893-3834

Jim & Beth Daniels
14018 N. Florida Ave
Tampa, FL 33613
(813) 960-7541
Fruit Jars

L.L. Linscott
3557 Nicklaus Dr.
Titusville, FL 32780
(305) 267-9170
Fruit Jars & Porcelain Insulators

GEORGIA

Michael D. (Mike) Newman
3716 Pebble Beach Drive
Augusta, GA 30907
(706) 868-8391
Southern Colored Sodas

Wayne's Bottles
Box 183
Butler, GA 31006
(912) 862-3699
Odd Colors & Shapes

Bob Brown
274 Riverhill Rd.
Cornelia, GA 30531
Saratoga Type Bottles

Keith Roloson
6220 Carriage Court
Cumming, GA 30130
(770) 781-5021
Insulators

Carlo & Dot Sellari
Box 888553
Dunwoody, GA 30338
(404) 451-2483

James T. Hicks
Rt. 4, Box 265
Eatonton, GA 31024
(404) 485-9280

Paul H. Irby
5862 Meadowview Lane
Flowery Branch, GA 30542
(770) 967-3946
Bottles & Insulators

Jim Scharnagel
3601 Laura Lane
Gainesville, GA 30506
(770) 536-5690
Inks & Female Medicines

Dave & Tia Janousek
2293 Mulligan Circle
Lawrenceville, GA 30245

Butch Alley
P.O. Box 358
Lithia Springs, GA 30057
(770) 942-4493
Bottles

Schmitt House Bottle Diggers
5532 Jane Rue Circle
Macon, GA 31206
(912) 781-6130

Ken Nease
Rt. 1, Box 149
Manassas, GA 30438
(912) 739-7355
Bottles

Bob & Barbara Simmons
152 Greenville St.
Newnan, GA 30263
(404) 251-2471

David Powell
Savannah, GA
(912) 354-3576
Bottles & Jars

Bill Wrenn
1060 Calls Creek Drive
Watkinsville, GA 30677
Mini Jugs

HAWAII
The Hawaiian Antique Bottle Shop
Kahuku Sugar Mill
P.O. Box 495
Honolulu, HI 96731
(808) 293-5581
Hawaiian Sodas, Whiskeys, Medicines,
and Milks

The Hawaii Bottle Museum
1044 Kalapaki Street
P.O. Box 25153
Honolulu, HI 96825
(808) 395-4671
Hawaiian Bottles, Oriental Bottles &
Pottery

IDAHO
John Cothern
Rt. 1
Buhl, ID 83316
(208) 543-6713

Jim & Barb Sinsley
1048 N. 14th Street
Coeur d'Alene, ID 83814
(208) 667-2211
Bitter Bottles

Rudy Burns
1238 Eagle Hills Way
Eagle, ID 83616

Idaho Hotel
Jordan St., Box 75
Murphy, ID
Silver City, ID 86350
(208) 495-2520

ILLINOIS
Ronald Selcke
4N236 8th Ave.
Addison, IL 60101
(312) 543-4848

Sean Mullikin
5014 Alicia Dr.
Alton, IL 62002
(312) 466-7506

Mike Spiiroff
1229 Alton St.
Alton, IL 62002
(618) 462-2283

Bob Kay
216 N. Batavia Ave.
Batavia, IL 60510
Miniature Bottles

Wayne & Jacquline Brammer
309 Bellevue Dr.
Belleville, IL 62223
(618) 213-8841

Marvin & Carol Ridgeway
450 W. Cart
Cerro Gordo, IL 61818
(217) 763-3271

Casad's Antique
610 South State St.
Champaign, IL 61820
(217) 356-8455
Milk Bottles

Tom & Gladys Bartels
5315 W. Warwick
Chicago, IL 60641
(312) 725-2433

Ernest Brooks
9023 S. East End
Chicago, IL 60617
(312) 375-9233

1st Chicago Bottle Club
P.O. Box A3382
Chicago, IL 60690

Jerry McCann
5003 West Berwyn
Chicago, IL 60630
(312) 777-0443
Fruit Jars

Joe Healy
3421 W. 76th St.
Chicago, IL 60652

William Kiggans
7747 South Kedzle
Chicago, IL 60652
(312) 925-6148

Carl Malik
8655 S. Keeler
Chicago, IL 60652
(312) 767-8568

Louis Metzinger
4140 N. Mozart
Chicago, IL 60618
(312) 478-9034

L.D. & Barbara Robinson
1933 So. Homan
Chicago, IL 60623
(312) 762-6096

Paul R. Welko
5727 S. Natoma Ave.
Chicago, IL 60638
(312) 229-0424
Blob Tops & Hutchinson Sodas

Al & Sue Verley
486 Longwood Ct.
Chicago, IL 60411
(312) 754-4132

Ray's & Betty Antiques
Box 5
Dieterich, IL 62424
(217) 925-5449
Bitters

Keith & Ellen Leeders
1728 N. 76th Ave
Elmwood, IL 60635
(708) 453-2085

Jeff Cress
3403 Morkel Dr.
Godfrey, IL 62035
(618) 466-3513

Jim & Jodi Hall
5185 Conifer Lane
Gurnee, IL 60031
(708) 541-5788
Bottles—All Types

Doug & Eileen Wagner
9225 S. 88th Ave
Hickory Hills, IL 60457
(312) 598-4570

Jim & Perry Lang
628 Mechanic
Hillsboro, IL 62049
(217) 532-2915

Art & Pat Besinger
611 Oakwood
Ingelside, IL 60041
(312) 546-2367

John Murray
301 Hillgrove
LaGrange, IL 60525
(312) 352-2199

Lloyd Bindscheattle
P.O. Box 11
Lake Villa, IL 60046

Russ & Lynn Sineni
1372 Hillcrest Rd.
Lemont, IL 60439
(312) 257-2648

Neal & Marianne Vander Zande
18830 Sara Rd.
Mokena, IL 60448
(312) 479-5566

Seve Kehrer
Box 151
New Memphis, IL 62266
(618) 588-7785
Fruit Jars

Joe Molloy
P.O. Box 225
Newton, IL 62448
(618) 783-8741
Miniature Bottles

Tom & Ann Feltman
425 North Oak St.
O'Fallon, IL 62269
(618) 632-3327

Vern & Gloria Nitchie
300 Indiana St.
Park Forest, IL 60466
(312) 748-7198

Ken's Old Bottles
119 East Lahon
Park Ridge, IL 60068
(312) 823-1267
Milks, Inks, Sodas, Whiskeys

Harry's Bottle Shop
612 Hillyer St.
Pekin, IL 61555
(309) 346-3476
Pottery, Beer, Sodas, Medicines

Oertel's Bottle House
Box 682
Pekin, IL 61555
(309) 347-4441
Peoria Pottery, Embossed Picnic Beer
Bottles, Fruit Jars

Bob Rhinberger
Rt. 7
Quincy, IL 62301
(217) 223-0191

Bob & Barbara Harms
14521 Atlantic
Riverdale, IL 60627
(312) 841-4068

Ed McDonald
3002 23rd
Sauk Village, IL 60511
(312) 758-0373

Jon & Char Granada
631 S. Main
Trenton, IL 62293
(618) 224-7308

Ben Crane
1700 Thompson Dr.
Wheaton, IL 60187
(312) 665-5662

Scott Garrow
2 S. 338 Orchard Rd.
Wheaton, IL 60187

Hall
940 E. Old Willow Rd.
Wheeling, IL 60090
(312) 541-5788
Sodas, Inks, Medicines

Steve Miller
623 Ivy Ct.
Wheeling, IL 60090
(312) 398-1445

Michael Davis
1652 Tappan
Woodstock, IL 66098
(815) 338-5147

Mike Henrich
402 McHenry Ave.
Woodstock, IL 66098
(815) 338-5008

INDIANA
Ed & Margaret Shaw
Rt. 1, Box 23
Boggstown, IN 46110
(317) 835-7121

Connie Hackman
11757 Whisper Bay Ct.
Carmel, IN 46033
(317) 846-3629
Miniature Bottles

Tony & Dick Stringfellow
714 Vine
Clinton, IN 47842
(317) 832-2355

Bob & Morris Wise
409 E. Main
Flora, IN 46929
(219) 967-3713

Annett's Antiques
6910 Lincoln Hwy., E.
Fort Wayne, IN 46803
(219) 749-2745

Gene Rice
61935 CR37, Rt. 1
Goshen, IN 46526

Wayne Wagner
23558 Creek Park Dr.
Goshen, IN 46526

George & Nancy Reilly
Rt. 10, Box 67
Greenfield, IN 46140
(317) 462-2441

John & Dianna Atkins
3168 Beeler Ave.
Indianapolis, IN 46224
(317) 299-2720

Herrell's Collectibles
265 E. Canal St.
Peru, IN 46970
(317) 473-7770

Fort Harrod Glass Works
160 N. Gardner Rd.
Scottsburg, IN 47170
(812) 752-5170

Harry & Dorothy Frey
5210 Clinton Rd.
Terre Haute, IN 47805
(812) 466-4642

Doug Moore
9 Northbrook Circle
Westfield, IN 46074
(317) 896-3015

IOWA

The Bottle Shop
206 Chestnut
Elkader, IA 52043
(319) 245-2359
Sarsaparilla & Bitters

John Wyss
1941 Grant Wood Drive
Iowa City, IA 52240
(319) 337-9965
Miniature Bottles

Ralph & Helen Welch
804 Colonial Circle
Storm Lake, IA 50588
(712) 732-4124

KANSAS

Mikey Stafford
507 On The Mall
Atchison, KS 66002
(913) 367-0056
Antiques and Books

Donald Haury
208 Main
Halstead, KS 67056
(316) 283-5876
(316) 835-2356

Mike Elwell
Rt. 2, Box 30
Lawrence, KS 66044
(913) 842-2102

Stewart and Sons Old Bottle Shop
610 E. Kaskaskia
Paola, KS 66071
(913) 294-3434
Drugstore Bottles, Blob-Top Beers

Joe & Alyce Smith
4706 West Hills Dr.
Topeka, KS 66606
(913) 272-1892

KENTUCKY

Michael & Kathy Kolb
6 S. Jefferson
Alexandria, KY 41001
(606) 635-7121

Paul Van Vactor
100004 Cardigan Dr.
Jeffersontown, KY 40299

Roy & Cordie Willis
Heartland of Kentucky
Lebanon Junction, KY 40150
(502) 833-2827
Jim Beam, Ski Country

Gene Blasi
5801 River Knolls Dr.
Louisville, KY 40222
(502) 425-6995

Jerry Phelps
8012 Deronia Ave.
Louisville, KY 40222
(502) 425-2561

Paul & Paulette Van Vavtor
300 Stilz Ave.
Louisville, KY 40299
(502) 895-3655

Earl & Ruth Cron
808 N. 25th St.
Paducah, KY 42001
(502) 443-5005

Sheldon Baugh
252 West Valley Dr.
Russellville, KY 42276
(502) 726-2712
Shaker Bottles

LOUISIANA

Sidney & Eulalle Genius
1843 Tudor Dr.
Baton Rouge, KY 70815
(504) 925-5774

Bobby & Ellen Kirkpatrick
7313 Meadowbrook Ave.
Baton Rouge, LA 70808

Sheldon L. Ray Jr.
P.O. Box 17238
LSU
Baton Rouge, LA 70893
(504) 388-3814

Hilly Trading Company
Bob Willett
3171 Highway 167
Dubach, LA 71235
(318) 255-6112 & (318) 777-3424

Cajun Pop Factory
P.O. Box 1113
Jennings, LA 70546
(318) 824-7078
Hutchinson, Blob-Tops, Pontil Sodas

Everett L. Smith
100 Everett Dr.
Monroe, LA 71202
(318) 325-3534
Embossed Whiskeys

Ralph & Cheryl Green
515 Elizabeth St.
Natchitoches, LA 71457

Bep's Antiques
3923 Magazine St.
New Orleans, LA 70115
(504) 891-3468
Import Bottles

Dr. Charles & Jane Aprill
484 Chestnut
New Orleans, LA 70118
(504) 899-7441

The Dirty Digger
1804 Church St.
Ruston, LA 71270
(318) 255-6112

MAINE

F. Barrie Freeman, Antiques
Paradise Hill Rd.
Bethel, ME 04217
(207) 824-3300

John & Althea Hathaway
Bryant Pond, ME 04219

Don McKeen Bottles
McKeen Way, P.O. Box 5A
E. Wilton, ME 04234

Spruce's Antiques
Main St., P.O. Box 295
Milford, ME 04461
(207) 827-4756

Morse and Applebee Antiques
US Rt. 1, Box 164
Searsport, ME 04974
(207) 548-6314
Early American Glass

Wink's Bottle Shop
Rt. 235
Waldoboro, ME 04572
(207) 832-4603

Daniel R. Winchenbaugh
RFD 4, Box 21
Waldoboro, ME 04572
(207) 832-7702

MARYLAND

Pete's Diggins
Rt. 40 West, RR3, Box 301
North East, MD 21901
(301) 287-9245

Fran & Bill Lafferty
Box 142
Sudlersville, MD 21668

MASSACHUSETTS

Gloria Swanson Antiques
611 Main St.
Dennis, MA 02675
(508) 385-4166

Joe & Kathy Wood
49 Surplus St.
Duxbury, MA 02332
(617) 934-2221

Metamorphosis
46 Teewaddle, RFD 3
Leverett, MA 01002
Hair Tonics & Medicines

Shop in My Home
211 East St.
Mansfield, MA 02048
(617) 339-6086
Historic Flasks

The Applied Lip Place
26 Linden St.
North Easton, MA 02356
(617) 238-1432
Medicines, Whiskeys

Carlyn Ring
59 Livermore Road
Wellesley, MA 02181
(617) 235-5675

Leo A. Bedard
62 Craig Dr., Apt. 7A
West Springfield, MA 01089
Bitters, Whiskeys, Medicines

MICHIGAN

John Wolfe
1622 E. Stadium Blvd
Ann Arbor, MI 48104
(313) 665-6106

Pat Keefe
2290 Hiller Rd. W.
Bloomfield, MI 48324
(313) 363-2068
Miniature Bottles

Jim & Robin Meehan
25 Valley Way
Bloomfield Hills, MI 48013
(313) 642-0176

Old Chicago
316 Ross Dr.
Buchanan, MI 49107
(616) 695-5896
Hutchinson Sodas, Blob-Top Beers

James Clengenpeel
316 Ross Dr.
Buchanan, MI 49107
(616) 695-5896

Fred & Shirley Weck
8274 S. Jackson
Clarklake, MI 49234
(517) 529-9631

Chief Pontiac Antique Bottle Shop
13880 Neal Rd
Davisburg, MI 48019
(313) 634-8469

Michael & Christina Garrett
19400 Stout
Detroit, MI 48219
(313) 534-6067

Ray & Hillaine Hoste
366 Main St.
Dundee, MI 48131
(313) 529-2193

E & E Antiques
9441 Grand Blanc Road
Gaines, MI 48436
(517) 271-9063
Fruit Jars, Beer Bottles, Milks

Dewey & Marilyn Heetderks
21 Michigan N.E.
Grand Rapids, MI 49503
(616) 774-9333

Sarge's
111 E. Hemlock
Iron River, MI 49935
(906) 265-4223
Old Mining Town Bottles,
Hutchinsons

Mark & Marty McNee
1009 Vassar Dr.
Kalamazoo, MI 49001
(616) 343-9393

Lew & Leon Wisser
2837 Parchmount
Kalamazoo, MI 49004
(616) 343-7479

The Jar Emporium
Ralph Finch
19420 Saratoga
Lathrup, MI 48076
(313) 569-6749
Fruit Jars

Chris & Becky Batdorff
516 Maple St.
Manistee, MI 49660
(616) 723-7917

Don & Glennie Burkett
3942 West Dunbar Rd.
Monroe, MI 48161
(313) 241-6740

Copper Corner Rock & Bottle Shop
4th and Lincoln
Stambaugh, MI 49964
(906) 265-3510
Beers, Hutchinsons, Medicines

Anvil Antiques
3439 Hollywood Rd.
St. Joseph, MI 49085
(616) 429-5132
Insulators

John & Kay Petruska
21960 Marathon Rd.
Sturgis, MI 49091
(616) 651-6400

MINNESOTA
Jim Conley
P.O. Box 351
Excelsior, MN 55331
(612) 935-0964

Steve Ketcham
P.O. Box 24114
Minneapolis, MN 55424
(612) 920-4205

Neal & Pat Sorensen
132 Peninsula Rd.
Minneapolis, MN 55441
(612) 545-2698

Doug Shilson
3308-32 Ave. So.
Minneapolis, MN 55406
(612) 721-4165
Bitters, Beers, & Sodas

Ron & Vernie Feldhaus
5117 W. 92nd St.
Bloomington, MN 55437
(612) 835-3504

MISSISSIPPI
Vieux Beloxie Bottery Factory
Restaurant
US 90 E.
Biloxi, MS 39530
(601) 374-0688
Mississippi Bottles

Robert A. Knight
516 Dale St.
Columbia, MS 39429
(601) 736-4249
Mississippi Bottles & Jugs

Robert Smith
623 Pearl River Ave.
McComb, MS 39648
(601) 684-1843

Jerry Drott
710 Persimmon Dr., P.O. Box 714
Starkville, MS 39759
(601) 323-8796
Liniments, Drug Store Bottles

Ted & Linda Kost
107 Columbia
Vicksburg, MS 39180
(601) 638-8780

MISSOURI
Dave Hausgen
Rt. 1
Elsberry, MO 63343
(314) 898-2500

Sam & Eloise Taylor
3002 Woodlands Terrace
Glencoe, MO 63038
(314) 273-6244

Bob & Debbi Overfield
2318 Chestnut St.
Hannibal, MO 63401
(314) 248-9521

Mike & Carol Robinson
1405 N. River
Independence, MO 64050
(816) 836-2337

Gary & Vickie Lewis
P.O. Box 922
Liberty, MO 64069
Soda Pop Bottles

Donald Kimrey
1023 W. 17th St.
Kansas City, MO 64108
(816) 741-2745

Robert Stevens
1131 E. 77th
Kansas City, MO 64131
(816) 333-1398

The Bottle House
Rt. 1, Box 111
Linn Creek, MO 65052
(314) 346-5890

Gene & Alberta Kelley
1960 Cherokee
St. Louis, MO 63126
(314) 664-7203

Jerry Mueller
4520 Langtree
St. Louis, MO 63128
(314) 843-8357

Terry & Luann Phillips
1014 Camelot Gardens
St. Louis, MO 63125
(314) 892-6864

Hal & Vern Wagner
10118 Schuessler
St. Louis, MO 63128
(314) 843-7573
Historical Flasks, Colognes, Early
Glass

Barkely Museum
U.S. 61
Taylor, MO 63471
(314) 393-2408

Joseph & Jean Reed
237 E. Morgan
Tipton, MO 65081
(816) 433-5937

Randy & Jan Haviland
American Systems Antiques
Westphalia, MO 65085
(314) 455-2525

MONTANA
Lavaur Scow
Box 959
Boulder, MT 59632
(406) 225-3290
Montana Embossed Bottles

NEBRASKA
Born Again Antiques
1402 Williams St.
Omaha, NE 68108
(402) 341-5177

Karl Person
10210 "W" St.
Omaha, NE 68127
(402) 331-2666

Fred Williams
5712 N. 33rd St.
Omaha, NE 68111
(402) 453-4317

NEVADA
Lost River Trading Co.
Larry Gray
401 W. Main
Beatty, NV 89003
(702) 553-2233

Tom George
P.O. Box 21195
Carson City, NV 89721
(702) 884-4766

Doug Southerland
Box 1345
Carson City, NV 89702

Loren D. Love
P.O. Box 412
Dayton, NV 89403
(702) 246-0142
Beer Cans, Bottles

Ed Hoffman
P.O. Box 6039
Elko, NV 89802
(702) 753-2435
Coins & Paper

Don & Opal Wellman
P.O. Box 521
Fallon, NV 89406
(702) 423-3490

The Gloryhole
Virginia Ridgway
P.O. Box 219, 115 Columbia
Goldfield, NV 89013

Coleen Garland
Mithell's Mercantile
Gold Point, NV 89440
Soda Pop & Beer Bottles

Anita's Antiques and Collectibles
2030 E. Charleston
Las Vegas, NV 89104
(702) 388-1969

Bottle Collector's Liquor Shop
1328 Las Vegas Blvd So.
Las Vegas, NV (702) 382-6645
Miniature Bottles

James Campiglia
4371 Lucas
Las Vegas, NV 89120
(702) 456-6855
Casino Collectibles, Postcards, Bottles

Frank Gafford
5716 West Balzar
Las Vegas, NV 89108

Joe Martin
2632 E. Harmon
Las Vegas, NV 89121
(702) 731-5004
Nevada Trade Tokens

Allen Wilson
P.O. Box 29
Montello, NV 89830
(702) 776-2511
Bottles

Bruce "Bogie" Bogaert
182 South C Street
Virginia City
(Mailing address:
2900 Vassar Street
Reno, NV 89502)
(702) 847-9300
Beer Collectibles

Ronald J. Freeman
450 Douglas Fir
Reno, NV 89511
(702) 849-9543
Miniature Whiskey Bottles

Marty Hall
15430 Sylvester Rd.
Reno, NV 89511
(702) 852-6045
Western Whiskeys & Nevada Bottles

Fred Holabird
14040 Perlite Drive
Reno, NV 89511
(702) 851-0836
Nevada Bottles & Paper Items

Richard Moritz
5025 S. McCarran Blvd.
Box 186
Reno, NV 89502
(702) 329-4358
Nevada Bottles

Larry & Jann Shoemaker
P.O. Box 50546
Reno, NV 89513
(702) 747-6095
Bottles

Willy Young
80 Promontory Pointe
Reno, NV 89509
(702) 746-0922
Fire Grenades

Pegasus Parlon
P.O. Box 33
Silver Peak, NV 89047
(702) 937-2314

Don & Bonnie McLane
1846 F. St.
Sparks, NV 89431
(702) 359-2171

Walt Walker
P.O. Box 21
Verde, NV 89439
(702) 345-0171
Bottles

Mark Twain's Museum of Memories
Joe Curtis
P.O. Box 449
Virginia City, NV 89440
(702) 847-0454
Rare Nevada Documents

Ann Hunt-Laird Antiques
119 North Main Street
Yerington, NV 89447
(702) 463-5641

NEW HAMPSHIRE

Dave & Carol Waris
Boston Post Rd.
Amherst, NH 03031
(603) 882-4409

Bob & Betty Morin
RD 3, Box 280
Dover, NH 03820

Lucille Stanley
9 Oak St.
Exeter, NH 03833
(603) 772-2296

Murray's Lakeside Bottle Shop
Benson Shores, P.O. Box 57
Hampstead, NH 03841
(603) 329-6969

Jim & Joyce Rogers
Harvey Rd., Rt. 10
Manchester, NH 03103
(603) 623-4101

House of Glass
25 High St.
Troy, NH 03465
(603) 242-7947

NEW JERSEY

Richard & Lesley Harris
Box 400
Branchville, NJ 07826
(201) 948-3935

Phil & Flo Alvarez
P.O. Box 107
Califon, NJ 07830
(201) 832-7438

Ed & Carole Clemens
81 Chester Pl., Apt. D-2
Englewood, NJ 07631
(201) 569-4429

John Orashen
RD 6, Box 345-A
Flemington, NJ 08822
(201) 782-3391

Tom & Marion McCandless
62 Lafayette St.
Hopewell, NJ 08525
(609) 466-0619

Howell Township
Bruce & Pat Egeland
3 Rustic Drive
Howell, NJ 07731
(201) 363-0556

Sam Fuss
Harmony Rd.
Mickleton, NJ 08056
(609) 423-5038

Old Bottle Museum
4 Friendship Dr.
Salem, NJ 08079
(609) 935-5631

NEW MEXICO

George Petroff
1401 Pennsylvania NE #3143
Albuquerque, NM 87110
(505) 875-0312
Miniature Bottles

Irv & Ruth Swalwell
8826 Fairbanks
Albuquerque, NM 87112
(505) 299-2977

Krol's Rock City & Mobile Park
Star Rt. 2, Box 15A
Deming, NM 88030
Hutchinson Sodas, Inks, Avons

Zang Wood
P.O. Box 890/#21 Road 3461
Flora Vista, NM 87415
(505) 334-8966
Seltzers, Hutchinsons

Tino Romero
2917 Canada del Humo
Santa Fe, NM 87505
(505) 474-6353
Poisons, Inks, Dr. Kilmer & New
Mexico

NEW YORK

Brewster Bottle Shop
297 South St.
Auburn, NY 13021
(315) 252-3246
Milk Bottles

Tom & Alice Moulton
88 Blue Spruce Lane, RD 5
Ballston Lake, NY 12019

Jim Chamberlain
RD 8, 607 Nowland Rd.
Binghamton, NY 13904
(607) 772-1135

Jo Ann's Old Bottles
RD 2, Box 638
Port Crane, NY 13833
(607) 648-4605

Edward Petter
P.O. Box 1
Blodgett Mills, NY 13738
(607) 756-7891
Inks

Old Bottle Shop
Horton Rd., P.O. Box 105
Blooming Grove, NY 10914
(914) 496-6841

Al Manuel
1225 McDonald Ave.
Brooklyn, NY 11230
(718) 253-8308
Miniature Bottles

J.J.'s Pontil Place
1001 Dunderberg Rd.
Central Valley, NY 10917
(914) 928-9144

John Kovacik
11 Juniper Dr.
Clifton Park, NY 12065
(518) 371-4118

Richard Strunk
RD 4, Grooms Rd.
Clifton Park, NY 12065
Flasks, Bitters, Saratogas

The Bottle Shop Antiques
P.O. Box 503
Cranberry Lake, NY 12927
(315) 848-2648

Leonard & Joyce Blake
1220 Stolle Rd.
Elma, NY 14059
(716) 652-7752

Tony Natelli
153-31 79th Street
Howard Beach, NY 11414
(718) 738-3344
Miniature Bottles

Kenneth Cornell
78 Main
Leroy, NY 14482
(716) 768-8919

The Bottle Shop
P.O. Box 24
Loch Sheldrake, NY 12759
(914) 434-4757

Manor House Collectibles
Rt. 42, South Forestburg
RD 1, Box 67
Monticello, NY 12701
(914) 794-3967
Whiskeys, Beers, Sodas

Chris Davis
522 Woodhill
Newark, NY 14513
(315) 331-4078
Bottles & Glass

David Byrd
43 E. Kenwood Dr.
New Windsor, NY 12550
(914) 561-7257

Chuck Moore
3 East 57th St.
New York, NY 10022

Bottles Unlimited
245 East 78th St.
New York, NY 10021
(212) 628-8769
18th & 19th Century Bottles

Schumer's Wine & Liquors
59 East 54th Street
New York, NY 10022
Miniature Bottles

Burton Spiller
169 Greystone Lane
Apt. 13, Rochester, NY 14618
(716) 244-2229

Robert Zorn
23 Knickerbocker Ave.
Rochester, NY 14615
(716) 254-7470

Dick & Evelyn Bowman
1253 LaBaron Circle
Webster, NY 14580
(716) 872-4015
Insulators

NORTH CAROLINA

Vieve & Luke Yarbrough
P.O. Box 1023
Blowing Rock, NC 28605
(704) 963-4961

Bob Morgan
P.O. Box 3163
Charlotte, NC 28203
(704) 527-4841

Clement's Bottles
5234 Willowhaven Dr.
Durham, NC 27712
(919) 383-2493
Commemorative Soft Drink Bottles

Howard Crowe
P.O. Box 133
Gold Hill, NC 28071
(704) 279-3736

Vernon Capps
Rt. 5, Box 529
Goldsboro, NC 27530
(919) 734-8964

Rex D. McMillan
4101 Glen Laurel Dr.
Raleigh, NC 27612
(919) 787-0007
North Carolina Blobs, Saloon Bottles,
Colored Drug Store Bottles

NORTH DAKOTA

Robert Barr
102 N. 9th Ave,
Mandan, ND 58554

OHIO

Don & Barb Dzuro
5113 W. Bath Rd.
Akron, OH 44313
(216) 666-8170

Jim Salzwimmer
3391 Tisen Rd.
Akron, OH 44312
(216) 699-3990

Allan Hodges
25125 Shaker Blvd.
Beachwood, OH 44122
(216) 464-8381

Schroll's Country Shop
3 Miles East of County Line Co.
Rd. 33
Bluffton, OH (419) 358-6121

Albert & Sylvia Campbell
RD 1, Box 194
Byesville, OH 43723
(614) 439-1105

Kenneth & Dudie Roat
7775 Kennedy Lane
Cincinnati, OH 45242
(513) 791-1168

Joe & Mary Miller
2590 N. Moreland Blvd.
Cleveland, OH 44120
(216) 721-9919

Don & Paula Spangler
2554 Loris Dr.
Dayton, OH 45449
(513) 435-7155

Roy & Barbara Brown
8649 Dunsinane Dr.
Dublin, OH 43017
(614) 889-0818

Roger Durflinger
P.O. Box 2006
Frankfort, OH 45628
(614) 998-4849

Gilbert Nething
P.O. Box 96
Hannibal, OH 43931
Hutchinson Sodas

R.J. & Freda Brown
125 S. High St.
Lancaster, OH 43130
(614) 687-2899

A. Waxman
1928 Camberly Dr.
Lyndhurst, OH 44124
(216) 449-4765
Miniature Bottles, Whiskey, Rye,
Scotch

John & Margie Bartley
160 South Main
North Hampton, OH 45319
(513) 964-1080

Bob & Dawn Jackson
107 Pine St.
Powhatan Point, OH 43942
(614) 795-5565

Bob & Phyllis Christ
1218 Creekside Place
Reynoldsburg, OH 43068
(614) 866-2156

Ballentine's Bottles
710 W. First St.
Springfield, OH 45504
(513) 399-8359

Larry R. Henschen
3222 Delrey Rd.
Springfield, OH 45504
(513) 399-1891

Tom & Deena Caniff
1223 Oak Grove Ave.
Steubenville, OH 43952
(614) 282-8918
Fruit Jars

Bob & Mary Ann Willamagna
711 Kendall Ave.
Steubenville, OH 43952
(614) 282-9029

Doug & Joann Bedore
1483 Ritchie Rd.
Stow, OH 44224
(216) 688-4934

Bob Villamagna
1518 Madison Ave., P.O. Box 56
Toronto, OH 43964
(614) 537-4503
Tri-State Area Bottles, Stoneware

Paul Stookey
3015 W. Tate Route 571
Troy, OH 45373
(513) 698-3392
Miniature Bottles

Bill Orr
1680 Glenwood Drive
Twinsburg, OH 44087
(216) 425-2365
Miniature Bottles

Michael Cetina
3272 Northwest Blvd. N.W.
Warren, OH 44485
(216) 898-1845

Al & Beth Bignon
480 High St.
Washingtonville, OH 44490
(216) 427-6848

The Bottleworks
70 N. Main St., P.O. Box 446
Waynesville, OH 45068
(513) 897-3861

Elvin & Cherie Moody
Trails End
Wellington, OH 44090
(216) 647-4917

Bill & Wanda Dudley
393 Franklin Ave.
Xenia, OH 45385
(513) 372-8567

OKLAHOMA

Ronald & Carol Ashby
831 E. Pine
Enid, OK 73701
Rare & Scarce Fruit Jars

Johnnie W. Fletcher
1300 S. Blue Haven Dr.
Mustang, OK 73064
(405) 376-1045
Kansas & Oklahoma Bottles

Joe & Hazel Nagy
3540 NW 23
Oklahoma City, OK 73107
(405) 942-0882

Larry & Linda Shope
310 W. 44th
Sandsprings, OK 74063
(918) 363-8481

OREGON

Juanita Rubio
4326 Old Stage Road
Central Point, OR 97502
Miniature Bottles

Tom & Bonnie Kasner
380 E. Jersey St.
Gladstone, OR 97027
(503) 655-9127
Insulators, Marbles, Bottles, Jars

Robert & Marguerite Ornduff
Rt. 4, Box 236-A
Hillsboro, OK 97123
(503) 538-2359

R.E. Barnett
P.O. Box 109
Lakeview, OR 97630
(503) 947-2415
Western Whiskey Bottles

Gerald M. Burton
611 Taylor St.
Myrtle Creek, OR 97457
(503) 863-6670

Alan Amerman
2311 S.E. 147th
Portland, OR 97233
(503) 761-1661
Fruit Jars

The Glass House
4620 S.E. 104th
Portland, OR 97266
(503) 760-3346
Fruit Jars

PENNSYLVANIA
R.S. Riovo
686 Franklin St.
Alburtis, PA 18011-9578
(610) 966-2536
Milk Bottles, Dairy Go-Withs

Ernest Hurd
5 High St.
Bradford, PA 16701
(814) 362-9915

Dick & Patti Mansour
458 Lambert Dr.
Bradford, PA 16701
(814) 368-8820

Claude & Ethel Lee
643 Bolivar Drive
Bradford, PA 16701
(814) 362-3663
Jars, Bottles, Pocket Knives

John & Mary Schultz
RD 1, Box 118
Canonsburg, PA 15317
(412) 745-6632

The Old Bottle Corner
508 South Main St.
Coudersport, PA 16915
(814) 274-7017
Fruit Jars, Blob Tops

James A. Hagenbach
102 Jefferson St.
East Greenville, PA 18041
(215) 679-5849

Jere & Betty Hambleton
5940 Main St.
East Petersburg, PA 17520
(717) 569-0130

Al & Maggie Duffield
12 Belmar Rd.
Hatboro, PA 19040
(215) 675-5175
Hutchinsons, Inks

Barry & Mary Hogan
3 Lark Lane
Lancaster, PA 17603

Ed Lasky
43 Nightingale
Levittown, PA 19054
(215) 945-1555

Harold Bauer Antique Bottles
136 Cherry St
Marienville, PA 16239

Chuck Henigin
3024 Pitch Fork Lane
McKees Rocks, PA 15136
(412) 331-6159

Harold Hill
161 E. Water St.
Muncy, PA 17756
(717) 546-3388

Allen Holtz
RD 1, 18947
Pipersville, PA 18947
(215) 847-5728

Carl & Gail Onufer
210 Newport Rd.,
Pittsburgh, PA 15221
(412) 371-7725
Milk Bottles

R.A. & Ester Heimer
P.O. Box 153
Roulette, PA 16746
(814) 544-7713

Butch & Gloria Kim
RD 2, Box 35
Strongstown, PA 15957

RHODE ISLAND

Wes & Diane Seemann
Box 49
Kenyon, RI 02836
(203) 599-1626

Normand Provencal
84 Rowe Ave.
Warwick, RI 02889
(401) 739-4148
Miniature Bottles

SOUTH CAROLINA

Bob Durham
704 W. Main St.
Eashey, SC 29640

Tony & Marie Shank
P.O. Box 778
Marion, SC 29571
(803) 423-5803

TENNESSEE

Charlie Barnette
100 N. Coffey St.
Bristol, TN
(615) 968-1437
Whiskeys, Druggists' Patent Medicines

Ronnie Adams
7005 Charlotte Dr.
Knoxville, TN 37914
(615) 524-8958

Terry Pennington
415 N. Spring St.
McMinnville, TN 37110
Jack Daniels, Amber Coca-Cola

Bluff City Bottlers
4630 Crystal Springs Dr.
Memphis, TN 38123
(901) 353-0541
Common American Bottles

Larry & Nancy McCage
3772 Hanna Dr.
Memphis, TN 38128
(901) 388-9329

Tom Phillips
2088 Fox Run Cove
Memphis, TN 38138
(901) 754-0097

TEXAS

Robert Snyder
4235 W. 13th
Amarillo, TX 79106

Mack & Alliene Landers
P.O. Box 5
Euless, TX 76039
(817) 267-2710

Bennie & Harper Leiper
2800 W. Dallas
Houston, 77019
(713) 526-2101

Gerald Welch
4809 Gardenia Trail
Pasadena, TX 77505
(713) 487-3057

Jimmy & Peggy Galloway
P.O. Drawer A
Port Isabel, TX 78578
(512) 943-2437

Chuck & Reta Bukin
1325 Cypress Dr.
Richardson, TX 75080
(214) 235-4889

Sam Greer
707 Nix Professional Bldg.
San Antonio, TX 78205
(512) 227-0253

Ken Malone
3110 Garfield
Wichita Falls, TX 76308
(817) 691-6397
New Mexico Bottles

UTAH

Betty's Antiques & Collectibles
1181 South Main
Cedar City, UT 84720
(801) 586-7221
Depression Glass & Pottery

Bruce Dugger
1617 W. 4800 So.
Salt Lake City, UT 84123

Dave Emett
1736 North Star Dr.
Salt Lake City, UT 84116
(801) 596-2103
Utah Crocks & Jugs

Shady Lane Antiques
Marie & Mont Bradford
276 W. St. George Blvd.
St. George, UT 84770
(801) 628-7716

Dark Canyon Trading Company
Janice & Gary Parker
W. 200N (24-4)
Blanding, UT 84511
Bottles, Pottery, Art

VERMONT

Kit Barry
88 High St.
Brattleboro, VT 05301
(802) 254-2195

VIRGINIA

A. E. Steidel
6167 Cobbs Rd.
Alexandria, VA 22310

Dick & Margie Stockton
2331 N. Tuckahoe St
Arlington, VA 22205
(703) 534-5619

Tom Morgan
3501 Slate Ct.
Chesterfield, VA 23832

White's Trading Post
Boutchyards Olde Stable
Fredericksburg, VA 22401
(703) 371-6252
Fruit Jars

Vic & Betty Landis
Rt. 1, Box 8A
Hinton, VA 22801
(703) 867-5959

Early American Workshop
Star Route
Huntly, VA 22640
(703) 635-8252
Milk Bottles

John Tutton
Rt. 1, Box 261
Marshall, VA 22115
(703) 347-0148

Lloyd & Carrie Hamish
2936 Woodworth Rd.
Richmond, VA 23234
(804) 275-7106

Jim & Connie Mitchell
5106 Glen Alden Dr.
Richmond, VA 23234

WASHINGTON

Kent Beach
1001 Harding Rd.
Aberdeen, WA 98520
(206) 532-8556
Owl Bottles & Related Items

Ron Flannery
1821 Jackson Dr NW
Bremerton, WA 98312
(360) 373-7514
Bottles

Pete Hendricks
3005 So. 302nd Pl.
Federal Way, WA 98023
(206) 874-6345
Owl Bottles

Ed Erickson
1602 143rd Pl. SE
Mill Creek, WA 98012
(425) 338-0890
Nevada Collectibles

Ed & Tami Barber
45659 SE 129th
North Bend, WA 98045
(206) 888-1179
Early American Bottles

John W. Cooper
4975 120th Ave. S.E.
Bellevue, WA 98006
(206) 644-2669
Bottles

WISCONSIN

Mike & Carol Schwartz
Rt. 1
Arlington, WI 53911
(608) 846-5229

Jeff Burkhardt
12637 N. River Forest Cir.
Mequon, WI 53092
(414) 243-5643

Bor Markiewicz
11715 W. Bonniwell Rd.
Mequon, WI 53092
(414) 242-3968

George Aldrich
3211 West Michigan Street
Milwaukee, WI 53208
(414) 933-1643
Miniature Bottles

Richard Schwab
65-5 Lareen Rd.
Oskosh, WI 54901
(414) 235-9962

Bill & Kathy Mitchell
703 Linwood Ave.
Stevens Point, WI 55431
(715) 341-1471

George & Ruth Hansen
Rt. 2, Box 26
Wautoma, WI 54962
(414) 787-4893

Foreign

AUSTRALIA

John Lynch
P.O. Box 78
Charters Towers QLD 4820, Australia

Stephen Trill
5 Acacia Avenue
Warwick, Australia 4370

CANADA

Ed Gulka
5901 44th Street
Lloydminster, Alberta T9V 1 V6
(403) 875-6677

Peter Austin
Off Road Bottles & Collectibles
P.O. 171
Pontypool, Ont., LOA 1KO
(705) 277-3704
Codd Bottles

Ron Nykolyshyn
8820-138 Avenue
Edmonton, Alberta T5E 2A8 Canada
Miniature Vodkas Bottles

ENGLAND

Rob Goodacre
44 Arundel Close, BH 25 SUH
New Milton Hants
Tel: 01425 620794
Overseas Direct Dial
011-441425-620794
Bitters, Whiskeys, Pictorial

Robin A. Gollan
6 Broom Mead
Bexleyheath, Kent
DA6 7NY England
011-441-1322-524246
Minature Cognac Bottles

NETHERLAND

Willy Van den Bossche
Kniplaan 3 NL
2251 Voorschoten, Nederland

CHINA

Hong Kong Miniature Liquor
Collection, Shop 107
Astor Plaza
380 Nathan Road
Kowloon, Hong Kong
Fax (852) 2314-8022
Miniature Bottles

Man's Chan
Dragon Empire Trading Co.
Bowa House
180 Nathan Road
Tsimshatsui, Kowloon, Hong Kong
Fax (852) 314-8022
Ph (852) 721-3200

Glossary

Amethyst-Colored Glass A clear glass that when exposed to the sun or bright light for a long period of time will turn various shades of purple. Only glass that contains manganese is subject to this process.

Amber-Colored Glass Nickel was added in the glass production to obtain this common bottle color. It was believed that the resulting dark color would prevent the sun from damaging the contents of the bottle.

Annealing The gradual cooling of hot glass in a cooling chamber or annealing oven.

Applied Lip On bottles manufactured before 1880 the lip was applied after removal from the blowpipe. This may be only a ring of glass trailed around the bottle neck.

Automatic Bottle Machine Invented in 1903, this machine revolutionized the bottle industry.

Aqua-Colored Glass The natural color of glass. The particular shade produced was dependent on the iron oxide used in the glass production. It was commonly produced until the 1930s.

Barber Bottle In the 1880s these colorful bottles decorated the shelves of barbershops and usually were filled with bay rum.

Batch A mixture of the ingredients necessary for the manufacture of glass.

Battledore A wooden paddle used by a glassblower to flatten the bottom or sides of a bottle.

Bitters An herbal, purportedly medicinal, mixture and flavoring, which contained a great quantity of alcohol, usually corn whiskey.

Black Glass This type of glass, produced between 1700 and 1875, is actually a dark olive green color created by the carbon used in the glass production.

Blob Seal A way of identifying an unembossed bottle. Manufacturers applied a molten coin-shaped blob of glass to the shoulder of this bottle, into which a seal with the logo, name of the distiller, date, or product name was impressed.

Blob Top A large thick blob of glass that was placed around the lip of soda or mineral water bottles. A wire held the stopper, which was seated below the blob and anchored the wire when the stopper was closed, to prevent the carbonation from escaping.

Blown-in Mold Process by which the gather of glass is blown into a mold to take the shape of the mold. The lips on these types of bottles were added later and the bases often have open pontil scars.

Blowpipe A hollow iron tube wider and thicker at the gathering end than at the blowing end. Glassblowers used them to pick up the molten glass, which was then blown in a mold or free-blown outside the mold. Pipes vary from 2½ to 6 feet in length.

Calabash A type of flask with a rounded bottom. These bottles are known as "Jenny Lind" flasks and were common in the 19th century.

Carboys Cylindrical bottles with short necks.

Cobalt-Colored Glass This color was used with patented medicines and poisons to distinguish them from other bottles. Excessive amounts resulted in the familiar "cobalt blue" color.

Codd A bottle enclosure that was patented in 1873 by Hiram Codd of England. A small ball is blown inside the bottle as a method of sealing the contents from the outside air.

Crown Cap A metal cap formed from a circular tin plate crimped on its edge to fit tightly over the rolled lip of a bottle. The inside of the cap was filled with a cork disk, which created an airtight seal.

Cullet Cleansed and broken glass added to the batch to bring about rapid fusion.

Date Line The mold seam or mold line on a bottle. The length of this line provides collectors with a clue to the bottle's approximate age.

Decolorizer A compound that is added to natural aquamarine bottle glass to render the glass clear.

Dip Mold A one-piece mold open at the top.

Embossed Lettering Raised print denoting the name of the product or manufacturer on the bottle.

Fire Polishing The reheating of glass to eliminate unwanted blemishes.

Flared Lip Bottles produced prior to 1900 have lips that have been worked out or flared out to reinforce the strength of the opening.

Flint Glass Glass composed of a silicate of potash and lead.

Free-Blown Glass Items of this nature are produced with a blowpipe and do not utilize a mold.

Gaffer The word for the master blower in the early glass houses.

Gather The gob of molten glass adhering to the blowpipe in the first stage of the free-blown process.

Glory Hole The small furnace used for the frequent reheatings necessary during the making of a bottle. The glory hole was also used in fire polishing.

Green Glass Refers to a composition of glass and not a color. The green color was caused by the iron impurities in the sand, which could not be controlled by the glassmakers.

Ground Pontil Refers to the smooth circle that remains when a rough pontil scar has been ground off.

Hobbleskirt The paneled shape used to describe Coca-Cola bottles.

Hutchinson A spring-type internal closure that seals soda bottles which was patented in 1879 by Charles Hutchinson.

Imperfections Include bubbles or tears of all sizes and shapes, bent shapes and necks, imperfect seams, and errors in spelling and embossing.

Improved Pontil Bottles having an improved pontil appear as reddish or blackish on the base.

Kick-up The deep indentation in the bottom of many bottles. This is formed by placing a projected piece of wood or metal in the base of the mold while the glass is still hot. Wine bottles are usually indented.

Laid-on Ring A bead of glass that has been trailed around the neck opening to reinforce the opening.

Lady's Leg Bottles that are shaped like long curving necks.

Lighting Closure A closure that used an intertwined wire bale configuration to hold the lid on fruit jars. This closure was also common with soda bottles.

Manganese Utilized as a decolorizer between 1850 and 1910. Will also cause glass to turn purple under extreme heat.

Melting Pot This was a clay pot used to melt silicate in the glass-making process.

Metal The molten glass.

Milk Glass Tin is added in glass production to obtain this colored glass, which was primarily used for cosmetic bottles.

Mold, Full-Height, Three-Piece The entire bottle was formed in the mold, and two seams run the height of the bottle to the lip on both sides.

Mold, Three-Piece Dip In this mold the bottom part of the bottle mold was one piece and the top, from the shoulder up, was two separate pieces. Mold seams appear circling the bottle at the shoulder and on each side of the neck.

Opalescence This is seen on the frosty bottle or variegated-color bottle that has been buried in mud or silt; the minerals in these substances have interacted with the glass to create these effects.

Painted Label Abbreviation for Applied Color Label (ACL), which is baked on the outside of the bottle; this was commonly used on soda pop bottles and milk bottles.

Paste Mold These were made of two or more pieces of iron and were coated with a paste to prevent scratches on the glass. The seams were eliminated as the glass was turned in the mold.

Pontil, Puntee, or Punty Rod The iron rod attached to the base of a bottle by a gob of glass to hold the bottle during the finishing.

Pontil Marks To remove the bottle from the blowpipe, an iron rod with a small amount of molten glass was applied to the bottom of the bottle for handling while the neck and lip were finished. A sharp tap removed the bottle from the pontil, leaving a jagged glass scar.

Potstone Impurities in the glass batch which when blown into a piece of finished glass resemble a white stone.

Pressed Glass Glass that has been pressed into a mold to take the shape of the mold or the pattern within the mold.

Pucellas Called "the tool" by glassmakers. This tool is essential in shaping both the body and opening in blown bottles.

Pumpkinseed A small round flat flask, often found in Western areas. Generally made of clear glass, the shape resembled the seed of the grown pumpkin. These bottles are also known as "Mickies," "Saddle Flasks," and "Two-Bit Ponies."

Round Bottom A soda bottle made of heavy glass designed in the shape of a torpedo. This enabled the bottle to lie on its side, keeping the liquid in contact with the cork, and preventing the cork from drying and popping out of the bottle.

Seal A circular or oval slug of glass applied to the shoulder of a bottle with an imprint of the manufacturer's name, initials, or mark.

Sheared Lip After the bottle was blown, a pair of scissorlike shears clipped the hot glass from the blowpipe. No top was applied and sometimes a slight flange was created.

Sick Glass Glass bearing a superficial decay or deterioration that takes on a grayish tinge caused by erratic firing.

Slug Plate A metal plate about two by four inches with a firm's name on it, which was inserted into a mold and customized bottles for a glasshouse's clients. By simply exchanging plates, the glasshouse could use the same mold for many companies.

Snap Case Also called a "snap tool." This tool replaced the pontil rod and enabled the worker to hold the bottle with a tool that had vertical arms curving out from a central stem. The snap case gripped the bottle and held it firmly during finishing of the neck and lip. The use of the snap case eliminated the pontil scars or marks; however, it did at times produce grip marks on the sides of the finished bottle.

Tooled Top Bottles manufactured after 1885 with tops that were a part of the original bottle mold

Whittle Marks Bottles formed in carved-wood molds have these distinctive marks. A similar effect was produced when forming hot glass on cold molds early in the morning. "Goose pimples" resulted on the surface of these bottles. As the day progressed and the mold warmed, later bottles were smooth.

Bibliography

Books

Agee, Bill. *Collecting All Cures*. East Greenville, PA: Antique Bottle & Glass Collector, 1973.

Albers, Marilyn B. *Glass Insulators from Outside North America, 2nd Revision*. Houston, TX: self-published, 1993.

Apuzzo, Robert. *Bottles of Old New York: A Pictorial Guide to Early New York City Bottles, 1680–1925*. New York, NY: R & L Publishing, 1997.

Ayers, James. *Pepsi-Cola Bottles Collectors Guide*. Mount Airy, NC: R. J. Menter Enterprises, 1998.

Arnold, Ken. *Australian Preserving & Storage Jar Pre-1920*. Chicago: McCann Publishing, 1996.

Barnett, R. E. *Western Whiskey Bottles, 4th Edition*. Bend, OR: Maverick Publishing, 1997.

Barrett II, William J. *Zanesville and the Glass Industry: A Lasting Romance*. Zanesville, OH: self-published, 1997.

Beck, Doreen. *The Book of Bottle Collecting*. Gig Harbor, WA: Hamlin Publishing Group, Ltd., 1973.

Berguist, Steve. *Antique Bottles of Rhode Island*. Cranston, RI: self-published, 1998.

Bound, Smyth. *19th Century Food in Glass*. Sandpoint, ID: Midwest Publishers, 1994.

Bredehoft, Tom and Neila. *Fifty Years of Collectible Glass 1920–1970: Identification and Price Guide, Volume I*. Dubuque, IA: Antique Trader Books, 1998.

Burnet, Robert G. *Canadian Railway Telegraph History*. Ontario, Canada: self-published, 1996.

Champlin, Nat. *Nat Champlin's Antique Bottle Cartoons*. Bristol, RI: self-published, 1998.

Cleveland, Hugh. *Bottle Pricing Guide, 3rd Edition*. Paducah, KY: Collector Books, 1996.

Creswick, Alice M. *Redbook Number 6: The Collector's Guide to Old Fruit Jars*. Grand Rapids, MI: privately published, 1992.

DeGrafft, John. *American Sarsaparilla Bottles*. East Greenville, PA: Antique Bottle & Glass Collector, 1980.

Diamond, Freda. *Story of Glass*. New York: Harcourt, Brace and Co., 1953.

Dodsworth, Roger. *Glass and Glassmaking*. London: Shire Publications, 1996.

Dumbrell, Roger. *Understanding Antique Wine Bottles*. Ithaca, NY: Antique Collectors Club, 1983.

Edmundson, Barbara. *Historical Shot Glasses*. Chico, CA: self-published, 1995.

Eilelberner, George, and Serge Agadjanian. *The Compleat American Glass Candy Containers Handbook*. Adele Bowden, 1986.

Ferraro, Pat and Bob. *A Bottle Collector's Book*. Sparks, NV: Western Printing & Publishing Co., 1970.

Ferguson, Joel. *A Collector's Guide to New Orleans Soda Bottles*. Slidell, LA: self-published, 1999.

Field, Anne E. *On the Trail of Stoddard Glass*. Dublin, NH: William L. Bauhan, 1975.

Fletcher, W. Johnnie. *Kansas Bottle Book*. Mustang, OK: self-published, 1994.

Fletcher, W. Johnnie. *Oklahoma Bottle Book*. Mustang, OK: self-published, 1994.

Gardner, Paul Vickens. *Glass*. New York: Smithsonian Illustrated Library of Antiques, Crown Publishers, 1975.

Graci, David. *American Stoneware Bottles: A History and Study*. South Hadley, MA: self-published, 1995.

Ham, Bill. *Bitters Bottles*. Downieville, CA: self-published, 1999.

Ham, Bill. *The Shaving Mug Market.* Downieville, CA: self-published, 1997.

Hastin, Bud. *AVON Products & California Perfume Co. Collector's Encyclopedia, 15th Edition 1998.* Kansas City, MO: Bud Hastin's Publications, 1995.

Holiner, Richard. *Collecting Barber Bottles.* Paducah, KY: Collector Books, 1986.

Hudson, Paul. "Seventeenth Century Glass Wine Bottles and Seals Excavated at Jamestown," *Journal of Glass Studies,* Vol. III. Corning, N.Y: The Corning Museum of Glass, 1961.

Holabird, Fred, and Haddock, Jack. *The Nevada Bottle Book.* Reno, NV: R. F. Smith, 1981.

Hudgeons III, Thomas E. *Official Price Guide to Bottles Old & New.* Orlando, FL: House of Collectibles, 1983.

Hunter, Frederick William. *Stiegel Glass.* New York: Dover Publications, 1950.

Husfloen, Kyle. *American Pressed Glass & Bottles Price Guide.* Dubuque, IA: Antique Trader Books, 1999.

Innes, Lowell. *Pittsburgh Glass 1797–1891.* Boston: Houghton Mifflin Company, 1976.

Jackson, Barbara and Sonny. *American Pot Lids.* East Greenville, PA: Antique Bottle & Glass Collector, 1992.

Jarves, Deming. *Reminiscences of Glass Making.* New York: Hurd and Houghton, 1865.

Kendrick, Grace. *The Antique Bottle Collector.* Ann Arbor, MI: Edwards Brothers Inc., 1971.

Ketchum, William C., Jr. *A Treasury of American Bottles.* Los Angeles: Rutledge Publishing, 1975.

Klesse, Brigitt, and Hans Mayr. *European Glass from 1500–1800: The Ernesto Wolf Collection.* Germany: Kremayr and Scheriau, 1987.

Knittle, Rhea Mansfield. *Early American Glass.* New York: Garden City Publishing Company, 1948.

Kovel, Terry and Ralph. *The Kovels' Bottle Price List, 11th Edition, 1999.* New York: Crown Publishers, 1996.

Kovill, William E., Jr., *Ink Bottles and Ink Wells*. Taunton, MA: William L. Sullwold, 1971.

Kosler, Rainer. *Flasche, Bottle Und Bouteille*. Ismaning, Germany: WKD-Druck Gmbh Publishing Company, 1998.

Lee, Ruth Webb. *Antique Fakes and Reproductions*, NorthBorough, MA: privately published, 1971.

Leybourne, Doug. *Red Book #8, Fruit Jar Price Guide*. North Muskegon, MI: privately published, 1998.

Maust, Don. *Bottle and Glass Handbook*. Union Town, PA: E. G. Warman Publishing Co., 1956.

Markota, Peck and Audie. *Western Blob Top Soda and Mineral Water Bottles*. Sacramento, CA: self-published, 1998.

Markowski, Carol. *Tomart's Price Guide to Character & Promotional Glasses*. Dayton, OH: Tomart Publishing, 1993.

McCann, Jerry. *1999 Fruit Jar Annual*. Chicago: J. McCann Publisher, 1999.

McDougald, John and Carol. *1995 Price Guide for Insulators*. St. Charles, IL: self-published, 1995.

McKearin, Helen and George S. *American Glass*. New York: Crown Publishers, 1956.

McKearin, Helen and George S. *Two Hundred Years of American Blown Glass*. New York: Crown Publishers, 1950.

McKearin, Helen, and Kenneth M. Wilson. *American Bottles and Flasks and Their Ancestry*. New York: Crown Publishers, 1978.

Megura, Jim. *Official Price Guide Bottles, 12th Edition*. New York: House of Collectibles, Ballantine, 1998.

Meinz, David. *So Da Licious,Collecting Applied Color Label Soda Bottles*. Norfolk, VA: self-published, 1994.

Milroy, Wallace. *The Malt Whiskey Almanac*. Glasgow,Scotland: Neil Wilson Publishing Ltd., 1989.

Monsen & Baer. *The Beauty of Perfume, Perfume Bottle Auction VI*. Vienna, VA: Monsen & Baer Publishing, 1998.

Mosen & Baer. *The Legacies of Perfume, Perfume Bottle Auction VII.* Vienna, VA:. Monsen & Baer Publishing, 1998.

Munsey, Cecil. *The Illustrated Guide to Collecting Bottles.* New York: Hawthorn Books, Inc., 1970.

Munsey, Cecil. *The Illustrated Guide to The Collectibles of Coca-Cola.* New York: Hawthorn Books, Inc., 1972.

Namiat, Robert. *Barber Bottles with Prices.* Radnor, PA: Wallace Homestead Book Company, 1977.

Newman, Harold. *An Illustrated Dictionary of Glass.* London: Thames and Hudson Publishing, 1977.

Nielsen, Frederick. *Great American Pontiled Medicines.* Cherry Hill, NJ: The Cortech Corporation, 1978.

Northend, Mary Harrod. *American Glass.* New York: Tudor Publishing Company, 1940.

Odell, John. *Digger Odell's Official Antique Bottle & Glass Price Guides, 1–11.* Lebanon, OH: Odell Publishing, 1995.

Odell, John. *Indian Bottles & Brands.* Lebanon, OH: Odell Publishing, 1998.

Ostrander, Diane. *A Guide to American Nursing Bottles.* York, PA: ACIF Publications, 1992.

Padgett, Fred. *Dreams of Glass: The Story of William McLaughlin and His Glass Company.* Livermore, CA: self-published, 1997.

Pepper, Adeline. *The Glass Gaffers of New Jersey.* New York: Charles Scribner's Sons, 1971.

Petretti, Alan. *Petretti's Coca-Cola Collectibles Price Guide, 10th Edition.* Dubuque, IA: Antique Trader Books, 1998.

Petretti, Alan. *Petretti's Soda Pop Collectibles Price Guide, 1st Edition.* Dubuque, IA: Antique Trader Books, 1998.

Putnam, H. E. *Bottle Identification.* New York: H.E. Putnam Publisher, 1965.

Ring, Carlyn, *For Bitters Only.* Concord, MA: The Nimrod Press, Inc., 1980.

Roller, Dick. *Fruit Jar Patents Volume III 1900–1942.* Chicago: McCann Publisher, 1996.

Roller, Dick. *Indiana Glass Factories Notes*. Chicago: McCann Publisher, 1994.

Russell, Mike. *Collectors Guide to Civil War Period Bottles and Jars, 3rd Edition*. Herndon, VA: self-published, 1998.

Schwartz, Marvin D. *"American Glass"* Antiques. Blown and Molded, Volume 1. Princeton, NJ: Pyne Press, 1974.

Seeliger, Michael. *H.H. Warner: His Company and His Bottles*. East Greenville, PA: Antique Bottle & Glass Collector,1974.

Sloan, Gene. *Perfume and Scent Bottle Collecting*. Radnor, PA: Wallace Homestead Book Company, 1986.

Snyder, Bob. *Bottles in Miniature*. Amarillo, TX: Snyder Publications, 1969.

Snyder, Bob. *Bottles in Miniature II*. Amarillo, TX: Snyder Publications, 1970.

Snyder, Bob. *Bottles in Miniature III*. Amarillo,TX: Snyder Publications, 1972.

Spaid, M. David, and Harry A. Ford. *101 Rare Whiskey Flasks (Miniature)*. Palos Verdes, CA: Brisco Publications, 1989.

Spiegel, Walter Von. *Glas*. Battenberg Verlag, Munchen,1979.

Spillman, Jane Shadel. *Glass Bottles, Lamps and Other Objects*. New York: Alfred A. Knopf, 1983.

Southard, Tom, and Mike Burggraaf. *The Antique Bottles of IOWA*. Des Moines: self-published, 1998.

Sweeney, Rick. *Collecting Applied Color Label Soda Bottles*. La Mesa, CA: Painter Soda Bottles Collectors Association, 1995.

Thompson, J. H. *Bitters Bottles*. Watkins Glen, NY: Century House, 1947.

Toulouse, Julian Harrison. *Bottle Makers and Their Marks*. Camden, NJ: Thomas Nelson Incorporated, 1971.

Townsend, Brian. *Scotch Missed (The Lost Distilleries of Scotland)*. Glasgow, Scotland: Neil Wilson Publishing Ltd., 1994.

Tyson, Scott. *Glass Houses of the 1800s*. East Greenville, PA: Antique Bottle & Glass Collector, 1971.

Tucker, Donald. *Collector's Guide to the Saratoga Type Mineral Water Bottles*. East Greenville, PA: Antique Bottle & Glass Collector, 1986.

Tutton, John. *Udderly Delightful*. Stephens City, VA: Commercial Press, Inc., 1996.

Umberger, Joe and Arthur. *Collectible Character Bottles*. Tyler, TX: Corker Book Company, 1969.

Van, P. Dale. *American Breweries II*. North Wales, PA: Eastern Coast Brewiana Association, 1995.

Van Rensselaer, Stephen. *Early American Bottles and Flasks*. Peterborough, NH: Transcript Printing Company, 1926.

Van Rensselaer, Stephen. *Early American Bottles and Flasks*. Stratford, CT: J. Edmund Edwards Publisher, 1969.

Watkins, Laura Woodside. *American Glass and Glassmaking*. New York: Chanticleer Press, 1950.

Watson, Richard. *Bitters Bottles*. New York: Thomas Nelson & Sons, 1965.

Watson, Richard. *Supplement to Bitters Bottles*. New York, NY: Thomas Nelson & Sons, 1968.

Wichmann, Jeff. *Antique Western Bitters Bottles*. Sacramento, CA: Pacific Glass Books Publishing, 1999.

Wilson, Betty and William. *Spirit Bottles of the Old West*. Wolfe City: Henington Publishing Company, 1968.

Wilson, Kenneth M. *New England Glass and Glass Making*. New York: Thomas Y. Crowell Company, 1972.

Wood, Zang. *New Mexico Bottle Book*. Flora Vista, NM: self-published, 1998.

Young, Susan H. "A Preview of Seventh-Century Glass from the Kourin Basilica, Cyprus." *Journal of Glass Studies*, Vol. 35. Corning Museum of Glass, 1993.

Zumwalt, Betty. *Ketchup, Pickles, Sauces*. SandPoint, ID: Mark West Publishers, 1980.

Periodicals

Bottles & Bygones, 30 Brabant Rd, Cheadle Hulme, Cheadle, Cheshire, SKA 7AU England.

Bottles & Extra Magazine, 1485 Buck Hill Dr., Southhampton, PA 18966.

British Bottle Review, 5 Ironworks Row, Elsecar Project, Wath Rd, Elsecar, Barnsley, S. York, S74, 8HJ, England.

FJN Publishers, *Fruit Jar Newletter.* 364 Gregory Avenue, West Orange, N.H. 07052-3743.

Hagenbuch, Jim. *Antique Bottle & Glass Collector,* 102 Jefferson Street, P.O. Box 187, East Greenville, PA 18041.

McDougald, Carol. *Crown Jewels of the Wire,* P.O. Box 1003, St. Charles, IL 60174-1003.

The Miniature Bottle Collector, P.O. Box 2161, Palos Verdes Peninsula, CA 92074, Brisco Publications.

Treasure Hunter's Gazette, 14 Vernon St., Keene, N.H. 03431, George Streeter—Publisher & Editor.

Auction Companies

ABIC Absentee Auctions
139 Pleasant Ave.
Dundas, Ontario, Canada L9H 3T9
Tim Denton (519) 443-4162
Mark Draak (905) 628-3433
E-Mail : info@auctionsbyabc.com
Website: http://www.auctionsbyabc.
com

Antique Bottle Connection
147 Reserve Road
Libby, Montana 59923
(406) 293-8442
E-Mail: letsgo@libby.org

Armans of Newport
207 High Point Avenue
Portsmouth, RI 02871

Robert Arner Auctioneer
Lehighton, PA
(717) 386-4586

B & B Auctions / Bottles & Bygones
30 Brabant Road
Cheadle Hulme, Cheadle
Cheshire England SK8 7AU
E-Mail: mike@bygones.demon.co.uk
Website: http://members.tripod.com/
~MikeSheridan/index.htm

BBR Auctions
5 Ironworks Row, Wath Rd.
Elsecar, Barnsley
S. Yorkshire, S74 844, England
PH: 01 226-745156

Bothroyd & Detwiler On Line Auctions
1290½ South 8th Ave.
Yuma, AZ
E-Mail: detwiler@primenet.com
Website: http://www.primnet.com/
~detwiler/index.html

Cerebro, Tobacco Ephemera Auctions
P.O. Box 327
East Prospect, PA 17317
(800) 695-2235
E-Mail: cerebrolab@aol.com
Website: http://www.cerebro.com

CB & SC Auctions
179D Woodridge Crest
Nepean, ON K2B 712, Canada
Rhonda Bennett (613) 828-8266

Collectors Sales & Services
P.O. Box 4037
Middletown, RI 02842
(401) 849-5012
E-Mail: collectors@antiquechina.com
Website: http://www.antiqueglass.
com/homepage.htm

Down-Jersey Auction
15 Southwest Lakeside Dr.
Medford, NJ 08055
(609) 953-1755
E-Mail: dja@skyhigh.com
Website: http://www.down-jersey.com

Garth's Auctions
2690 Stratford Rd.
Box 369
Delaware, OH 43015
(614) 362-4771
E-Mail; info@garths.com
Website: http://www.garths.com

GLASSCO Auctions
102 Abbeyhill Drive
Kanata, Ontario, Canada K2L 1H2
(613) 831-4434
E-Mail: phil@glassco.com

Glass Works Auctions
Box 187
East Greenville, PA 18041
(215) 679-5849
E-Mail: glswrk@enter.net
Website: http://www.glswrk-auction.
com

Gore Enterprises
P.O. Box 158
Huntington, VT 05462
William D. Emberley
(802) 453-3311

Harmer Rooke Galleries
32 East 57th Street
New York, NY 10022
(212) 751-1900

Norman C. Heckler & Co.
79 Bradford Corner Road
Woodstock Valley, CT 06282
(203) 974-1634
E-Mail: heckler@neca.com
Website: http://www.hecklerauction.
com

KIWI Auctions
128 Tancred Street
Avonside, Christchurch, New Zealand
(645) 336-846
E-Mail: kiwi.auctions@extra.co.nz

Leslie's Antiques & Auctions
934 Main Street
Newberry, SC 29108
(888) 321-8600
E-Mail: frleslie@interpath.com
Website: http://www.antiqueusa.com

McMurray Antiques & Auctions
P.O. Box 393
Kirkwood, NY 13795
(607) 775-2321

Wm. Morford
Rural Route #2
Cazenovia, NY 13035
(315) 662-7625
E-Mail: morf2bid@aol.com
Website: http://morfauction.com

NSA Auctions/R. Newton-Smith
Antiques
88 Cedar St.
Cambridge, Ontario, Canada
N1S IV8
E-mail: nsa@mgl.ca
Website: http://www.mgl.ca/~nsa

Don Osborne Auctions
33 Eagleville Rd.
Orange, MA 01354
(978) 544-3696

Pacific Glass Auctions
1507 21st Street, Suite #203
Sacramento, CA 95814
(916) 443-3296
E-Mail: info@pacglass.com
Website: http://www.pacglass.com

Howard B. Parzow
Drug Store & Apothecary Auctioneer
P.O. Box 8464
Gaithersburg, MD 20885-3464
(301) 977-6741

Pop Shoppe Auctions
10556 Combie Road #10652
Auburn, CA 95602
(530) 268-6333
E-Mail: PopShoppe@aol.com

Carl Pratt Bottle Auctions
P.O. Box 2072
Sandwich, MA 02563
(508) 888-8794

Shot Glass Exchange
Box 219 BE.
Western Springs, IL 60558
(708) 246-1559

Skinner Inc.
63 Park Plazza
Boston, MA 02116
(617) 350-5400
E-Mail: info@skinnerinc.com
Website: http://www.skinnerinc.com

Mike Smith's Patent Medicine Auction
Veterinary Collectibles Roundtable
7431 Covington Hwy.
Lithonia, GA 30058
(770) 482-5100
E-Mail: Petvetmike@aol.com

Stuckey Auction Co.
315 West Broad Street
Richmond, VA 23225
(804) 780-0850

T.B.R. Bottle Consignments
P.O. Box 1253
Bunnell, FL 32110
(904) 437-2807

Victorian Images
Box 284
Marlton, NJ 08053
(609) 985-7711

Bruce & Vicki Waasdorp
Decorated Stoneware Auctions
P.O. Box 434
Clarence, NY 14031
E-Mail: msvicki@fcs-net.com
Website: http://www.antiques-stoneware.com